Thomas Eakins
and the Uses of History

Thomas Eakins

and the Uses of History

AKELA REASON

PENN

University of Pennsylvania Press

Philadelphia

Published by
University of Pennsylvania Press
Philadelphia, Pennsylvania 19104-4112

Printed in the United States of America on acid-free paper

10 9 8 7 6 5 4 3 2 1

Library of Congress Cataloging-in-Publication Data

Reason, Akela.
Thomas Eakins and the uses of history / Akela Reason.
p. cm.
Includes bibliographical references and index.
ISBN 978-0-8122-4198-3 (alk. paper)
1. Eakins, Thomas, 1844–1916—Criticism and interpretation. 2. History in art. I. Eakins, Thomas, 1844–1916. II. Title.
N6537.E3R43 2010
759.13—dc22

2009027549

Contents

Illustrations

INTRODUCTION

The value of these works is permanent. They have nothing to do with passing or evanescent Art moods. They are outside of fad or fashion.
—Cecilia Beaux[1]

Cecilia Beaux (1855–1942) drafted this appreciation of the work of fellow Philadelphia artist Thomas Eakins on the occasion of the memorial exhibition held in his honor at the Metropolitan Museum of Art in 1917. Although Beaux had studied at the Pennsylvania Academy of the Fine Arts while Eakins was teaching there, she claimed to have avoided his "magic circle" of student devotees, preferring to watch him "from behind staircases, and corners." Beaux respected Eakins's realist work and yet found it "deeply alien" to her own temperament.[2] Indeed, the two artists had completely different careers. Beaux, hailed in her day as the "greatest living woman painter," became a successful portraitist particularly sought after for her elegant depictions of society women. Eakins was a portraitist too, but he had far fewer commissions and a number of dissatisfied sitters. Yet Beaux understood that Eakins's failings as an artist, marked by his lack of financial and sometimes critical success, were the products of a man who sought to become what he called a "big painter," an artist who transcended "evanescent Art moods" in order to establish a permanent legacy.

Unlike many of his peers, Eakins never painted to earn a living. He did not come from wealth but had an unusually supportive father in Benjamin Eakins, who encouraged his only surviving son to become a painter. Benjamin made Eakins's career possible by supplementing his son's meager income and providing him with room and board. Eakins lived in his father's house for most of his adult life and remained there after his father's death in 1899. Benjamin funded

Eakins's artistic education in France at the Ecole des Beaux-Arts between 1866 and 1870. He subsidized Eakins's unpaid teaching posts at the Philadelphia Sketch Club and the Pennsylvania Academy and was no doubt proud when his son eventually became the director of the Academy's schools in 1882.[3]

With Benjamin's support, there was no need for Eakins to paint within the confines of "fad or fashion." This circumstance, coupled with what Beaux called his "integrity of purpose," sent Eakins in artistic directions that few others pursued.[4] He painted scenes from contemporary life: doctors performing surgery, men rowing on the Schuylkill River, baseball players, and the like. He painted these not only because they were part of his world but also because he believed that all great artists depicted their own time. And it is these images that most resonate with today's viewers. However, Eakins also painted and sculpted historical subjects throughout his life. The focus of these images on the past has frequently set them apart in larger evaluations of his career. As a result, these projects have often been viewed as anomalous episodes in an otherwise realist career, but they constitute a crucial aspect of Eakins's worldview as an artist. If great artists depicted their own time, they also took on epic themes that linked them to their predecessors.

Since his death, Eakins has become an American Old Master largely because of realist images such as *The Gross Clinic* (Figure 1), which depicts the Philadelphia physician Samuel D. Gross surgically removing a piece of dead bone from a young patient's leg. Indeed, when Jefferson Medical College controversially decided to sell the painting in 2006, Earl A. Powell III, director of the National Gallery in Washington, D.C., termed it "America's *Night Watch*"—referring to Rembrandt's well-known masterpiece in the Rijksmuseum.[5] Although Eakins's contemporaries acknowledged the power of the painting, they also found it disturbing. However, Eakins valued his historical images as much as, if not more than, the portraits and contemporary genre pictures that we admire him for today. For example, in 1900, when Eakins wrote to John W. Beatty of Pittsburgh's Carnegie Institute that he intended to send his "best painting" to the institute's upcoming exhibition, he referred to *Crucifixion* (1880), his largest history painting and the only overtly religious work that he ever completed.[6] Modern observers might find *Crucifixion* an unusual choice for "best painting" in a career so devoted to realism, but Eakins created this painting with the same ambition with which he painted *The Gross Clinic.*

Eakins painted both *The Gross Clinic* and *Crucifixion* without the certainty of any financial reward, as he had not received a commission for either of these large pictures. However, in the case of *The Gross Clinic*, Eakins clearly hoped that his daring and monumental image would appeal to Jefferson Medical College and that it also might bring him patrons appropriately desirous of such

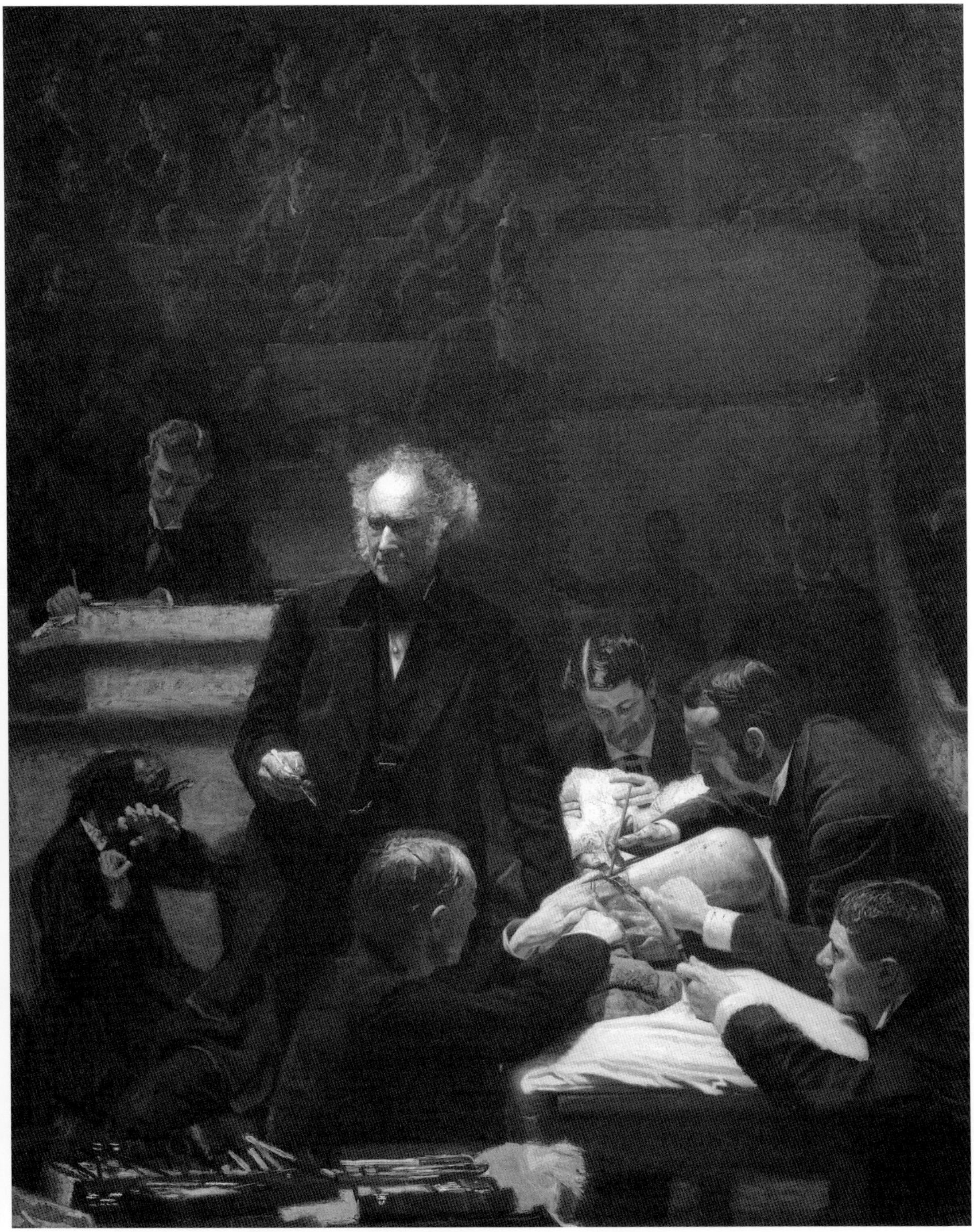

1. Thomas Eakins, *Portrait of Dr. Samuel D. Gross (The Gross Clinic)*, 1875. Oil on canvas, 96 × 78½ in. Courtesy of the Pennsylvania Academy of the Fine Arts, Philadelphia. Gift of the Alumni Association to Jefferson Medical College in 1878 and purchased by the Pennsylvania Academy of the Fine Arts and the Philadelphia Museum of Art in 2007 with the generous support of more than 3,500 donors.

ambitious work. In this case, Eakins was able to find a home for the painting when the alumni association of Jefferson Medical College raised a meager two hundred dollars for its purchase a few years after its completion. *Crucifixion* was quite a different matter. In spite of the religious subject, *Crucifixion* is no church altarpiece. In fact, Protestant and Catholic viewers alike could find reason to object to Eakins's audacious reinvention of the centuries-old iconography. Many critics found the work as displeasing as *The Gross Clinic* for its representation of a realist Jesus, with clawlike hands, dirty feet, and caked-on blood. Eakins sent the work to numerous exhibitions conscious that it did not meet contemporary expectations for religious art. The painting never sold and often encountered negative press, yet Eakins maintained that it was his best work. *Crucifixion*, like many of his historical works, allowed Eakins to engage in a dialogue with the art historical past, and he hoped that it would one day be recognized as his masterpiece.

This book explores Eakins's complex reasons for choosing historical themes. More specifically, it proposes that he used these subjects to advance some of his most deeply held professional aspirations. Historical subjects were part of what he called "big painting"—timeless works that engaged with the art of previous centuries. Through these works, it is possible to see how his consciousness of the art historical tradition influenced his teaching as well as guided the trajectory of his career. With respect to this tradition, he felt that a core set of artistic beliefs bound all great artists together—past, present, and future. Eakins's insistent placement of the historical works in major exhibitions alongside his powerful images of doctors and rowers reflects his desire to carve out a place within this tradition. Moreover, his partiality for these historical images makes clear that he envisioned his artistic legacy in different terms than those by which twentieth-century art historians have typically defined his art.[7]

In keeping with his historical subject choices, Eakins developed a meticulous working method rooted in some of the oldest recorded artistic practices. For example, at a time when many of his peers were achieving success with bravura brushwork, he crafted tightly composed images that often built on a perspectival grid worthy of a Renaissance master. His technique was the result of many years of study.[8] However, he would only realize the importance of such time-honored methods when he traveled to Paris to study at the Ecole des Beaux-Arts. It was there that Eakins began to feel the depths of the tradition that had shaped the artistic profession for centuries. In Europe, he came to appreciate the work of the Old Masters and began to focus on producing the best work that he could "outside of fad or fashion." But he would not rely exclusively on tried and true artistic practices; he sought to integrate modern ideas into both his technique and his teaching—notably through the use of photography. Eakins felt that these innovations were critical to the continuing development of the art historical tradition into the modern age.

The following chapters examine how Eakins explored historical subject matter throughout every decade of his career in order to present his beliefs about his profession and his relationship to the art historical past. These subjects engage with the past in myriad ways, and my use of the term *history* will necessarily be fluid. As Randall Griffin has proposed, even in historical images "Eakins deliberately confronted the popular view that American themes were provincial and less interesting than foreign ones."[9] As a consequence of this overarching belief in American subjects and in order to better integrate the historical subjects into Eakins's career, this study will include images of contemporary themes that relate to his historical works. Eakins's historical projects, like most of his works, are starkly different from those of his American contemporaries. The themes he chose were frequently obscure, sometimes requiring explanation. His method could seem at odds with his subject matter, as in the case of his Arcadian images, which are Greek in subject but almost anticlassical in style. Even when he chose a familiar theme like the Crucifixion, he created such an unusual composition that it sparked a great deal of criticism and debate in its own time and remains a bit of an enigma today.

This volume begins with Eakins's first fully realized history painting, *William Rush Carving His Allegorical Figure of the Schuylkill River.* When Eakins began the painting in 1875, he was primarily known for his contemporary genre scenes and for his portraits. Although admired for these works today, critics in the 1870s often regarded Eakins's attraction to these contemporary subjects as eccentric. Such critics typically acknowledged Eakins's tremendous ability as a draftsman but hoped someday to see his talent put to better use.[10] Eakins attempted to meet this challenge with *William Rush,* a complex work that is equal parts portrait, genre, and history painting. The painting also boldly elaborates upon well-established European art historical precedents. Initiated as he was completing the Rembrandtian *Gross Clinic,* this image reflects upon the career of one of the first native-born sculptors in America, an American Old Master, in the days before anyone knew that such a person could exist. Eakins's reasons for focusing on Rush have to do with the understanding of art history that Eakins developed as an art student in Paris. In the painting, Eakins defined sculpture as the pinnacle of the arts and boldly elevated an American sculptor to a position of distinction within the medium. Eakins developed the idea for this picture as the notion of an American art history was just coalescing. In addition, he addressed the position of the model within the Western tradition, particularly the associations, dating back to antiquity, of immorality with the female models who posed for sculptors. By referring to an American past, a classical past, and his own time, Eakins suggested a new role for the female nude model—recasting her as a noble and virtuous woman.

Continuing into the 1880s, Eakins used the colonial past to reconsider the position of the burgeoning group of female students attending his classes at the Pennsylvania Academy in a series of works that feature women knitting, spinning, and sewing in old-fashioned dress. Eakins's advocacy of women in the arts was marred by a deeper ambivalence about their capabilities. In his depictions of colonial women, Eakins tapped into contemporary theories regarding nervous exhaustion among educated women by glorifying a simpler past when robust women engaged in traditional women's work. His colonial images gradually evolved into classical ones. With slight modifications of costume and setting, he soon became immersed in a fully classical idiom.

Eakins's classicizing Arcadian subjects reflect a new approach to teaching that he began to explore at the Pennsylvania Academy in the mid-1880s. He derived his new method from the writings of the little-known French artist Horace Lecoq de Boisbaudran. Lecoq achieved notoriety for the innovative curriculum he developed for the Ecole Gratuite de Dessin in Paris. While his system emphasized the cultivation of memory in budding young artists, it was also rooted in the classical tradition. Lecoq's students studied models in classical attire in interiors and completely nude out-of-doors. Beginning around 1882, Eakins also began dressing models in classical costume and studying nude bodies outdoors. Eakins presented his adaptation of Lecoq's ideas to the Academy when he painted *Swimming*, a contemporary genre scene that evokes classical subjects, for one of its directors in 1885. Shortly thereafter, Eakins's experiment was curtailed by his forced resignation from his teaching position at the Academy in 1886.

As Elizabeth Milroy has shown, Eakins painted *Crucifixion* in 1880 as a demonstration of his skill as a mature professional artist.[11] Eakins took this staple of Old Master painting and crafted a new iconography, which he based on liberal religious texts that presented Jesus as a historical figure. Eakins's image depicts a human Jesus, stripped of his divinity, enduring physical torment on the cross. Eakins's modern Jesus created a stir among critics, garnering him more attention in the press—both positive and negative—than he had ever before received for any of his works. In the year after his dismissal from the Academy, Eakins may have invested the painting with a poignant new meaning as he came to identify with Jesus and used the work as a symbol of his own martyrdom. Shortly thereafter, Eakins continued to assert the value of the painting as his best work by placing it almost exclusively in international venues, where it could be seen in the context of a broader art historical tradition.

Eakins's most ambitious and public venture into historical terrain came in the 1890s with his work on two large Beaux-Arts sculpture projects: the Trenton

Battle Monument and Brooklyn's Soldiers and Sailors Memorial in Grand Army Plaza. Although little known today, Eakins hoped that his public sculptures would become the crowning accomplishments of his career. In these works, Eakins reasserted the beliefs that he had outlined two decades earlier in his painting of William Rush, namely, that sculpture was the most difficult, and therefore the most significant, achievement any artist could master. Eakins labored over these sculptures in an effort to endow them with the strength of classical art. Unfortunately, Eakins's fastidious technique brought him into conflict with his patrons and effectively severed his ties with those who might have helped him gain additional sculpture commissions.

In spite of such disappointments, sculpture remained on Eakins's mind, and around 1908 he returned again to the theme of William Rush carving his allegorical figure of the Schuylkill River. By this point, Eakins's critical reception had begun to change, with many of the works that had formerly faced negative reviews now hailed as masterpieces. In this period, critics even began to compare Eakins to the Old Masters. Eakins revisited Rush from this new vantage point. In an unprecedentedly large number of sketches and unfinished compositions, Eakins reworked the Rush subject, concluding it with an image in which he made the Federal sculptor, an American Old Master, resemble himself.

The arrangement of the chapters is roughly chronological; however, because I am interested in the reception of the images and consider the exhibition history of these works critical to their meaning, I have not strictly adhered to placing works within the book according to their date of execution. The most significant deviation is seen in the third and fourth chapters, which are reversed in terms of creation dates. Because I see the Arcadian works as important to understanding the beliefs that led to Eakins's departure from the Academy in 1886, I felt it useful to discuss these works before *Crucifixion*. In addition, because *Crucifixion* remained important to Eakins after his 1886 resignation, I view that work as crucial to his effort to restore his reputation in subsequent decades. Therefore it seems appropriate to situate this work after the Arcadian themes and *Swimming*, which remained little known and unexhibited after 1886.

Although I have framed the chapters as case studies of individual iconographic themes, I see these works as forming a cohesive project through which Eakins ruminated upon his profession and his place within the art historical tradition. Far from aberrations, these works were of great importance to Eakins and central to his artistic development. While he may have attained his Old Master status through paintings like *The Gross Clinic*, he envisioned his legacy differently. The historical images reflect Eakins's preoccupation with creating a permanent legacy apart from "evanescent Art moods." In this way, Eakins crafted his backward-looking historical works with an eye to the future.

CHAPTER ONE

William Rush and the History of Art

Thomas Eakins completed his first history painting, *William Rush Carving His Allegorical Figure of the Schuylkill River* (Figure 2), in 1877.[1] He spent roughly two years on this work—a paean to a Federal-era Philadelphia sculptor and ship carver—carefully considering the subject and plotting its composition with a large number of sketches and sculptural models. The slow gestation of the image suggests deliberation; the investment of so much time and thought underscores the work's importance to the artist. Eakins's final image shows the fashionably attired Rush practicing life study, carving the wooden figure of a nymph from the nude female model who poses in the foreground. The model, Louisa Vanuxem, was the unmarried daughter of an esteemed Philadelphia merchant and was celebrated for her beauty. Rush's finished sculpture, known today as *Water Nymph and Bittern* (Figure 3), was unveiled in 1809 as the centerpiece of a public fountain that stood in front of the city's waterworks pumphouse at Centre Square until the 1820s, when it was moved to the new waterworks in Fairmount.

Eakins's painting of Rush is now part of the American art canon and has been the subject of rich interpretation by scholars. Particularly relevant to this study is Elizabeth Johns's examination of the painting in terms of Eakins's desire to link both Rush and himself with an academic tradition in order to "root his 'modernity' in what had gone before."[2] Not only did Eakins focus on the past in his choice of subject, but as Johns and others have shown, *William Rush* closely adheres to a centuries-old European tradition of representing artists, particularly Old Masters, in their studios. However, for this painting, as Johns noted, Eakins chose "an Old Master who was in virtually no one's canon but his own."[3]

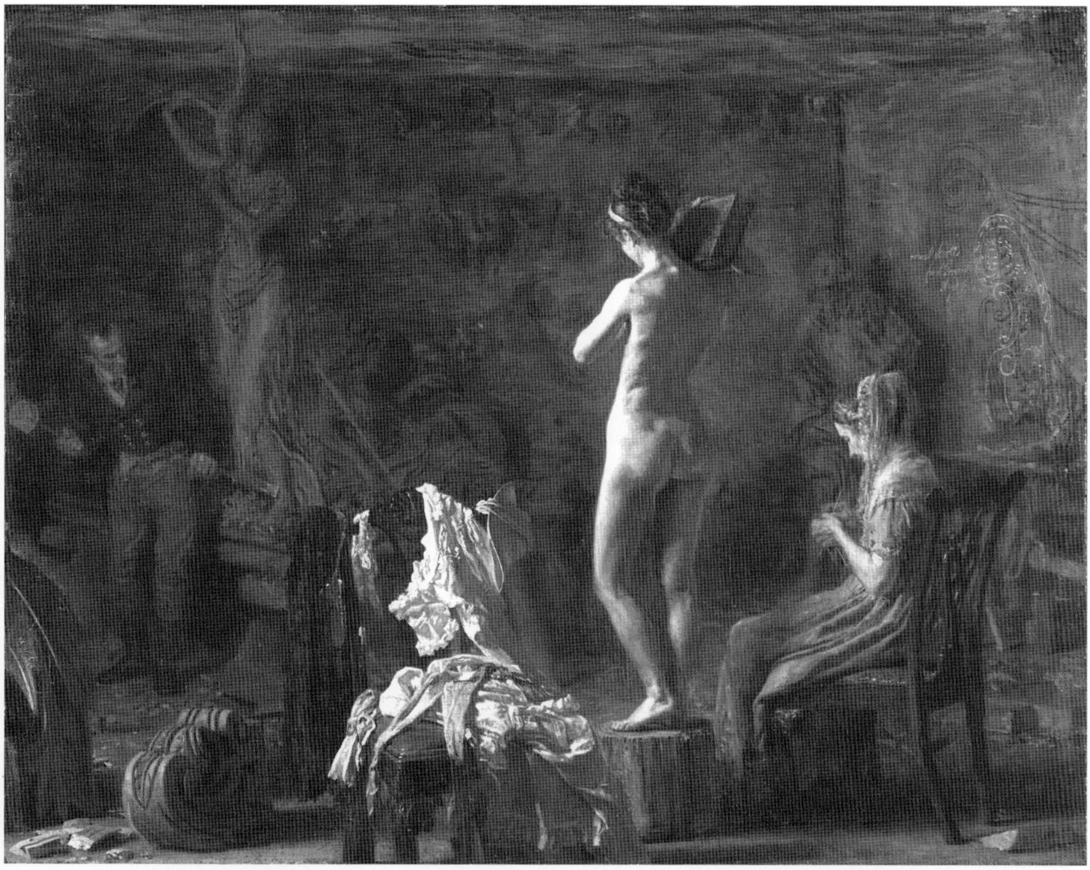

2. Thomas Eakins, *William Rush Carving His Allegorical Figure of the Schuylkill River*, 1876–77. Oil on canvas, 20 1/8 × 26 1/8 in. Philadelphia Museum of Art. Gift of Mrs. Thomas Eakins and Miss Mary Adeline Williams, 1929.

Only dimly remembered by the 1870s, Rush had been one of the most successful American sculptors of the 1810s and 1820s. The son of a Philadelphia ship's carpenter, Rush assisted his father as a child. In his teens, he apprenticed with the London-trained carver Edward Cutbush and opened his own shop in his native city around 1774. After serving with a militia during the American Revolution, he returned to Philadelphia and reopened his business. Shortly thereafter, Rush became the city's leading carver of figureheads and scrolls for merchant and naval vessels. After 1808, possibly due to a decline in shipbuilding, Rush shifted his attention to portraiture and freestanding allegorical figures. Several of his life-size figures adorned Philadelphia landmarks. In spite of his success as a sculptor, Rush remained rooted in his artisanal origins, carving only in wood, never marble, and expanding his range of materials only in the use of terra-cotta for portrait busts.[4]

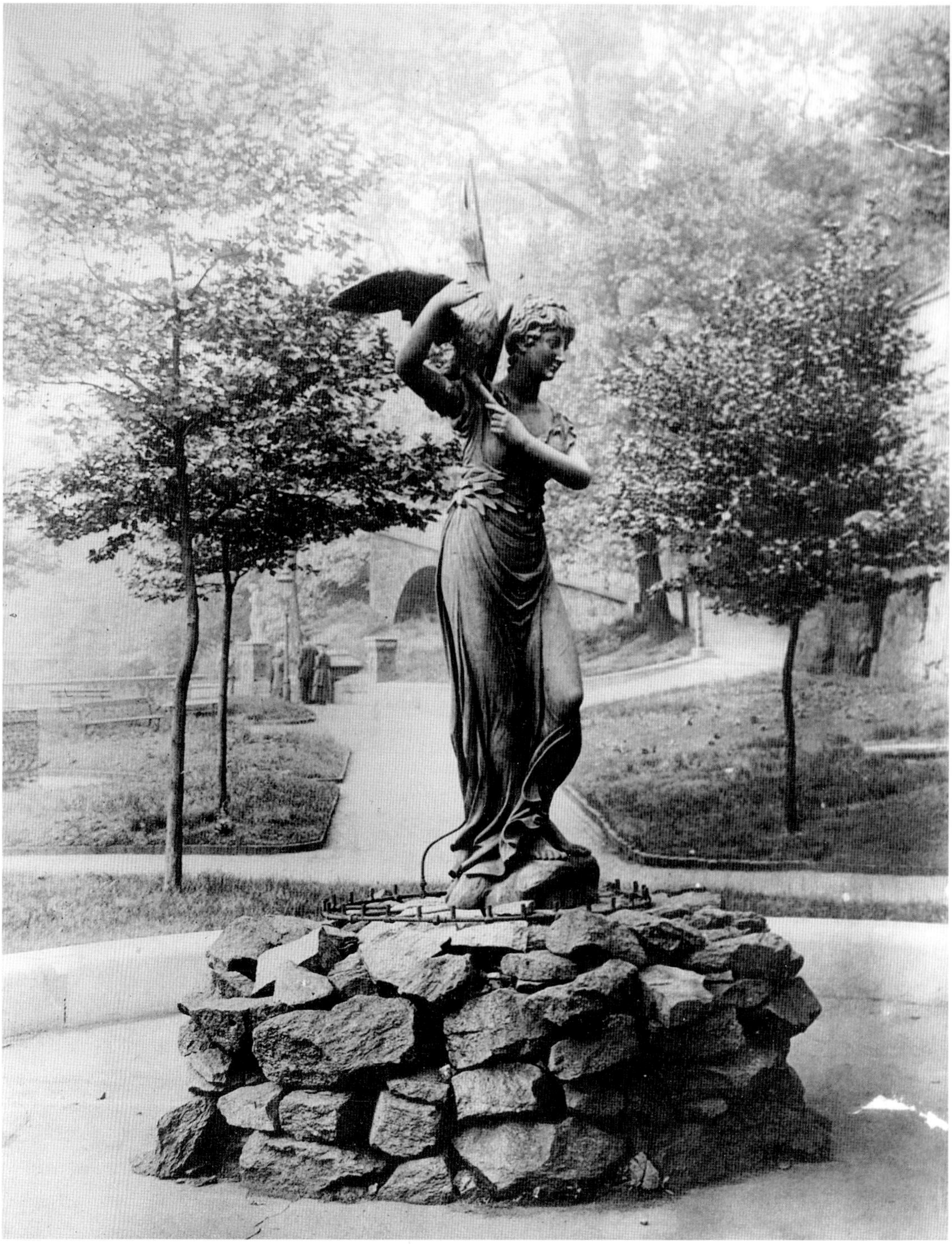

3. William N. Jennings, *Water Nymph and Bittern Statue in Fairmount Park*, ca. 1895. Gelatin silver print, 10 × 8 in. The Library Company of Philadelphia.

Like many of the sitters in Eakins's contemporary portraits, Rush had played an active role in Philadelphia's civic life. He became a founding member of the Pennsylvania Academy of the Fine Arts and served as a director of that institution for all but one year from 1805 until his death in 1833. Rush was among the group of academicians who instituted the first life class at the Academy, and he regularly exhibited his work in its annuals. In addition to his professional accomplishments, he held positions on the city's Select and Common Councils. He also served with Louisa Vanuxem's father, James, on the Watering Committee, which oversaw the waterworks providing clean drinking water to the city.

In order to create an image that presents a particular moment, showing Rush in the act of creating one of his better-known public sculptures, Eakins studied the artist's work and undertook a great deal of historical research. To establish the setting, Eakins visited with woodcarvers and spoke with some elderly Philadelphians who remembered Rush's long-gone workshop. In the painting, the dimly lit interior of the shop is filled with woodworking tools and examples of Rush's sculpture, including the ship's scrolls that were among the sculptor's earliest professional works. Eakins studied each of the large sculptures carefully, making sketches, taking photographs, and even modeling them in wax. In spite of such apparent concern for accuracy in the effort to resurrect Rush's reputation, several key elements of the painting are fictional or anachronistic. Rush would not have carved a sculpture in the gentleman's attire that he wears in the painting.[5] Moreover, in 1809, Rush had not yet conceived of the two sculptures visible in the background: *George Washington* (1815) and *Allegory of the Waterworks* (1825). And, perhaps most important, Rush probably would not have used a female life model and most definitely did not model Louisa Vanuxem nude.[6]

Yet, in spite of the painting's title, it is Vanuxem rather than Rush who is the focal point of the painting. Her nude form occupies the center of the composition and is more brightly illuminated than that of the sculptor, who toils in the darker recesses of the workshop on the left side of the image. Underscoring Vanuxem's state of undress, Eakins included a masterful still life of her discarded clothes unceremoniously piled on a Chippendale chair to her left. The elderly matron knitting on the right (often misidentified by critics as Vanuxem's mother) acts as the model's chaperone. Her absorption in her task and consequent inattention to the modeling session suggests her confidence that the artist will in no way compromise her vulnerable charge's reputation. Her presence is intended to dispel any sense of impropriety.

There is no question that Eakins used *William Rush* to assert the central beliefs of his realist art and teaching. His friend, the critic Earl Shinn, emphatically declared the picture's didactic message in an 1878 review, writing, "The painter of the fountain seemed to have a lesson to deliver—the moral, namely, that good sculpture, even decorative sculpture can only be produced by the most uncompromising, unconventional study and analysis from life."[7] Indeed, life study was at the core of Eakins's art: it was the cornerstone of the education he had received at the Ecole des Beaux-Arts in France in the 1860s, and it became the basis of his teaching at the Pennsylvania Academy of the Fine Arts. Art historians have further explored the implications of Eakins's "lesson," regarding *William Rush* as "an assertion of the legitimacy of Eakins' own artistic methods."[8] More specifically, because Eakins began teaching at the Academy in 1876, while he was working on his image of Rush, the painting has also been viewed as a visual defense of the use of nude models at the school.[9]

Yet some nagging questions remain: namely, why did Eakins frame his defense of life study in the past? He could have used his teacher Jean-Léon Gérôme or another respected artist of the period to make his point—an approach, one could argue, he used in *The Gross Clinic*, or even in his earlier image of contemporary athleticism, *Max Schmitt in a Single Scull (The Champion Single Sculls)*. The fact that he defended his profession through the use of history suggests something about the way Eakins regarded his craft that has yet to be fully explored.

While Eakins's interest in Rush was deeply personal, he also situated the sculptor in a broader context. In the painting, Eakins fashioned an American precedent for his belief that life study was not just a critical component of contemporary artistic training but the guiding principle behind all great artistic achievement. Of particular importance to the development of the painting was his belief that life study originated in antiquity. In 1879, he suggested that Phidias, the fifth-century BCE sculptor of the Parthenon, was among the earliest artists to use models.[10] Nude subject matter flourished during the classical period. Although Greek sculptors generally favored the male body, they also pioneered the female nude. This perhaps suggests why Eakins chose to represent a sculptor for his first major historical painting even though he had yet to complete a single exhibition sculpture. He may have conceived of the painting as establishing an American historical precedent for his contemporary artistic practice, but he selected a sculptor in order to reach back further into the art historical past.

Eakins introduced the fiction that Rush studied Vanuxem from life not only to illustrate the importance of life study but also to emphasize the professionalism of the artist, whose gaze is directed at his work instead of the nude body before him. Indeed, professionalism is at the heart of the image and reflects favorably upon all of the participants. As a contemporary critic observed, "Its principle charm lies in the air of earnest restraint that pervades the whole. The perfect absorption of the carver in his work, the simple dignity of the mother [chaperone] at her knitting, the delightful air which all, even the posing model, have for caring more for what they are doing than for displaying themselves while doing it."[11] Eakins imparts a gravitas to each of his three human figures that speaks to the integrity of the artist-model relationship.

Building upon the work of Elizabeth Johns and others, this chapter will examine how *William Rush* laid the foundation for Eakins's larger interest in historical subject matter. In particular, the painting illustrates two important concerns that preoccupied Eakins throughout his career: first, his belief that American art could be integrated into the grand tradition of Western art and, second, his need to assert the professionalism of artists within American culture to make the first claim possible. Life study, as it was practiced in Europe, would not become acceptable in America without the perception of the artist as a trained professional. Only a professional would be able to view a nude body without submitting to base sexual desires. Since Eakins believed that life study was essential to the creation of great works of art, the relationship between the artist's professional status and the ability for Americans to enter the canon were intertwined.

"Big Painting"

William Rush Carving His Allegorical Figure of the Schuylkill River builds upon a European iconographic precedent, and it also derives from the understanding of the history of art that Eakins gained while he was an art student at the Ecole des Beaux-Arts in Paris from 1866 to 1870. Although he was eager to become a professional artist, his appreciation of the fine art of the past was slow in coming. In 1866, the day after entering the atelier of the French academic painter Jean-Léon Gérôme, Eakins wrote about his first visit to the galleries of the Louvre in a letter to his sister Frances (Fanny). After briefly mentioning the paintings, which he jokingly referred to as "nice funny old pictures," he began to describe the museum's "curiosities," which he appreciated for their "great historical interest." Eakins teasingly assured Fanny that he believed his taste had "been very much improved" by his encounter with art, but he mentioned not a single work by name, nor did he espouse any preferences for particular artists or periods.[12]

While Eakins may have assumed a jocular tone in order to amuse his younger sister, it was also typical of his first two years in France that historical relics, public amusements, opera, and musical performances proved more attractive to him than Paris's artistic offerings. Although he had benefited from the rigorous curriculum of Philadelphia's Central High School, followed by study at the Pennsylvania Academy, then one of the best art schools in the United States, Eakins's early letters betray his provincialism when faced with European art and culture.

A few months later, in a letter to his father, Eakins explained his inability to describe the art that he had seen on his visits to the Palais du Luxembourg and the Louvre, claiming that "the pleasure in seeing a picture cannot be conveyed in writing." The best he could do was to suggest a comparison with the paintings he had seen at Philadelphia's Sanitary Fair of 1864, some of which he felt "have never . . . been surpassed," but, he continued, "I see many here just as good."[13] At this early stage of his career he could only assess one of the greatest art collections in Europe by situating it against what he had known in Philadelphia. Experience would convince him of the greatness of certain European masters, but he confidently maintained that Americans also belonged within that pantheon.

During Eakins's first two years in Paris, when he discussed art at all in his letters home he spoke primarily of his teachers at the Ecole des Beaux-Arts and of their contemporaries.[14] However, as he struggled to master oil painting after several years of drawing, he developed an appreciation for earlier European art. By 1868, in anticipation of launching a professional career as a painter, Eakins defined the type of artist that he hoped to become with an eye to the past. While professing that an artist who emulated others instead of looking to nature would fail to become a "big painter," Eakins's concept of the "big painter" expressed his heightened awareness of the European artistic tradition.[15] Although he never made oil copies of other artists' work, as many of his peers did, he began to admire certain Old Masters for their adherence to nature. Henceforth, gaining the skills needed to produce important paintings became Eakins's primary aspiration.

Becoming a "big painter" meant something different to Eakins than attaining financial success with his work. He alluded to this distinction in a letter to his father, in which he wrote that, although he thought that he could "earn a respectable living . . . painting heads," he still felt like "a little child . . . alongside of the big painters around me and fear that I will be for some time yet, but I will try my best."[16] Months later he reported on his progress, writing that he believed he could at least "equal the work . . . [that] some of the big painters" had done during their own youthful apprenticeships. He continued by expressing his disdain for the "namby pamby fashion painters" and hoped that he might one day "find poetical subjects & compositions like Raphael."[17] At this early stage of his career, Eakins dismissed conventional indications of artistic success—quick sales and immediate public recognition—in favor of a more enduring legacy. As he approached the end of his student days, he again wrote to his father about his goals, stating that, more than anything else, "worthy painting is the only hope of my life and study."[18]

Eakins gratified his appetite for "worthy painting" during a trip to Madrid in 1869. In the galleries of the Prado Museum, Eakins encountered masterworks that "I had always thought ought to have been done and what did not seem to me impossible."[19] Contrasting sharply with his first visit to the Louvre, Eakins was enthralled by the Prado's collection. During his visits to the museum, he filled a small notebook with his observations of Old Master technique, citing specific artists and paintings. He compared these works, assessing faults and strengths as he saw them. He particularly admired the Spanish Baroque master Diego Velázquez, calling his *Fable of Arachne (Las hilanderas)* "the finest piece of painting I have ever seen." And yet Eakins did not frame all of his scribblings in the "Spanish notebook" in the past—he constantly compared passages of the Prado's Old Master paintings with the work of contemporary French painters, including those of his teachers Gérôme and Léon Bonnat. He also had not lost any of his regard for American artists, making a note to himself to examine the work of Gilbert Stuart for comparison with that of Spanish painter Francisco de Goya. Eakins felt that at his best "Goya's drawing can be as exquisite as a Stuart."[20]

American Subjects

Among the works that Eakins most admired at the Prado were large-scale history paintings. Upon his return to the United States, Eakins soon began to develop ideas for his own history subjects. As he considered the composition of *William Rush Carving His Allegorical Figure of the Schuylkill River*, he also made studies for three historical pictures: *Hiawatha*, *Robert E. Lee Defeated*, and *Columbus in Prison* (*Columbus in Chains*). Together, these sketches illustrate how Eakins's interest in history evolved as he developed *William Rush.*[21] In each of these works Eakins conceived a traditional history painting based on American subject matter. In the end, he abandoned these ideas in favor of *William Rush*, a traditional iconographic theme newly envisioned through an American lens.

Throughout Eakins's search for a history subject, he remained wedded to finding it in the American past. Near the end of his life, he famously advised American artists, "If America is to produce great painters and if young art students wish to assume a place in the history of the art of their country, their first desire should be to remain in America to peer deeper into the heart of American life."[22] This statement can be viewed as a summation of his career—an affirmation of his investment in realism and in contemporary American subject matter—yet he expressed a similar view in 1881 when he was at work on several historical subjects.[23] In that year the *Philadelphia Evening Telegraph* declared, "Mr Thomas Eakins is an artist who has theories. One of his theories is that an American artist cannot do better than to treat American subjects, for the reason that no better subjects than American subjects exist."[24] Shortly after the publication of this article, Eakins exhibited two works at the Pennsylvania Academy that illustrate his point. In this exhibition, Eakins showed the contemporary genre painting *Mending the Net* and *William Rush*, which appeared in Philadelphia for the first time. The two works together seem not only to reflect his intentions to "treat American subjects" but also suggest that he did not think of them solely in terms of contemporary life. Indeed, he exhibited his historical subjects regularly and considered them vital to his reputation as an artist.[25]

Eakins began his exploration of historical subject matter with the 1874 watercolor *Hiawatha*.[26] Although the work was destroyed in the 1940s, an oil of the subject (Figure 4), which may have been a study for the watercolor, survives.[27] Eakins based his image on Henry Wadsworth Longfellow's enormously popular poem *The Song of Hiawatha* (1855). Eakins's oil depicts a scene from "Hiawatha's Fasting (Canto V)," in which the Ojibwa leader fasts and prays in the forest for a solution to the starvation facing his people. During this seven-day fast, Hiawatha has several visions. In the first of these appear the animals hunted by his people: deer, rabbits, pheasants, squirrels, pigeons, and geese. Eakins painted the forms of several of these animals in the sunset clouds of his painting, but he also deviated from Longfellow's text by illustrating animals not mentioned in the poem. Hiawatha cries out to the "Master of Life" and asks, "Must our lives depend on these?" On the fourth day, the corn spirit, Mondamin, appears before Hiawatha to teach him how to gain what he has prayed for. For three days, Hiawatha and Mondamin wrestle at sunset, until on the seventh day of the fast, "Suddenly upon the greensward, All alone stood Hiawatha."[28] Eakins shows Hiawatha at this moment, silhouetted against the sunset in a posture evocative of Donatello's *David*.[29] In the poem, Hiawatha buries the benevolent spirit and cultivates the cornstalks that grow over the grave, introducing corn to his people.

Eakins told his friend Earl Shinn that he intended to exhibit the watercolor with the American Society of Painters in Water Colors in New York. Artists were attracted to Longfellow's poem but typically opted to portray scenes involving either dramatic action or the more sentimental plotline relating to Hiawatha's love for the maiden Minnehaha. Eakins instead selected a significant but contemplative moment in the poem. In spite of the potential popularity of the theme, he did not complete the picture. Eakins suggested to Shinn that

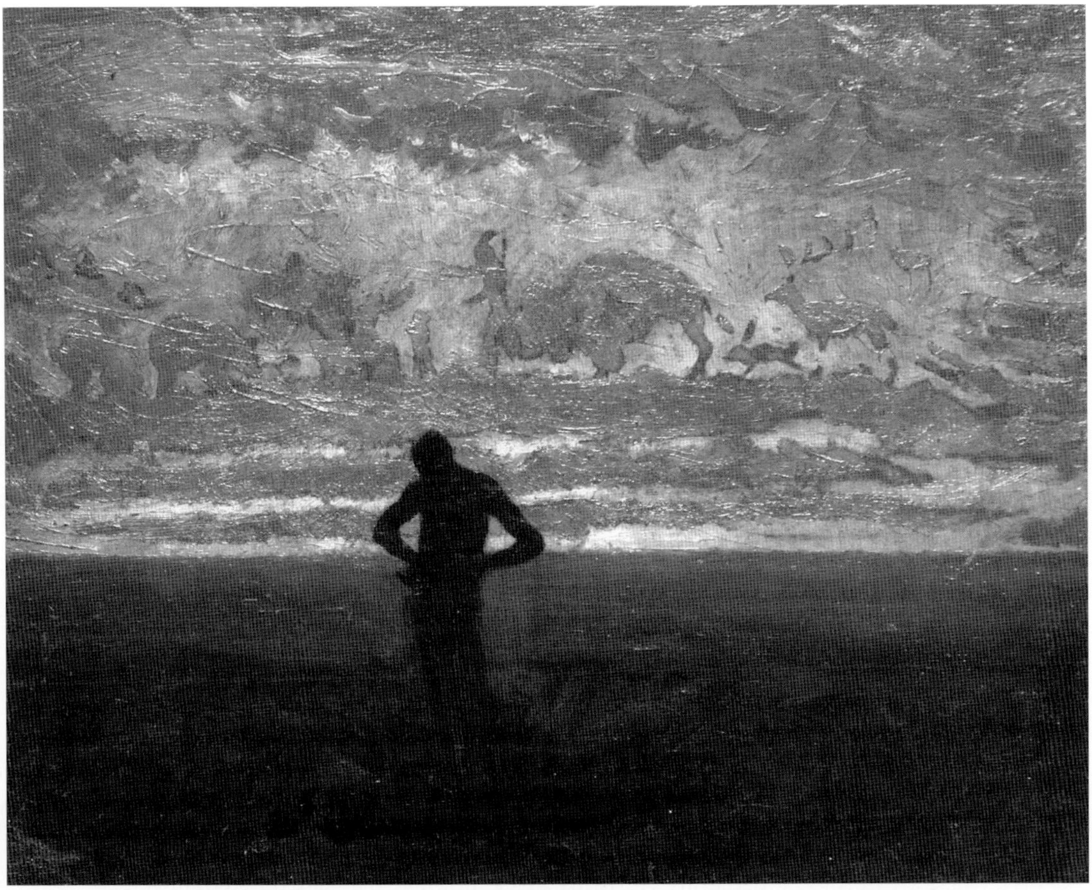

4. Thomas Eakins, *Hiawatha*, ca. 1874, Oil on canvas mounted on wood panel, 14⅛ × 17⅝ in. Hirshhorn Museum and Sculpture Garden, Smithsonian Institution. Gift of Joseph H. Hirshhorn, 1966.

artistic bohemianism had gotten the better of him in taking up such a poetic subject, writing, "I guess maybe my hair was getting too long for on having it cropped again I could not have been induced to finish it."[30]

Around the time that he painted *Hiawatha*, Eakins, perhaps not coincidently, began writing to Shinn of his interest in the art market. In rare high spirits, Eakins boasted of his talent to Shinn, proclaiming that he could paint a better figure painting than anyone in New York.[31] In the same letter to Shinn in which he discussed *Hiawatha*, Eakins outlined a plan to visit New York to show his pictures to "three or four principal N.Y. dealers" and to see a painting in a private collection by his former teacher Bonnat.[32] After showing his pictures in New York, he hoped to send them on to Gérôme in Paris. In similarly buoyant tones, Eakins mused a few months later, "There is no particular harm done by

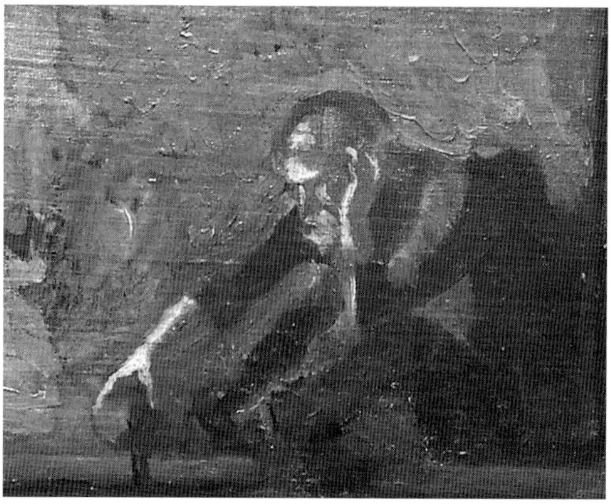

5. Thomas Eakins, *Columbus in Prison*, ca. 1876. Oil on canvas, 5⁵/₈ × 7³/₈ in. Courtesy of Kennedy Galleries, New York.

exhibiting if it calls attention to my name."[33] Because there are so few surviving letters dating to this period, there is no way of knowing whether Eakins acted on this plan. He had, however, remained in touch with both Bonnat and Gérôme throughout this period, occasionally seeking their approval and advice on the management of his blossoming career.

Although Eakins abandoned *Hiawatha* at this time, he did not give up on the idea of crafting an American history painting. Eakins attempted two other American historical subjects before completing *William Rush*. Unlike *Hiawatha*, these two projects, depicting Christopher Columbus and the Confederate general Robert E. Lee, did not develop beyond preliminary studies. Of the two subjects, the Civil War theme remains among the most enigmatic of his career. Two surviving images, depicting Lee's surrender to General Ulysses S. Grant at Appomattox, probably once formed a single composition that was later divided.[34] The sketches focus on a recent event following in the tradition of Benjamin West, whose *Death of General Wolfe* of 1770 depicted a scene that had occurred only eleven years prior. The theme of Southern defeat may have been suggested by Winslow Homer's success with *Prisoners from the Front*, which was shown at the Exposition Universelle in Paris in 1867. However, the failure of Pennsylvania history painter Peter F. Rothermel's epic *Battle of Gettysburg*, which was nearly universally condemned when it appeared at the Centennial Exhibition, may have led Eakins to reconsider the development of his own Civil War image.[35] Eakins would not revisit Civil War subject matter until the 1890s, when he created two life-size relief sculptures for the Soldiers and Sailors Memorial in Brooklyn.

As with his sketch of Lee, the Columbus study (Figure 5) shows an accomplished man facing declining fortunes. Although Columbus was a popular subject, as attested to by the roughly ten images on view at Philadelphia's 1876 Centennial Exhibition, Eakins again selected an unusual scene within the larger narrative.[36] Like *Hiawatha*, Eakins's subject came from a literary source: Washington Irving's *History of the Life and Voyages of Christopher Columbus*, published in 1828. Rather than illustrating one of the many heroic episodes from Irving's narrative of the life of the celebrated explorer, Eakins depicted Columbus after he was arrested in Hispanola and sent in irons to Spain following his third voyage to America. In this little sketch, an aged Columbus appears seated on the floor of his cell gazing at the ball shackled to his leg.[37]

As he considered the Columbus theme, Eakins studied earlier works of American art. During the late summer and fall of 1877, Eakins traveled to Washington, D.C., to undertake a portrait of President Rutherford B. Hayes commissioned by Philadelphia's Union League. While in Washington, Eakins made sketches of American paintings and sculptures in a small notebook. Notable among these images are three figures of Columbus taken from separate compositions in the United States Capitol building, a rich site for viewing artists' interpretations of American historical subjects. Eakins copied two of the figures from sculptor Randolph Rogers's panels for the bronze doors at the east entrance of the Capitol (modeled 1856–58). One of these sketches (Figure 6) was based on Rogers's version of *Columbus in Chains*. Eakins also sketched John Vanderlyn's large painting *The Landing of Columbus* in the Capitol rotunda (installed 1847).[38] This sketch appears to have been intended as a costume study, for it includes a textual description of the clothing worn by the explorer. Vanderlyn, whose *Ariadne Asleep on the Island of Naxos* (1809–14) had been exhibited many times in Philadelphia, may also have interested Eakins because he was among the first American artists to study in France. In any case, none of these pencil sketches influenced the Columbus oil study, which may have preceded Eakins's trips to Washington.[39] However, the Vanderlyn and Rogers sketches suggest that Eakins continued to contemplate a Columbus subject as he was completing the painting of William Rush.

As Kathleen Foster has shown, the Washington sketchbook indicates that studies made on his fall trip to the city contributed to the development of the Rush picture.[40] The sketchbook contains notes and sketches for the painting done in Philadelphia as well as in the capital. For example, the book includes a number of early nineteenth-century costume studies made in Washington from works by the French sculptor Jean-Antoine Houdon and the Federal-era American painters Thomas Sully (Figure 7), Chester Harding, and Gilbert Stuart. Also in the sketchbook are measurements taken directly from Rush's sculptures in Philadelphia, as well as drawings for some of the props featured in the 1877 painting.

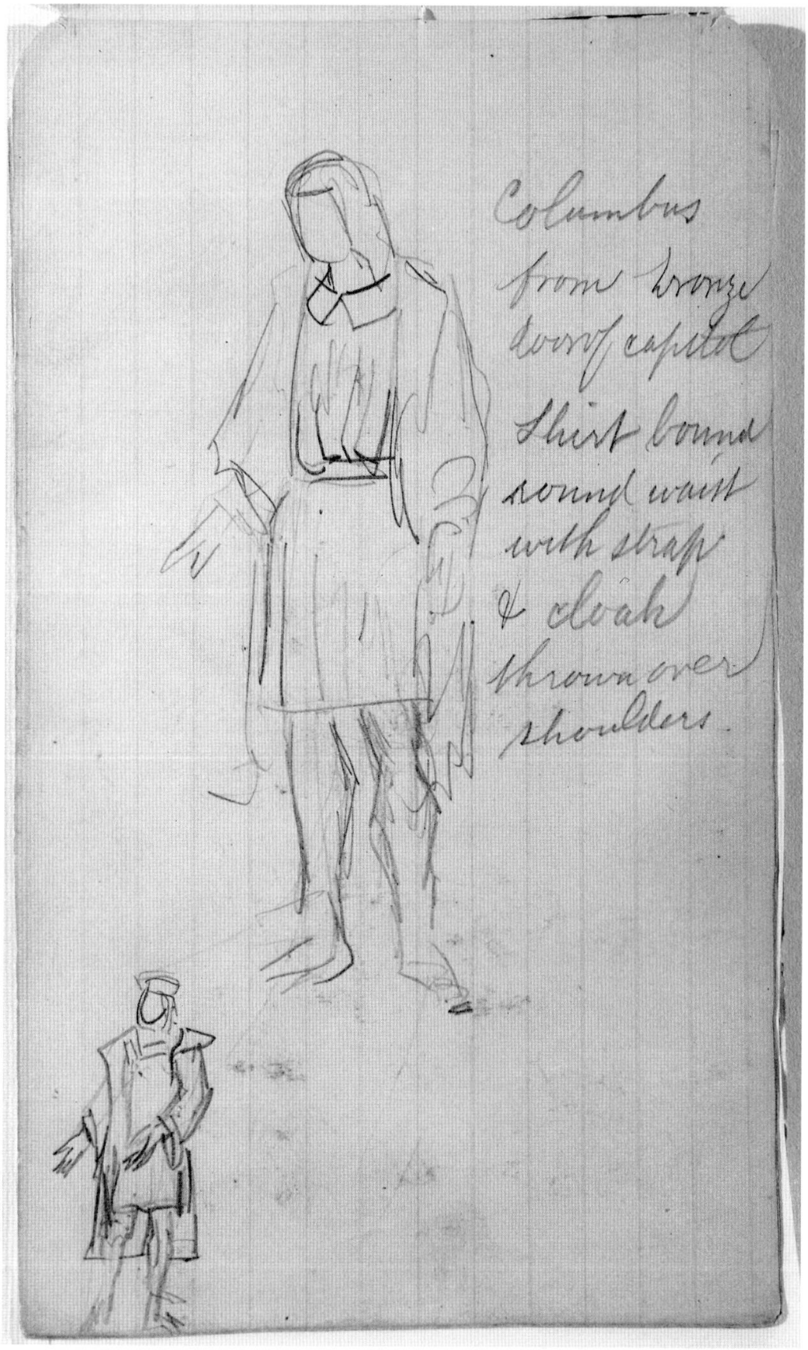

6. Thomas Eakins, *Washington Sketchbook: Christopher Columbus* (two views; verso), 1876–78. Graphite on blue-lined machine-made paper, 4½ × 7½ in. Courtesy of the Pennsylvania Academy of the Fine Arts, Philadelphia. Charles Bregler's Thomas Eakins Collection. Purchased with the partial support of the Pew Memorial Trust and the John S. Phillips Fund.

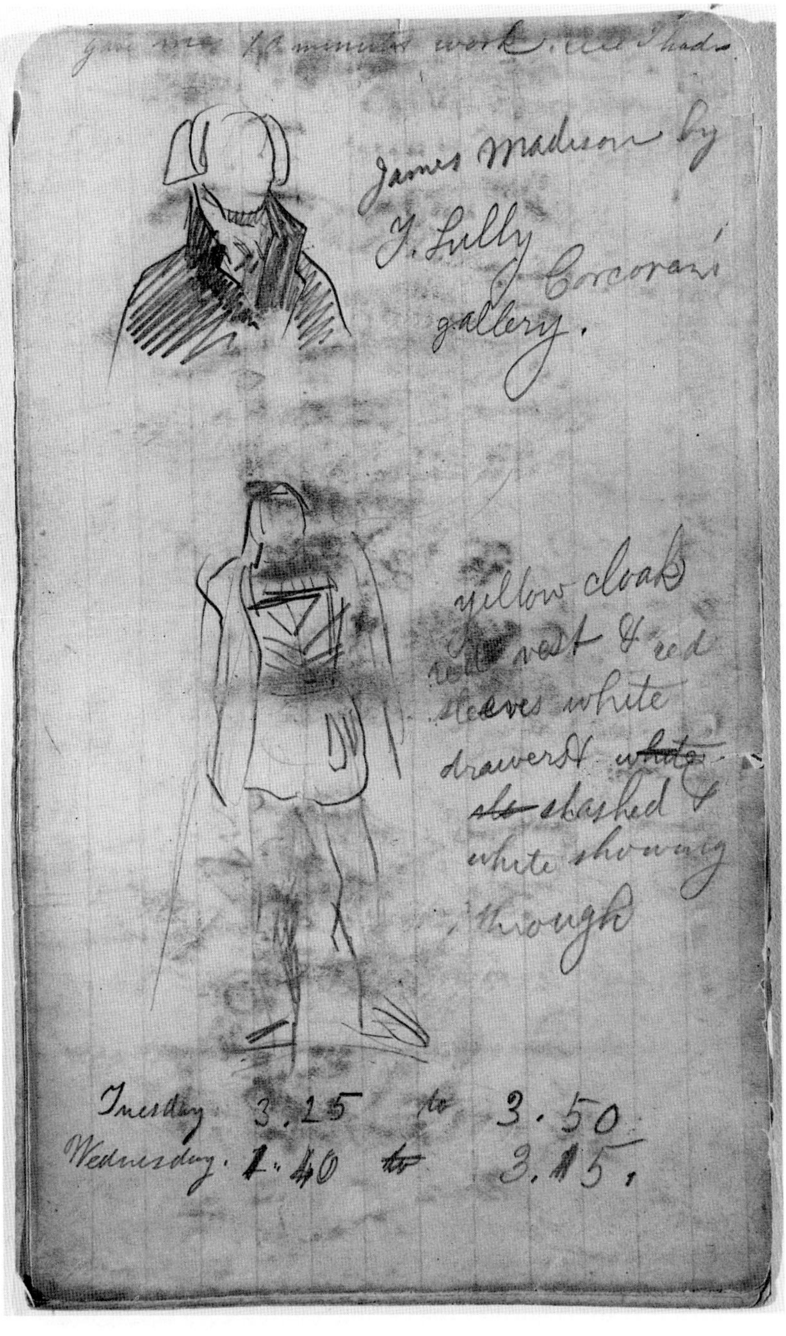

7. Thomas Eakins, *Washington Sketchbook: Costume Studies; after Thomas Sully's "James Madison"; after John Vanderlyn's "Columbus"* (verso), 1876–78. Graphite on blue-lined machine-made paper, 4½ × 7½ in. Courtesy of the Pennsylvania Academy of the Fine Arts, Philadelphia. Charles Bregler's Thomas Eakins Collection. Purchased with the partial support of the Pew Memorial Trust and the John S. Phillips Fund.

While Eakins's sketches of earlier American paintings lack the textual descriptions found in the "Spanish notebook," they suggest a similar sense of observation and technical interest throughout. They also reflect Eakins's shift from an exploration of American history to the specific interest in the history of American art that he visualized in *William Rush*. As the drawings in the Washington sketchbook demonstrate, *William Rush Carving His Allegorical Figure of the Schuylkill River* was shaped by Eakins's growing awareness of American art of the past. A further example of this is a list, interleaved in the sketchbook between technical studies for the Rush painting and preceding the Columbus sketches from the Capitol, that Eakins compiled of seventy-five Philadelphia artists, past and present. The list reflects Eakins's growing consciousness of the city's lengthy artistic heritage. The roster of artists is intriguing for some unusual inclusions of now little-known painters, such as Edward Dalton Marchant (1806–87), and for the notable omissions of some of Eakins's closest friends, such as William Sartain (1843–1924). Although it is impossible to know what compelled Eakins to make such a list, it suggests his concern with an American art historical tradition and his understanding of Philadelphia's place within this tradition.[41]

In *William Rush*, Eakins selected a theme that was at once obscure but also epic in its capacity to illustrate the ideals that he sought to uphold throughout his professional life. In abandoning the Hiawatha and Columbus paintings, Eakins rejected two fashionable subjects that might have been salable. By painting Rush as an American Old Master, Eakins asserted an idea that was just gaining ground in the 1870s, namely, that America had an artistic past worthy of study.

America's Old Masters

Eakins's contemplation of the art historical past began in earnest at the Prado, where he found Old Master paintings so close to nature that he declared them to be "free from every affectation."[42] Unfortunately, the "big painting" of Europe was, by and large, not to be found in the United States. Nor did Americans pay much attention to their own Old Masters. However, by the 1870s, a few significant events heralded a growing interest in the American artistic tradition. This period witnessed the rapid growth of specialized journals and illustrated magazines that would help to professionalize the field of art criticism. As a consequence, the number of books and articles on American art expanded greatly in these years, with many, particularly around the year of the Centennial, focusing on art of the past. Another significant development at this time was the expansion of exhibition venues within the United States, allowing more frequent opportunities to view historical American art. This accompanied the professional credentialing of American artists in academies at home and abroad. All of these influences helped to shape a growing consciousness of an American art historical tradition.[43]

As early as 1834, William Dunlap's *History of the Rise and Progress of the Arts of Design in the United States* provided an in-depth, albeit anecdotal, guide to the lives of the artists of the United States—past and present. Yet it would not be followed by significant writings in the field until the 1860s. Henry Theodore Tuckerman's *Book of the Artists* of 1867 picked up where Dunlap left off and urged American artists to consider native subject matter. Following Dunlap's model, Tuckerman chose a largely biographical approach. Despite this limitation, the book provided invaluable reference material for the more critical evaluations of the field that succeeded it. By the time Eakins began his painting of William Rush, several additional studies of American art had become available.[44]

Eakins's friend Earl Shinn was among those to benefit from the expansion of magazine publishing following the Civil War, writing art criticism for several periodicals and eventually becoming art editor for *The Nation*. In 1872, Shinn took the occasion of the demolition of the old Pennsylvania Academy building to write about the institution's history for *Lippincott's Magazine*. In addition to praising the foresight of its founders (including William Rush), Shinn wrote of the hardships young artists faced in acquiring basic artistic training from the fledgling Academy. Like Dunlap before him, Shinn perpetuated stories about the difficulties that American artists, including Pennsylvanians such as Benjamin West and Thomas Sully, had in finding opportunities to study.[45] The demolition of the old Academy and the building of a new one may have contributed to Eakins's interest in American art of the past and the artistic tradition of his native Philadelphia.

There were also increasing opportunities to see historical American art in this period. In 1872, the Brooklyn Art Association held what it called "The First Chronological Exhibition of American Art," which intended to illustrate "a history of art in this country from the earliest period . . . to the present time."[46] Although American art exhibitions frequently included older works, the Brooklyn show, with more than 250 paintings, was an early effort to present a historical survey of American art. The works in the show spanned a broad historical range, from the colonial portraiture of John Smibert to the landscapes of the recently deceased Hudson River School painter John Kensett. In spite of the chronological sweep of the exhibition, it was far from comprehensive. Having drawn extensively from the collections of a small group of private lenders and institutions, the show ultimately offered an eclectic view of American art.[47]

Another difficulty for the viewer was that, in spite of the title of the exhibit, the arrangement was not chronological—making a progressive visual survey impossible.

Eakins may not have seen the Brooklyn exhibition, but in Philadelphia he had access to a growing collection of historical American art at the Pennsylvania Academy. In addition, he most likely became familiar with the private collections of the institution's supporters, such as John Sartain, Fairman Rogers, James Claghorn, and Joseph Harrison. Not only did the Academy possess outstanding examples of American art, it also had several major American history paintings, including such large grand manner pictures as Washington Allston's *The Dead Man Restored to Life by Touching the Bones of the Prophet Elisha* (1811–13), Charles Robert Leslie's *Murder of Rutland by Lord Clifford* (1815), and Benjamin West's *Death on a Pale Horse* (1817). From these works and those of living artists such as Peter F. Rothermel and Christian Schussele, Eakins could have developed a familiarity with an American history painting tradition. However, the Academy had to move its collection to cramped temporary quarters after the sale of its old Chestnut Street building in 1870. According to Shinn, the works remained accessible to students but they were only intermittently available to the public.[48] With the reopening of the school in April 1876 in its new building, designed by Frank Furness, Eakins continued his research for the William Rush painting using the Academy's collections.[49] For example, he probably modeled his image of Rush upon the Academy's terra-cotta self-portrait of the sculptor. He also made extensive costume sketches from John Lewis Krimmel's 1812 painting *Fourth of July in Centre Square* (Figure 8), which shows Philadelphians celebrating the holiday with Rush's *Nymph* in the background.[50]

While Eakins was working on his painting of Rush, he visited at least two other Philadelphia collections, those of the Union League Club and Independence Hall. Each offered him the ability to study a range of American art extending back to the eighteenth century. Although neither had an overtly artistic mission, both institutions had, through the accretion of gifts, obtained significant historical collections of American art, including holdings by the Peale family, Thomas Sully, and Gilbert Stuart. Independence Hall, which owned Rush's 1815 sculpture of *George Washington*, actually witnessed a dramatic expansion of its collection of historical portraits in the 1870s under the stewardship of the antiquarian Frank M. Etting.[51] At Independence Hall, Eakins made studies of Rush's *Washington* and sketched from a lifetime portrait of William Rush (ca. 1813) attributed to Rembrandt Peale. The latter provided the inspiration for the costume that Rush wears in Eakins's painting.[52]

Philadelphia's Centennial Exhibition of 1876, America's first world's fair, offered another opportunity to showcase American art of the past. The organiz-

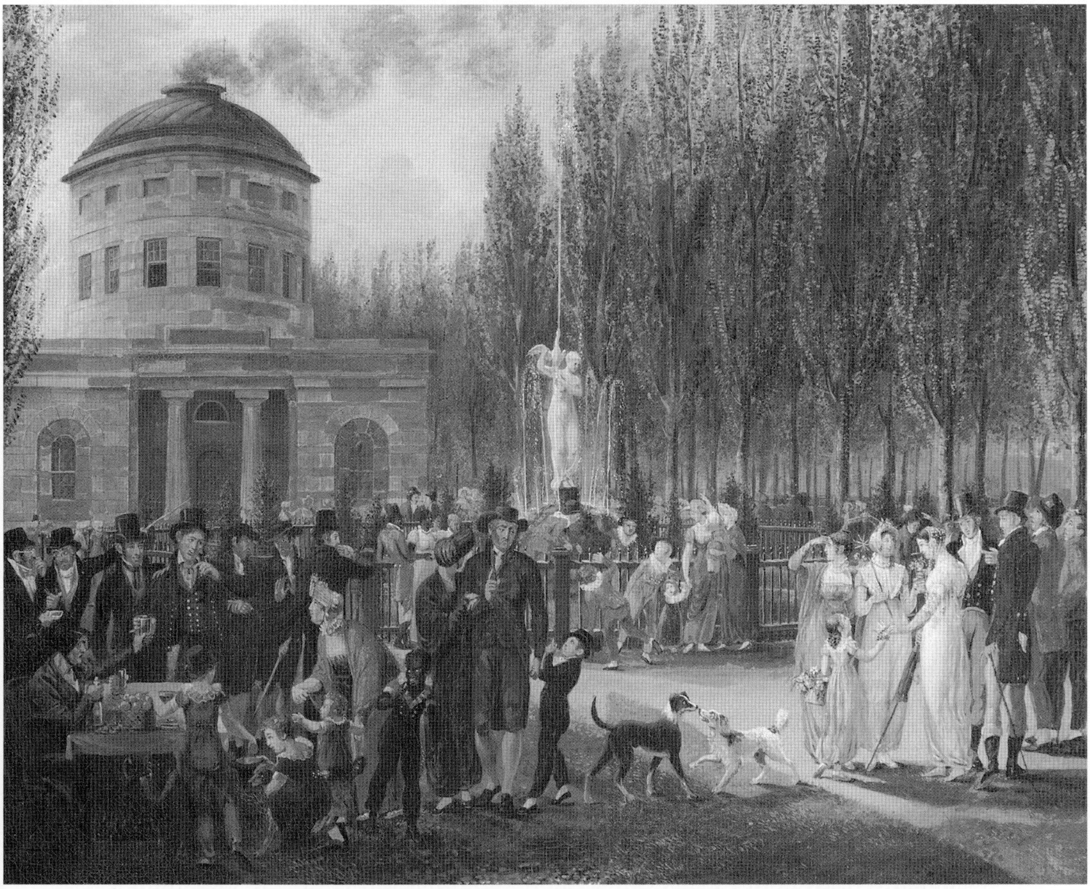

8. John Lewis Krimmel, *Fourth of July in Centre Square*, 1812. Oil on canvas, 22¾ × 29 in. Courtesy of the Pennsylvania Academy of the Fine Arts, Philadelphia. Pennsylvania Academy purchase (from the estate of Paul Beck Jr.).

ers of the fine art exhibit at the Centennial, headed by Eakins's sometimes mentor, the artist John Sartain, included a selection of historical American art, helping to fulfill the fair's mission to celebrate one hundred years of American progress. This display faced many of the problems witnessed by the earlier Brooklyn show and, in fact, included several works borrowed from the same handful of collections. Following the Brooklyn exhibition by only four years, the Centennial display seemed to confirm that America had an artistic tradition worthy of appreciation. It also featured a small exhibit of earlier American sculpture, insufficient for constructing a history of the medium, but notable for its inclusion of work by William Rush.[53] As the first international art exhibition held in the United States, the Centennial marked a turning point in the history of American art. Although many critics complained of the mediocrity of the art on view at the fair, American artists hoped that their contributions would rival those of their European counterparts.[54]

The fair may have inspired Eakins to consider America's artistic heritage in other ways. As a celebration of the nation's first one hundred years, the Centennial provided ample opportunities for members of newly professionalized fields, artists among them, to reflect upon their origins and consider the progress they had made.[55] As Sarah Burns has argued, following the Civil War, American artists increasingly eschewed bohemian eccentricities in order to cultivate an image of "competence, discipline, social skill, organization, and managerial acumen."[56] Accompanying this move to professionalization was the rapid expansion of academic institutions for artists. Having once suffered from inadequate training, American artists now had access to academies at home and abroad that offered a systematic means of preparing students for professional careers. Amy Werbel has suggested that, by the 1870s, even Eakins "could have looked back at his own experiences as an art student in Philadelphia with a sense of great accomplishment. In place of the previous 'program' of intermittent criticism by local artists, students now engaged in a coherent, full-time curriculum overseen by prominent experts in the field."[57] American artists had arrived.

Reviving William Rush

By the time Eakins completed his painting of William Rush, he had gained a familiarity with both the art of his nation and that of his city. In preparation for *William Rush Carving His Allegorical Figure of the Schuylkill River*, Eakins supplemented his broader exploration of earlier American art with a thorough study of Rush's sculptures. For this purpose, he sketched each of the works that appear in his painting: the ship's scrolls, *Water Nymph and Bittern*, *George Washington*, and *Allegory of the Waterworks*. He also gained a solid comprehension of Rush's forms by making three-dimensional wax models of each of the figurative sculptures.

Even though Rush's preferred materials—wood and terra-cotta—were inherently fragile, many of his sculptures had endured to Eakins's day. All three of the figurative works that Eakins included in his painting remained in the public eye, suggesting that, while Philadelphians might no longer have recalled Rush's authorship of these sculptures, they remained familiar with the works themselves. Rush's *Nymph* and his statue of George Washington were frequently mentioned in travel accounts and guidebooks. *Allegory of the Waterworks* was another highly visible public sculpture, one of two figures that Rush carved for the entrances to the millhouse of the new waterworks in Fairmount in 1825, which remained a popular public attraction in the 1870s.[58]

Apart from the continuing presence of Rush's public sculptures, Eakins personally encountered Rush's legacy in other ways throughout his negotiations of the city of Philadelphia. Eakins would surely have felt Rush's presence at the Pennsylvania Academy. As a founding member of the institution, Rush's name was part of Academy lore. The Academy owned significant examples of Rush's work, having a particularly rich collection of his bust-length portraits of leading Philadelphians.[59] Rush was also buried conspicuously close to the Eakins family plot in Woodlands Cemetery, where Eakins's mother was interred in 1872. Furthermore, Rush remained sufficiently present in Philadelphia that Eakins was able to visit the site of the sculptor's old Front Street shop, where he "found some very old people who still remembered it and described it" for him. From an elderly woodcarver, Eakins borrowed one of Rush's old sketchbooks, which may have provided the imagery for the sketches on the wall of Rush's workshop and for the ship's scrolls that appear in the foreground of the final painting.[60]

Through such diligent study, Eakins probably became his era's foremost expert on Rush's work. However, the question remains, why did Eakins select the sculptor as his subject? According to Elizabeth Johns's research, Rush had become an obscure figure by the 1870s, a point that seems validated by the fact that Eakins prepared a précis of Rush's life and work to accompany his painting.[61] Whether or not viewers ever saw all of the text that he drafted is unclear, but shortened versions of this text appeared in exhibition catalogues. For example, when the painting was shown at the Pennsylvania Academy in 1881 (before the audience most likely to have heard of Rush), the catalogue included an abridgment of the longer description and a sketch by Eakins that acted as a visual key to the painting.[62]

Scholars have interpreted these texts as evidence that Eakins hoped to revive the reputation of the little-known sculptor with his painting.[63] However, a closer reading of the texts reveals that Eakins drafted an idiosyncratic biography for Rush in which he omitted large portions of the sculptor's career, such as his extensive work as a portraitist. Instead, Eakins highlighted the sculptor's devotion to life study, his civic commitments, his professional standing, and the enduring legacy of his public monuments. Eakins's approach to Rush's biography suggests his goal was not simply to rekindle interest in the sculptor but to fashion a professional role model to stand at the beginning of the American sculptural tradition.

In order to draft his text, Eakins probably read biographical accounts of Rush's life. Johns found that early writers characterized Rush in two distinct ways, the first defined him as a ship carver and, the second, portrayed him as an artist.[64] The most readily available source of the first type of interpretation was John Fanning Watson's *Annals of Philadelphia*, an invaluable city history first published in 1830, with revised editions printed well into the twentieth century. Watson also provided source material for Rush biographies appearing in subsequent histories, such as Henry Simpson's 1859 *The Lives of Eminent Philadelphians, Now Deceased.* Watson touted Rush's international renown, citing the flocks of European admirers who would come to view his figureheads when American ships sailed into British ports. Watson declared that Rush "surpasses any other American, and probably any other ship-carver in the world!" Although by 1830 Rush had long distinguished himself as a sculptor of free-standing works, he remained for Watson the carver whose figureheads excited "admiration in foreign ports." Watson considered this international recognition noteworthy for a humble American who, according to the author, had reached the pinnacle of his career some thirty years earlier when an English firm commissioned two figureheads from him.[65] Given his focus, it is not surprising that Watson made no mention of the *Nymph.*

In contrast to Watson, William Dunlap, in his *History of the Rise and Progress of the Arts of Design in the United States*, positioned Rush as an artist rather than an artisan.[66] Accordingly, Dunlap focused on Rush's portrait busts and full-length figurative works. Dunlap placed less value on Rush's work as a ship carver, which he considered a time-consuming obstacle to Rush's attainment of skill as a stonecutter. In the era of neoclassical sculpture, Dunlap lamented that Rush had never turned to marble. Dunlap also published what is perhaps the only scrap of evidence to support Eakins's belief that Rush studied from life. According to Dunlap, "Mr. Rush was observing in his study of the human figure," and he quoted the sculptor as saying, "'When I see my boys bungling in the carving of a hand, I tell them look at your own hands—place them in the same position—imitate them and you must be right. You always have the model at *hand.*'" Although Dunlap's coverage of Rush was brief, he listed "the Water Nymph at 'Fair Mount'" among the artist's accomplishments.[67]

Rush's posthumous reputation seems to have faltered by the mid-nineteenth century as a generation of neoclassical sculptors gained ascendancy.[68] Eakins's painting, without question, raised Rush's profile. However, as Johns has shown, Eakins himself became so closely identified with Rush that aspects of his own biography erroneously began to permeate stories about Rush and his sculpture.[69] In fact, Rush's relative obscurity lent a certain malleability to his biography, which Eakins manipulated for his own purposes. Through his emphases and omissions in both painting and text, Eakins fashioned a Rush in his own image, leading to confusion in later years as writers ascribed his traits to the earlier artist.

In his lengthiest text, Eakins effectively crafted a new interpretation of William Rush's career. In Eakins's hands, Rush became a ship carver who gained the commission for the Centre Square *Nymph* because of the international renown of his figureheads. In other words, Eakins argued that Rush's solid reputation as a talented artisan was rewarded with sculptural commissions, echoing the personal ambitions he shared with Earl Shinn.[70] While Rush made the leap from carver to sculptor in Eakins's extended text, Eakins blurred any sense that this represented a significant professional advance by returning to a discussion of Rush's ship-carving shop before shifting back again to the other freestanding sculptures included in his picture. In this version of the text, Eakins completely ignored the portrait busts that Rush regularly exhibited at the Academy, speaking only of Rush's public projects: "figure heads, scrolls for vessels, ornamental statues and tobacco signs called Pompeys."[71] Eakins elevated anything in Rush's oeuvre that had been on public view—linking tobacco signs and ship's scrolls with "high art." In doing so, Eakins failed to acknowledge the nineteenth-century hierarchy, which asserted that an artist's intellectual accomplishments were superior to the manual labor of artisans such as ship carvers. Yet Rush could not be so easily defined—he was, unlike many neoclassical sculptors, both a skilled artisan and a creative artist.

Rush and the American Sculptural Tradition

By the 1860s, Rush's place as a first-rate American artist was compromised by the very artisanal origins of his fame. Given that all of his large-scale projects were carved from wood, a material typically associated with the decorative arts, questions could be raised as to whether he was a sculptor at all. An 1867 publication was typical in its praise of Rush's *George Washington* (1815) as "a monument of the aspiration for native art awakened by the new national life," while at the same time proclaiming that "no American sculptor of ability had [yet] risen" in this period. The author further noted that "it was not until about 1830 or 1840 that works of sculpture began to appear which proved that ere long a rich harvest in this department of art was to be the growth of American soil."[72] Rush had become a curiosity, not quite a full-fledged sculptor by virtue of his chosen media. In the 1870s, as American sculptors increasingly left marble for work in bronze, Eakins challenged the assumption that the American sculptural tradition began with marble, a material that he never used himself.

The history of sculpture in the United States was in many ways more complicated than that of painting. Sculpting materials in the early Republic were rare and costly; the opportunities for training, few and inadequate. Such obstacles led the painter John Trumbull to warn sculptor John Frazee in 1816 that "sculpture would not be wanted here for a century."[73] Most nineteenth-century discussions of American sculpture acknowledged antecedents such as Rush or the wax sculptor Patience Wright, but Frazee, as a stonecutter, was typically upheld as the founder of the American school of sculpture. Yet Frazee's untutored work was usually presented as an "interesting" and somewhat primitive prelude to the neoclassical sculptors. As Johns has demonstrated, most studies credited Hiram Powers, Horatio Greenough, and their neoclassical cohort in Italy as the first significant native school of sculpture.[74]

However, neoclassicism had fallen out of favor by the 1870s, causing some critics to reevaluate the state of sculpture in the United States. Shifting tastes and political strife in Italy helped contribute to the decline of the Italianate neoclassical style, but the emergence of a younger generation of Parisian-trained sculptors ended the dominance of neoclassicism altogether. Beaux-Arts sculptors such as Augustus St. Gaudens led the move to bronze and to a more naturalistic mode of sculptural representation. Materials aside, the Italian and French schools of sculpture were viewed as irreconcilably opposed to one another on aesthetic and methodological grounds. Neoclassical artists emulated antique sculpture and relied on the skill of Italian stonecutters to execute their designs. By contrast, many Beaux-Arts-trained sculptors rejected the ideal compositions of their neoclassical predecessors in favor of a bold naturalism based on close study of the human figure.

The writer Charles Akers struck at the heart of the matter by accusing neoclassical sculptors of adhering to foreign models instead of working from nature. Akers suggested that neoclassical sculptors vainly struggled to "produce something equal to the Quoit-thrower of Myron or the Apollo Belvedere." Furthermore, he questioned whether neoclassical sculptors should even be considered Americans, declaring them to be "denationalized," because their subjects "are strange to the people, and the workmanship foreign."[75] Although Eakins admired the classical sculptor Phidias, he never advocated emulating his work and felt that the Greek artist's talent was the product of his adherence to nature. As Eakins stated, "I don't like a long study of casts even of sculptors of the best Greek period. At best, they are only imitations, and an imitation of imitations cannot have so much life as an imitation of nature itself."[76] Although he was referring to the time-honored tradition of sketching from casts as part of an artist's training, it was a philosophy that he brought to all of his work, including sculpture. Eakins, who hated stylistic "affectation," would likely have faulted neoclassical sculptors for emulating the work of other artists instead of looking to nature.

Eakins also voiced a pronounced bias against marble. During his first visit to the Louvre, he complained that the marble statues there made him "shiver." He also rejected the notion that a stone carver could accurately translate a highly trained artist's work. In part, this issue revolved around Eakins's belief that artists, like doctors or lawyers, were skilled professionals. Eakins's opinions on the subject surfaced throughout his career but were most clearly articulated in the 1890s in an exchange with Augustus St. Gaudens over the creation of a posthumous cast of sculptor Edmund Austin Stewardson's *The Bather* for the collection of the Pennsylvania Academy. St. Gaudens argued that, as it had been the artist's intention to carve the piece, marble was a more appropriate medium for the replica. But Eakins believed that, following the artist's death, bronze would be best because it more faithfully recorded the artist's hand. Eakins felt that even the most "expert workman in the country" would "ruin [the sculpture's] refinement."[77] Here the word *workman* highlights the gulf between sculptor and stonecutter—the stonecutter in Eakins's eyes was a technician, not an artist. Years earlier, during a controversy over his own *Knitting* and *Spinning* reliefs, Eakins had already made clear the importance that he placed on his academic training over the manual abilities of stone carvers, writing to his patron, "How can any stone cutter unacquainted with the nude follow my lines? . . . How could the life be retained?" He then asked that the panels be cast "in iron or bronze . . . so that good work and good money may not be thrown away."[78] Eakins's suggestion that Rush worked from life, coupled with his ability as a woodcarver to work his own materials, marked him as an artist rather than an artisan and distinguished him from the neoclassical sculptors who surpassed him in fame.[79]

Eakins also availed himself of the opportunity to study Rush's work in bronze, perhaps allowing him to more easily distance the artist from neoclassical marble sculptors. Sometime around 1872 a bronze cast of Rush's wooden nymph was installed near the Callowhill Street bridge. The cleaned and whitewashed original was returned to the forebay at Fairmount. The text that Eakins drafted for *William Rush* discusses this process in some detail, suggesting that he either witnessed it or had some direct contact with someone who had. Although Eakins studied both versions of the *Nymph*, he made most of his sketches from the Callowhill Street bronze, which was possible to observe from multiple vantage points.[80] Eakins likely felt that bronze offered the best means of preserving Rush's work. Yet this meant that Eakins prepared most of the studies for the sculpture of a carver from a cast.

In turning to the subject of William Rush, Eakins was not only reclaiming Rush's reputation but also asserting a new origin for American sculpture. He placed Rush at the beginning of a native sculptural tradition that did not emulate foreign models or rely on foreign workmanship. Although Rush's allegorical nymph was, in fact, influenced by the classical tradition, Eakins made the point of clarifying in his text that it represented a Philadelphia subject: the Schuylkill River and not "Leda and the Swan" as "the idle and unobserving have . . .

now generally so miscalled" her. Although he distanced Rush's sculpture from classical subject matter, Eakins acknowledged that the work was influenced by French artists (who favored the neoclassical style at that time).[81] However, given the tension between Italian and French trained sculptors that emerged in the 1870s, Eakins may have considered the French neoclassicists in rather different terms than he did the Italians. In addition, Jean-Antoine Houdon, the only French neoclassical sculptor who he ever mentioned while he was studying in France, was well-known for his realistic portraits and his devotion to anatomical study. By connecting Rush to a French tradition, even a neoclassical one, Eakins allied the woodcarver with his own background as a French-trained artist. In showing Rush engaged in life study and by studying his *Nymph* in bronze, Eakins associated the sculptor with his own Beaux-Arts training—placing Rush at the head of an American school of sculpture that he could then link with his own artistic methods.

No Smirking Goddess

Of course, William Rush is not the only subject of Eakins's painting. In order to make life study the focus of the work, Eakins placed equal, if not greater, emphasis on the sculptor's nude female model. Yet as a student in Paris, when confronted with academic paintings of nude women, many of them based on classical Greek subjects, Eakins felt he could "conceive of few circumstances wherein I would have to make a woman naked." He complained of the contrivances that artists used to reveal the female body under the guises of "Phrynes, Venuses, nymphs, hermaphrodites, houris & Greek proper names." He castigated the artists' "mutilation" of these "smiling smirking goddesses"—presumably through the idealized elimination of pubic hair, also a common practice of neoclassical sculptors. Significantly, when Eakins painted his first nude figure in *William Rush*, he portrayed her not as one of these "smirking goddesses" but as an unidealized woman posing for an artist.[82]

Although William Rush was a member of the life committee of the Columbianum, a short-lived artist's association founded in Philadelphia in 1794, and a director of the Pennsylvania Academy when it instituted its first life class in 1813, he probably did not have any opportunities to study nude female models. Finding men willing to pose partially draped was difficult enough in the early Republic; nude female models were practically unheard of. In his history of the Academy for *Lippincott's*, Earl Shinn recounted a popular anecdote about the artist Charles Willson Peale's baring his own chest for the life class because of the scarcity of male models.[83] The problem of obtaining models seems to have little improved by 1832, when Fanny Trollope, in her travelogue *Domestic Man-*

ners of the Americans, recalled, "One young artist, whose circumstances did not permit his going to Europe, but who being nevertheless determined that his studies should, as nearly as possible, resemble those of the European academies, was about to commence drawing the human figure, for which purpose he had provided himself with a thin silk dress, in which to clothe his models, as no one of any station, he said, could be found who would submit to sit as a model without clothing."[84] Of course, this does not preclude the use of models of "no station"; however, there is scant evidence for this practice.

Some progress may have been made by the mid-nineteenth century. Two drawings dating to the 1850s by the painters Christian Schussele and Peter F. Rothermel provide the earliest evidence of female models posing nude at the Pennsylvania Academy.[85] Female models were still a rarity at the Academy in the 1860s when Eakins first trained there.[86] They remained difficult to obtain into the 1870s when Eakins began teaching at the school. In spite of a perpetual deficit of female models, Eakins made life study of a woman the focus of *William Rush Carving His Allegorical Figure of the Schuylkill River.*

Moreover, just as Eakins hoped to revive interest in Rush with his textual accompaniments to the painting, he was equally intent on restoring the identity of the model. In the longest of his texts, he all but gave her name, referring to her as "the daughter of [Rush's] friend and colleague in the water committee, James Vanuxem, an esteemed merchant."[87] Although he stopped just short of giving the full name of the model, he unambiguously asserted her familial identity and class. Even without the aid of Eakins's text, the image clearly presents Rush's model as a respectable woman, who has chosen to pose for the artist but not out of financial need. Just as Rush's gentlemanly attire asserts his decorum and professionalism, the unusual prominence of the model's discarded, but highly fashionable, clothing in the foreground of the painting reinforces her class status.[88]

Tradition holds that James Vanuxem's eldest daughter, Louisa, was the model for the *Nymph.*[89] Eakins's painting cemented this tradition, but it also embellished upon it by depicting her nude. Yet, aside from Eakins's painting, there is no indication that anyone prior to 1877 believed that Vanuxem had posed nude. As Elizabeth Johns has demonstrated, the majority of the stories that circulated about Rush and his nude model grew out of Eakins's image.[90] As early as 1884, written accounts claimed that the sculpture had been "denounced when first erected as immodest."[91] In subsequent decades, versions of the modeling story suggested that Vanuxem had created a public scandal by posing nude for Rush.[92] If Vanuxem, a young, unmarried women from a respectable family, had posed nude, the scandal would surely have tainted Rush and his work in addition to ruining her reputation. The notion that the *Nymph* was regarded as a salacious work is not borne out by the favorable descriptions of the figure that appeared around the time it was installed in Centre Square. Admired for its "graceful attitude and attire," the sculpture became a major public attraction, visited by everyone from Fanny Trollope to devout Moravian sisters. Further, Krimmel's *Fourth of July in Centre Square* clearly illustrates that the sculpture was not shunned by women and children, even if the Quaker parents in the foreground appear unnerved by their son's scrutiny of the figure.[93]

Not only would Vanuxem's nude modeling have been considered immodest, but it also would have been highly unusual due to the scarcity of female models in this period. In addition, it would not even have been necessary given Rush's methods. In the final sculpture, the *Nymph* is fully clothed in a simple gown. Although there are some effective passages of wet drapery around the breasts and thighs, the anatomy of the nymph's midsection remains obscured by drapery folds. While Beaux-Arts-trained artists such as Eakins often sculpted their figures nude before clothing them to ensure anatomical accuracy, Rush would not have been able to apply this modeling technique to the subtractive method of woodcarving. Rush may have wanted to consult a (draped) model in order to maintain correct proportions during the planning stages of his work, but he would not have carved the final sculpture from a nude model. Eakins, conversely, would work directly from life for his later sculpted works—fashioning clay models that could be altered before casting into bronze. Rush's more direct method did not allow for this possibility. Eakins again used Rush to reflect his own practices.

Eakins may well have invented the story of Rush working from a nude life model to assert "the legitimacy of [his] own artistic methods," but his identification of the model went beyond this intention. As late as 1879, most of the female models at the Academy concealed their identities, coming to the school "closely veiled" and appearing "before the classes with a mask over their faces." It was even stated that "one or two that have been coming for several years are not known except as models, even to the actuary of the Academy."[94] Eakins made a sketch of one such masked model (Figure 9) during his early study at the Pennsylvania Academy in the 1860s.[95] For Eakins, Louisa Vanuxem—perhaps even more than Rush—asserted the legitimacy and professionalism of his method of life study through her respectability and class background. The women who posed as life models during Eakins's early career were women with questionable reputations, who often came from the ranks of the working class or who earned their livings as prostitutes. Eakins's identification of Vanuxem as a life model rejects the widespread belief that artists' models were disreputable or sexually available women.[96]

As Earl Shinn lamented, Rush's "Philadelphia had no Piazza di Spagna with

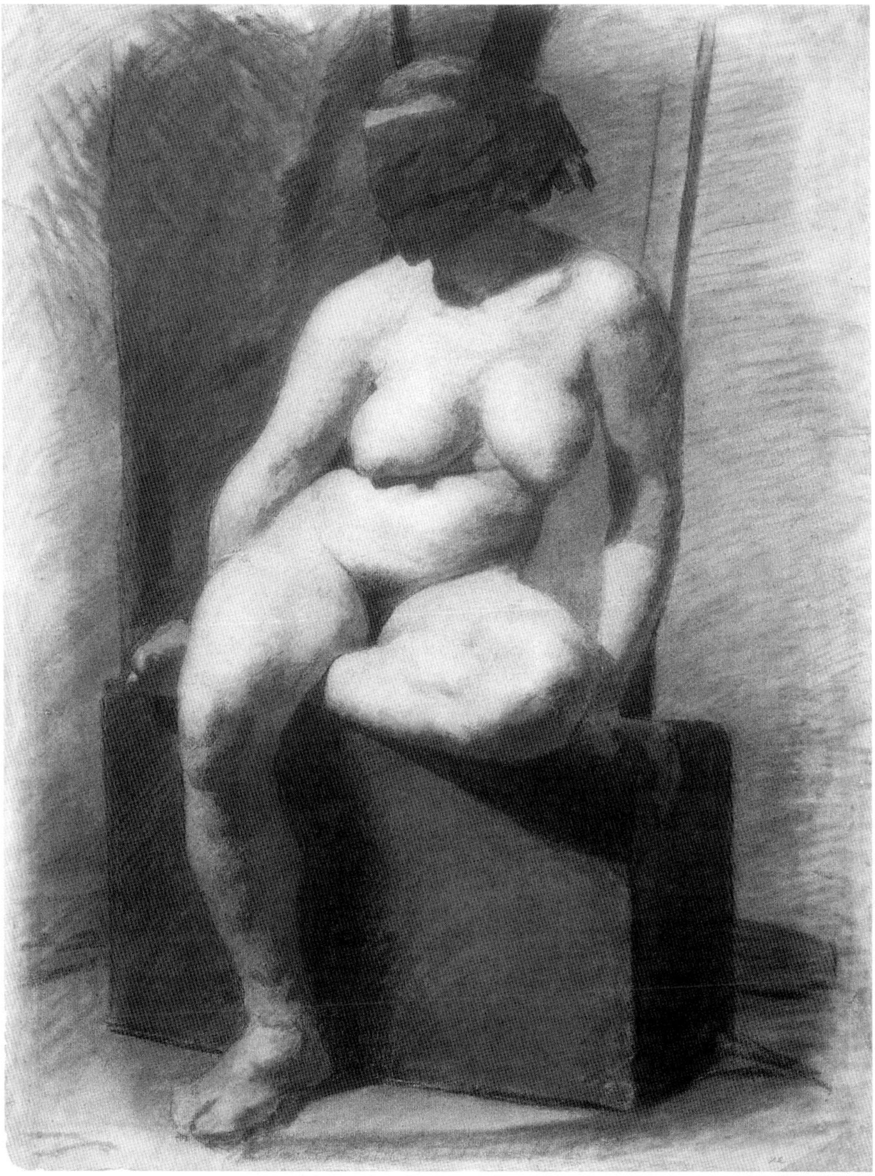

9. Thomas Eakins, *Seated Nude Woman Wearing a Mask*, ca. 1863–66. Charcoal and crayon with stumping on paper, 24¼ × 18⅝ in. Philadelphia Museum of Art. Gift of Mrs. Thomas Eakins and Miss Mary Adeline Williams, 1929.

groups of professional models."[97] By 1879 the situation had improved, but it still remained difficult to find female models. The report of the Academy's annual stockholders meeting described the situation: "Not less than a score of people [both male and female] make a living by posing before the classes. The female model is not easy to obtain, at least such ones as present good studies of the human form divine."[98] Two years earlier, Eakins had urged the Academy's directors to consider adopting new methods for attracting more respectable women. He proposed that the school's Committee on Instruction advertise in the *Public Ledger* for "Female Models for the Life Schools. . . . Applicants should be of respectability and may on all occasions be accompanied by their mothers or other female relatives." In order to make his case, he disparaged the previous method of acquiring models from "low houses of prostitution" as not only "degrading" but as attracting "flabby, ill formed & unfit" women who did not make good models.[99] While there is no evidence that the Academy advertised for models, other schools did.

In 1883, artists' model Charlotte Adams described the progress of the previous decade: "It is little more than ten years since models were something of a rarity even at the Academy of Design," but that "by means of advertising" and enhanced competition "a number of models were brought together."[100] These women came from varied backgrounds but were generally distinguished by their social and physical refinement. Such "amateur" female models attained a degree of respectability and even celebrity, unknown to their predecessors. The typically sensational tabloid the *National Police Gazette* even ran stories vouching for the modesty of these "ladylike" women.[101] The morality of the nude figure was still called into question in the late nineteenth century, but several of the women who posed for artists were willing to have their names published in the press. In spite of the apparent increase in women willing to pose for artists and art schools, *professional* artists' models—those who made a living modeling, often for large classes—remained a questionable group, linked with shopgirls, actresses, and dancers as women of suspect morals. As Susan Waller has observed, during the 1860s when Eakins was studying in France, similar distinctions were being made between professional models and the occasional or amateur model, particularly in Edouard Manet's Realist circle.[102]

Throughout his career Eakins avoided professional models almost entirely. He relied instead on amateurs who were close at hand—often using family, friends, or students. The anecdote of Rush's invitation to the daughter of a colleague and peer to pose for his *Nymph* provided an analogue to Eakins's own penchant for asking family friends to pose. The painting itself reflected Eakins's preferences, as the model who posed for the figure of Vanuxem was Anna W. ("Nannie") Williams, a family friend and schoolmate of Eakins's sisters. Williams became one of Eakins's favorite models in this period. Eakins also suggested her to George T. Morgan in 1876 when he was looking for a woman to pose for the head of Liberty on the obverse of the new silver dollar. Her role as the model for the coin soon became publicly known, though it appears that her more controversial nude modeling for Eakins was not disclosed until decades later.[103] Williams, a schoolteacher who later became director of Philadelphia's public kindergartens, would have represented more than just Vanuxem's body to Eakins—she also suggested her respectability.

Ironically, many interpreted Eakins's desire to use "respectable" women as models as lascivious behavior. Encouraging such women to expose their bodies to an artist's gaze was considered degrading. Life study had become a recognized part of an artist's training, but Eakins's practices challenged accepted limitations about who should pose nude.[104] Throughout his career he pressured many of his female friends and acquaintances to model nude for him—most of them refused. Eakins also made the act of modeling an important part of his pedagogy by encouraging his students to pose nude for one another instead of hiring professional models. He strongly believed that anyone in a life class should be willing to pose. Practicing what he preached, Eakins offered his own body as an example, in one instance lowering his pants before a student to show "the movement of the pelvis."[105] Eakins's tenacious insistence that respectable individuals pose proved one of the most controversial methods that he introduced to the students at the Academy.

Phryne and *A Sculptor's Model*

In challenging ideas about who should pose, Eakins confronted an old art historical tradition, one particularly associated with sculpture. Nude models had been equated with loose women since antiquity. The first model identified in the Western tradition was the courtesan Phryne, who posed for Praxiteles' Late Classical sculpture the *Aphrodite of Knidos.* Regarded by art historians as the first life-size freestanding female nude sculpture, Praxiteles' famed rendering of the Greek goddess of love stood in her temple at Knidos in the fourth century BCE. The original sculpture has long since disappeared. It was last recorded in Constantinople in the palace of Lausos, which was consumed by fire in the fourth century CE. The composition of the Knidia, identified through coins and textual references, survives in later Roman copies, the best known of which is, perhaps, the Colonna version in the Vatican Collection (Figure 10). The fame of the sculpture in antiquity was such that it spawned several variants that further explored the possibilities of the female nude.[106]

Phryne was identified as Praxiteles' model in the second century CE, centuries after the Knidia was carved. Echoing the myth of Pygmalion, whose sculpture of a beautiful woman became flesh through the intervention of Aphrodite, Phryne was characterized as Praxiteles' lover and muse. Stunningly beautiful and capricious, Phryne is also known from Hellenistic and Roman literary sources, which describe two instances in which she brazenly displayed her naked

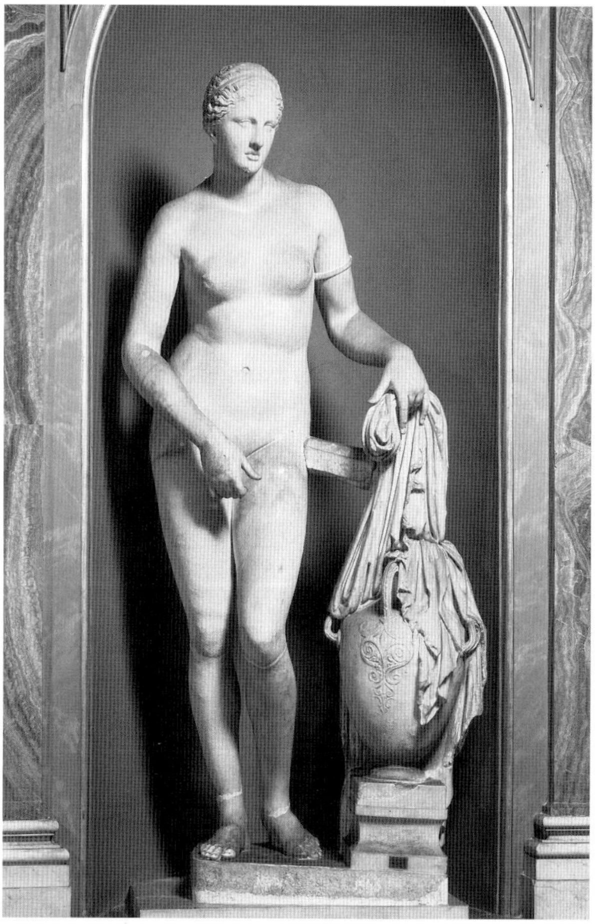

10. Praxiteles, *Cnidian Venus (Aphrodite of Knidos)*. Roman copy after Greek original, ca. 350–330 BCE. Museo Pio Clementino, Vatican Museums. Photo: Scala/Art Resource, New York.

form publicly. In one of these tales, Phryne, or alternately her lawyer, successfully used her nude body as a defense in a trial. The identification of the sacred Knidia with the profane courtesan Phryne had decided implications for later understandings of the sculpture and the female nude in general.

Although created for a religious context, several ancient writers presented the Knidia as an object of lust. As early as the first century CE, Pliny the Elder described the seductive power of the statue in an anecdote that claimed that the Knidia had been stained by the ejaculation of one male viewer who found himself unable to resist her charms. There were also stories that the temple had a second entrance "for those who wish to see the goddess directly from the back."[107] The Hellenistic period (when Phryne was identified as the model for the statue) introduced new eroticizing nude Aphrodites derived from the Knidia. On account of these textual and visual traditions, Praxiteles' Knidia gradually became associated with male lust. And it was this notion of the statue and its model that held greatest sway in the nineteenth century when Eakins painted Rush and Vanuxem.[108]

Nineteenth-century scholars of Greek art denigrated Praxiteles because of his identification with the first female nude. In comparison with Phidias, whose work was perceived as elevated and noble, Praxiteles was thought to appeal to "less refined sympathies . . . undecorous fancy and prurient tastes."[109] In her study of the reception of the Aphrodite of Knidos, Christine Mitchell Havelock attributes the nineteenth century's negative perception of the Knidia with Phryne's reputation as a prostitute. Eakins never mentioned Praxiteles or his work in any of his surviving letters. What he would have made of the tradition is unclear, but he did include "Phrynes" in his list of the objectionable types of female nudes included in the French Salons. Of all of the classical sculptors, Eakins held Phidias in the highest regard, and in many ways Phidias, known for "grandeur and solemn dignity," was considered the opposite of Praxiteles.[110] Given his own thoughts about prostitute models, it remains possible that Eakins shared the opinions of his contemporaries with respect to Phryne and the Knidia.

Phryne had become a popular subject with French and British artists in the later nineteenth century. Perhaps more than any other classical figure popularized in the period, Phryne was depicted as an object of unvarnished lust, possessing no ennobling qualities beyond her physical charms. Gustave Boulanger's *Phryne* (Figure 11) placed the nude courtesan in a distinctly erotic context on a disheveled bed, fingering her necklace and distractedly holding a mirror, a symbol of her vanity, as she provocatively gazes at the viewer. Similarly, Eakins's teacher Jean-Léon Gérôme's *Phryne before the Tribunal* (Figure 12) depicts the climatic scene in Phryne's trial when her body is exposed before the judges. In Gérôme's rendering of the subject, Phryne shields her face, becoming merely an exquisite body displayed for the delectation of her exclusively male audience. Gérôme exhibited the painting in 1867 at the Exposition Universelle in Paris while Eakins was studying in his atelier.

Eakins may have intended *William Rush Carving His Allegorical Figure of the Schuylkill River* as a defense of his use of nude models at the Pennsylvania Academy, but the painting also challenged the tradition that the female nude was morally bankrupt. Neither Louisa Vanuxem nor Nannie Williams suggests the temptresses associated with the nude model—in either ancient Greece, the neoclassical period, or the later nineteenth century. Eakins's consciousness of the negative connotations of the female nude is suggested by a newspaper article, "The Nude in Art," which he clipped from the *Evening Telegraph* in 1878, shortly after he completed *William Rush*. Not merely a discussion of the nude, the article addressed a specific controversy that had erupted in Liverpool over

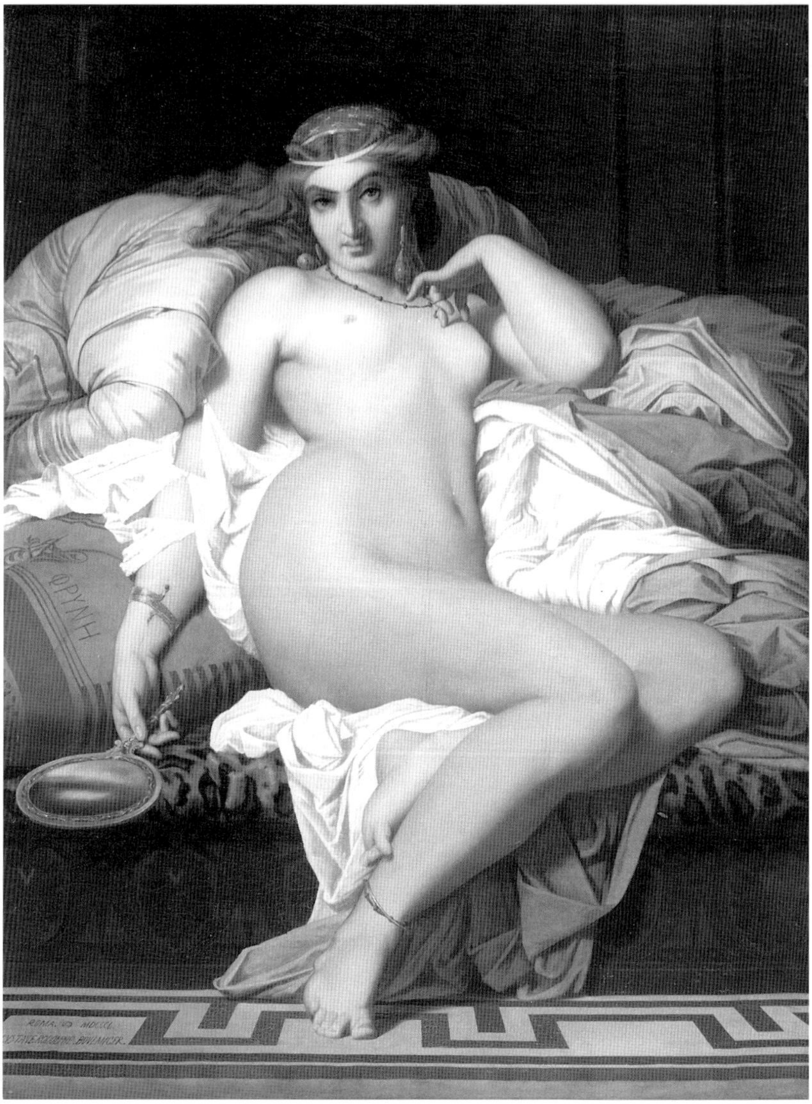

11. Gustave Boulanger, *Phryne*, 1850. Oil on canvas, 51 1/8 × 41 3/4 in. Amsterdam, Van Gogh Museum.

the public exhibition of the English painter Lawrence Alma-Tadema's *A Sculptor's Model* (Figure 13). The article summarized a paper read by P. H. Rathbone, one of the exhibit's organizers, at the Social Science Congress in Cheltenham. Rathbone spoke in response to a series of letters that had appeared in the Liverpool press attacking the painting for its immorality. Rathbone associated such purist attitudes with uneducated and unrefined tastes and championed the nude as "the noblest and most elevating of all subjects that art can treat."[111]

Alma-Tadema took as his subject a nude female model posing in a sculptor's

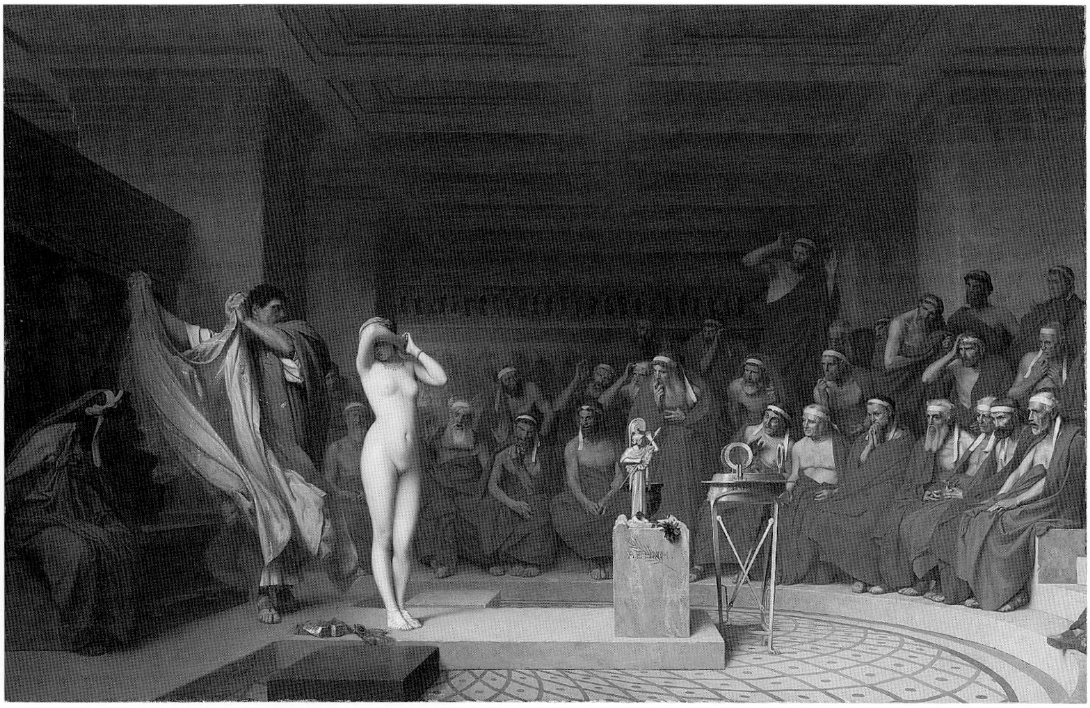

12. Jean-Léon Gérôme, *Phryne before the Tribunal*, 1861. Oil on canvas, 31½ × 50⅜ in. Hamburger Kunsthalle, Hamburg, Germany. The Bridgeman Art Library.

studio in ancient Greece. The model stands with her elegant form facing the viewer, as the sculptor admires her from behind. Defending the work from the charge that it was likely to cause "mischief" for young men, Rathbone felt the work a healthy example of ideal feminine beauty unaltered by modern fashion, such as binding corsets and high heels. Rathbone acknowledged that "in French art, there have been questionable nude figures exhibited: but the fault was not that they were nude, but that they were the portraits of ugly immodest women."[112]

Eakins would have agreed with Rathbone's defense of the nude in art, but Alma-Tadema's painting reiterated the less savory connotations of the female nude that Eakins rejected in *William Rush*. The pose of Alma-Tadema's model was based on the recently excavated *Venus Esquilina*.[113] Although the authorship of this sculpture was still debated when Alma-Tadema painted the subject—the notion of a classical Greek artist admiring his model for the goddess of love from behind echoed the stories of Praxiteles' Aphrodite and Phryne. Eakins's *William Rush* set out to confront these associations with the female nude. Eakins's model does not possess the smooth, marmorean contours of Alma-Tadema's figure. Indeed, as many critics of Eakins's painting noted, Nannie

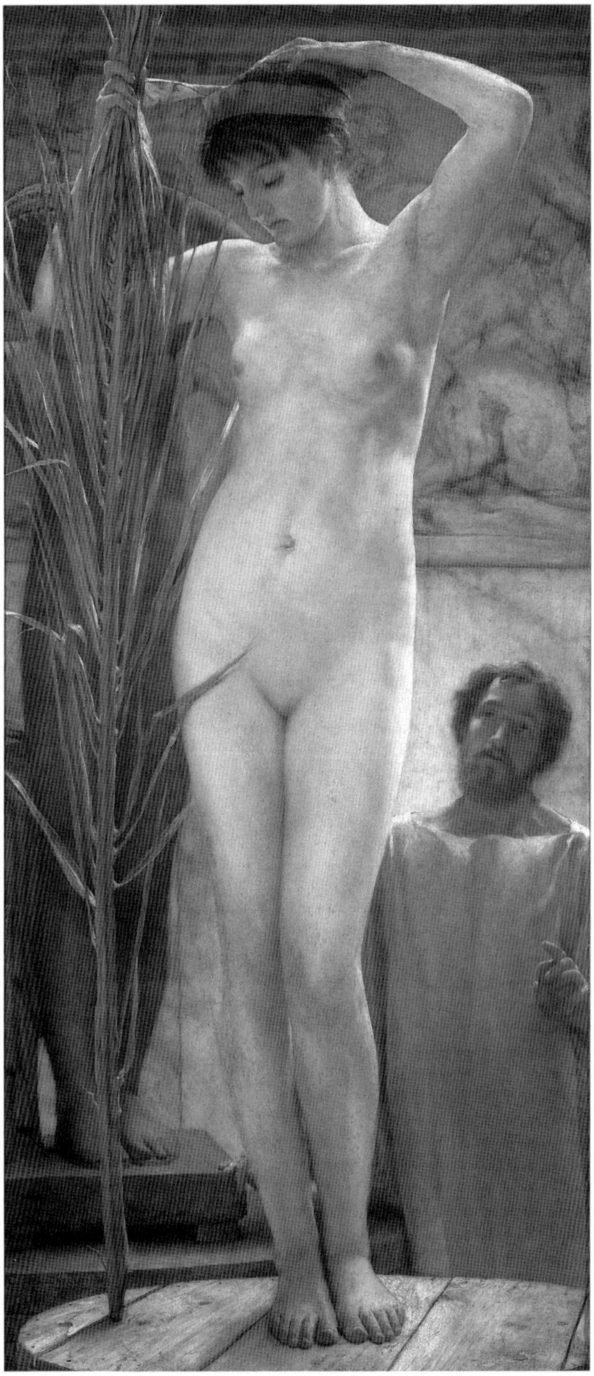

13. Sir Lawrence Alma-Tadema, *A Sculptor's Model*, 1877. Oil on canvas, 77 × 33 in. Private collection, The Bridgeman Art Library. Photo © Christie's Images.

Williams's form did not resemble the Greek ideal but rather reflected an actual body that was both beautiful and imperfect.[114]

Further, Alma-Tadema's tight composition implies an almost too intimate relationship between artist and model. Alma-Tadema placed the model close to the picture plane, effectively blocking out her marble counterpart with the large palm that she holds in her right hand. The model stands exposed and alone, sandwiched between the admiring sculptor behind her on the right and the viewer in front. In spite of the defense of the work in press, *A Sculptor's Model* contains at least a kernel of the prurient tendencies of which critics and moralists complained.

Eakins, by contrast, used several means to make the relationship between the model and the sculptor thoroughly professional and therefore chaste. First, he made the correlation between woman and statue markedly clear; Rush, in the act of carving, does not gaze at Vanuxem's body outside of the professional context in which she poses. Indeed, Rush appears so intent upon his task that he barely notices the nude woman. In addition, Rush stands at some remove from Vanuxem's nude form. Situated in the deepest corner of the composition, Rush is not only spatially distant but physically separated from Vanuxem by his own work—Rush carves with the statue between himself and the model. Last, and perhaps most significantly, Vanuxem does not stand alone before the sculptor. At her side, more proximate to her than Rush, sits the industrious matron who acts as her chaperone.

Through these compositional choices Eakins affirmed the professional behavior both of the artist and the model. *William Rush Carving His Allegorical Figure of the Schuylkill River* did not merely advocate the legitimacy of nude modeling as an artistic practice but further asserted its propriety. In doing so, Eakins contended with a tradition, rooted in antiquity but equally present in his own day, that models were sexually available women. Here the soberly clad chaperone provided a critical buffer to counter any talk of scandalous behavior on the part of either artist or model. Her serious mien and her absorption in her knitting suggest that she has no concern that the young model is in any moral danger.

It seems fitting that *William Rush Carving His Allegorical Figure of the Schuylkill River* began Eakins's exploration of historical subject matter. In its look backward, the painting confronted the traditions as well as the modern concerns of his profession in a period when writers were beginning to take note of America's art historical past. In this painting Eakins fashioned an American Old Master as the progenitor of the Beaux-Arts methods that he himself followed. As Eakins pursued his vocation as an artist, he used this history painting to assert the professionalism of his calling, while simultaneously drawing attention to the role of the model. Rejecting the entrenched view of the female nude as inherently lascivious, Eakins depicted a respectable alternative. However, American attitudes about the life model could not be as easily shaped as William Rush's biography. Although female nudes became commonplace in American exhibitions and female models more plentiful, Eakins's use of friends, family, and students as life models would ultimately lead to the greatest disappointments of his life.[115]

CHAPTER TWO

Thomas Eakins and the Colonial Revival

Between 1876 and 1883, Eakins produced about a dozen colonial revival images, the majority of which focus on women engaged in old-fashioned domestic tasks.[1] In these simple, modestly scaled genre subjects, Eakins uncharacteristically pursued a highly fashionable theme. In fact, Eakins had some of the greatest successes of his career with the series. Critics praised these works for their "fine drawing" and "charming" compositions. Eakins received his first professional honor when he won a silver medal at the Massachusetts Charitable Mechanics Association exhibition in 1878 for two watercolors, including the colonial revival image *Fifty Years Ago*.[2] The significance of the theme in Eakins's career is further highlighted by the fact that biographical dictionaries continued to mention the artist's "many small pictures of domestic life in the early days of America" into the twentieth century, decades after he had ceased painting them.[3]

The swift purchase of three of the colonial revival paintings, an otherwise infrequent occurrence in Eakins's career, also reflects their positive reception. In 1878, *Seventy Years Ago* sold during its exhibition with the American Water Color Society in New York. Around the same time, the Philadelphia physician Horatio C. Wood acquired the unfinished oil *The Courtship* directly from the artist. But the crowning achievement of Eakins's success with colonial revival subject matter came in 1879 when Smith College purchased *In Grandmother's Time* (Figure 14), which became the first of his paintings to enter a museum collection.

Scholars have often considered the anniversary of the nation's founding, celebrated in Philadelphia's Centennial Exhibition of 1876, as the inspiration for

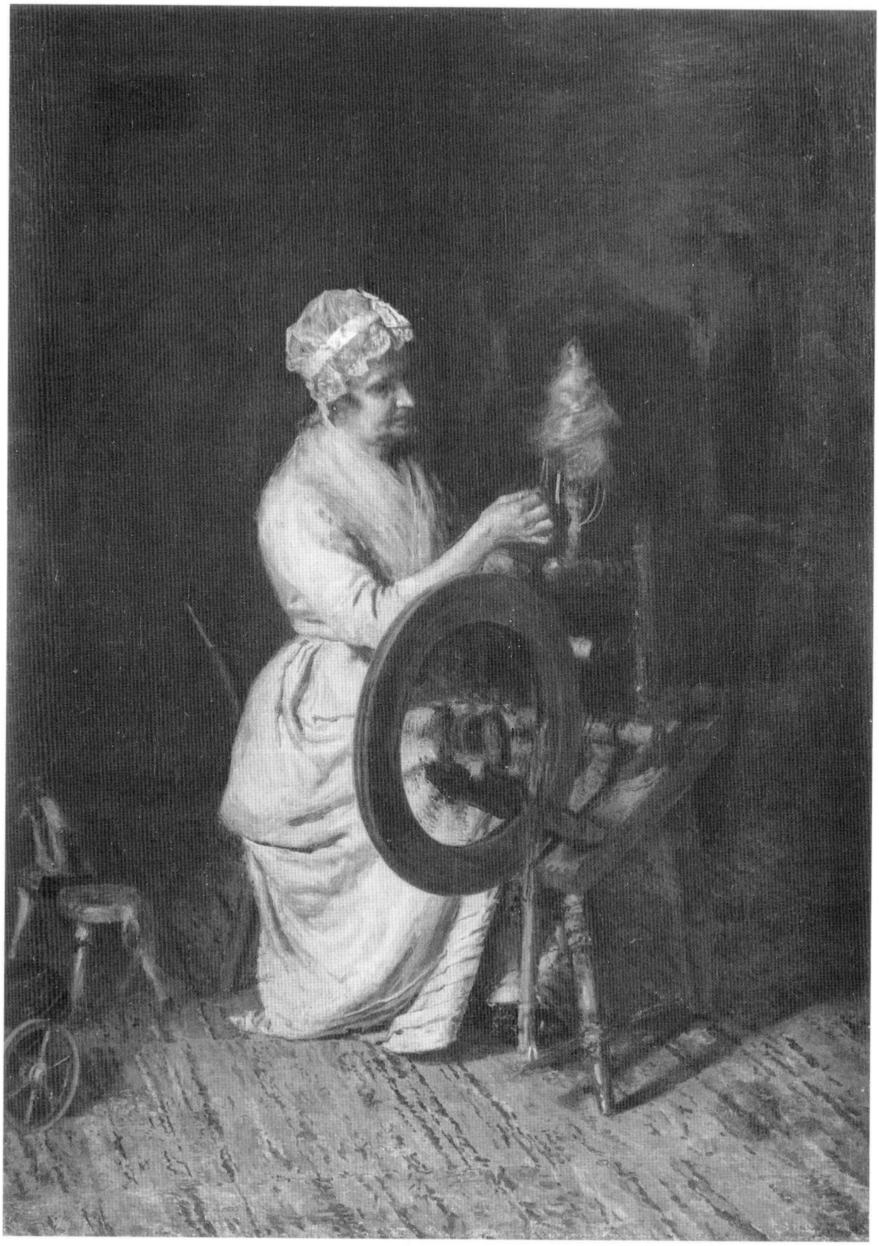

14. Thomas Eakins, *In Grandmother's Time*, 1876. Oil on canvas, 16 × 12 in. Smith College Museum of Art, Northampton, Massachusetts.

these nostalgic images of industrious women.[4] This may well be the case for the first work in the series, *In Grandmother's Time*, which dates precisely to the year of the Centennial. However, Eakins's continued development of this feminine theme over the next six years also coincided with his increased teaching responsibilities at the Pennsylvania Academy of the Fine Arts, where he faced a female student body for the first time. Eakins's choice to depict women of an earlier era at this particular moment may reflect his ambivalence about his role as an educator of women at a time when physicians warned that academic study could compromise mental well-being. The acquisition of *In Grandmother's Time* by a women's college further suggests a means of understanding the series as it relates to contemporary concerns regarding women's education.

While several scholars have noted that Eakins's psychologically probing portraits reveal his awareness of "nervous disease," or neurasthenia, the colonial revival series has not often been situated in this context.[5] Yet doctors specializing in the treatment of these disorders explicitly contrasted the heartiness of colonial women with the fragility of their modern counterparts. An examination of the circumstances of Eakins's personal and professional life at the time he was preparing this series provides insight into his complex reasons for turning to this subject at just this moment in his career.

The Centennial and a National History

The Centennial Exhibition probably inspired Eakins's initial interest in colonial themes. Indeed, the 1876 fair is generally regarded as the starting point for the colonial revival movement.[6] As America's first world's fair, the Centennial sought to position American goods and culture in an international context, but it also celebrated the nation's first one hundred years by recollecting its past. As Eakins skated and rowed in Fairmount Park, he likely witnessed firsthand its transformation into the vast fairgrounds of the Centennial. Eakins submitted six paintings to the fair's fine art exhibit. This ample selection demonstrated his abilities not only as a portraitist but also as a genre painter. In spite of the disappointing placement of *The Gross Clinic* in an army medical display, the fair offered Eakins his first significant opportunity to exhibit a large number of paintings in an international milieu.[7]

While the majority of the displays at the fair celebrated progress, a number of small but popular exhibits focused on history. Peppered among these were genuine colonial artifacts such as John Alden's desk, as well as Revolutionary-era objects, including George Washington's camp equipment. The Centennial additionally presented objects of iconic rather than historical significance, including countless "liberty bells" fashioned from an astonishing array of consumer goods or the items made from the seemingly inexhaustible Charter Oak.

These historical displays offered a symbolic salve to a nation still haunted by the Civil War by recollecting its shared past. In the aftermath of war, the colonial era—broadly defined as ranging from early European colonization through the Federal period—was perceived as a time of national harmony. The appeal of a reunited country celebrating a common past cannot be overstated, particularly in Philadelphia, where loyalties had been divided by the war. As one journalist put it, "If the Centennial celebration in 1876 were to serve no other purpose than that of bringing the people of the North and South together again in friendly relation, every dollar spent, and every hour devoted would be invested in a cause as glorious as the mind of man ever conceived. . . . Past issues are dead and the opportunity is now offered to sink them for ever in oblivion. We meet the people of the South on the Anniversary of the Birth of Our Country, which is theirs, too, as men who were brave as foes and ever generous and kind as friends."[8]

The nostalgia in evidence at the Centennial had antecedents in the Sanitary Fairs of the 1860s. These fund-raisers, organized on behalf of the United States Sanitary Commission, were staged in several Northern cities in order to raise funds for the Union cause. A popular feature of the Sanitary Fairs, including the one held in Philadelphia's Logan Circle in 1864, was the "colonial kitchen"—suggesting a direct connection between the Civil War and the colonial revival movement. These kitchens, precursors to modern living-history displays, included homey re-creations of colonial hearths with costumed women cooking and often serving visitors hearty "colonial fare." Virtually every colonial kitchen featured a woman seated before the fireside spinning at her flax wheel.[9]

The Sanitary Fairs laid the groundwork for some of the displays that would be incorporated into the Centennial Exhibition more than a decade later. Indeed, the Centennial's most overtly colonial exhibit was its much admired New England kitchen of the Massachusetts Pavilion (Figure 15). Characterized by one writer as a structure with "realism about it," this log dwelling provided a demonstration of outdated technology that could be contrasted with an adjacent modern kitchen. Yet the charmingly anachronistic colonial kitchen easily surpassed its modern counterpart in popularity. Outfitted with old furnishings, the kitchen had "the added attraction of two or three buxom girls in old-time costume, to loll in the rocking chairs, and twirl the spinning-wheel."[10] William Dean Howells offered an eloquent description of his visit to the Pavilion:

> Massachusetts, through the poetic thoughtfulness of one of her women, had done far better in the erection of the Old Colony House of logs,

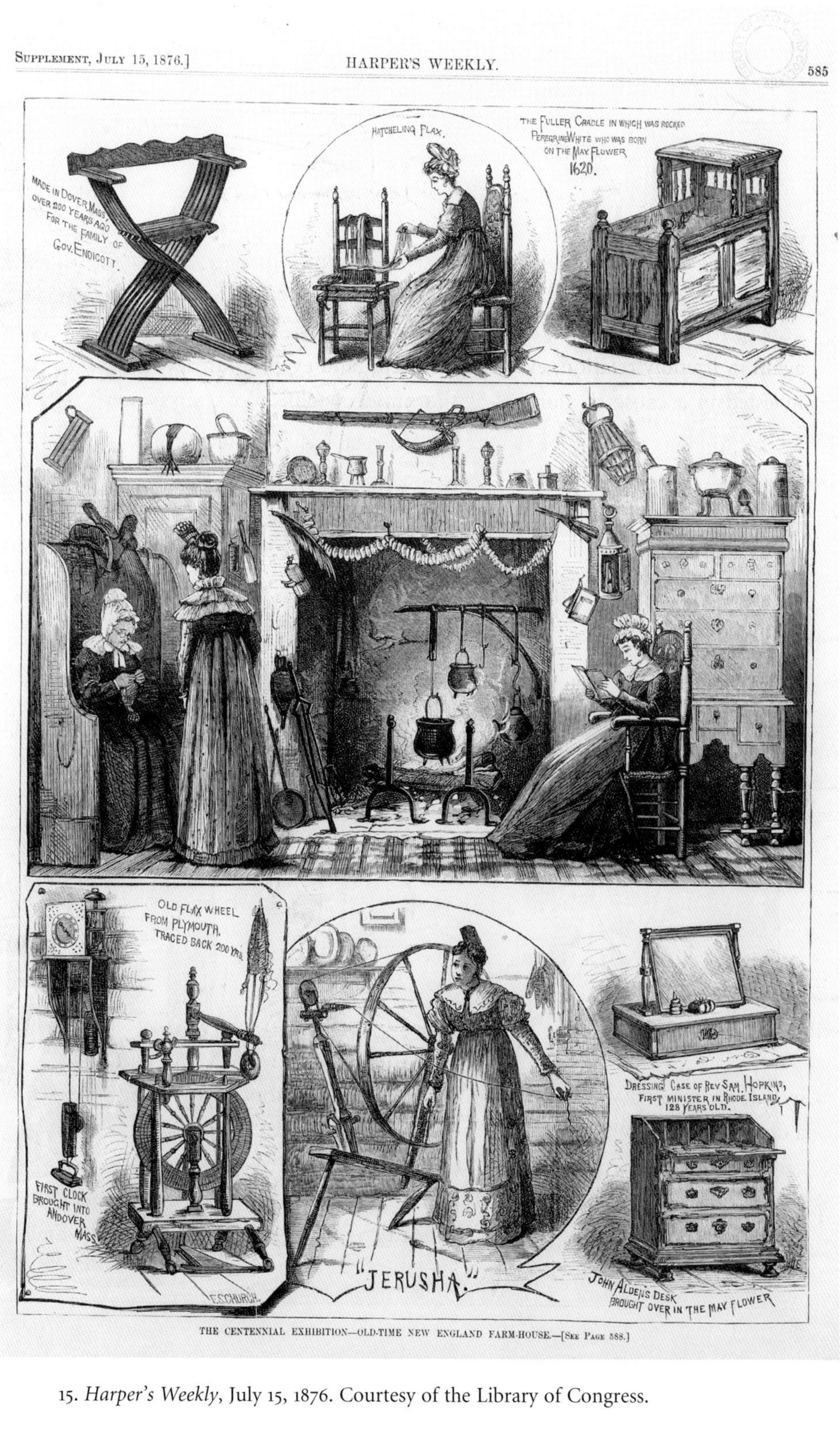

SUPPLEMENT, JULY 15, 1876.] HARPER'S WEEKLY. 585

THE CENTENNIAL EXHIBITION—OLD-TIME NEW ENGLAND FARM-HOUSE.—[SEE PAGE 588.]

15. *Harper's Weekly*, July 15, 1876. Courtesy of the Library of Congress.

> which we found thronged by pleased and curious visitors. . . . [A]t the corner of the deep and wide fire-place sat Priscilla spinning—or some young lady in a quaint, old fashioned dress, who served the same purpose. I thought nothing could be better than this, till a lovely old Quakeress, who had stood by, peering critically at the work through her glasses, asked the fair spinster to let her take the wheel. She sat down beside it, caught some strands of tow from the spindle, and with her long-unwonted fingers tried to splice the broken thread; but she got the thread entangled on the iron points of the card, and there was a breathless interval in which we all hung silent about her, fearing for her success. In another moment the thread was set free and spliced, the good old dame bowed herself to her work, and the wheel went round with a soft, triumphant burr, while the crowd heaved a sigh of relief. That was altogether the prettiest thing I saw at the Centennial.[11]

Howells's account not only documents the interest of Centennial visitors in the colonial display, and particularly its coterie of spinners, but also highlights the fact that at least a few women remembered the "colonial" tradition of spinning well into the 1870s.

The first of Eakins's colonial revival images, *In Grandmother's Time*, is nearly a visual counterpart to Howell's description. Eakins began the painting in 1876 as he prepared sketches for *William Rush Carving His Allegorical Figure of the Schuylkill River*. Like nearly all of the other images in the series, *In Grandmother's Time* focuses on a lone woman in old-fashioned dress diligently absorbed in traditional women's work. In this instance, the elderly woman at the center of the composition spins at a flax wheel. The model, who had posed for the similarly industrious chaperone in the Rush picture, was "Aunt Sally" King, a relative of Eakins's then fiancée Kathrin Crowell. She became a favorite model, appearing in at least two additional colonial revival works.[12]

As Eakins's first exploration of the theme, *In Grandmother's Time* shows a hesitancy in representing the past that is not evident in other works in the series. It also differs from his contemporary genre scenes, where typically every background detail is precisely rendered. The setting of the colonial image is instead dark and indistinct. A Boston critic recognized this when he noted that while the figure was "admirably drawn," the interior remained "a whirl of indefiniteness."[13] Although the outdated costume of the woman and her task link her to the colonial period, details of the room, probably in the Eakins home, betray the 1870s date of the picture. The scattered toys on the floor, for example, are not "colonial," even in the broad sense with which most artists used the idiom. Also of more recent vintage is the Jacobean revival chair dimly

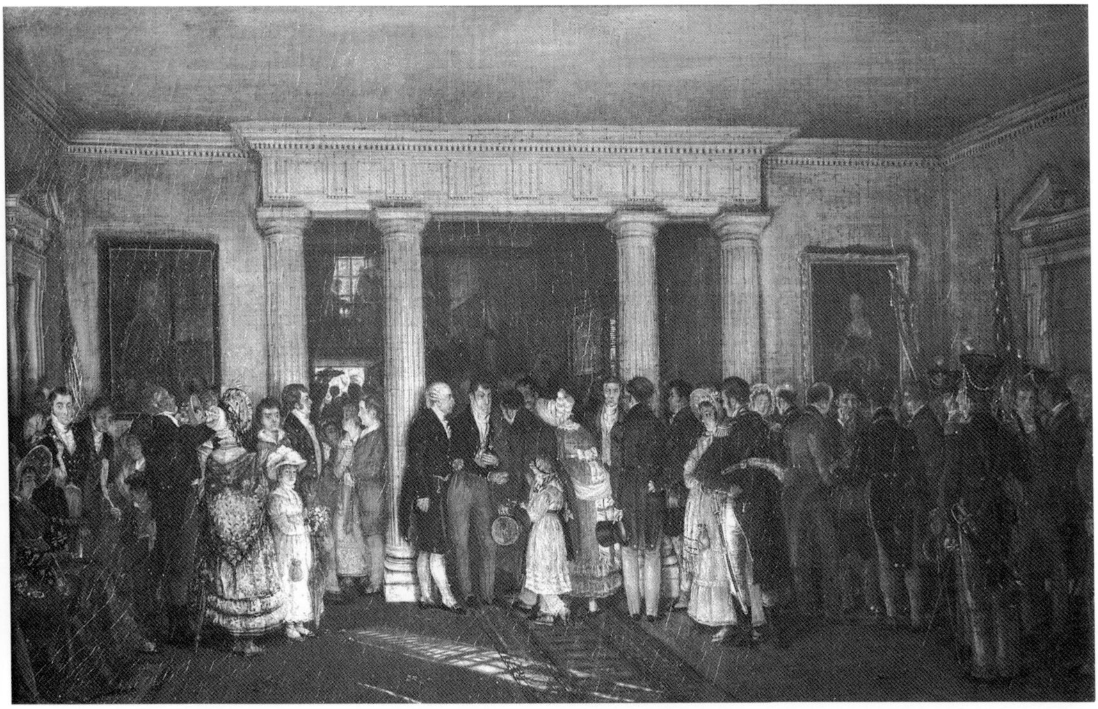

16. Edward Lamson Henry, *The Lafayette Reception*, 1874. Oil on canvas, 17 × 27$^{3}/_{8}$ in. Courtesy of Cliveden, a National Trust Historic Site.

visible in the murky background. Eakins frequently used this chair as a prop in his portraits and domestic genre paintings of the period. As Eakins developed the theme, he would decrease the number of objects composing the settings for the series while simultaneously tightening their historical scope.[14]

Despite the seeming conservatism of such old-fashioned subject matter, young artists exhibited colonial revival images in significant numbers at the fine art display at the Centennial.[15] These works also adorned the walls of progressive art organizations, including the American Watercolor Society and the fledgling Society of American Artists. However, artists of different schools had disparate concerns when treating such themes. Genre painters such as Enoch Wood Perry and Edward Lamson Henry filled their colonial revival images with a highly detailed profusion of antique objects. Crucial to their work was the creation of an "authentic" setting. As a result, many of these images seem to revolve around architecture and the marshaling of period artifacts. Even when historical events inspired their work, as in Henry's *The Lafayette Reception* (Figure 16), the period room and the appropriately costumed crowd overwhelm the central figure of the Marquis de Lafayette. It is history writ small.

By contrast, figure painters, William Merritt Chase, J. Alden Weir, and

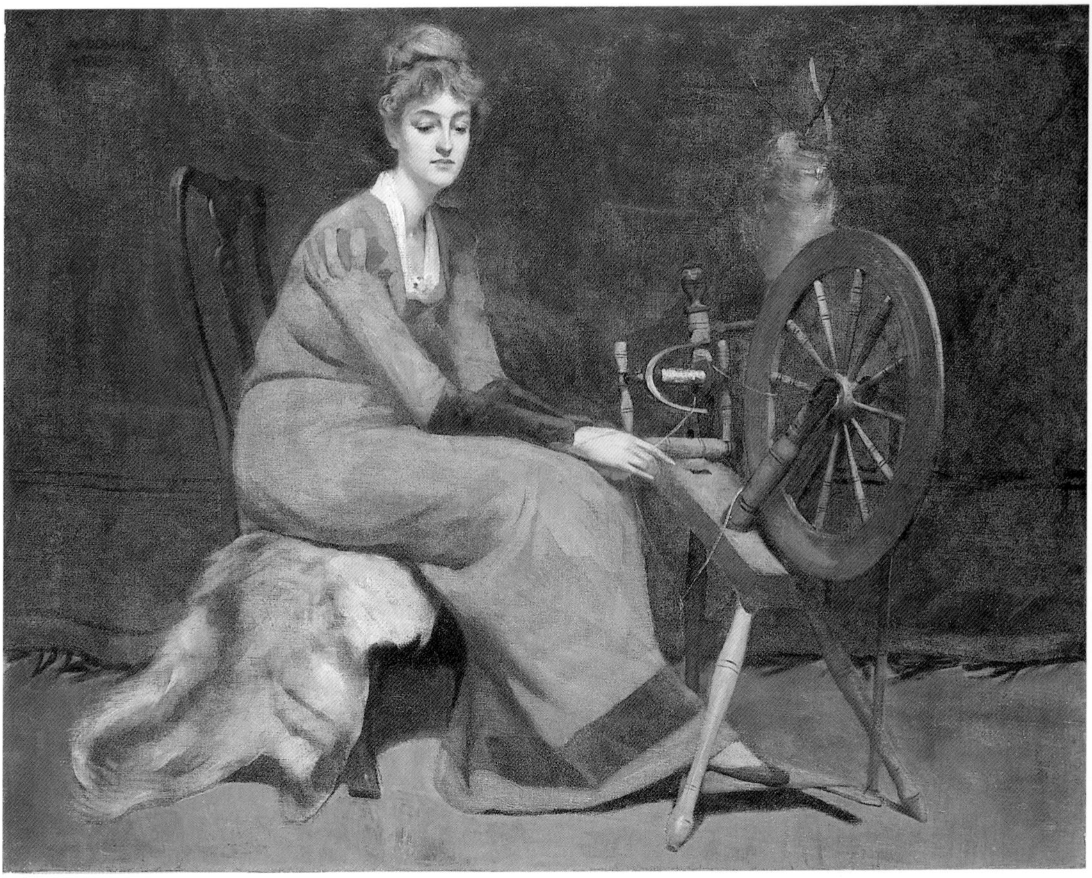

17. Thomas Wilmer Dewing, *The Spinner*, 1880. Oil on canvas, 42 × 54 in. Brigham Young University Museum of Art. Gift of Donald Greenwood.

Thomas Wilmer Dewing (Figure 17) among them, pared down the anecdotal detail and focused on costumed figures and aestheticized still lifes.[16] The figure painters also tended to eschew actual history painting in favor of historical genre images featuring pretty young women, as well as sage old dames, often situated within the domestic sphere. In comparison with Henry or Perry's work, Eakins's colonial interiors are spare. As a figure painter, Eakins tended to dispense with artifacts in favor of his female subjects. This emphasis on costumed women makes the images some of the most aestheticizing that he would ever produce. Yet Eakins's colonial women, particularly his spinners, are rarely mere pretty objects. Unlike Dewing, for example, Eakins never depicts his spinners idle at the wheel; they are instead industrious women intent upon their tasks.

The two watercolors, *Fifty Years Ago* and *Seventy Years Ago*, which were the first of the colonial revival works that Eakins exhibited, illustrate the simplicity of his compositional choices.[17] In *Fifty Years Ago* (Figure 18), a contemplative

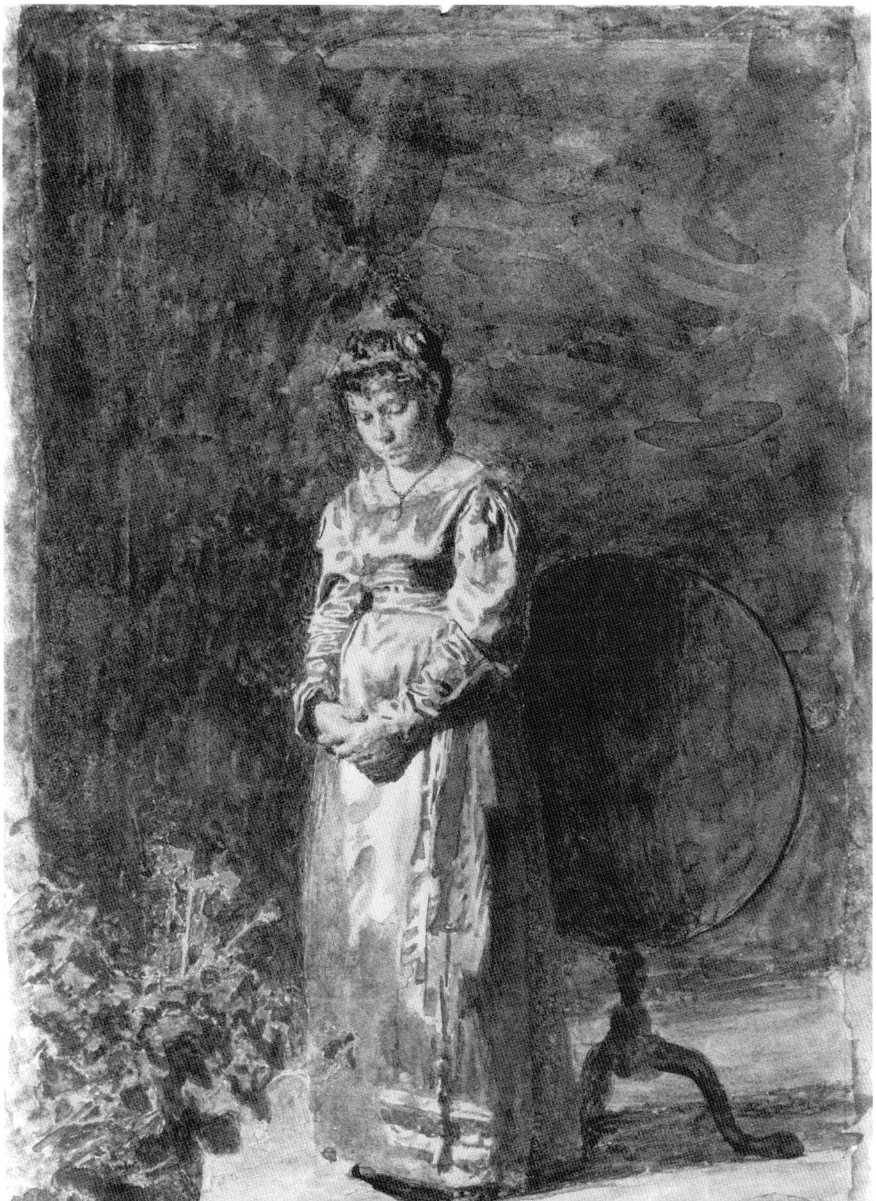

18. Thomas Eakins, *Young Girl Meditating (Fifty Years Ago)*, 1877. Watercolor and gouache on off-white wove paper, $9\frac{9}{16} \times 6\frac{1}{8}$ in. The Metropolitan Museum of Art, Fletcher Fund, 1925 (25.97.2).

young woman wearing a high-waisted Empire gown of the 1820s stands in a spartan interior—a rare example of an unproductive colonial woman. The primary prop used to establish the setting is an antique Philadelphia tilt-top table behind the woman on the right. In the left foreground is a geranium, an imported plant associated with eighteenth-century Philadelphia horticulture.[18] In *Seventy Years Ago* (Figure 19), an elderly woman (Sally King) knits in a Chippendale chair. Behind her to the left is a spinning wheel, while the same tilt-top table figured in *Fifty Years Ago* appears on the right. Though not intended as visual pendants—*Fifty Years Ago* is much smaller than its counterpart—the titles certainly imply a relationship between the two.

As Marc Simpson has suggested, "The use of the word 'ago' impos[es] a sense of process, of both now and then, on the spectator."[19] Indeed, it is unclear if Eakins intended us to view these images as historical re-creations in the present, or if we are to perceive these works as windows on the past.[20] In either case, the ambiguity engenders a sense of remembrance, of memory, a process that is by nature "both now and then." In his selection of these titles, Eakins echoed language that appeared in newspapers and magazines in the years just before and after the Centennial that featured countless stories of life "a hundred years ago."[21] While these articles suggested a sense of progress, they also expressed nostalgia for a simpler time.

Eakins's Family Ties

The grandmother of *In Grandmother's Time* may indeed be a figure who expresses the "now and then" that Simpson observes. On the one hand, she is "Aunt Sally" King; on the other, she evokes Eakins's own paternal grandmother, Fanny Fife Eakins. In this way, Eakins may have personalized his colonial revival subjects by alluding to his own family history. It is well known that Eakins's father, Benjamin, earned his living as a writing master, engrossing documents and teaching penmanship in Philadelphia-area schools. However, his daughter Frances (Fanny) referred to him as a "country boy." Benjamin moved to Philadelphia as an adult in the late 1830s in order to learn penmanship from his cousin William Fife. But he was born and raised near Valley Forge, Pennsylvania, the son of Alexander Eakins, a Scots Irish tenant farmer whose primary trade was weaving.[22]

The manufacture of homemade cloth in the eighteenth and early nineteenth centuries usually involved an entire family, as it took a great deal of physical labor to prepare the fibers for use. While men often did the weaving and finishing of the cloth, women typically spun the wool or flax into yarn.[23] As one would expect, Alexander Eakins's estate included a loom. In addition, he owned

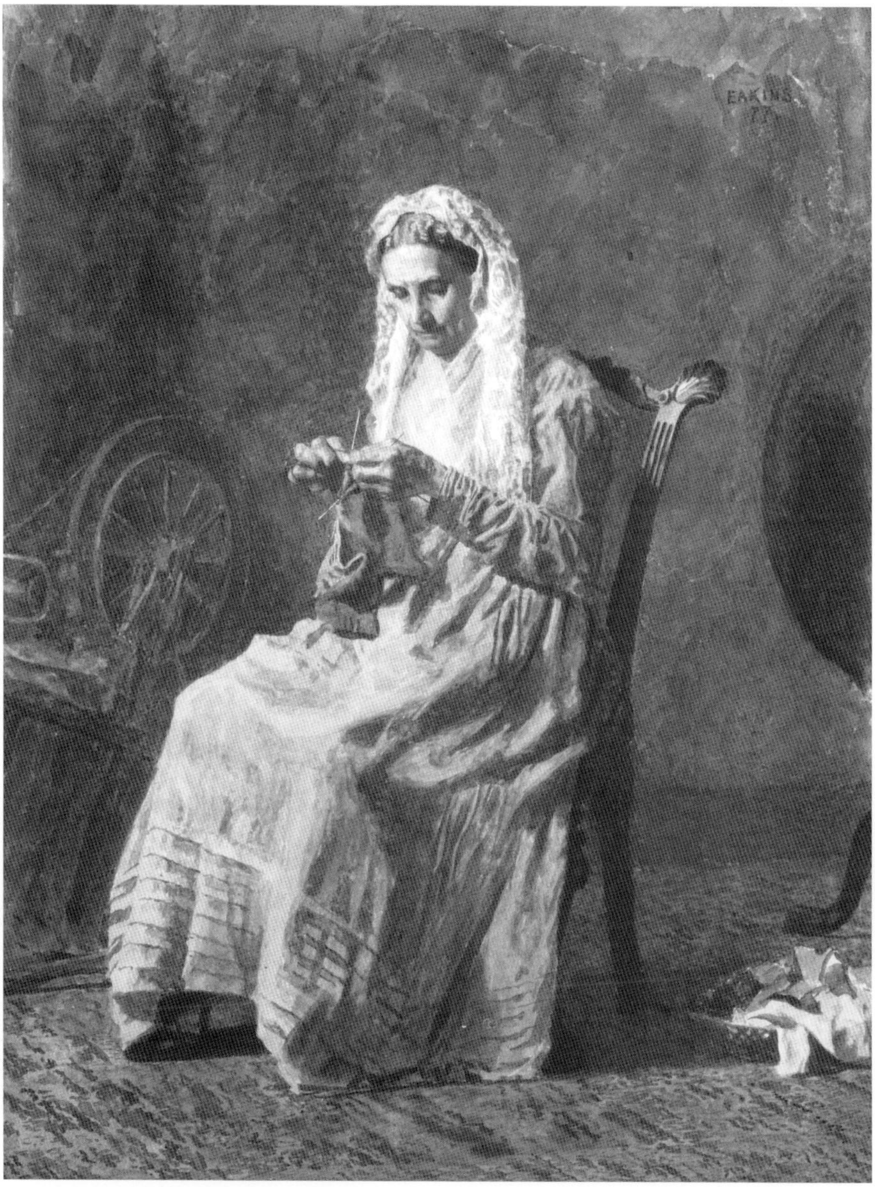

19. Thomas Eakins, *Seventy Years Ago*, 1877. Watercolor and gouache on cream wove paper with graphite border, $15\frac{11}{16} \times 10\frac{13}{16}$ in. Princeton University Art Museum. Gift of Mrs. Frank Jewett Mather Jr.

at least two spinning wheels and a "reel" for winding yarn. His estate inventory also notes an unspecified quantity of homespun yarn. These last three items indicate that spinning was done in the household.[24] Therefore it is likely that Benjamin's mother and his two sisters were themselves spinners. While Eakins never knew his paternal grandparents, who died before he was born, he surely knew of them from his father, who nostalgically returned to Valley Forge in 1874, spending nine hours visiting all of his childhood haunts.[25]

According to Lloyd Goodrich, the costumes in Eakins's colonial revival paintings "were brought down from trunks in the attic," suggesting that they had been worn by an earlier generation of Eakins women.[26] It is likely that the spinning wheel that Eakins depicted was also a family relic, perhaps from Alexander Eakins's estate. In a manner of speaking, the artist "claimed" the spinning wheel as his own by signing *In Grandmother's Time* and at least two other works in the series on the bench of the wheel itself. By signing the wheel, Eakins directly associated the object with his paternal ancestors.[27]

The colonial revival images also bear the influence of other facets of Eakins's domestic life. Compositionally, they resemble the depictions of female friends and family members in interiors that Eakins made during the first half of the 1870s. Eakins painted these quiet pictures of somber women deeply absorbed in simple tasks in the same years that he was producing active male-dominated images of rowers and hunters. *Kathrin* (Figure 20), completed in the midst of the rowing series, is typical of this genre. In this painting, Eakins figured Kathrin Crowell, who would become his fiancée two years later, seated in the Jacobean revival chair seen in the background of *In Grandmother's Time.* Her attention is directed at a kitten in her lap. Her dress, with its bows, lace, and ruffles is distinctly feminine, her form romantically lit, with an open fan adding an aesthetic touch.

Women in Eakins's colonial revival subjects are similarly preoccupied in domestic spaces, but there are also notable differences in how the artist approached his historical material. Nearly all of Eakins's colonial women are deeply absorbed in some activity related to clothing manufacture: spinning, knitting, or sewing. Their industry results in functional domestic products. By contrast, in his paintings of his sisters and their friends, including that of his future fiancée, Kathrin Crowell, the women are typically engaged in middle-class leisure activities. Whether they are playing with a pet or playing the piano, the women in his contemporary domestic scenes are not participating in "useful" labor.[28]

This distinction is an important one, as part of the appeal of the colonial revival was the valorization of "old tyme" feminine labor. Spinning was particularly associated with feminine virtue. As Laurel Thatcher Ulrich has observed, "Celebrations of spinning almost always portrayed a good housewife who worked to clothe her family." This notion had biblical sanction in the often quoted "Proverbs 31, which described 'a virtuous woman,' presumably Solomon's mother, who 'seeketh wool, and flax and worketh willingly with her hands.'"[29]

Middle- and upper-class women of the 1870s and 1880s, like Kathrin Cro-

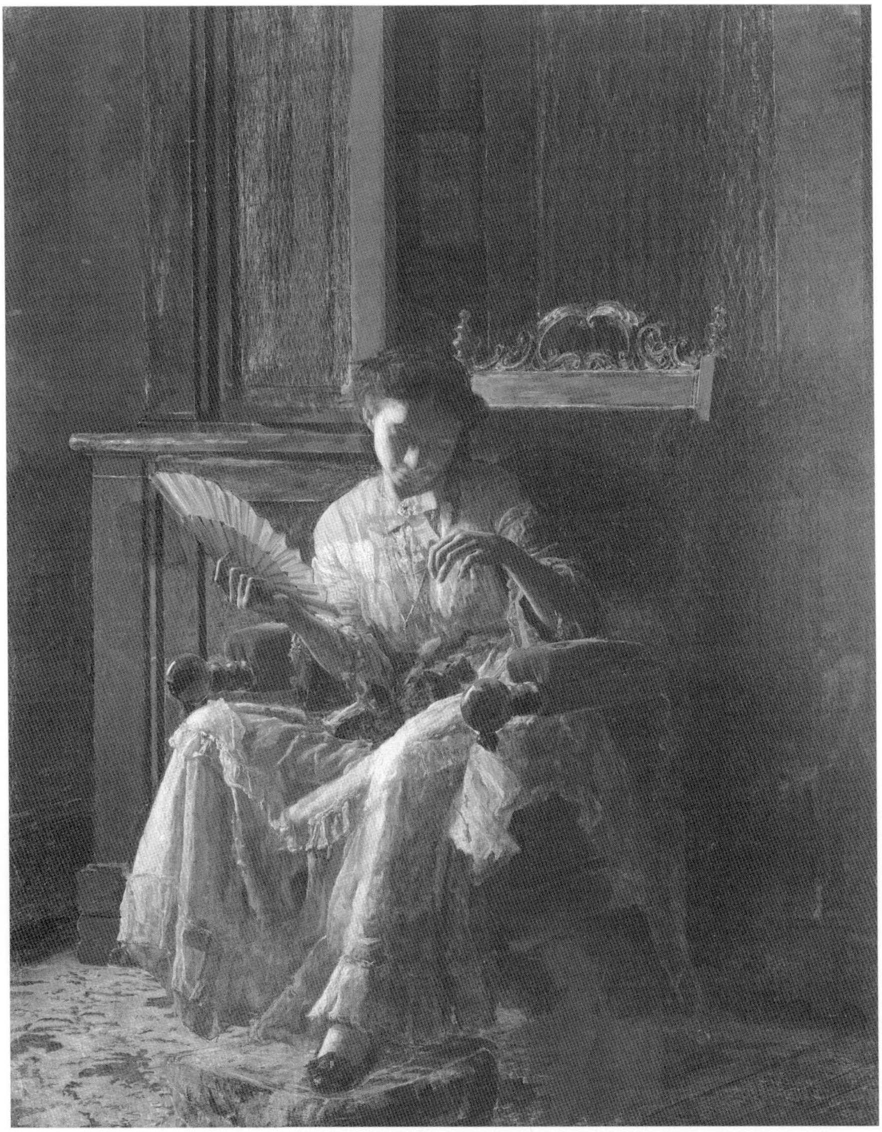

20. Thomas Eakins, *Kathrin*, 1872. Oil on canvas, 65 × 52½ in. Yale University Art Gallery. Bequest of Stephen Carlton Clark, B.A., 1903.

well, had both more and less to do than their colonial ancestors. Modern conveniences and industrialized urban life allowed these women significant leisure time. But they also had increasing opportunities for education and employment. The Centennial's Women's Pavilion, the first display of its kind, highlighted many of these advances and opportunities. Women raised funds for the pavilion and filled its cavernous hall with impressive examples of feminine ingenuity, from traditional domestic crafts to industrial displays involving complex feats of engineering. Through its exhibits, the Women's Pavilion explored the growing number of professional and educational options available to women, as well as the additional leisure time afforded to upper- and middle-class women through "time-saving" modern inventions.[30]

Not everyone was pleased by women's changing social roles. Critics of modern femininity suggested that so-called New Women were over-reaching and unfeminine. Doctors provided substantial "evidence" that women were biologically ill suited to compete with men. Others worried about their idleness. Some physicians cautioned that such new opportunities as those celebrated in the Women's Pavilion presented a danger, because in extreme cases they could—or so the theory went—produce mental illness or outright madness.

Eakins's shift to nostalgic images of colonial women may have been influenced by the difficulties faced by the women closest to him. In June 1872, Eakins's mother, Caroline Cowerthwait, died of "exhaustion from mania" following what appears to have been a prolonged bout of mental instability. Eakins was deeply affected by his mother's illness, as a family friend noted in April 1871, "Tom Eaken [*sic*] has been at home since July 4th. Since early autumn he has never spent an evening from home as it worried his Mother . . . they never leave her a minute."[31] This was the first of Eakins's several encounters with mentally ill women and no doubt one that made a profound impression upon him.

Two years after his mother's death, Eakins became engaged to Kathrin Crowell, but the two never married. A friend of the family speculated that Eakins prolonged the engagement due to a lack of enthusiasm for his betrothed, but a document written by Kathrin's brother William suggests that illness may have prevented the marriage.[32] Kathrin died in 1879 of meningitis but apparently, several years earlier, had "nearly succumbed to an attack of the typhoid," from which William believed that she had never fully recovered.[33] Eakins's depiction of Kathrin alludes to the fragility that ultimately claimed her young life. By contrast, the elderly "Aunt Sally," Eakins's favorite colonial revival model, represented a hardier generation of Crowell women.

Mental Exhaustion

During the development of the colonial revival series, Eakins became friendly with Horatio C. Wood and Silas Weir Mitchell, two physicians famous for their treatment of "mental exhaustion."[34] This condition—known by many names, including the term *neurasthenia*, coined by Dr. George M. Beard in 1869—would today encompass several affective mood disorders, including major depression. Beard postulated that the disease was a direct consequence of modern life: "Both anemia and neurasthenia are most frequently met with in civilized, intellectual communities. They are a part of the compensation of our progress and refinement."[35] This notion may have been particularly resonant in 1876, as the exhibits at the Centennial provided some of the best evidence that modern life was moving too fast. Its technological wonders astounded visitors. Yet the fair's nostalgia for a simpler past is also relevant to the diagnosis and treatment of mental exhaustion.

Mitchell and Wood built upon Beard's work in their own extensive publications on mental disease. In addition, each developed his own specialized treatment regimen to combat mental exhaustion. Wood's "camp cure" required that his patients leave behind modern stress and comfort to live outdoors in a rural environment.[36] Mitchell chose a different approach, becoming best known for his "rest cure." In its most extreme form, Mitchell's treatment depended on the patient's isolation from family and friends and a complete lack of activity. Massage, electric stimulation, and a high-fat diet were also prescribed by Mitchell to address the physiological causes of the illness. Charlotte Perkins Gilman, Mitchell's most famously dissatisfied patient, wrote a vivid description of the doctor's methods in the short story "The Yellow Wallpaper." Gilman's disturbing tale of a woman's descent into madness *because* of Mitchell's treatment, offers an alternative perspective to the success stories touted by Mitchell himself, who specialized in treating women.

Physicians attributed mental collapse to a diverse array of causes that were tied to gender. For men, overwork was thought to cause most breakdowns. In these cases, the disease could be triggered by the stresses of business combined with insufficient physical activity. The situation for women was slightly more complex. Doctors argued that excessive mental stimulation should be avoided, particularly in the developmental stages of puberty when menstruation and physical development allegedly strained the female mind and body. Although thinking too much could lead to breakdown, a lack of physical activity could do the same. However, women had to be careful, because too much activity could be as detrimental as none. Doctors recommended a balance between the mental and the physical. This balance can be observed in Eakins's colonial revival images, which show "physical labor driven by mental concentration."[37]

An intriguing aspect of Eakins's friendship with Mitchell and Wood is that both medical men had connections to his colonial revival paintings. Wood offered unequivocal support for the colonial revival series by purchasing Eakins's painting *The Courtship* (Figure 21) in 1878. According to the doctor's son James, his father was so eager to acquire the work that he "took the painting away from Eakins before it was finished, fearing that he would spoil it."[38] The image features a young woman spinning at a flax wheel with a male admirer

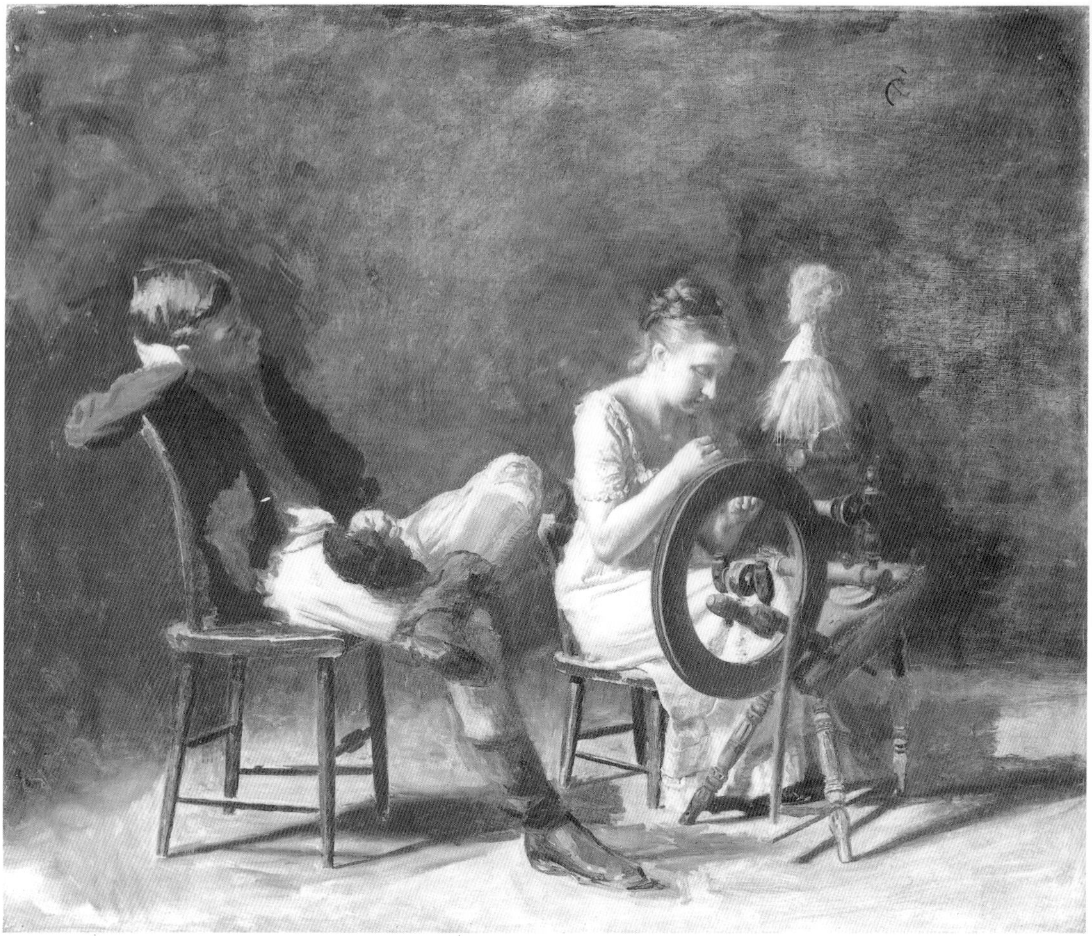

21. Thomas Eakins, *The Courtship*, ca. 1878. Oil on canvas, 20 × 24 in. Fine Arts Museums of San Francisco, Museum purchase. Gift of Mrs. Herbert Fleishhacker, M. H. de Young, John McLaughlin, J. S. Morgan and Sons, and Miss Keith Wakeman, by exchange, 72.7.

gazing at her, lost in thought. Eakins again signed his work on the wheel itself.[39] As the only image in the series to include a male figure, there is a curious tension in the painting absent from the others, although the emphasis remains on the industrious female.

The painting suggests a greater narrative dimension than other works in the series and may have been inspired by Henry Wadsworth Longfellow's poem *The Courtship of Miles Standish.*[40] The scenario evokes the poem's John Alden brooding upon his charge to ask Priscilla Mullins, whom he loves, to marry his friend Captain Miles Standish. However, the painting does not exactly illustrate the text, as the costumes worn by Eakins's figures postdate the Pilgrim context of the narrative. It is unclear whether Wood commissioned the work, but his interest in the subject finds a parallel in his treatment of mental disease. In his book *Brain-Work and Overwork* of 1880, Wood contrasted colonial vigor with the sedentary complexities of modern life: "Stern Miles Standish, at the head of his Puritan bands, roaming the wild woods in search of the wilder savage, no doubt would have smiled grimly had any one suggested that recreation of some sort is a necessity for the highest development of man."[41] The colonial era, while fraught with physical danger, seemed to Wood a salutary period for mental health.

Mitchell similarly characterized the colonial past as an ideal era from the standpoint of mental health. In *Wear and Tear or Hints for the Overworked*, Mitchell noted that "the settlers, here as elsewhere, had ample room, and lived sturdily by their own hands, little troubled for the most part with those intense competitions which make it hard to live nowadays and embitter the daily bread of life."[42] Although Mitchell did not purchase a colonial revival painting from Eakins, he owned an extensive collection of "relics" from the period, including furniture and letters.[43] He also wrote several novels, mostly historical romances set in the Revolutionary or Federal periods. As his contribution to Eakins's series, Mitchell lent the artist a Philadelphia Chippendale chair, which appears in several of the colonial revival paintings, sculptures, and photographs. In gratitude for this loan, Eakins intended to give Mitchell a "gelatine cast" of the colonial revival sculpture *Knitting* (Figure 22), which features Mitchell's chair.[44]

In terms of mental health, Mitchell extolled the virtues of the past, praising its home-based economies, agrarian trades, physical labor, and limited opportunities for intellectual exhaustion. It seemed to Mitchell that our ancestors lacked "the thousand intricate problems to solve which perplex those who struggle to-day in our teeming city hives."[45] The implicit nostalgia of this philosophy manifested itself in Eakins's colonial revival images, which celebrate domestic cloth production as the fruit of skilled, but not intellectual, labor. The therapeutic value of such domestic handicraft was widely acknowledged. The needle was likened by one writer to a lightning rod in its power to act as "a conductor off for concealed disturbance." The author further suggested that imagery of these tasks could even have a salubrious effect: "Sewing, knitting, netting, spinning, are all most graceful occupations. They are sweet, quiet, happy-looking things; they give a man rest even to think of them."[46]

The condition of female mental health was especially imperative to Mitchell, because he felt that "if the mothers of a people are sickly and weak, the sad inheritance falls upon their offspring."[47] One wonders if Eakins had any anxiety regarding his own mental health in the wake of his mother's illness—or if he

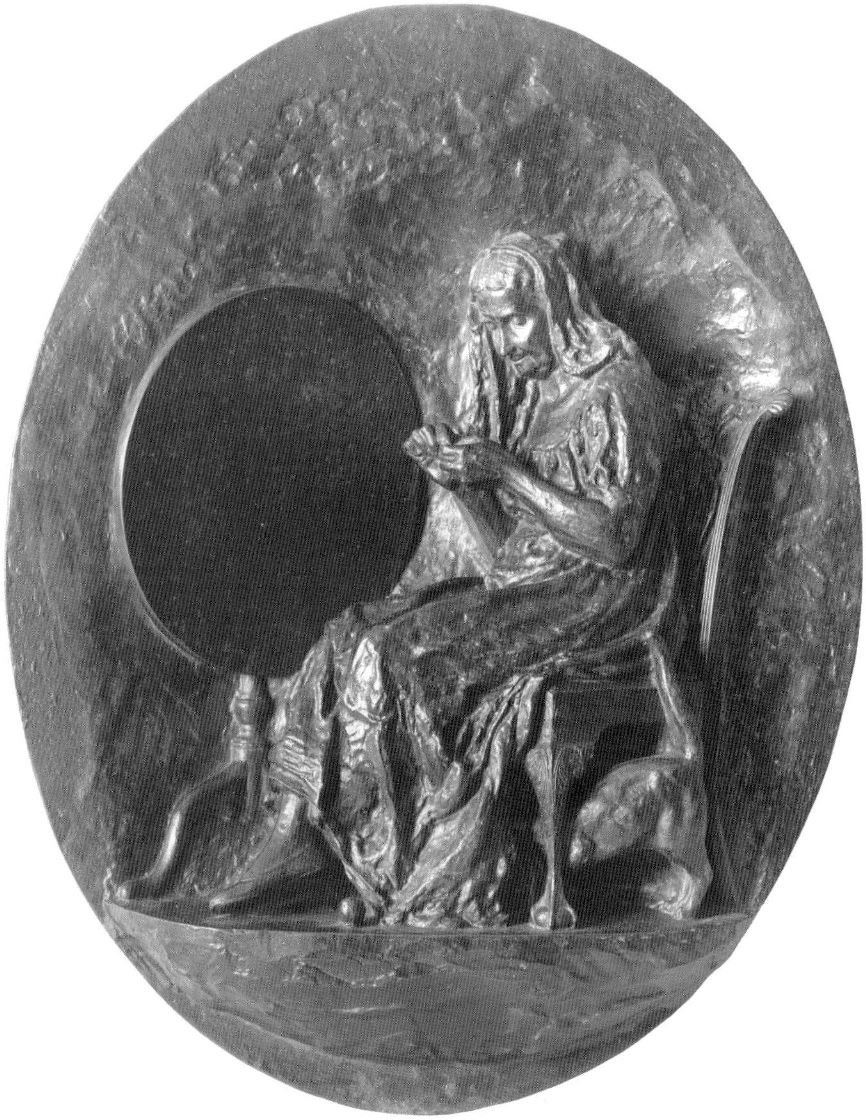

22. Thomas Eakins, *Knitting*, 1882–83 (sand cast in 1886). Bronze, 20 × 16½ × 5 in. Courtesy of the Pennsylvania Academy of the Fine Arts, Philadelphia. Gift of Edward H. Coates.

felt any concern for his three sisters, who often served as his models.[48] And what of his increasingly prominent role as an educator at an institution with a growing female student body? Art education at the Pennsylvania Academy offered a unique opportunity for women to follow the same course of study as the male pupils. Yet the progressive nature of the program led to tensions between Eakins and his students. As Eakins was concluding the colonial revival series, the Academy began to receive complaints about his teaching—these complaints came from female students or their parents.[49]

The Colonial Revival and Women's Education

In 1874, Eakins was invited to offer his professional expertise to members of the Philadelphia Sketch Club. This constituted his first regular, albeit unpaid, teaching position. Over the next several years, Eakins also volunteered his services at the Pennsylvania Academy, assisting the ailing professor of painting and drawing, Christian Schussele. By the time he attained a permanent teaching position at the Academy in 1879, Eakins ostensibly had years of teaching experience behind him. And yet, nearly all of his work had been on his own terms as a volunteer. Although Eakins had been fully in charge at the Sketch Club, the all-male enclave was vastly different from the student body Eakins would encounter at the Academy. In order to pay its bills, the Academy accepted a good number of dilettantes into its classes—many of them women. While Eakins professed a healthy tolerance of female artists and even encouraged some of his best women students to become teachers themselves, his thoughts on the matter were clearly ambivalent.

In his youth, Eakins's behavior toward women, particularly his own sisters, could be exasperatingly patronizing. According to Margaret McHenry, Eakins disapproved of higher education for women to the extent that he discouraged his talented eldest sister, Frances, from attending high school.[50] However, his thinking seems to have evolved during his tenure at the Academy, where he had many female students, several of whom became lifelong friends. As Eakins observed, "Although professional privileges are more tardily accorded to women than to men, and with reason, yet there is a decided advance . . . with respect to the education of women especially in America." Although he did "not believe that great painting or sculpture or surgery will ever be done by women," he did feel that "good enough work is continually done by them to be well worth doing."[51]

These statements place Eakins in a progressive position in terms of late nineteenth-century art instruction, yet they fall short of a complete endorsement of women's abilities. Given his qualification that women's education had lagged behind men's "with reason" and his less than forceful acknowledgment that women did only "good enough work," it appears that he had continued ambivalence regarding the accomplishments of his female pupils. Further, Eakins qualified his statement: "As the population increases, and marriages are later and fewer, and the risks of losing fortunes greater; so increases the number of women who are or may be compelled at some time to support themselves, and figure painting is not now so dishonorable to them." This, along with other comments he made, indicates that he was speaking primarily of unmarried women. Eakins distained "lady painters" and hoped to train women to become self-supporting professional artists. Yet this training did not come without a price, for he wholeheartedly believed that any woman seeking a career as an artist could not expect to live "the conventional life."[52]

Eakins's friend Mitchell believed that women's growing access to education contributed to the increasing number of nervous breakdowns he witnessed through his practice. He wondered, "Does any physician believe that it is good for a growing girl to be so occupied seven or eight hours a day? Or that it is right for her to use her brains as long a time as the mechanic employs his muscles?"[53] In answer to his own questions, Mitchell observed, "The cases I see of breakdown among women between sixteen and nineteen who belong to normal schools or female colleges are out of all proportion larger than the number of like failures among young men of the same ages."[54] Not only were "city-bred" women generally failing "to fulfil all the natural functions of mothers," but their "future womanly usefulness" was being compromised by education.[55] Affirming his belief that things were better in the past, Mitchell again asserted that this epidemic stemmed from progress, in that the educational demands made upon contemporary women were "vastly more exacting" than those made "half a century ago."[56]

Eakins's female pupils had unparalleled access to fine arts education in a period when women were still not admitted to the Ecole des Beaux-Arts.[57] Under his stewardship, the Academy expanded its curriculum to include additional life study opportunities for women. Eakins also increased the number of hours devoted to women's study of anatomy. As Amy Werbel has shown, Eakins encouraged his female students to engage in dissections when even medical schools frequently denied female medical students access to cadavers.[58] To maintain decorum, women at the Academy nearly always viewed nude models and cadavers in classes separate from those of the male pupils, yet the conditions were to be identical to the men's class. This environment offered women and men virtually equal access to art education. The most successful women to train at the Academy under this program went on to become professional artists or teachers.

Eakins's curriculum was not unlike that offered by some of the leading women's colleges in its attempt to provide women with the same opportunities given to men. So why, then, did Laurenus Clarke Seelye, president of Smith College, purchase Eakins's nostalgic colonial revival image *In Grandmother's Time* for the progressive school's new art collection? From the beginning, Seelye had made the establishment of an art collection a priority for the pioneering women's college.[59] A traditional range of European prints and casts were acquired for the school, but, more unusually, Seelye decided to build a collection of contemporary American art as well. Seelye was assisted in this endeavor by the artist James Wells Champney, the school's professor of art and a well-known painter residing in nearby historic Deerfield. Whether Seelye or Champney selected Eakins's work is not known, nor is it clear why *In Grandmother's Time* was chosen to represent the young artist. Champney's interest in the past, witnessed by his own nostalgic paintings of Deerfield, may have been a factor, or perhaps the subject seemed an appropriate exemplar for young college women.

Another possibility is that Seelye embraced the theme due to his familiarity with the sorts of arguments against women's higher education put forth by Mitchell and others. In *Wear and Tear*, Mitchell made his concerns clear by naming Vassar as an example of a women's college that, while "careful" in "guarding the health" of its students, still upheld a dangerous standard for "health and endurance" that did not acknowledge the limits of feminine life.[60] Smith would have raised even greater concerns for Mitchell, as the school intended its admission standards to equal those held by male colleges. Unlike many of its sister institutions, Smith did not modify its curriculum or offer preparatory courses to compensate for a lack of adequate training. Instead, in its first class, the college admitted only the few female applicants who could meet its stringent requirements.

On account of these policies, Smith was subject to intense criticism in its early years, forcing Seelye to explicitly acknowledge the fears regarding women's health and mental labor in his annual report for the college in 1875–76. While stating that during the course of the term none of his students appeared "as yet, to have been injured by study," he recognized the need for caution, stating that, "in this respect, however, they need greater care than young men." He admitted that his charges were "more disposed to study and less inclined to exercise" and outlined the measures he had taken to ensure that the young women were not "shirking physical exercise." This environment cultivated New Women while acknowledging the commonly held belief in their physical and mental limitations. Seelye felt that their growth was possible only with considerable care but that under these circumstances women would prove to "have both the mental and physical ability to gain a high intellectual culture."[61]

As president of a progressive women's institution, Seelye chose a pragmatic approach in his public advocacy of women's education. While he was determined to collect American art for the college, he notably did not collect work by women artists. In this context, the selection of *In Grandmother's Time* for the school's collection seems entirely in keeping with Seelye's attention to the ongoing critique of women's education. Eakins's image celebrates the ideal balance of body and mind for women advocated by Mitchell and Wood, but its identification with the past prevented it from being too assertive a model for young women of the late nineteenth century.

Compared with the male-dominated subjects that Eakins painted just prior to and during his work on the colonial revival images—doctors, rowers, hunters, and fishermen—men who are actively "doing," his colonial women seem unusually anachronistic. Yet they are perhaps not quite so different in that they address equally modern concerns. As Elizabeth Johns and Martin Berger have shown, one of the virtues of a task like rowing was that it required a balance between physical and mental labor of the sort that Mitchell and others prescribed to maintain good health.[62]

Margaret and Penelope

As Eakins concluded his series of colonial revival images, he turned to a new model: his middle sister, Margaret (Maggie), who posed for the watercolors *Homespun* (Figure 23) and *Spinning*. Each shows Margaret working at a spinning wheel. A robust example of modern womanhood, Margaret was intelligent but not bookish, and she was also a superb athlete. Unmarried, she acted as Eakins's "manager," assisting him with correspondence and keeping the records of his exhibitions before his marriage to Susan Macdowell in 1884. In this way, she helped her brother without threatening him or compromising her sex.

Eakins's depictions of Margaret at the wheel differ from his other colonial revival images in that she is not quite in colonial dress. In fact, her garb has often been characterized as "classical."[63] Indeed, her dress most closely resembles the classicizing costumes seen in photographs that Eakins took of women posing with antique casts and with his own Greek influenced *Arcadia* sculpture. Although Goodrich argued that there was "no loss of authenticity" in Eakins's colonial revival images, the artist mixed incongruous historical styles in the final works of the series.[64] As in his earlier colonial revival scenes, the room in which Margaret is situated is modestly furnished with only the essentials necessary to establish the setting. The focus is on Margaret and her actions at the wheel. Because Margaret so captivates our attention in this American interior, her dress is all the more curious. Eakins was moving in a new direction and would soon embark on a classical or Arcadian series, which may have originated with these later colonial revival subjects.

There was a precedent for linking the "colonial" past with the classical. The Federal period was rife with classical imagery. In public discourse, direct comparisons were often made between the neoclassical period and ancient Greece. In 1809, for example, one "Will Homespun" published an article in the

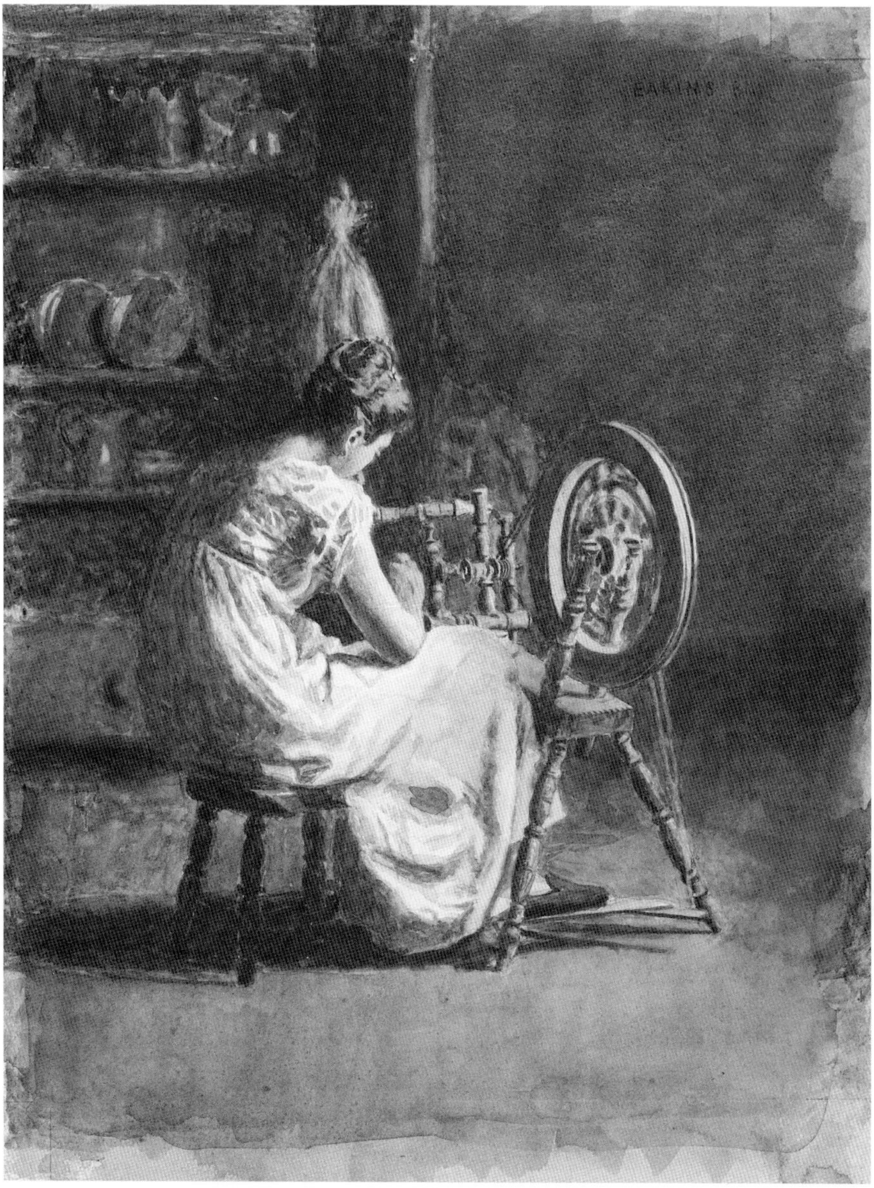

23. Thomas Eakins, *Homespun*, 1881. Watercolor on off-white wove paper, 13⅞ × 10¾ in. The Metropolitan Museum of Art, Fletcher Fund, 1925 (25.97.4).

Aurora in which he advocated domestic cloth production over the importation of foreign goods. As he wrote, "The daughters of Columbia will feel a virtuous pride in taking up the spindle and the loom when they reflect that they are imitating the example of the virtuous Penelope, wife of the sage chief of Ithaca."[65] Here the author tied the manufacture of homespun cloth with the Homeric story of Penelope, the faithful wife of Odysseus, who kept her suitors at bay by telling them that she would only remarry after completing a shroud for her aging father-in-law, Laertes. Each night she prolonged her work by deceptively unraveling a portion of the shroud.

Although known more for her weaving rather than spinning, Penelope's virtue and industry was often intertwined in the popular consciousness with the notion of yarn production through spinning. Following the Centennial, *Appleton's Journal* published an article titled "Arachne and Penelope," which focused on women's handicraft, encompassing sewing, lace making, spinning, and weaving. The article suggested that "the modern Penelope" could trace her roots back to "great-grandmamma."[66] In other words, the classical and the colonial were linked by the inherent moral value of women's work.

Eakins reused the composition from the watercolor *Homespun* for one of his earliest finished sculpted works, *Spinning* (Figure 24). The sculpture was commissioned through the architect Theophilus Chandler as a decorative embellishment for a mantel in the Walnut Street home of sugar refiner James P. Scott. *Spinning* was to be paired with *Knitting*, a sculpture whose composition derived from his earlier colonial revival painting *Seventy Years Ago*. However, Margaret died while Eakins was preparing *Spinning*, forcing him to continue his work on the image with another model, chosen from the ranks of his female pupils. But he kept the costume in the same classical vein.

Although, as Simpson noted, the two sculpted panels share formal similarities with eighteenth-century mantel designs, the shift to sculpture may have further inspired Eakins to move in a classical direction and to leave the colonial behind.[67] As Eakins wrote, "[Chandler] wished me to undertake myself the ornamentation of the chimney piece and easily induced me, for the work was much to my taste." Coming at the end of the colonial revival series, it was clearly not the subject matter alone that was "to his taste," but the medium. Eakins averred, "Relief work too has always been considered the most difficult composition and the one requiring the most learning."[68]

When Scott balked at Eakins's price for the reliefs, Eakins referred his patron to classical Greek works as his benchmark for both sculptural accomplishment in general and for what he was attempting in his own panels. To affirm the value of his colonial revival panels, Eakins directed Scott to "stop at the Academy of Fine Arts" so that he might "examine there casts of the most celebrated reliefs in the world, those of the frieze of the Parthenon." He continued, "Now this frieze, just twice as large as mine (linear measure), was placed on the temple nearly 40 feet high while my panel is not I think more than 3 feet above the eye. Hence to view the frieze at as favorable an angle as my panel you would have to go 12 times as far off."[69] In this passage Eakins suggested a comparison between

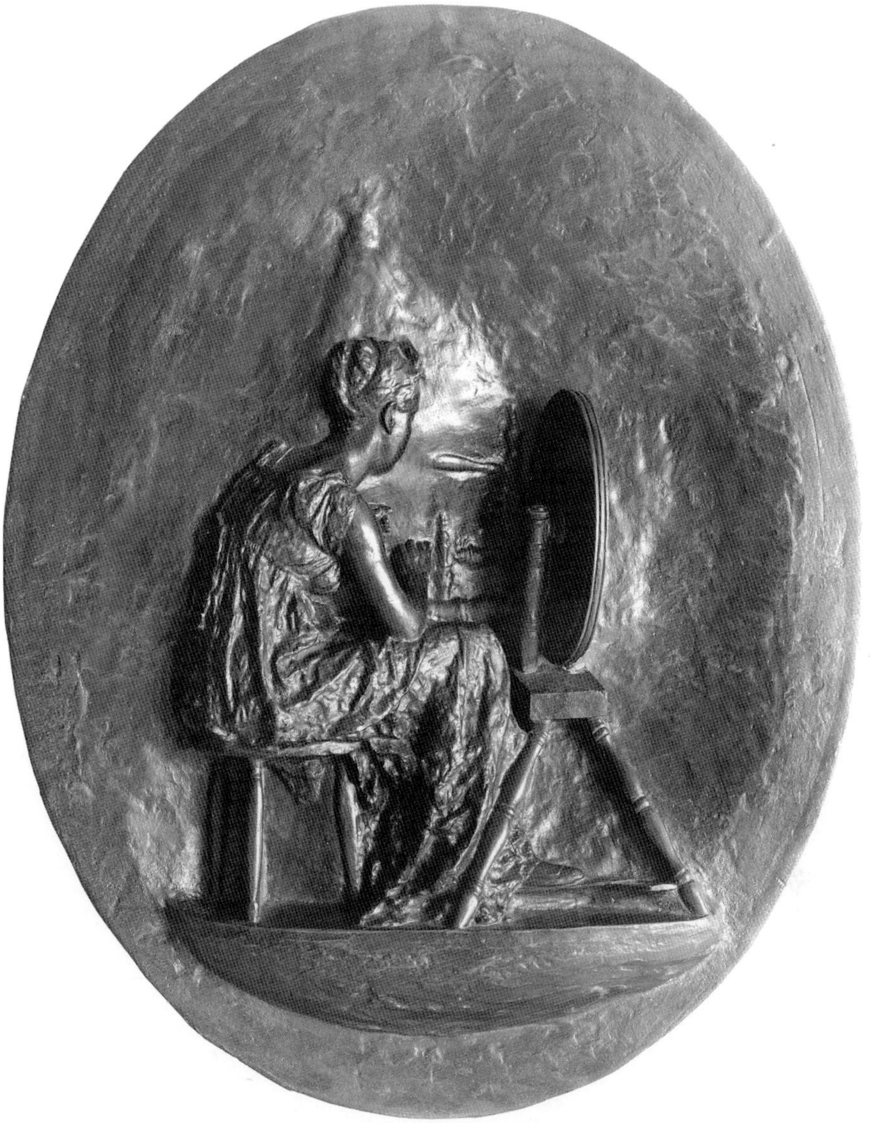

24. Thomas Eakins, *Spinning*, 1882–83 (sand cast in 1886). Bronze, 20 × 16½ × 3 in. Courtesy of the Pennsylvania Academy of the Fine Arts, Philadelphia. Gift of Edward H. Coates.

Phidias's great antique work, done in a relatively low relief, with his own decorative high-relief colonial revival panels. It seems unlikely that Scott ever visited the Academy to see the Parthenon casts, because if he had, he would perhaps have been puzzled by the formal differences between the works. Eakins's comparison suggests that relief sculpture may have inspired the new classical direction of his work.

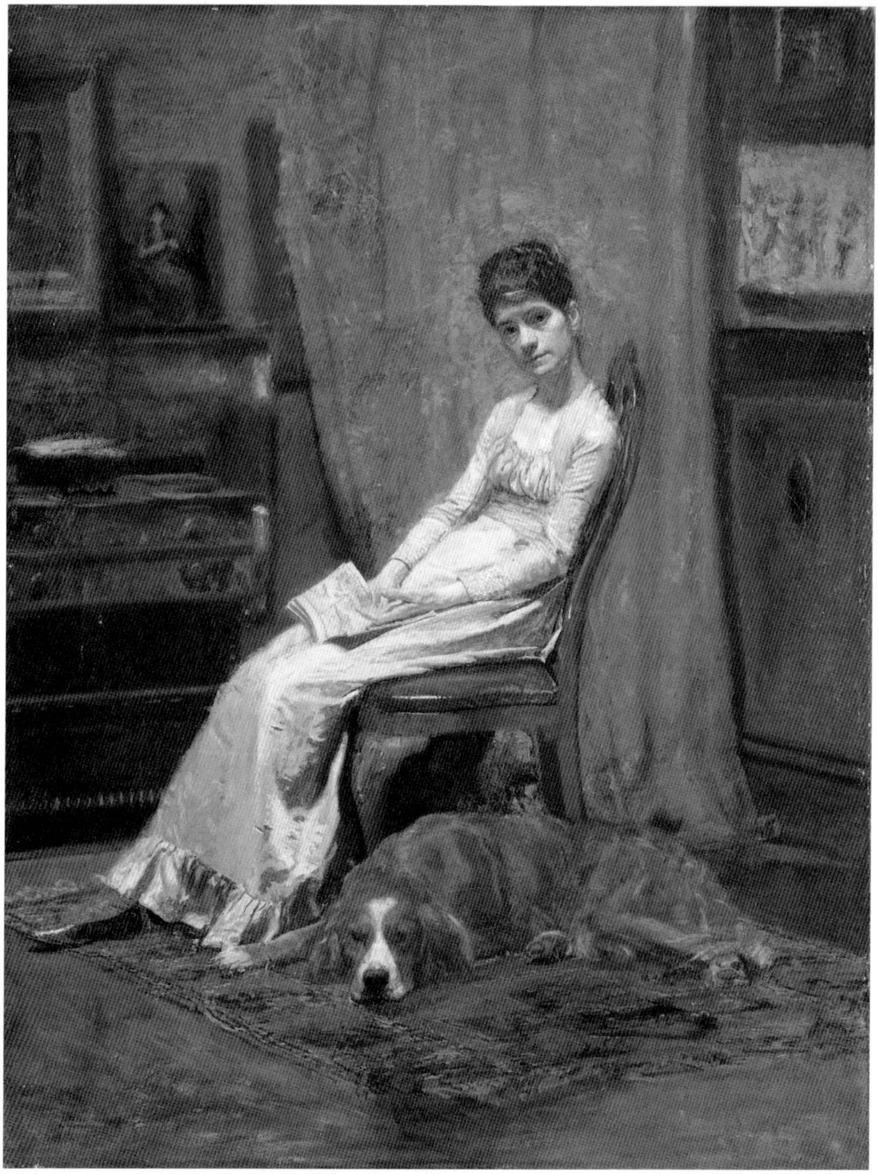

25. Thomas Eakins, *The Artist's Wife and His Setter Dog*, ca. 1884–89. Oil on canvas, 30 × 23 in. The Metropolitan Museum of Art, Fletcher Fund, 1923 (23.139).

The Artist's Wife

Eakins had finished depicting colonial revival imagery with *Knitting* and *Spinning*, yet echoes of the theme can be seen in his 1884–89 painting *The Artist's Wife and His Setter Dog* (Figure 25). The work further illustrates the tension that exists between Eakins's advocacy of artistic training for women and his use of female pupils as models, particularly in his historical images. Arguably, none of Eakins's female students in this period was more talented or more susceptible to her teacher's influence than his future wife, Susan Macdowell. Of all of Eakins's students, Susan's work was most like her teacher's. Susan's paintings were not only stylistically similar to Eakins's own, but at times she even used his models to illustrate the same subjects. For example, her watercolor *Spinning* depicts "Aunt Sally" from a slightly different vantage point than that seen in Eakins's *In Grandmother's Time.*[70] Susan embraced the colonial revival theme in works such as *The Old Clock on the Stairs* (lost), a painting commissioned by Academy director Fairman Rogers and derived from Longfellow's nostalgic poem of the same title. The work featured an "old-fashioned mansion, with an old-fashioned standard clock on the landing above, and with a youth and a maid seated on the steps."[71] An impressive foray into the colonial idiom, Susan received the Academy's Charles Toppan Prize for the painting.[72]

Susan also served as a model for Eakins beginning with the colonial revival series. On June 15, 1881, she noted in her diary "that group of infant waist dressed Acad. girls taken in Trot's yard."[73] In this entry Susan referred to a group of outdoor photographs attributed to Eakins that were probably taken in fellow Academy student Mary K. Trotter's backyard. These show several female Academy students, including Susan and her sister Elizabeth, dressed in Empire costume (Figure 26). The haphazard arrangements of the figures and inattention to the 1880s details of the backyard in which they were taken suggest that Eakins meant these photographs to function as studies, perhaps for some unrealized project or for teaching. The women pose singly or in groups, dancing, conversing, or standing. The images relate to other photographic studies that Eakins made of costumed models indoors. In one of these, Elizabeth Macdowell coyly poses in eighteenth-century dress (Figure 27). The act of using students as models, while fulfilling a need for good models, in the case of his female pupils, forced them into the more traditional role granted women in the arts—that of subject or muse. By dressing them in outdated costume, Eakins further negated the complex identity of the female artist.

Although few of Eakins's photographs of women in costume yielded finished paintings, they did inform his work of the period. One important correspondence exists between two photographs of an unidentified woman in a laced-bodice dress and Eakins's painting of Susan, *The Artist's Wife and His Setter Dog.*[74] In the photographs, the model wears a stylistically undefined gown, which appears vaguely antiquated on account of the lacing through the bodice. Eakins carefully arranged a setting for his model even if he left it somewhat incomplete. In one of the images (Figure 28), the woman sits in a Queen Anne chair that has been positioned on an old carpet; behind her is a sofa upholstered

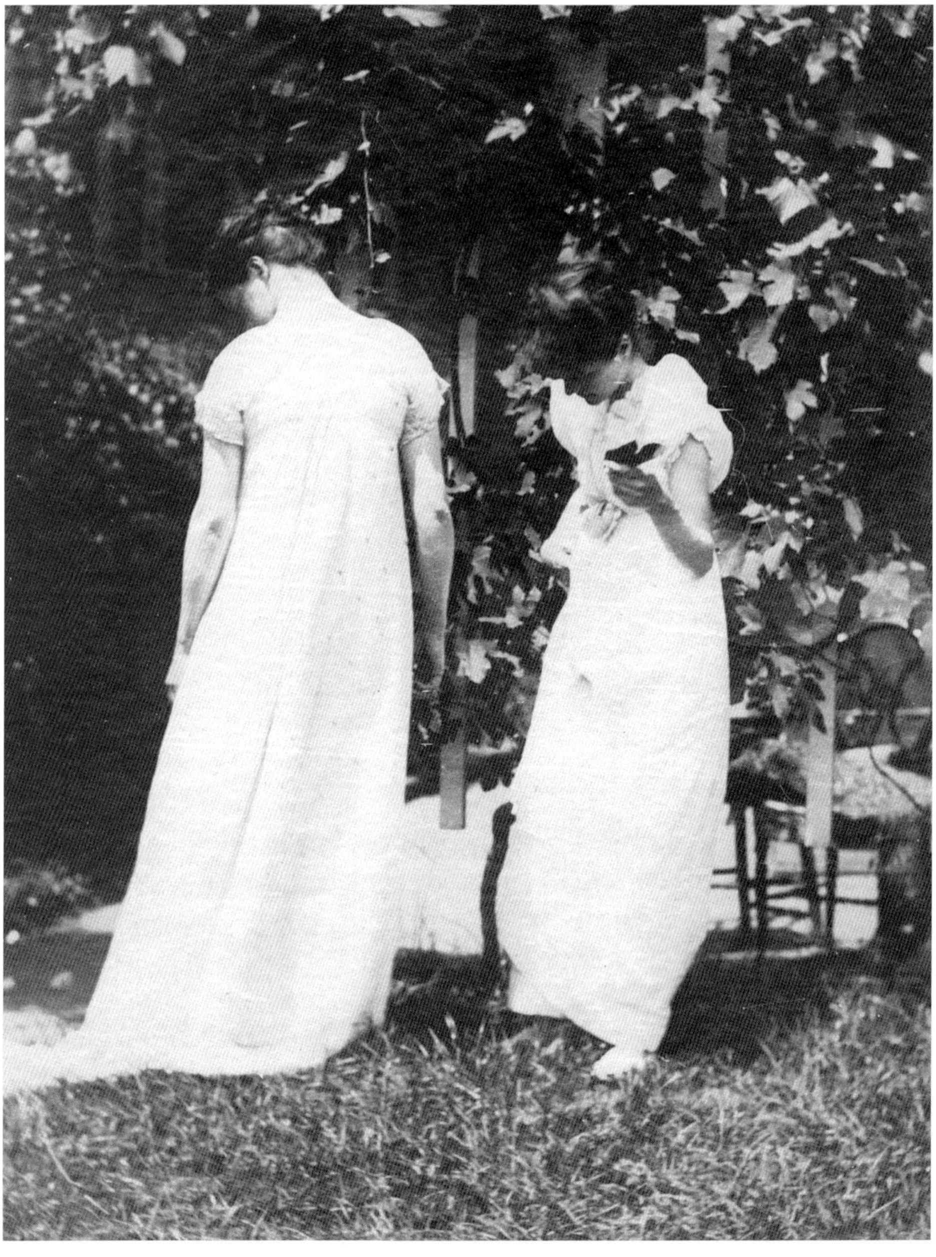

26. Thomas Eakins, *Elizabeth Macdowell and Susan Macdowell in Empire Dresses*, 1881. Albumen print, 7$^{5}/_{16}$ × 5$^{3}/_{4}$ in. Bryn Mawr College Library, Pennsylvania, Seymour Adelman Collection.

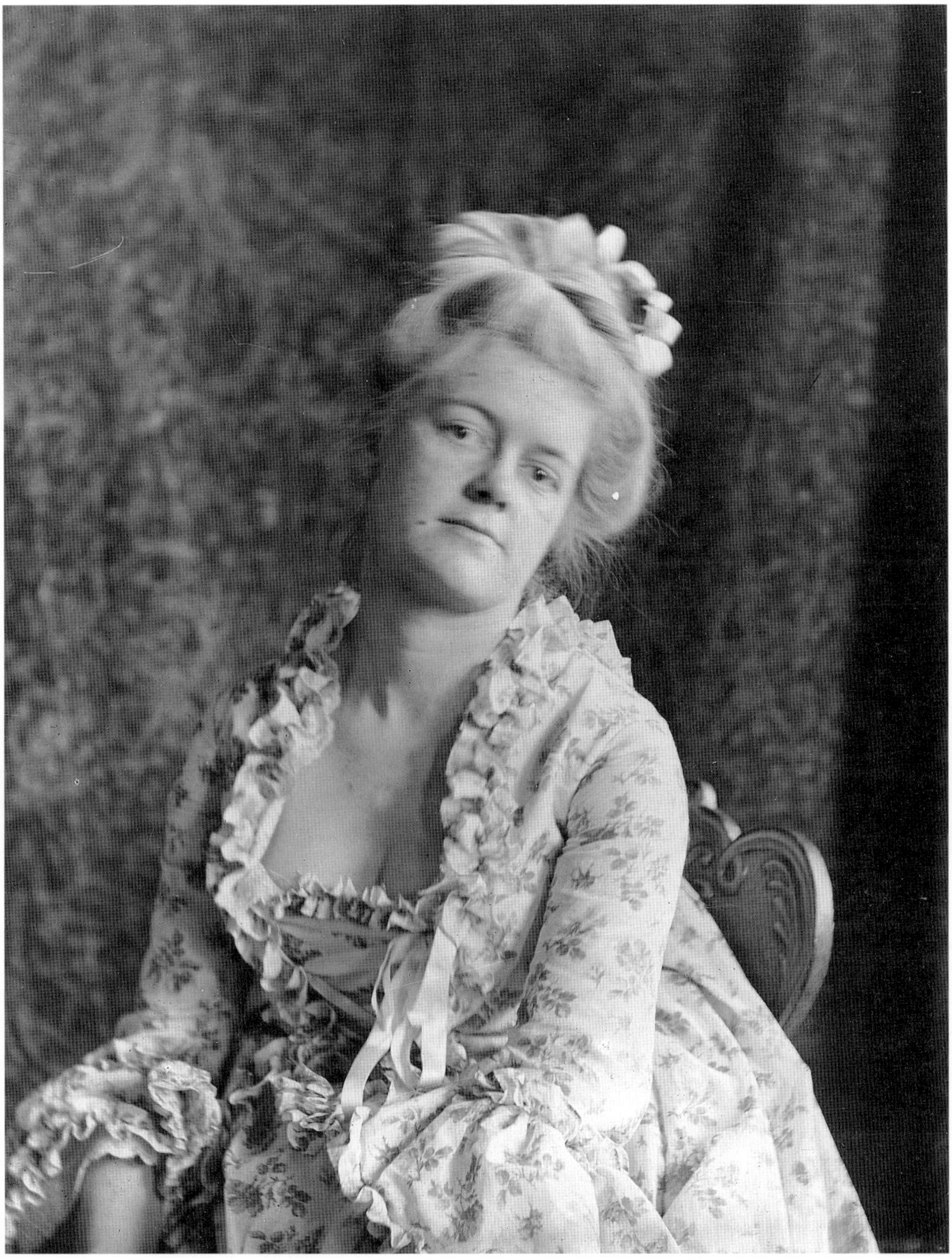

27. Thomas Eakins, *Elizabeth Macdowell in Eighteenth-Century Dress*, ca. 1885. Dry-plate glass negative, 4 × 5 in. Courtesy of the Pennsylvania Academy of the Fine Arts, Philadelphia. Charles Bregler's Thomas Eakins Collection. Purchased with the partial support of the Pew Memorial Trust.

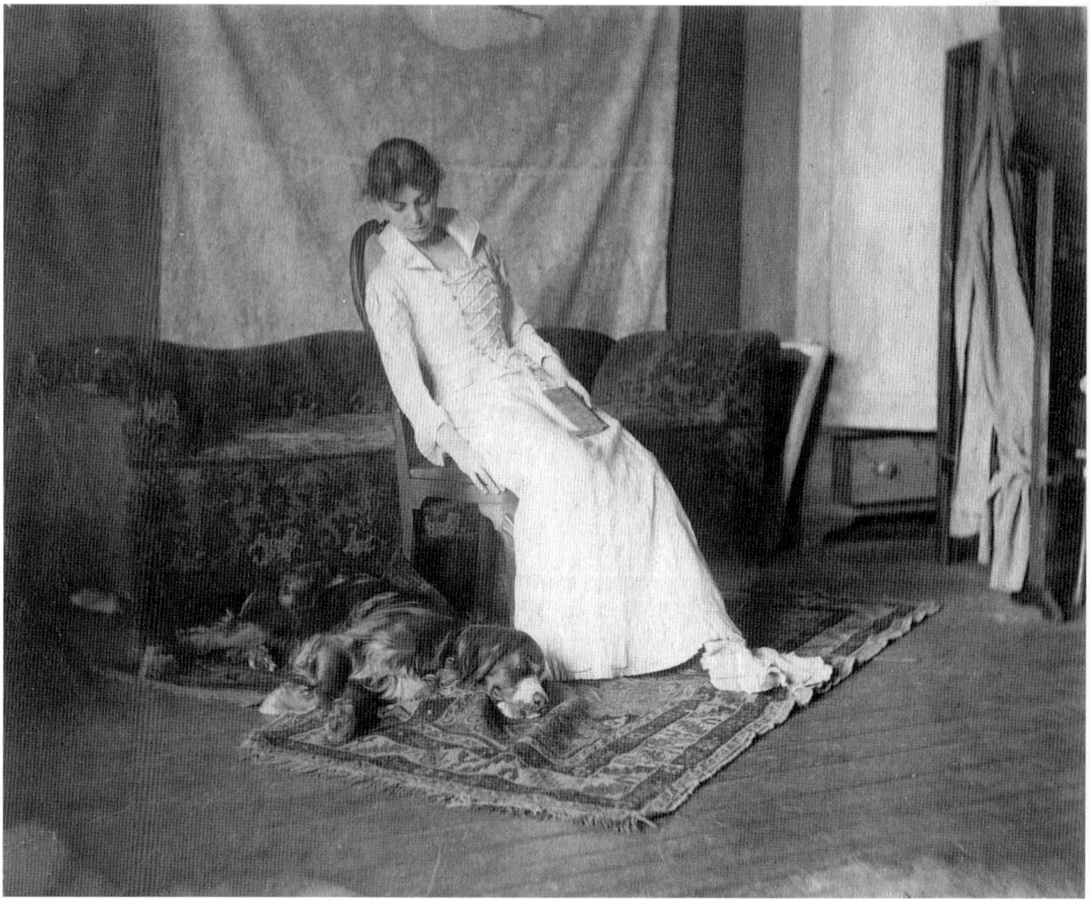

28. Thomas Eakins, *Woman in Laced-Bodice Dress, Sitting with Setter at Her Feet*, ca. 1883. Albumen print, 3 9/16 × 4 1/2 in. Courtesy of the Pennsylvania Academy of the Fine Arts, Philadelphia. Charles Bregler's Thomas Eakins Collection. Purchased with the partial support of the Pew Memorial Trust.

in a damask print, and in the background hangs some patterned drapery. Sleeping at the woman's feet is the artist's dog, Harry. The woman holds an unidentifiable book in her hand. The use of old-fashioned props and patterned fabrics link this painting with Eakins's interest in aestheticism and the colonial revival.

This photograph was one of several works that Eakins used to develop the composition of the *Artist's Wife and His Setter Dog*. However, he rearranged the elements for the oil, turning the figure to the left instead of the right and clothing Susan in an entirely different gown, one that resembles the Empire dresses worn by the women posing "in Trot's yard." The setting is also different, being the interior of Eakins's own private studio on Chestnut Street. But the basic notion of the image remains: a woman with a book seated in a Queen Anne chair, with a dog at her feet, and a patterned drape behind.[75] It is significant that Eakins began with such an overtly historicizing aesthetic image as the basis for a portrait of his new wife and former pupil. Although he placed Susan in a contemporary context, the two objects most closely associated with her—the chair and the dress—remain rooted in the past.

Eakins had begun the process of bringing his colonial subjects into the present with the painting *Retrospection* (Figure 29), which also shares compositional similarities with his painting of Susan. In this image, Eakins seated his model, a Mrs. Perkins, in Mitchell's Chippendale chair facing right. The setting is nonexistent, yet defined as a space by Eakins's unusually intense use of chiaroscuro. Eakins exhibited this work at least twice with the unromantic title *Study (Mrs. Perkins Sitting on Dr. M's Chair).* Through this title Eakins identified his sitter as a contemporary and suggested that she not be seen as a figure from the past. Likewise, his abbreviated mention of Mitchell indicates that this is a Chippendale chair in 1880, not 1780. The moodiness of the lighting lends a melancholy air that, if we follow contemporary diagnoses of mental exhaustion, could also be related to her inactivity. Unlike most of the other images in the series, the woman in *Retrospection* is both unproductive and distinctly of the present, despite her dress.

Eakins similarly cast a melancholy cloud over the painting of his wife, noticeably heightened when he reworked Susan's face after 1886, making her seem older, more tired, and weaker than she initially did.[76] In consequence, the painting bears the hallmarks of Eakins's least marketable qualities: his uncompromising realism, which critics found particularly unappealing in his depiction of Susan.[77] Yet there are indications that Eakins intended the painting as a highly aestheticized work. The setting is artfully composed. Autoradiographs suggest that "the arrangement of objects in the studio was altered several times."[78] The colorful Japanese book in Susan's lap overtly refers to the Japonisme then fashionable with his contemporaries and to the collection of Japanese objects that Susan and her sister Elizabeth owned.[79] Two of the sketchily rendered artworks behind Susan can be identified as historical images. On the right is Eakins's classically inspired sculpture, *Arcadia.* The work on the left appears to be *Figure Study: Woman Sewing* (Figure 30), a colonial revival sketch by Susan that depicts a woman in early nineteenth-century dress sewing in a chair with a spinning wheel behind her.[80] Susan's gown also hints at aestheticism—the style is contemporary but with revivalist overtones. Possibly inspired by the vogue for early American dress that followed in the wake of the Centennial fair, Susan's gown, paired with her bright red stockings, positions her as an "artistic" woman.[81]

The Artist's Wife and His Setter Dog has often been compared to William Merritt Chase's paintings of women in his own studio and to his portrait of

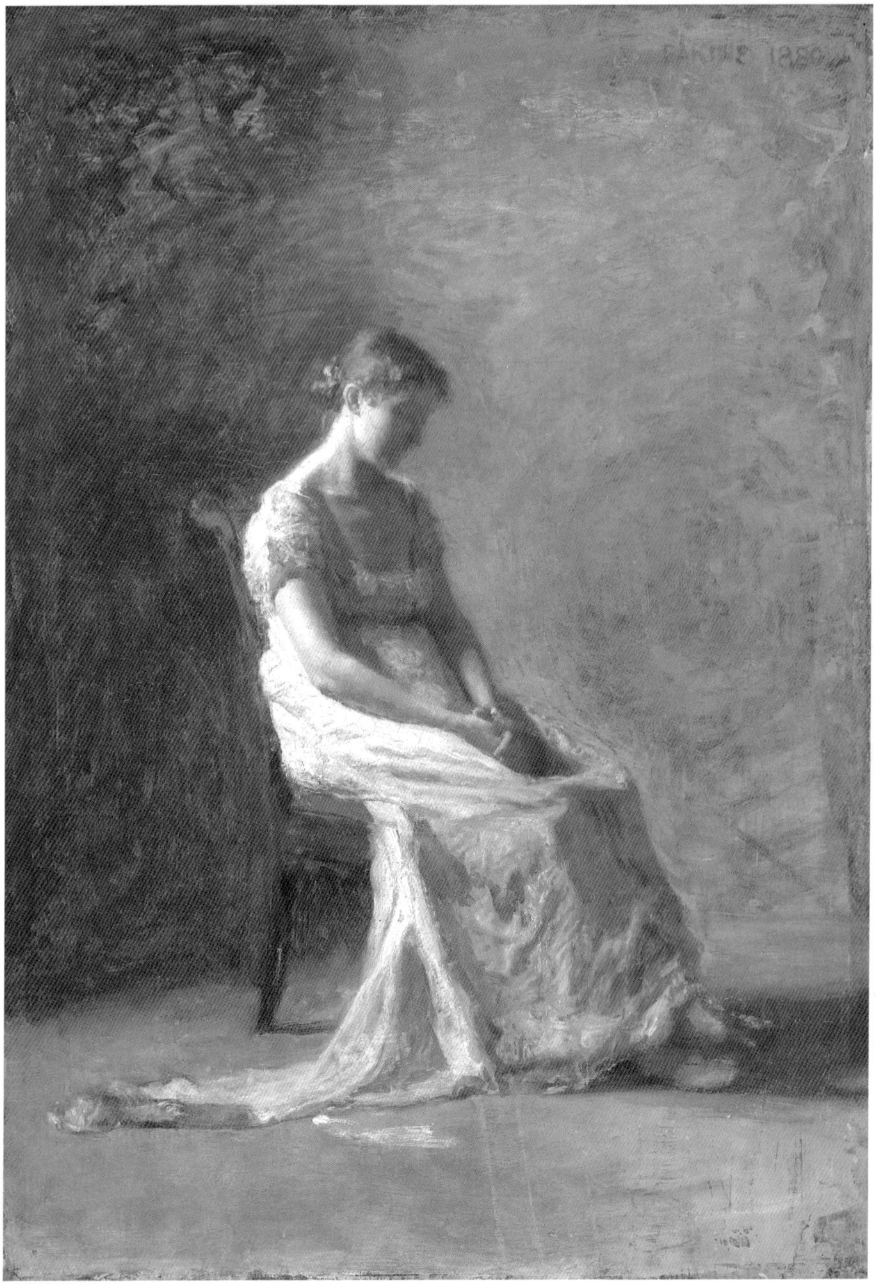

29. Thomas Eakins, *Retrospection*, 1880. Oil on wood, 14½ × 10⅛ in. Yale University Art Gallery. Bequest of Stephen Carlton Clark, B.A., 1903.

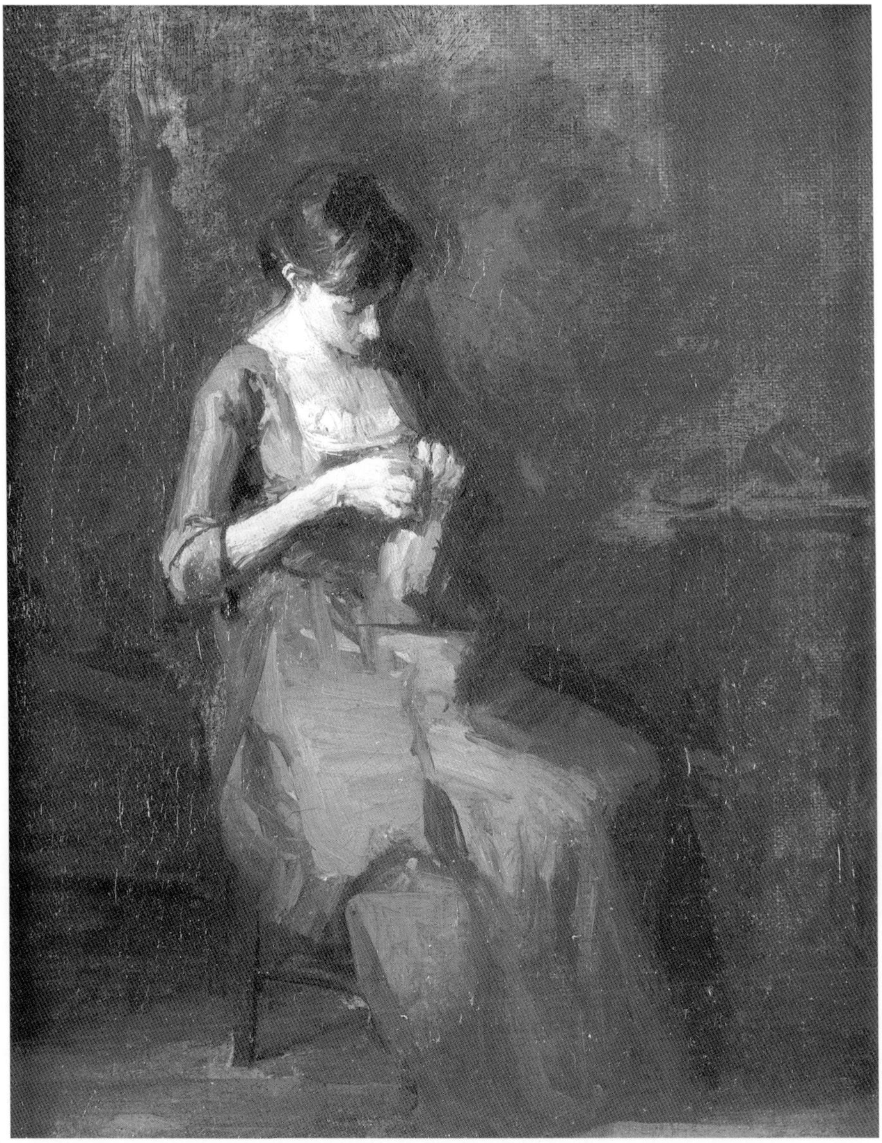

30. Susan Macdowell Eakins, *Figure Study: Woman Sewing*, ca. 1882–84. Oil on canvas, 10 1/16 × 8 1/16 in. Courtesy of the Pennsylvania Academy of the Fine Arts, Philadelphia. Charles Bregler's Thomas Eakins Collection. Purchased with the partial support of the Pew Memorial Trust and the Henry C. Gibson Fund.

Dora Wheeler (Figure 31).[82] Indeed, there are clear affinities between Chases's works and Eakins's painting of his wife. The yellow drape, the turn of the chair, and Susan's outward gaze and basic pose echo Chase's portrait of Wheeler, who was *his* pupil. Yet there are also several notable differences. Karal Ann Marling has called Chase's portrait "a sympathetic and optimistic tribute to a young

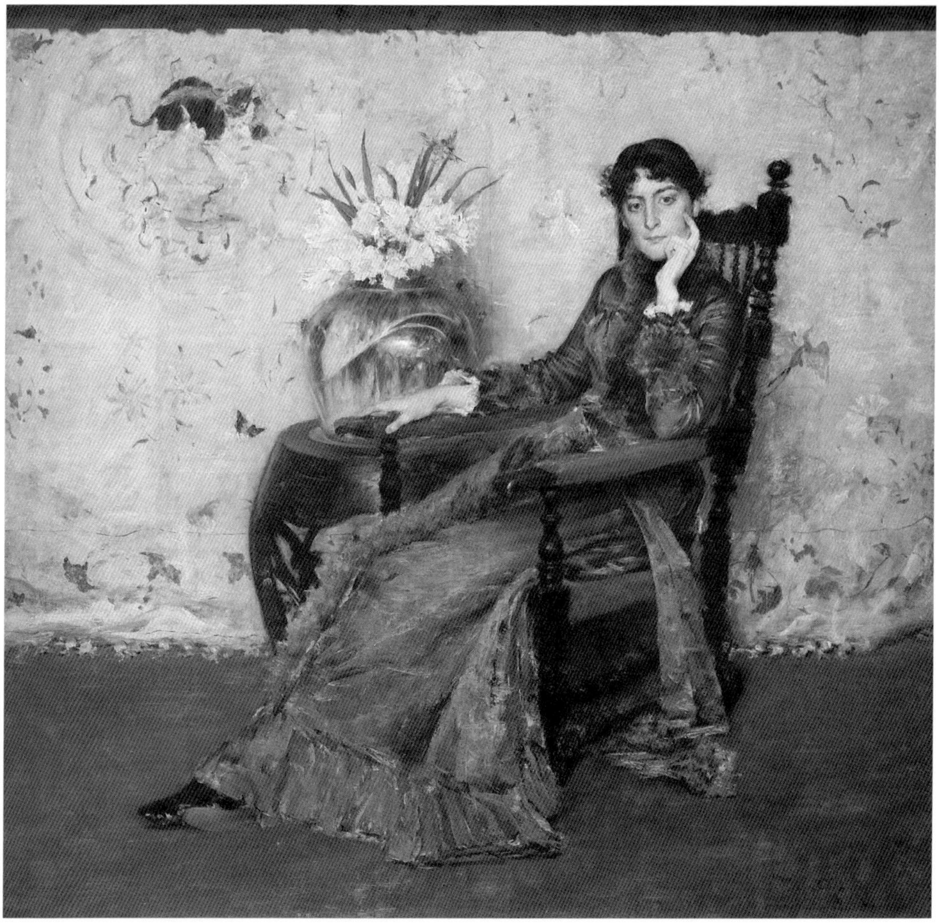

31. William Merritt Chase, *Dora Wheeler*, 1882–83. Oil on canvas, 159 × 165.5 × 11.5 cm. The Cleveland Museum of Art. Gift of Mrs. Boudinot Keith in memory of Mr. and Mrs. J. H. Wade.

woman artist poised on the brink of great things to come."[83] Chase accomplished this by asserting his student's presence as an individual. She appears confident and self-possessed, unlike Susan, who seems small and withering by comparison. Wheeler is surrounded by objects—the richly embroidered textile hanging, the Chinese taboret, and the blue ceramic bowl—that allude to her professional status as a decorative artist.[84] The setting also asserts her success as an artist, for it is Wheeler's own studio.

Eakins likely intended to depict Susan as an artist. He shows her in bohemian dress and included one of her works in the background. However, she does not seem to be on the verge of a brilliant career. Rather, she appears as a possession in the artist's studio, not unlike a costumed model. Although *The*

Artist's Wife and His Setter Dog was not Eakins's title for the painting, it was the one that Susan gave when the Metropolitan Museum of Art purchased the painting from her.[85] Her own preference for the possessives in the title may provide a context for viewing the image. Although Susan continued to paint after her marriage, she essentially ceased being a professional artist, rarely exhibiting her work. As Laura Prieto has observed, "She remained an artist, but not a fully professional one. That is, regardless of how much she painted in private, Susan's professional activity as an artist was decidedly curtailed during the marriage, while Thomas's was not."[86] She became "the artist's wife" rather than the artist herself. Even after her husband's death, when she returned to painting more regularly, Kirsten Swinth suggests that "she had difficulty conceiving of herself as a professional, referring in several letters to her 'little paintings' and expressing embarrassment at putting a price on her work."[87]

Wheeler's career differed in significant ways from Susan's. Although Wheeler aspired to become a figure painter, she instead achieved success as a decorative artist. Throughout her career, Wheeler continued to paint but became best known for her book and magazine illustrations, Christmas card designs, and textile work. Following in the footsteps of her talented mother, Candace, Wheeler designed a number of tapestries for Associated Artists, the firm her mother founded. Yet in spite of her success as a professional artist, Wheeler ultimately did not contest the importance of household industry. Wheeler perpetuated the link between women and handicraft through her production of high-end needlework.

With its ties to the colonial revival series, *The Artist's Wife and His Setter Dog* raises questions about Eakins's thoughts about women's education and the specter of mental illness. Susan's revivalist dress allies her with the colonial figure in the painting behind her. However, Eakins's placement of this painting invites a visual comparison between his wife and the productive colonial woman. In the colonial image, the young costumed woman mirrors Susan's pose, but unlike Susan, whose hands rest idly upon the book, the woman in the painting is focused on her sewing—the action of her hands being clearly visible. Susan is as quiescent as Kathrin Crowell with her kitten. That Susan is seated with a book in a contemporary setting and, further, that we know she is Susan Eakins, former pupil of Thomas Eakins, heralds her as a New Woman, and yet she appears enervated and inert. Eakins's reworking of the painting increased the shadows on Susan's face, making her seem more worn and frail—leading some scholars to suggest that she appears ill and dejected, rather like a neurasthenic.[88] Was Eakins, on some level, depicting the consequences of female education in his portrait of Susan?

Susan's appearance echoes Mitchell's descriptions of modern "city-bred" women as weak and "merely pretty to look at," whose unfortunate "destiny is the shawl and the sofa, neuralgia, weak backs and the varied forms of hysteria."[89] Although Susan was by most accounts a good-natured companion, not prone to mental illness, her potential as a professional artist put her at risk. This is not to suggest that Eakins consciously depicted his wife as a neurasthenic but rather that his ambivalence about educated professional women, especially those who married, made it impossible to represent her as a confident individual.[90]

The Artist's Wife and His Setter Dog may specifically express Eakins's ambivalence about Susan's status as a married woman artist. By the time Eakins altered his wife's appearance in the painting, it must have been clear that she would not bear him any children, placing her in the same category of women who, according to Mitchell, were unable "to fulfill all the natural functions of mothers."[91] Carroll Smith-Rosenberg has studied this tendency in Victorian culture, writing, "Society, late-nineteenth-century physicians warned, must protect the higher good of racial health by avoiding situations in which adolescent girls taxed their intellectual faculties in academic competition. Pointedly, they compared the robust fertility of early-nineteenth-century women with the relative barrenness of their granddaughters—New Women."[92]

In his student years, Eakins espoused strong views regarding motherhood, writing that "the noblest & most beautiful sight in the world is the father and mother of strong children & the most ignoble & contemptible a bride & bridegroom." He continued, "If ever I marry it will be only for the delight of raising children."[93] Not only was Susan Eakins unsuccessful as an artist, but, by Victorian standards, she had also failed as a wife by not producing children.

Eakins's colonial revival images reflect a complex amalgam of concerns, some national, some quite personal. Inspired by the Centennial, Eakins went on to use the colonial past to reconsider the position of the burgeoning group of female students attending his classes at the Pennsylvania Academy. Eakins's advocacy of women artists, including his own wife, was marred by a deeper ambivalence about their capabilities. In his depictions of colonial women, Eakins tapped into contemporary theories regarding nervous exhaustion among educated women by glorifying a simpler past when robust women engaged in traditional women's work.

CHAPTER THREE

Reenacting the Antique

Thomas Eakins followed the colonial revival *Knitting* and *Spinning* panels with three more sculptures, which he said were made "after the Greek methods of relief."[1] The works he referred to, *Youth Playing the Pipes*, *An Arcadian*, and *Pastoral (Arcadia)* (Figure 32), depict nude and classically draped figures, some playing antique-style pipes. The reliefs otherwise in no way resemble the classical Greek sculptures that Eakins admired, all three panels being small, intimate scenes of roughly modeled individuals who do not possess the idealized physiques preferred by classical sculptors. Never meant for marble, all three works survive as plasters intended for bronze. In addition to these Greek-influenced sculptures, Eakins took many photographs of costumed and nude models and made two Arcadian paintings, all with similarly classical subject matter.[2] Why did Eakins, the realist devoted to "American subjects," suddenly turn to these antique historical themes?

As a teacher at the Pennsylvania Academy, Eakins objected to his students' copying too long from plaster casts of antique sculptures. His opposition to this long-held artistic tradition became a well-known and ultimately controversial part of Eakins's pedagogical philosophy. In place of study from classical casts, Eakins advocated extended study of the life model. The Academy's emphasis on life study went well beyond that of any other American art school of the period—so much so that critics and students complained that Eakins's program fell short in other areas, such as landscape painting.[3] However, this attention to the life model was part of what Eakins meant by "Greek methods." Eakins felt certain that all great artists, including the classical sculptor Phidias, produced their timeless works only through similarly scrupulous life study.

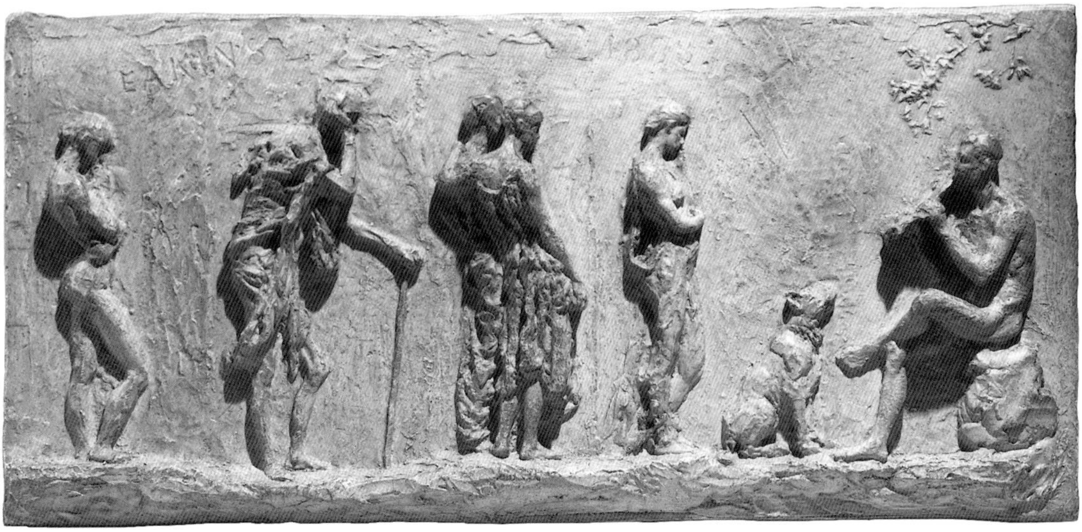

32. Thomas Eakins, *Pastoral (Arcadia)*, 1883–84. Plaster with transparent brown patina, 11¾ × 24 × 2³⁄₁₆ in. Philadelphia Museum of Art. Purchased with the J. Stogdell Stokes Fund, 1975.

Eakins paid homage to this link between life modeling and the classical tradition in his Arcadian works and in the genre picture *Swimming* (Figure 33), commissioned in 1884 by Edward Hornor Coates, the newly appointed chairman of the Committee on Instruction at the Academy. *Swimming* shows a group of male nude models, nearly all of whom were Academy students, outdoors at Dove Lake, near Bryn Mawr, Pennsylvania. Although ostensibly a contemporary subject, the nudity of the men and the influence of classical sculpture on the arrangement of the figures tie *Swimming* to the Arcadian works.[4] However, *Swimming* seems more formal and, with its one diver frozen in midair, ironically, more static, than the overtly historicizing Arcadian works. Some of this, perhaps, accounts for Coates's rejection of the painting in favor of *Singing a Pathetic Song* (Figure 34).

Eakins began his Arcadian series shortly after he was made director of the Academy's schools in February 1882. Following years of precarious employment by the Academy, this promotion afforded Eakins the opportunity to take the school's artistic program fully in hand and craft it according to his personal artistic vision. In doing so, Eakins applied the pedagogical theories of the French artist and theorist Horace Lecoq de Boisbaudran. Both the Arcadian series and *Swimming* provide visual evidence of the influence of Lecoq's theories through their emphasis on classical themes and the use of nude models outdoors.[5] The integration of Lecoq's pedagogical ideas into *Swimming* suggests another possi-

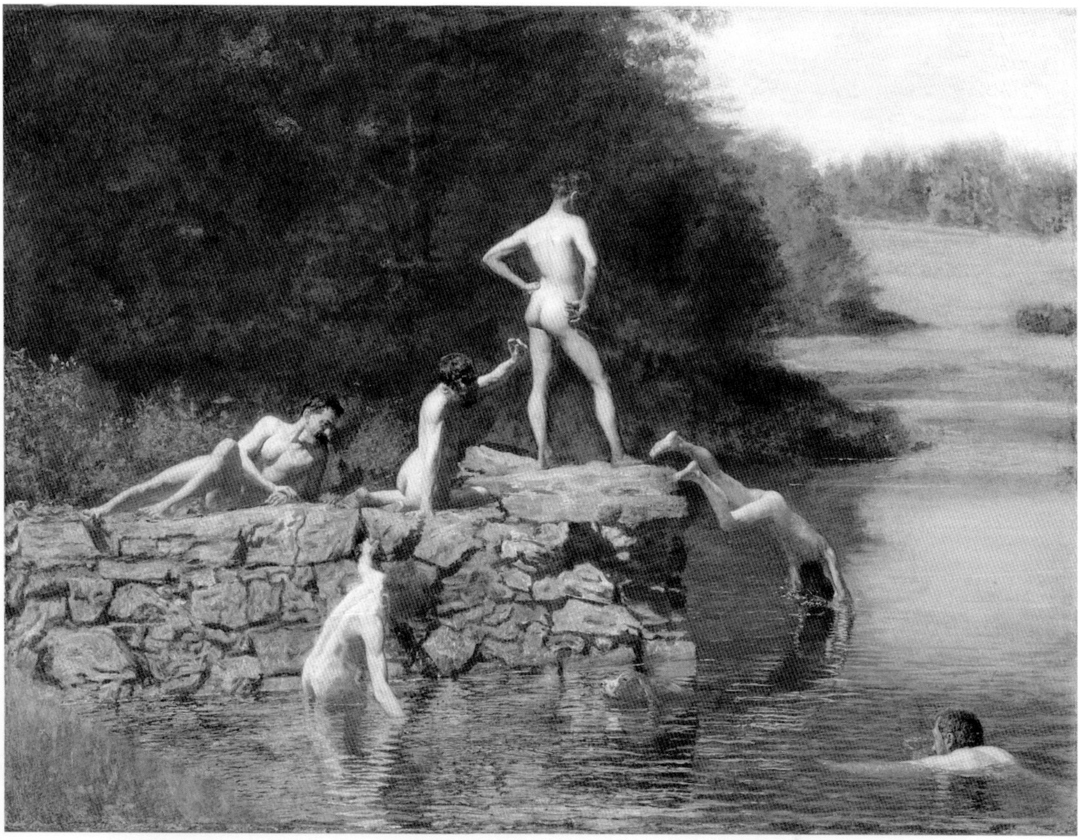

33. Thomas Eakins, *Swimming*, 1885. Oil on canvas, 27$^{3}/_{8}$ × 36$^{3}/_{8}$ in. Amon Carter Museum, Fort Worth, Texas. Purchased by the Friends of Art, the Fort Worth Art Association, 1925; acquired by the Amon Carter Museum, 1990, from the Modern Art Museum of Fort Worth through grants and donations from the Amon G. Carter Foundation, the Sid W. Richardson Foundation, the Anne Burnett and Charles Tandy Foundation, Capital Cities/ABC Foundation, Fort Worth Star-Telegram, The R. D. and Joan Dale Hubbard Foundation, and the people of Fort Worth (1990.19.1).

ble reason for Coates's rejection of the painting. Acceptance would have meant tacit approval.

Arcadian Themes

Eakins's attraction to classical subject matter grew out of his popular colonial revival series. As noted in the previous chapter, Eakins's late colonial revival images anachronistically depict figures wearing classical costumes in early American interiors. The colonial revival series also provided Eakins with his first opportunity to work in relief sculpture, a medium that he would continue

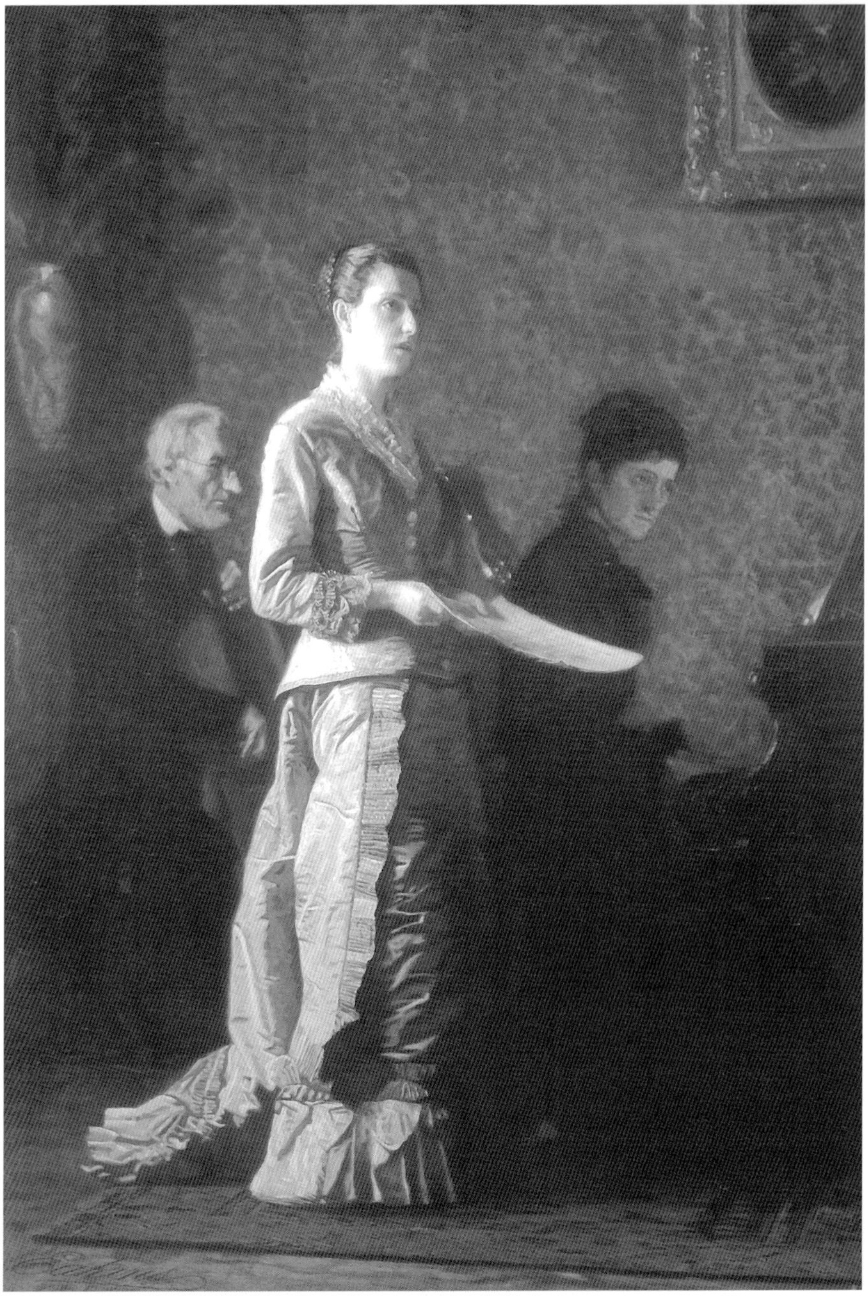

34. Thomas Eakins, *Singing a Pathetic Song*, 1881. Oil on canvas, 45 × 32½ in. Corcoran Gallery of Art, Washington, D.C. Museum Purchase, Gallery Fund.

to explore with the Arcadian series. As with his colonial revival subjects, Eakins's classically inspired works reflected a contemporary interest in this type of historicizing subject matter. With their moody, almost tonalist, landscapes and idyllic figures, the Arcadian paintings resemble those of his more successful contemporaries.[6] Yet Eakins chose not to reap the benefits that might have come from exhibiting such timely works.

Because most of the Arcadian works were never exhibited and some remained unfinished, they were virtually unknown during Eakins's lifetime. As a consequence, they have been regarded by some twentieth-century scholars as an experiment or, less charitably, as an artistic dead end.[7] If true, this would have been remarkable, for although Eakins occasionally abandoned individual works (such as *Hiawatha*), the Arcadian subjects would be the lone example in his oeuvre of an entire series failing to bear fruit. Furthermore, Eakins invested several years in this seemingly profitless pursuit. In order to explain why Eakins chose not to finish and exhibit the Arcadian subjects, some scholars have suggested that he cast them aside when he received the more important commission for *Swimming*. An alternate theory postulates that Eakins's increased teaching duties during this period curtailed further development of the theme.[8]

In either case, because the Arcadian pictures directly precede *Swimming*, they have usually been viewed as precursors to the later image. Indeed, most discussions of the Arcadian works have surfaced in studies of *Swimming*. But this also highlights perceived differences between Eakins's "realist" works and those that are ideal. *Swimming* has been deemed a canonical realist work because the figures are identifiable as specific individuals situated in a verifiable location outside of Eakins's Philadelphia—the picture is "real." Scholars have regarded the more lyrical Arcadian works in an entirely different light, often as anomalous, because they appear to be an unsuccessful venture into an unusually romantic historical mode of painting.[9]

As easy as it might be to dismiss the Arcadian subjects, not only were they critical to the development of *Swimming*, but they also held some special significance for Eakins. His ambition for the series is apparent from the way that he pursued the subject over three years in different media, creating several sketches, two large works in oil, three relief sculptures, and numerous photographs. *Arcadia*, the more finished of the two paintings, is notably larger than many of his exhibition oils, including *Swimming*, which suggests that Eakins intended it for public display. Although it remained unfinished, he did think highly enough of the work to give it to the artist William Merritt Chase. The Arcadian works also represent Eakins's most daring exploration of the nude because some of the images feature male and female figures interacting in the same setting.[10]

The largest of Eakins's three Arcadian reliefs, *Pastoral (Arcadia)*, provides further evidence of the importance of the series to Eakins. This relief has the most complex composition of the entire series, including six figures, a dog, and elements of a landscape setting. In October 1883, Eakins sent the sculpture to New York where he exhibited it as *Sketch in Plaster (Pastoral)* at the American Art Association's Second Annual Exhibition of Sketches and Studies. This sole exhibition generated little contemporary criticism that might give an indication of how the Arcadian series would have been received by a nineteenth-century audience.[11] But Eakins must have felt confident about his progress on the relief to exhibit it publicly, especially in New York, where it would have been seen by his peers.

The work again appeared before the public, albeit indirectly, when Eakins exhibited the painting *The Artist's Wife and His Setter Dog* in 1887. In this image, the relief is one of a handful of works displayed in the studio interior, appearing to the right of Eakins's wife, Susan. Eakins exhibited *The Artist's Wife and His Setter Dog* during his lifetime three times in New York (1887, 1892, 1915), once in Chicago (1889), and once in Paris (1891). The painting was also reproduced as a photogravure in Mariana van Rensselaer's 1886 volume, *The Book of American Figure Painters.* Eakins's figuration of the relief within another of his works is highly unusual and underscores the important place that it held in his oeuvre. Eakins similarly photographed models in classical costumes posing with the relief. He also gave replicas of the plaster to close students and friends.[12]

The relief has been subject to a range of interpretations by scholars. Lloyd Goodrich saw *Pastoral (Arcadia)* as a reflection of Eakins's "admiration for Greek art, particularly Phidias and the sculptures of the Parthenon," and also as an affirmation of his pedagogical insistence upon the study of the nude figure.[13] Elizabeth Johns read the work as an extension of Eakins's interest in music, but "removed from the ephemeral trappings of contemporary life." In the relief she found evocations of larger "truths about human life," represented within the panel as both the ages of man as well as the states of solitude, friendship, and passion.[14] More recently, Henry Adams has viewed the sculpture "in family terms," representing "Eakins's dog, his three sisters, his father, and finally somewhat removed from the rest, his mother."[15]

Marc Simpson has written the most extensive study of *Pastoral (Arcadia)*, in which he discussed a range of iconographic sources for the panel, citing works by Phidias, Ghiberti, and Thomas Wilmer Dewing as influences. Simpson related the relief to the death of Eakins's sister, Margaret, in December 1882.[16] Margaret's death no doubt influenced Eakins's work in 1883, and the mood of the relief is somber. Yet Eakins chose not to include overt references to death, despite contemporary precedents for memorial works. Eakins's title, *Pastoral*, is

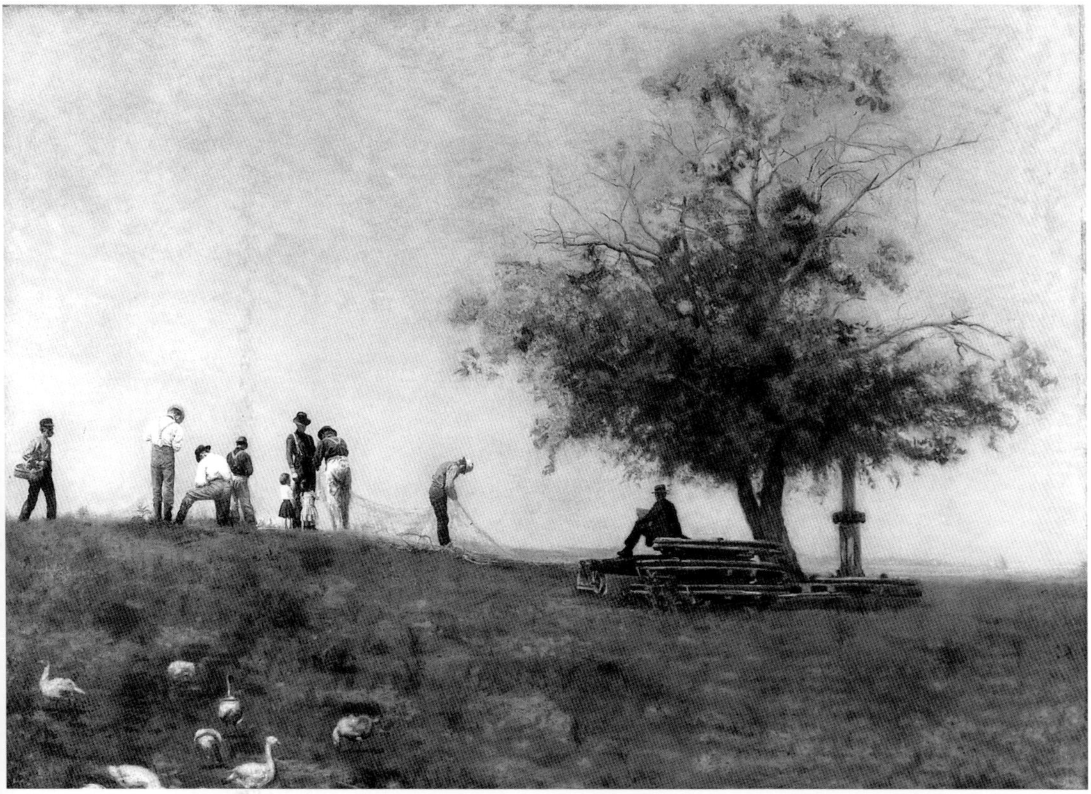

35. Thomas Eakins, *Mending the Net*, 1881. Oil on canvas, 32⅛ × 45⅛ in. Philadelphia Museum of Art. Gift of Mrs. Thomas Eakins and Miss Mary Adeline Williams, 1929.

also more benign than funerary images such as Elihu Vedder's explicit 1879 *In Memoriam*, which was made as a memorial tribute to his son Philip.[17]

Eakins and the Camera

Process was perhaps as important to the development of *Swimming* and the Arcadian series as the shift to classical subject matter. The most significant change that Eakins made to his working methods at this time was his embrace of photography. Shortly after acquiring a camera in 1881, Eakins began photographing costumed models outside for his colonial revival works.[18] Eakins also studied fully clothed figures both on the rooftop of his studio and on the Gloucester shore for a series of paintings that he made of New Jersey fishermen, among them *Shad Fishing at Gloucester on the Delaware River* and *Mending the Net* (Figure 35). The period between 1883 and 1886, when Eakins was working on Arcadian themes, is marked by a profusion of photographic studies, many of them featuring nude or costumed models. These photographs relate to the Arcadian paintings and sculptures in their evocation of Greek subjects, either overtly or indirectly. However, unlike his Gloucester photographs, these generally did not aid in the development of other works of art. Apart from a handful of photographs that were used to craft Eakins's two Arcadian paintings, most of these images were not used as studies for paintings or sculptures.

Kathleen Foster has noted that the sheer variety of sizes and processes that Eakins used "seem to demonstrate an affection for these images as photographs, quite apart from their use in painting."[19] However, this does not mean that they functioned as independent art objects. Although Eakins lived in one of the great centers of amateur photography, he steadfastly avoided adding his images to this culture. Despite his apparent fondness for these photographs, he chose never to exhibit them. Of course, in the case of the nudes, there may have been a desire to protect the identities of the models. However, among the negatives that Eakins favored with multiple printings are several featuring fully clothed models in classical dress. Some of these subjects loosely resemble the aestheticized photographs of contemporary pictorial photographers. Had Eakins cared to tidy up his studio to create a more consistently historical setting with greater aesthetic appeal, he could surely have exhibited these images with some success. That he chose not to pay greater attention to the settings indicates that, as one would expect of Eakins, the models themselves interested him more than the medium.

The most unusual and controversial aspect of the Arcadian photographs is that many of them feature nude models, some of them posing for the artist outdoors. As discussed earlier, Eakins also photographed clothed models outdoors. And in 1880 he took his nearly nude student J. Laurie Wallace outdoors to pose as Christ for his painting *Crucifixion.* Unlike these earlier efforts, the Arcadian works marked the first time that he had taken entirely nude models outside. At this time, Eakins photographed his models—mostly Academy students—in a variety of poses: some seemingly candid, others staged to resemble classical sculptures, and still others engaging in classicizing athletic feats ranging from boxing to tug-of-war and, ultimately, swimming (Figure 36). These active poses further relate to Eakins's concurrent interest in motion photography.

In addition to photographing nude models outdoors, Eakins continued photographing models indoors—this time with a classical focus. Indoors, Eakins photographed more athletic nudes as well as models assuming the poses of well-known antique sculptures. He also photographed models in classical dress. In many of these images, the models pose before the Academy's antique cast collection. Through these studies, Eakins seems to have been

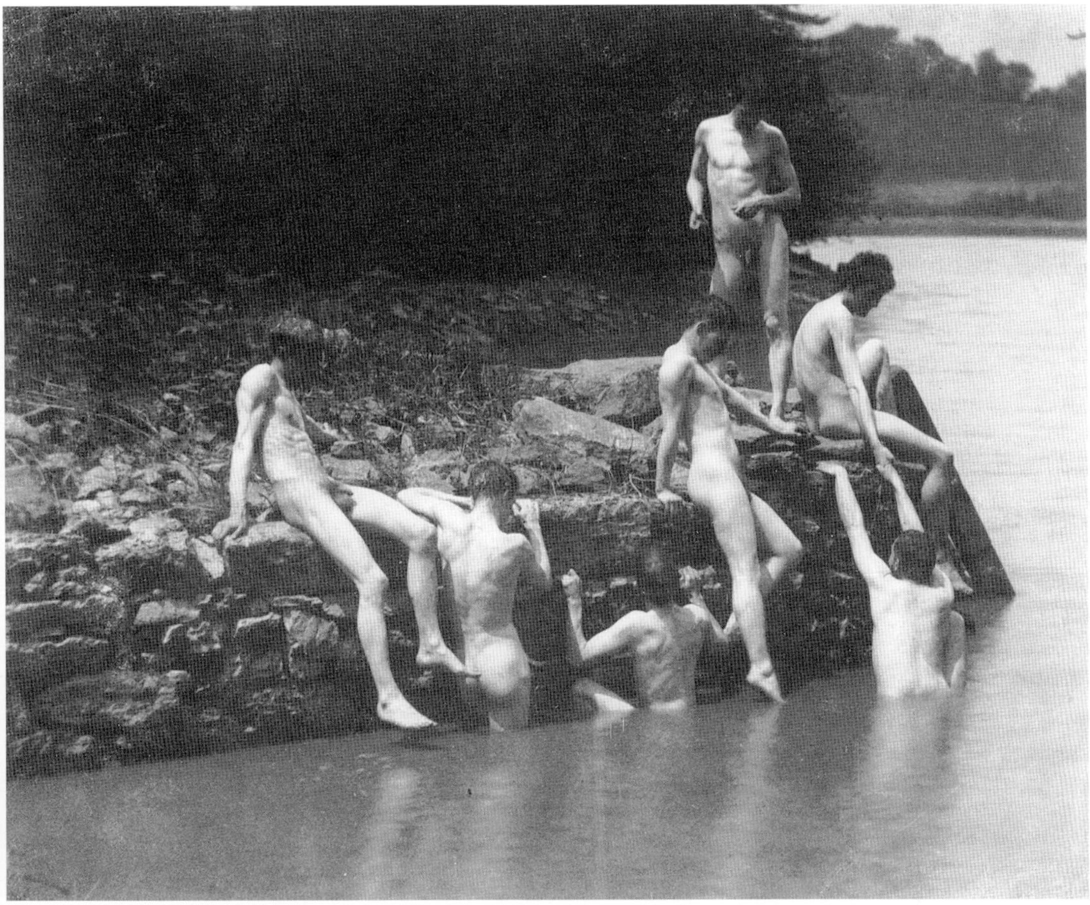

36. Thomas Eakins, *Thomas Eakins and Students, Swimming Nude*, ca. 1883. Platinum print, 8 15/16 × 11 1/16 in. Courtesy of the Pennsylvania Academy of the Fine Arts, Philadelphia. Charles Bregler's Thomas Eakins Collection. Purchased with the partial support of the Pew Memorial Trust.

making a comparison between living models and ancient sculpture—a theme that he would develop in *Swimming*. In spite of this juxtaposition, Eakins's Arcadian models retain their modernity and individuality throughout the photographs. Even in instances where the models' poses reference specific antique sculptures, they do not appear to have been selected for their ideal classical form. Eakins's flirtation with the past was about method and not the appropriation of an aesthetic style.

But why did Eakins take so many photographs that he did not exhibit or use in the development of other works? Marc Simpson has suggested that the Arcadian works "may be seen as a vehicle for exploring and synthesizing the major professional and pedagogic concerns of the artist's academy years, from

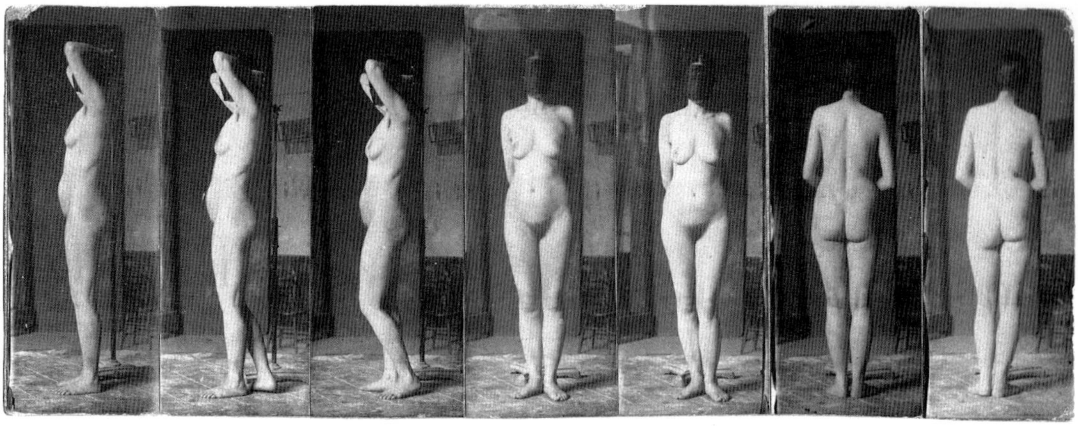

37. Thomas Eakins, *Naked Series: Female with Dark Mask, Poses 1–7*, ca. 1883. Seven albumen prints mounted on blue board, each 3¹⁄₁₆ × 1³⁄₁₆ in. Courtesy of the Pennsylvania Academy of the Fine Arts, Philadelphia. Charles Bregler's Thomas Eakins Collection. Purchased with the partial support of the Pew Memorial Trust.

1876–1886."[20] Photography was both critical to the development of the Arcadian works and a vital aspect of Eakins's teaching in the 1880s. By 1883, Eakins had begun using photographs in his teaching at the Academy. Around this time, he and his students began photographing nude models in standardized poses for what has become known as the "Naked Series" (Figure 37). Eakins mounted these photographs on cards to enable his students to study a wide variety of body types assuming the same seven stances. Because Eakins gave several of the Arcadian images to his students, it seems that these photographs also served as teaching tools. For example, he must have given prints from the swimming session to his student, the photographer Eva Watson, as she lent two Eakins photographs, both titled *Bathers*, to the Loan Exhibition of the Camera Club of New York in December 1899. Furthermore, when Eakins left the Academy in 1886, he took many of the photographs from the Arcadian and swimming modeling sessions with him. Significantly, these photographs adorned the walls of Eakins's private academy, the Art Students League of Philadelphia (Figure 38), where he taught in the later 1880s and 1890s.

The combination of classical subject matter with nude modeling sessions outdoors and at the Academy relate to practices advocated by French pedagogue Horace Lecoq de Boisbaudran. However, Eakins innovatively introduced photography into the curriculum developed by Lecoq. If Eakins abandoned the Arcadian series in favor of his commission for *Swimming*, he did not discard the new methods he developed for the series—*Swimming* marks the fullest integration of Lecoq's theories into his art.

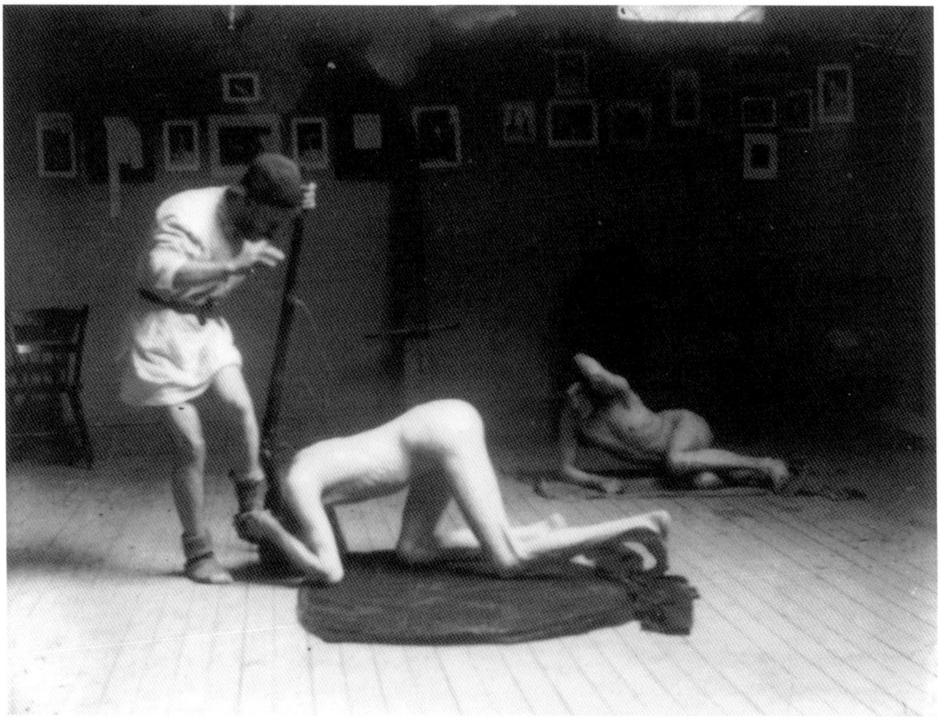

38. Circle of Thomas Eakins, *Male Students Posing at the Art Students League of Philadelphia*, ca. 1890. Digital inkjet print from the original gelatin dry-plate negative, 4 × 5 in. Philadelphia Museum of Art. Purchased with funds contributed by Mr. Seymour Adelman, 1981.

Horace Lecoq de Boisbaudran, Memory, and the Photograph

Though little known today, Horace Lecoq de Boisbaudran (1802–97) was an influential art teacher in Paris when Eakins was studying there during the late 1860s. Lecoq entered the Ecole des Beaux-Arts as a student in 1819. Throughout the 1830s, he exhibited portraits and religious subjects at the French Salons. Although he continued to paint until his death at the age of ninety-five, he stopped exhibiting altogether in 1844 to devote himself to teaching. In 1847, while teaching at the Ecole Gratuite de Dessin, known as the "Petite Ecole," Lecoq introduced an experimental method of artistic training whereby he required his students to reproduce images from memory as a supplement to the school's standard drawing instruction. The students were given graduated exercises, starting with the reproduction of simple lines and progressing to complex compositions, with the most proficient students finally advancing to drawing from moving figures outdoors. Lecoq believed that the practice of memory training would help artists record the fleeting effects of light, weather, motion, and color. He detailed the success of his memory experiments at the Petite Ecole in his 1847 pamphlet *L'Éducation de la mémoire pittoresque*.[21]

In contrast to the fine arts–oriented Ecole des Beaux-Arts, the Petite Ecole emphasized the decorative and industrial arts. Accordingly, Lecoq's first exercises with his students focused on form. But in 1862 he expanded his text to include sections on memory studies of color and light, leading the architect and writer Eugéne Emmanuel Viollet-le-Duc to suggest its implementation at the Ecole des Beaux-Arts. Viollet-le-Duc hoped that Lecoq's method would act as a corrective to a system of art education that he felt only encouraged pupils to perpetuate their master's style. In a second pamphlet, *Coup d'oeil sur l'enseignement des beaux-arts*, published in 1872, Lecoq similarly argued that the Ecole had forgotten "that the great masters, whose example it was continually quoting, were not satisfied to merely accept tradition as handed to them by their predecessors, but sought to combine it with the living elements of their own age, and thus become creators in their turn."[22] While the Ecole never adopted the program, several artists experimented with the system, including Henri Fantin-Latour, Léon Lhermitte, Auguste Rodin, Jean-Charles Cazin, and the Régamey brothers: Félix, Guillaume, and Frédéric.

When Eakins began his studies at the Ecole des Beaux-Arts in 1866, Lecoq had just become director of the Petite Ecole. Following his appointment, Lecoq proceeded to reform the curriculum of the school according to the tenets of his system. Lecoq's ideas received their greatest notoriety in 1867 when he presented them before the Education and the Fine Arts Committees at the Exposition Universelle. These two bodies, in turn, formed a committee to carry out tests of Lecoq's method at the Ecole des Beaux-Arts.[23] Although criticism of Lecoq's curriculum eventually forced his resignation from the Petite Ecole in 1869, he remained influential and continued to teach both privately and at other institutions. He published a final pamphlet, *Sommaire d'une methode pour l'enseignement du dessin et de la peinture: Lettres à un jeune professeur*, in 1876, which further outlined his teaching methods. Lecoq's three texts, each of which expands upon and complements the others, were united in a single volume in 1879.

Eakins could have become acquainted with Lecoq's ideas at any time during his studies in Paris. His fluency in French gave him advantages that other American art students often lacked. On occasion, he even read French artistic texts in their original language.[24] He was also friendly with a number of the French students in Gérôme's atelier, some of whom may have been knowledgeable about the activities at the Petite Ecole. Eakins certainly must have heard of Lecoq's controversial methods from his close friend William Sartain, who studied at the Petite Ecole sometime in 1869, the year in which Lecoq was fired.[25] In addition, it seems likely that Eakins either witnessed or heard about the demonstration at the Ecole in 1867, for in that year he began to discuss memory in his letters home.

Eakins first alluded to the influence of Lecoq's system of memory training in a letter to his father that November: "I see much more ahead of me than I used to, but I believe I am seeing a way to get at it & that is to do all I see from memory."[26] Eakins was still working from memory in January 1868, writing again to his father, "After painting a model I paint it from memory."[27] A few months later, Eakins outlined a notion of picture making that had memory and imagination at its heart, writing that if a painter "makes a hot day he makes it like a hot day he once saw or is seeing, if a sweet face a face he once saw or which he imagines from old memories or parts of memories and his knowledge."[28] This often quoted letter parallels a passage in *L'Éducation de mémoire pittoresque*: "Except in our memories, how can we ever hope to reconstruct nature's endless happy groupings once they are broken and scattered."[29]

That Lecoq's theories inspired more than a passing interest in the young Eakins is clear from letters written by Susan Macdowell Eakins after her husband's death. In one dating from the 1930s, Susan wrote to Mrs. Lewis R. Dick about Eakins's student years in Paris, recalling, "When weary from class study, he would stop his painting in the school, and try to memorize the work he had been doing in the school, working alone in his lodging room. He considered this a good tax for the mind."[30] In another letter to her niece Peggy Macdowell, Susan wrote of her husband's training, "He also studied independently of anyone, and often reviewed by memory in his little living room, what he had done in the schools. Memory work was excellent he said, good for the mind. He advised strain your brain more than your eyes."[31] As Eakins did not know Susan Macdowell during his years in Paris, he must have recounted his experiences to her years later. The fact that he mentioned study from memory to his wife suggests that it held an important place in his training. Eakins's continuing concern with memory reemerged later in his career in the advice that he offered a student in 1906 to "frequent the life schools and reproduce from memory what you do there at home."[32]

After his years in Paris, Eakins's interest in Lecoq's work was likely revived by his contact with Félix Régamey, one of Lecoq's most devoted pupils.[33] Régamey came to the United States to work as an illustrator for *Harper's Weekly* in 1873. He visited Philadelphia's Centennial Exhibition for *Harper's* in 1876. Perhaps more significantly, in June of that year Régamey attended a meeting of the Philadelphia Sketch Club, where Eakins was teaching.[34] As an acknowledged Francophile, Eakins would have been eager to meet this progressive Frenchman while he visited Eakins's hometown. That they did meet, probably in the fall of 1879, is established by the 1881 publication of Régamey's *L'Enseignment du Dessin Aux Etats-Unis.* In preparation for the book, which discussed the curricula of several art schools in the United States, Régamey visited the Pennsylvania Academy, where Thomas Eakins had recently been made a professor following the death of Christian Schussele.[35]

Since Eakins traveled little after his return to the United States, few letters exist from the critical period of his artistic maturation to establish his knowledge of contemporary theories. New discoveries about Eakins's technique, particularly the revelation that he sometimes directly transcribed photographs into his paintings, indicates that Eakins did not always document his methods and even went to some effort to hide them.[36] Therefore the works themselves must be used as evidence. The Arcadian series and *Swimming* offer the best proof of Lecoq's influence on Eakins, but there are indications that Lecoq's work had an impact even earlier in Eakins's career.

Douglass Paschall has suggested that Eakins used memory in his 1881 painting *Mending the Net*, which he considers "Eakins's reconstruction of a scene that must have transpired much earlier" rather than as "a glimpse of a contemporary encounter."[37] Although Paschall does not link the painting with Lecoq's theories, Eakins's extensive use of photography in the creation of *Mending the Net* provides a clue about Eakins's evolving relationship with artistic memory. Eakins relied on a range of traditional preparatory methods throughout the 1870s, including oil sketches, meticulous perspective drawings, commercial photographs, and even three-dimensional models. But by the 1880s he had become increasingly dependent on photographs taken by himself and his students.

Lecoq did not incorporate photography into his method, but Eakins's use of photographs in *Mending the Net* conforms to one of the memory techniques described in his texts. Eakins constructed the painting's composition from several photographs taken at different sites, which he then projected onto his canvas.[38] The painting therefore represents a composite of details from these individual photographs. In order to create a coherent whole, Eakins transcribed individual elements of the photographs onto his canvas while simultaneously subjectively reconfiguring these elements into an entirely original compositional arrangement. Lecoq encouraged this approach, writing, "Memory and imagination are so closely linked that imagination can only use what memory has to offer her, producing, like chemistry from known elements, results completely new."[39]

In *Mending the Net*, Eakins assembled his "known elements" from photographs to create a "completely new" composition. Picture making, not mere mimesis, was the ultimate goal of Lecoq's memory training. In fact, he hoped that the subjective nature of memory would be of help in filtering out extraneous and distracting details. In *Mending the Net*, as in the Arcadian works that followed, Eakins's photographs act as something more than *aides-mémoires*; they actually substitute for memory itself. Eakins, who was always interested in finding scientific solutions to the imprecision of perception and cognition, used photography as a shortcut for Lecoq's training of memory.

While memory was at the heart of Lecoq's method, several other aspects of his program would have appealed to Eakins. In fact, the course of study that Eakins implemented at the Pennsylvania Academy had several points of direct correspondence with Lecoq's curriculum. An exploration of the correlations between Lecoq's writings and Eakins's program illuminates the reasons behind Eakins's attraction to Lecoq's theories. Further, the seemingly disparate themes that informed Eakins's art in the 1880s, manifesting themselves fully in the Arcadian series and *Swimming*, can also be found in Lecoq's texts. A careful comparison of these themes in the work of both Eakins and Lecoq is critical to understanding Eakins's art and his pedagogical practices prior to his dismissal from the Academy in 1886.

Anatomy and Motion

Although anatomy played a vital role in the French artistic curriculum, both Lecoq and Eakins advocated a central position for it in artistic training that exceeded even what the Ecole des Beaux-Arts offered its students. Lecoq asserted that anatomical study should be "the basis of all teaching in all schools, and should come before any specialization, for it is the parent-stem of all branches of art." Further, he believed that "knowledge of the structure of the human body" was the "resume of all the forms in nature" and thus "should be considered a sort of syntax for the art of drawing, and as such should be learnt by heart."[40] Eakins similarly placed the human body at the center of his program of instruction at the Academy. As an 1882–83 circular for the school, probably written by Eakins, unequivocally declared, "The course of study is believed to be more thorough than that of any other existing school. Its basis is the nude human figure."[41]

In order to understand the human body, Lecoq encouraged his students to attend dissections and thoroughly learn the names and functions of every muscle group. This would give the student a general understanding of human anatomy, which could then be taken into account when studying an individual model. As Lecoq warned, "The deltoid of every model is somewhat different in appearance, and it is the infinite variations of this individual character which the student must always be ready and able to express."[42] Eakins similarly believed that "a man's hand no more looks like another man[']s than his head like another's."[43]

Eakins made dissection and anatomical study essential to the curriculum at the Academy. Lectures on anatomy, given by the physician Dr. William W. Keen, complemented student work in the dissection room. Eakins also made plaster casts of flayed human body parts for his students to use in their study of anatomy. Eakins defended the practice in an 1879 interview with critic William Brownell: "To draw the human figure it is necessary to know as much as possible about it, about its structure and its movements, its bones and muscles, how they are made, and how they act."[44] Although Eakins assured Brownell that the Academy did not turn out physicians, Amy Werbel has argued that Eakins developed an "anatomist's view of the body," a view that was closer to a physician's than an artist's. This understanding of the body often placed a barrier between him and his audience.[45] However, the program of anatomical study that Eakins embraced had sanction in the writings of Lecoq.

Expert knowledge of anatomy was critical to Lecoq because the students who mastered this "syntax for all drawing" would advance to studying both humans and animals in motion, quickly reproducing actions and forms from memory. Although Lecoq felt that traditional life study remained an important building block in an artist's development, he also understood its limitations. Static models quickly lost "all the movement and expression of the pose," causing "the muscles to lose their shapeliness."[46] A posed life model only approximated life; a moving figure, by contrast, remained true to nature in revealing the fluidity and functionality of the body.

Eakins would undoubtedly have been interested in an artistic method that espoused greater truthfulness to nature and involved the study of movement. An unusual feature of *Swimming* is the moving figure of the diver leaping from the rocks into the lake. This frozen diver culminated Eakins's years of study of bodies in motion. Eakins had become deeply invested in the representation of moving figures by 1879. In that year, Eakins undertook a commission from Fairman Rogers, an Academy director, to depict his four-in-hand coach in motion. Rogers, a civil engineer and amateur photographer, headed the Committee on Instruction during Eakins's least controversial years at the Pennsylvania Academy.

From the studies that Eakins made at Rogers's Newport home, it seems likely that the commission was more collaboratively conceived than Eakins's later arrangement with Coates. In any case, Rogers graciously accepted the finished painting, *A May Morning in the Park* (Figure 39), which shows Rogers and his wife, along with two other couples, coaching in Fairmount Park. Eakins accurately rendered the horses' legs in their differing phases of motion, a conceit

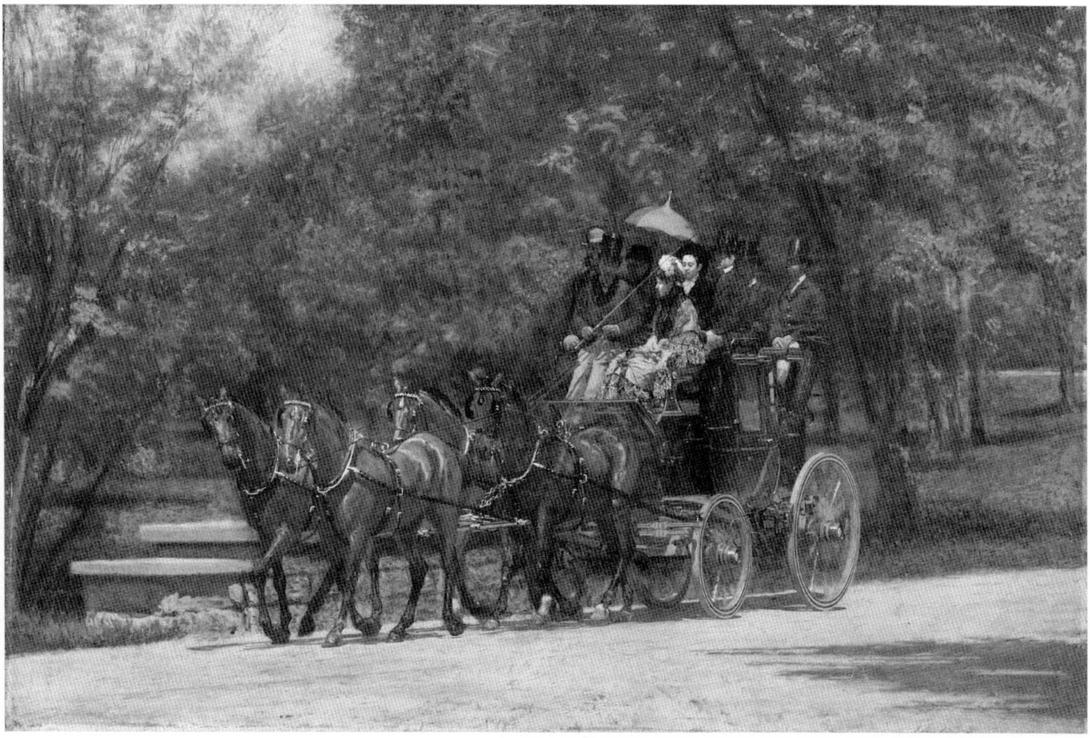

39. Thomas Eakins, *A May Morning in the Park (The Fairman Rogers Four-in-Hand)*, 1879–80. Oil on canvas, $23^{3}/_{4} \times 36$ in. Philadelphia Museum of Art. Gift of William Alexander Dick, 1930.

that owes a debt to photographs of horses in motion published by the photographer Eadweard Muybridge.[47] Perhaps more obviously symbolic of forward motion are the blurred spokes of the wheels of the coach. However, as Michael Leja has observed, although Eakins borrowed much from Muybridge, the blur of the wheels deviates from "instantaneous" photography in an effort to signify motion, creating "a decisive rift between knowledge and appearances."[48]

Contemporary critics recognized this, with a writer for the *North American* pointedly suggesting that the falseness of the wheels was less the problem than the scientifically accurate poses of the horses, whose limbs are frozen by the "immobility of the camera." But time more than motion makes the painting so curiously out of synch. Eakins attempted to render what was known through photography but impossible to witness with the naked eye. His representation of motion was considered a failure, the result of having "forsaken the old method of representing quick action" in favor of "the very different mode of progression revealed by the camera."[49] In order to "fix" the image, which he constructed from his awareness of empirical evidence, Eakins fashioned a painting that was photographic in its timing. Lecoq's memory training suggested an alternative, yet Eakins adhered to his attachment to the camera while simultaneously adopting other aspects of Lecoq's program.

Eakins started making his own photographic studies of human locomotion alongside Muybridge at the University of Pennsylvania in the 1880s. Undertaken at the height of his teaching career at the Academy, Eakins began to think about the uses of motion photography in his role as a teacher.[50] In addition to taking photographs of moving figures, Eakins also made a zoetrope available to his students. When spun, this cylindrical device could be used to animate photographs of "men walking and horses galloping."[51] The impact of Eakins's interest in motion on his Academy students is difficult to assess. However, in 1881, the members of the Philadelphia Sketch Club, many of whom were Eakins's students, began proposing moving subjects at their evening sketches. In this year, the Sketchers abruptly switched from more evocative subjects such as "Reverie" and "A Quiet Nook" to sketches of single figures undertaking very specific movements: "A Boy Jumping," "A Man Pulling a Stake from the Ground," "A Man in His Undershirt Looking under the Bureau"—hardly the typical themes of high art but, in fact, similar to the sorts of images that Muybridge would eventually produce.[52]

The 1883–84 circular for the Academy included a report on the previous season, indicating that Eakins had also begun photographing models from the life class "in cases in which the model was unusually good or had any peculiarity of form or action which would be instructive."[53] Ellwood C. Parry III has taken this to refer to the Naked Series, the photographs that Eakins took of models in seven standardized poses.[54] But the static poses of the Naked Series do not convey "action." The circular must have been referring to another group of photographs.

Around this time, Eakins and his students took just such a group of action photographs for the Arcadian series and *Swimming*. These photographs were distinctly different from the Naked Series and his later motion studies. They show nude men, probably students, engaged in a range of athletic activities including boxing (Figure 40), wrestling, swimming, and tug-of-war. Although the models performed for Eakins's camera, their poses were not predetermined as in the Naked Series. Focused on their tasks, these men became less conscious of the camera's presence than Eakins's inactive subjects. The men in these photographs have been arrested in motion, but unlike the sequential shots of Muybridges's motion studies made with multiple cameras, here the shutter of the camera effectively freezes the action, while still suggesting movement through the slight blurring of the figures.

Eakins also on occasion photographed a kind of arrested movement. For

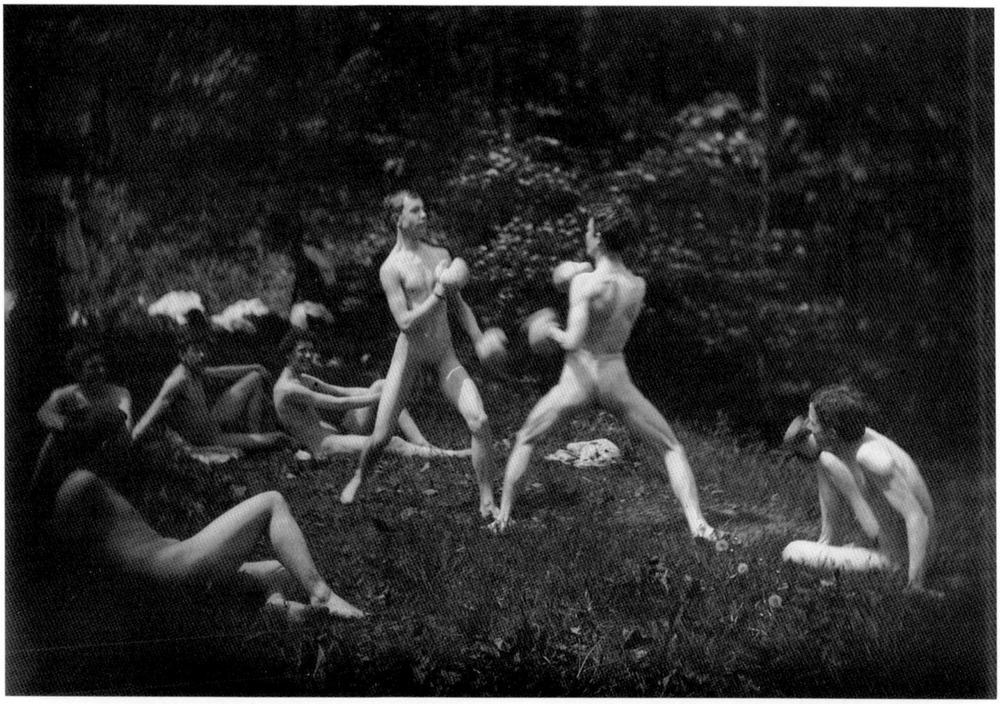

40. Thomas Eakins, *Seven Males, Nude, Two Boxing at Center*, ca. 1883. Dry-plate glass negative, 4 × 5 in. Courtesy of the Pennsylvania Academy of the Fine Arts, Philadelphia. Charles Bregler's Thomas Eakins Collection. Purchased with the partial support of the Pew Memorial Trust.

example, he took shots of two different male models, each stopped in the act of carrying or throwing stones (Figure 41).[55] An analogous stoppage of movement appears in Lecoq's writings. In order to help his students mentally capture an image, Lecoq allowed them to stop the moving model and "beg him to stay in some chance attitude that struck us all."[56] Unlike the photographs of athletes, Eakins's stone throwers are not engaged in continuous motion. These images are instead studies of specific movements stilled before the photographs were taken, the artistic value being in the visible response of the muscles to an actual weight. These images may relate to one of the exercises given by Lecoq in his *Lettres à un jeune professeur*. In this passage, Lecoq describes the disadvantage of observing an artificially posed figure instead of one undertaking a real action: "Instead of saying to a model, for instance, Take the pose of a man carrying a stone, we shall say, Carry this stone from here to there. The students who are observing him, as he crosses the room, will be watching a series of movements always real, and because they are natural and right, almost always beautiful. In fact the model will lift the stone with exactly the effort it demands, will walk as

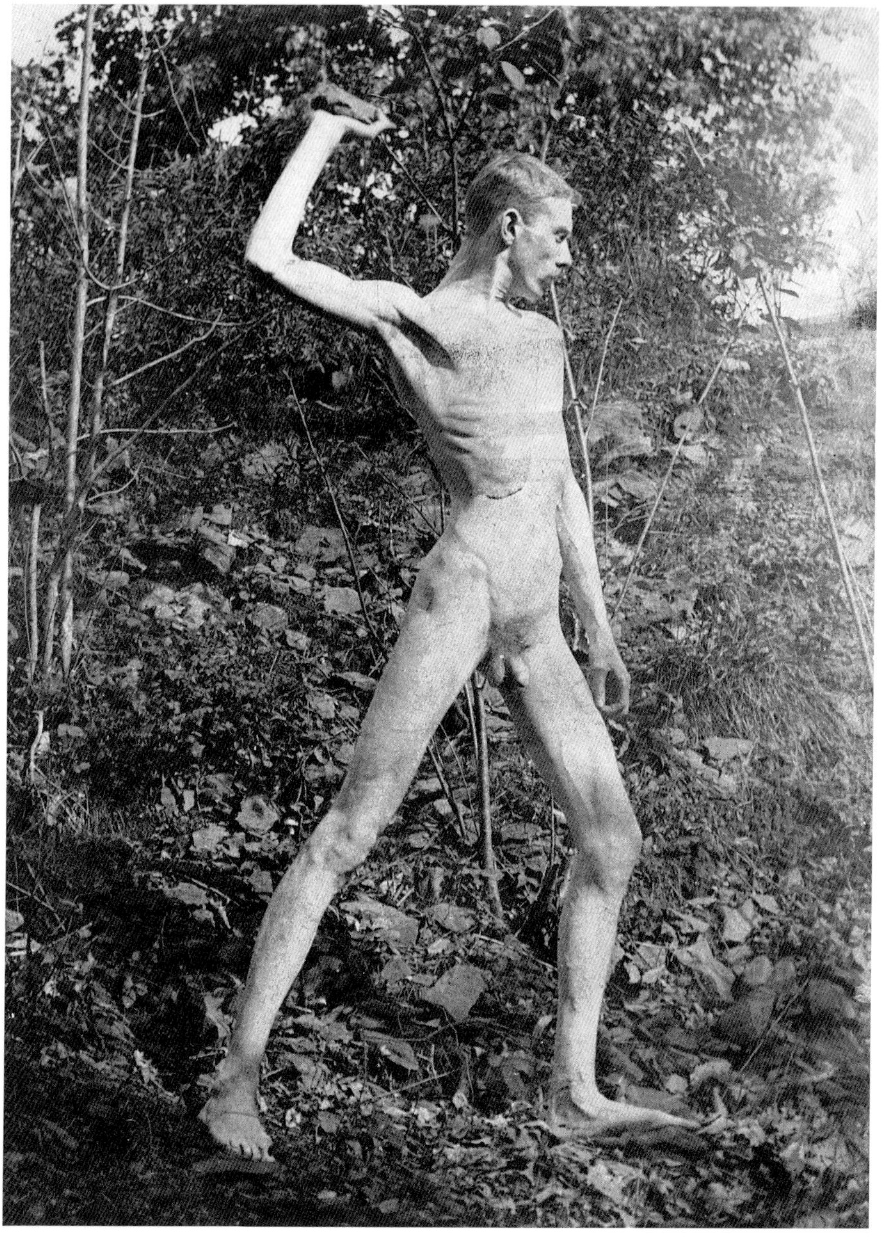

41. Thomas Eakins, *Male Nude, Poised to Throw Rock, Facing Right, in Wooded Landscape*, ca. 1883. Albumen print, 11 × 8 1/8 in. Courtesy of the Pennsylvania Academy of the Fine Arts, Philadelphia. Charles Bregler's Thomas Eakins Collection. Purchased with the partial support of the Pew Memorial Trust.

a person walks when carrying a burden of that size and weight, and his action will necessarily be true again when he puts the stone down at the required point."[57] Eakins's photographs suggest a variant of the exercise proposed by Lecoq.

While the primary interest of many of Eakins's Arcadian photographs appears to be the study of movement, the antique is ever present in these works. The athleticism of the figures and their nudity easily evoke antique statuary. Ancient Greek athletes exercised nude, and the male nude figure became the foundation of Greek art. Eakins believed that he could re-create the conditions under which the ancient Greek sculptors had produced their best works through the photographic study of athletes in motion. Lecoq describes how anatomical and motion studies could suggest the classical tradition in his observation "What could be more useful in the study of anatomy, or more in accordance with tradition, than the close observation of nude models at exercise *in imitation of the ancient athletes?*"[58]

Greek Methods

That so many of Eakins's photographs from this period feature nude models outdoors—hardly a common practice in the 1880s—is particularly noteworthy. In *L'Éducation de la mémoire pittoresque*, Lecoq indicated that once his pupils had mastered the basics of memory training, they should be taken outside to continue their work with life models. By moving outdoors, his students would be relieved of the monotonous conditions of studio life study. As Lecoq wrote of one outdoor excursion, "The poor hirelings of the life-class were transfigured, as it were by their splendid living setting. Here were no stiff, fagged models perched on the traditional throne, weighing heavily on the traditional stick or string; here was man, the chosen of life's creatures, in all his strength."[59] Once outdoors, Lecoq's students faced models in fluid moving poses, seen under variable natural lighting conditions, which also created subtle changes in color over time—all factors requiring a quick memory to render on canvas.

Instead of relying on memory alone, when Eakins followed Lecoq's method and ventured outdoors with his unclothed models for the Arcadian series, he took his camera with him. The figures in the paintings, *Arcadia* (Figure 42) and *An Arcadian*, derive from specific photographs, replicating the method that Eakins had used in *Mending the Net*. Each of these paintings contains lush, verdant landscapes, populated by incongruously crisp, precisely rendered people.[60] The precision of the figures reflects Eakins's reliance on photography as a replacement for Lecoq's memory training. As with *Mending the Net*, each of the models in the Arcadian series posed at different times, possibly at different sites.

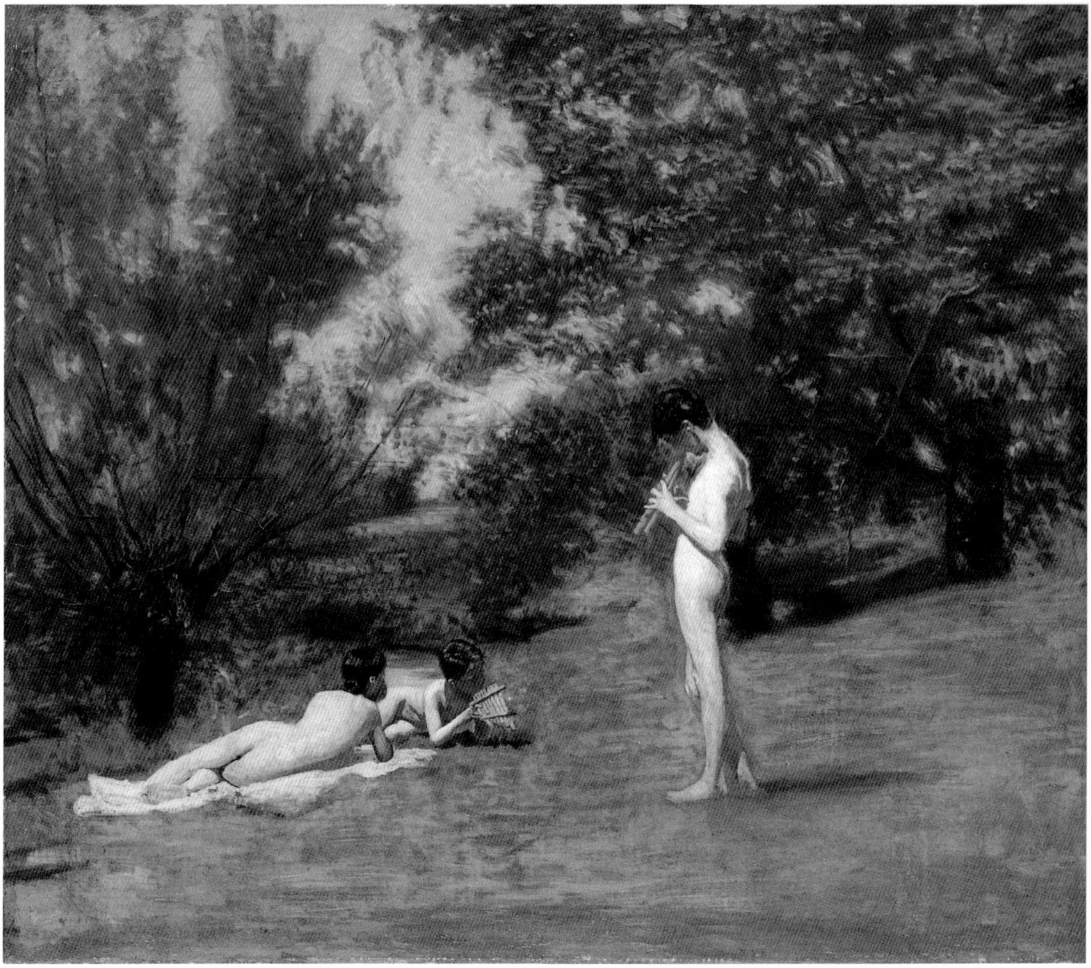

42. Thomas Eakins, *Arcadia*, ca. 1883. Oil on canvas, 38⅝ × 45 in. The Metropolitan Museum of Art. Bequest of Miss Adelaide Milton de Groot (1876–1967), 1967 (67.187.125).

For *Arcadia*, Eakins used at least three photographs to construct the final image. The reclining boy playing the pan pipes derives from a photo of Eakins's nephew Ben Crowell (Figure 43).[61] Similarly, Eakins modeled the reclining woman in *Arcadia* from an image of his fiancée, Susan Macdowell (Figure 44). Eakins also used a study of his student J. Laurie Wallace as the model for the standing piper in *Arcadia*. However, here, as Marc Simpson has suggested, Eakins's transcription was less exacting; the painted piper is leaner, more youthful, and positioned slightly differently than Wallace appears in the photograph (Figure 45). Although Wallace clearly served as the model, and the painted figure retains much of the feel of the photographs, the resulting figure does not

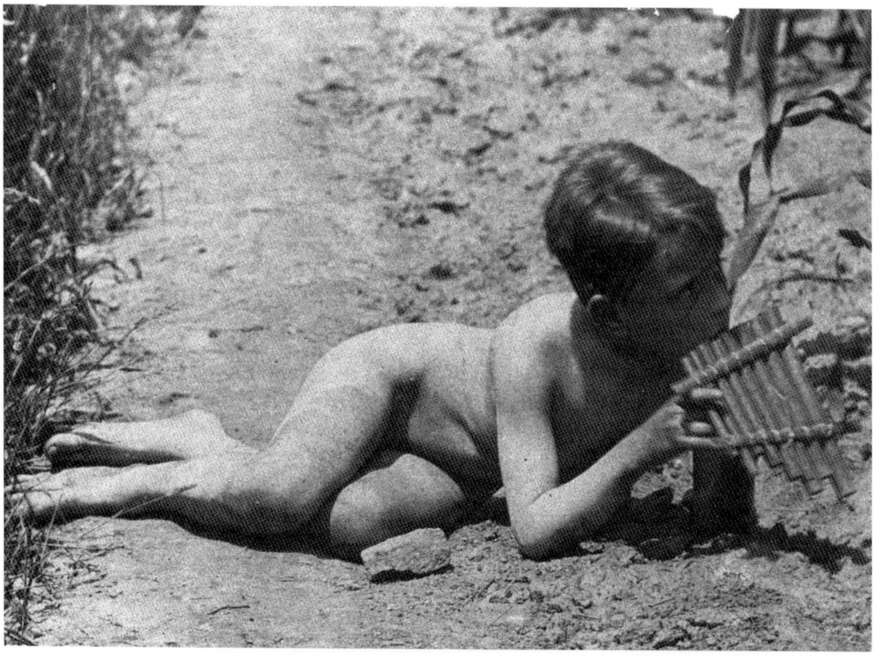

43. Thomas Eakins, *Ben Crowell (Study for "Arcadia")*, ca. 1883. Platinum print on paper, 4¼ × 5¹³⁄₁₆ in. Hirshhorn Museum and Sculpture Garden, Smithsonian Institution. Gift of Joseph H. Hirshhorn, 1966.

resemble Wallace.[62] Eakins employed the synthesis of memory and imagination described by Lecoq to craft the image.

Aside from the photographs used directly in the creation of the *Arcadia* oil, Eakins took several other images that explore overtly classical themes. Most are single figure studies using a limited and close-knit group of models including Wallace and Susan Macdowell. Eakins himself appears in some of the photographs, posing, like Wallace, with pipes. Resembling the more static figures in *Swimming*, all of the models in these photographs are posed and still. There is little suggestion of motion, arrested or otherwise. Also, like the figures in *Swimming*, some of the poses in the Arcadian photographs are based on specific classical types. For example, a few of the images of Wallace deliberately evoke antique sculpture. In one instance, he emulates the *Faun with Pipes*, a cast of which was in the Academy's collection (Figure 46). The pose is not identical, but the inclusion of the stump at Wallace's side, a common supporting device used by Roman copyists of Greek bronzes, makes the allusion to classical sculpture unmistakable.[63] Likewise, one of the rock-throwing models also posed for a standing adaptation of the Greek *Spinario* (*Thorn-puller*) (Figure 47).[64] Later, when he became a teacher in the Midwest, Wallace would photograph a female

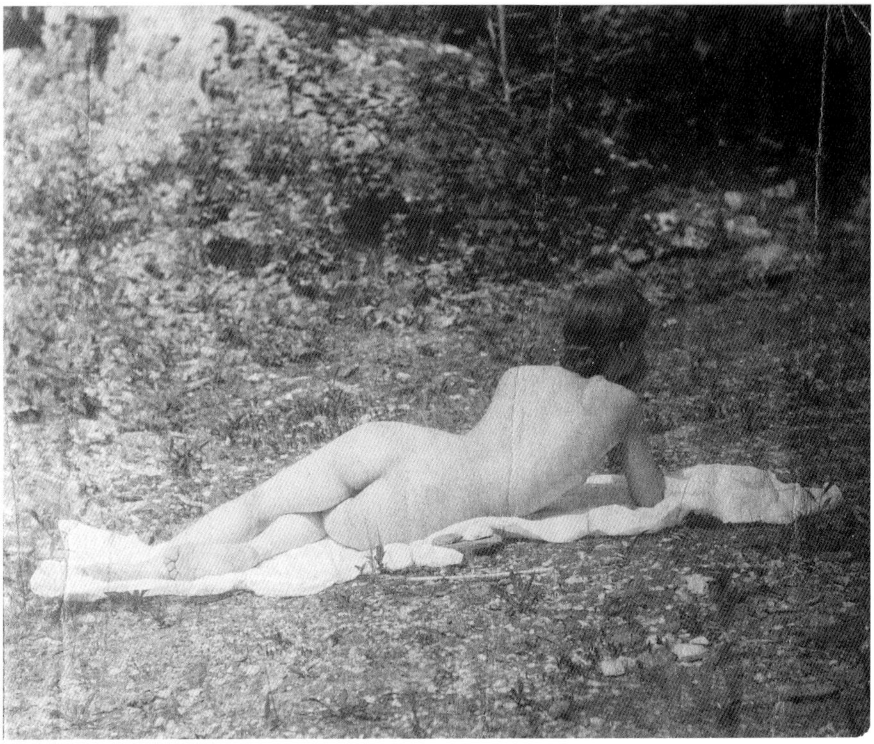

44. Thomas Eakins, *Susan Macdowell Nude, Reclining on Elbow, from Rear*, ca. 1883. Albumen print, 3¼ × 4 in. Courtesy of the Pennsylvania Academy of the Fine Arts, Philadelphia. Charles Bregler's Thomas Eakins Collection. Purchased with the partial support of the Pew Memorial Trust.

model posing outdoors in the same position (Figure 48), suggesting the transmission of Eakins's teaching practices to his students.

Eakins's specific allusions to Greek sculpture may seem at odds with his well-known objection to extended study from plaster casts, but his admiration of classical art found a place in his teaching. What he argued against was the second-hand knowledge of the body acquired by sketching from the antique. He felt that the best way to emulate the classical masters was through life study, not mimicry of classical compositions. Eakins suggested this to William Brownell, stating, "The Greeks did not study the antique: the 'Theseus' and 'Illyssus' and the draped figures in the Parthenon pediment were modeled from life, undoubtedly. And nature is just as varied and just as beautiful in our day as she was in the time of Phidias."[65] Therefore the classicism of the Arcadian images should not be regarded as antithetical to, but rather as a vital element of, his realism. In the Arcadian series, Eakins consciously set out to reenact "the Greek method" through the study of the nude figure.

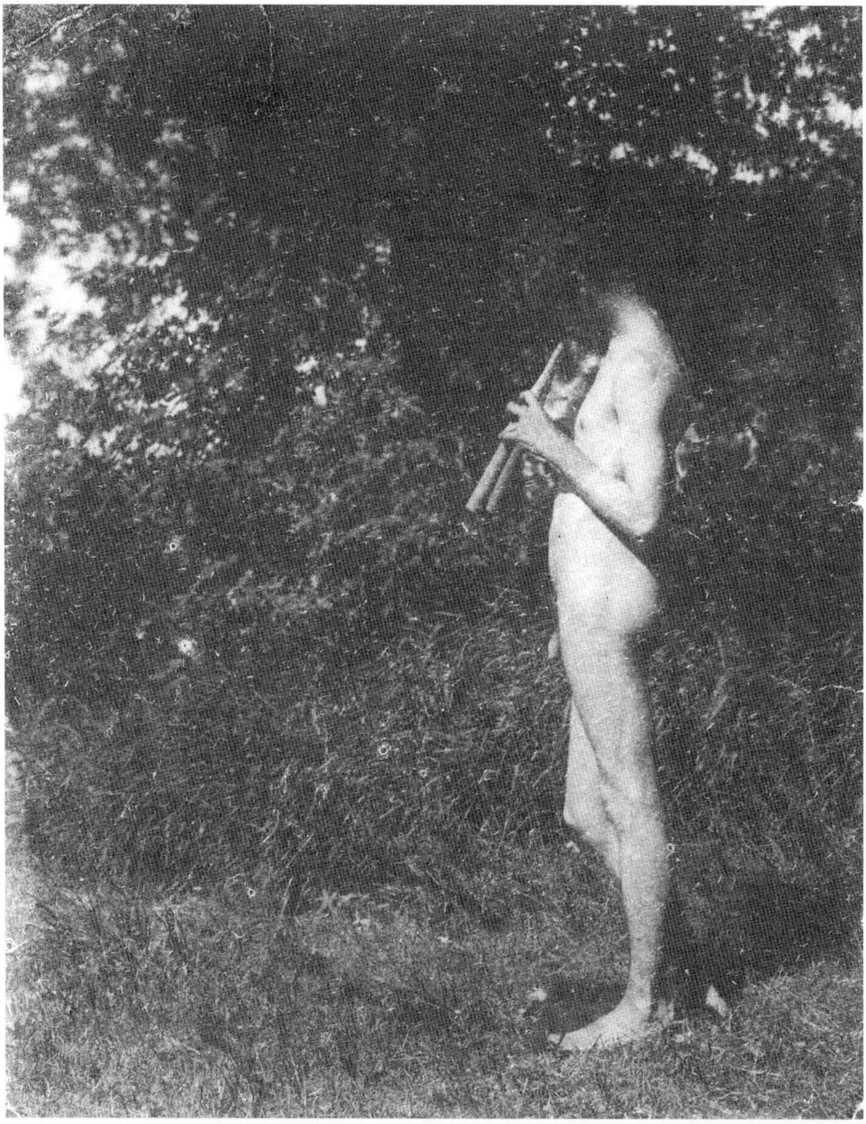

45. Thomas Eakins, *J. Laurie Wallace Nude, Playing Pipes, Facing Left, in Front of Leafy Background*, ca. 1883. Platinum print, 3³/₈ × 2¹¹/₁₆ in. Courtesy of the Pennsylvania Academy of the Fine Arts, Philadelphia. Charles Bregler's Thomas Eakins Collection. Purchased with the partial support of the Pew Memorial Trust.

Lecoq similarly believed that careful observation of nature would keep students from affected imitation of other artists.[66] Only through this method would a student develop his or her own style, following the same path as the Old Masters. Both Lecoq and Eakins cited Phidias as the paragon of realist originality, with Lecoq writing, "As one admires the cavalry of the Parthenon frieze one

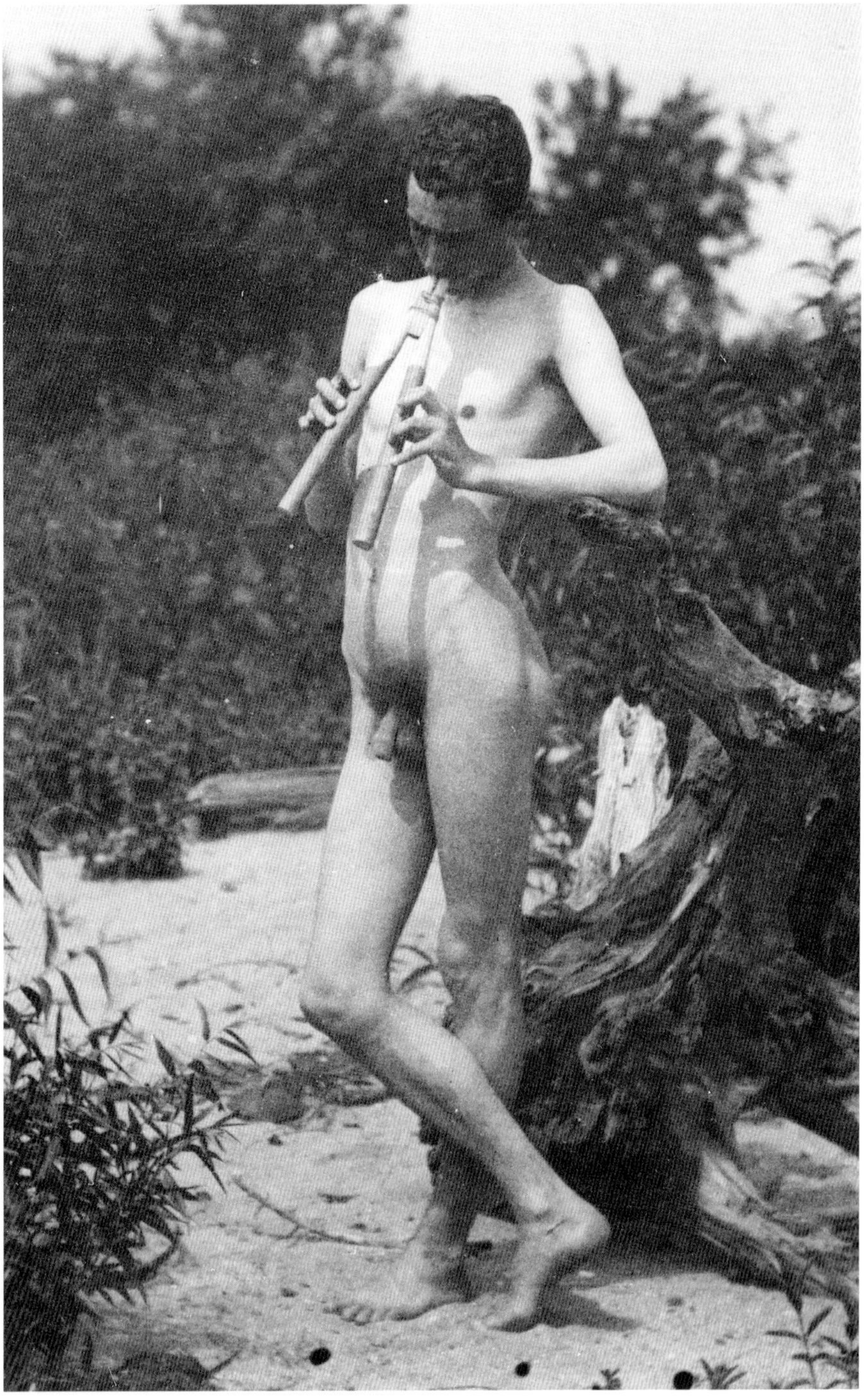

46. Thomas Eakins, *J. Laurie Wallace (Study for "Arcadia")*, ca. 1883. Platinum print on paper, 6⅝ × 3⅞ in. Hirshhorn Museum and Sculpture Garden, Smithsonian Institution. Gift of Joseph H. Hirshhorn, 1966.

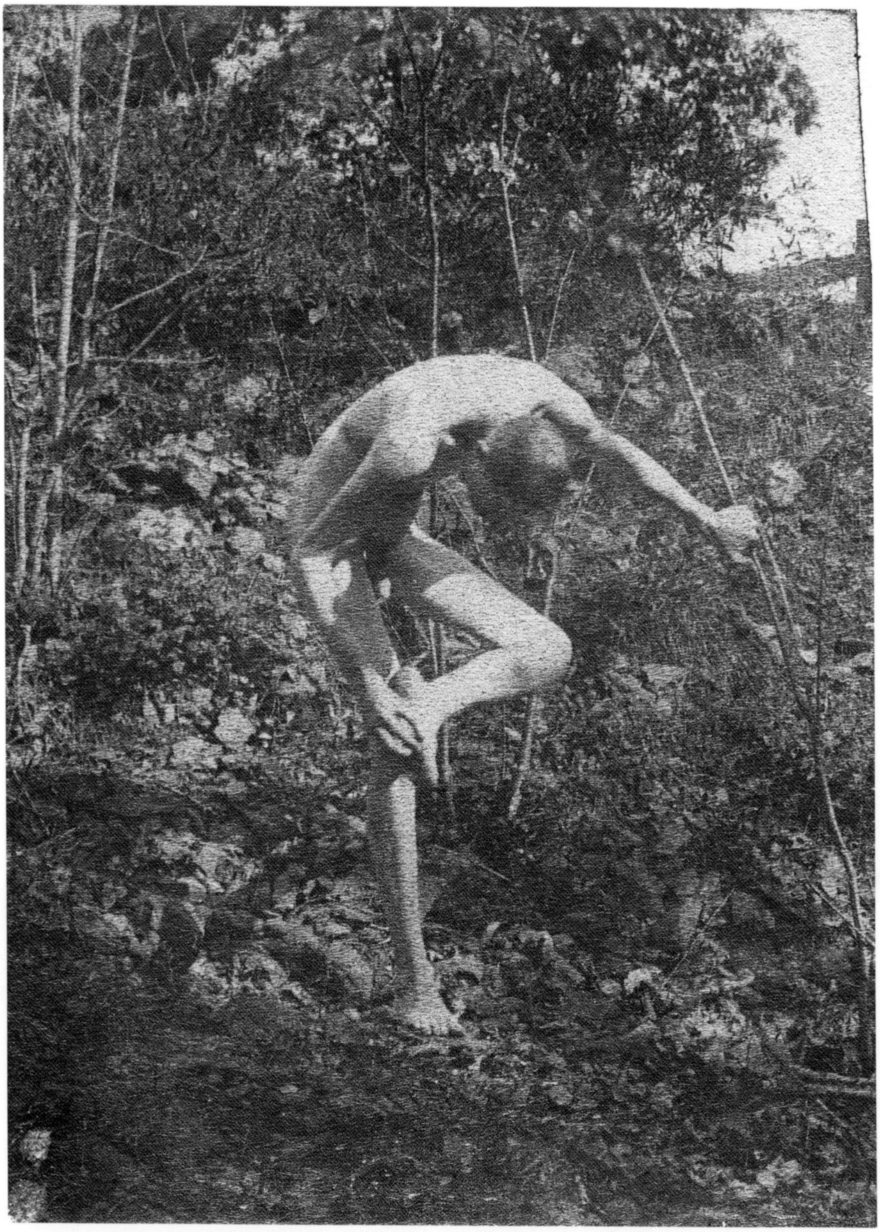

47. Thomas Eakins, *Male Nude, Standing on One Leg, in Wooded Landscape*, ca. 1883. Albumen print, 3⅝ × 2$^{11}/_{16}$ in. Courtesy of the Pennsylvania Academy of the Fine Arts, Philadelphia. Charles Bregler's Thomas Eakins Collection. Purchased with the partial support of the Pew Memorial Trust.

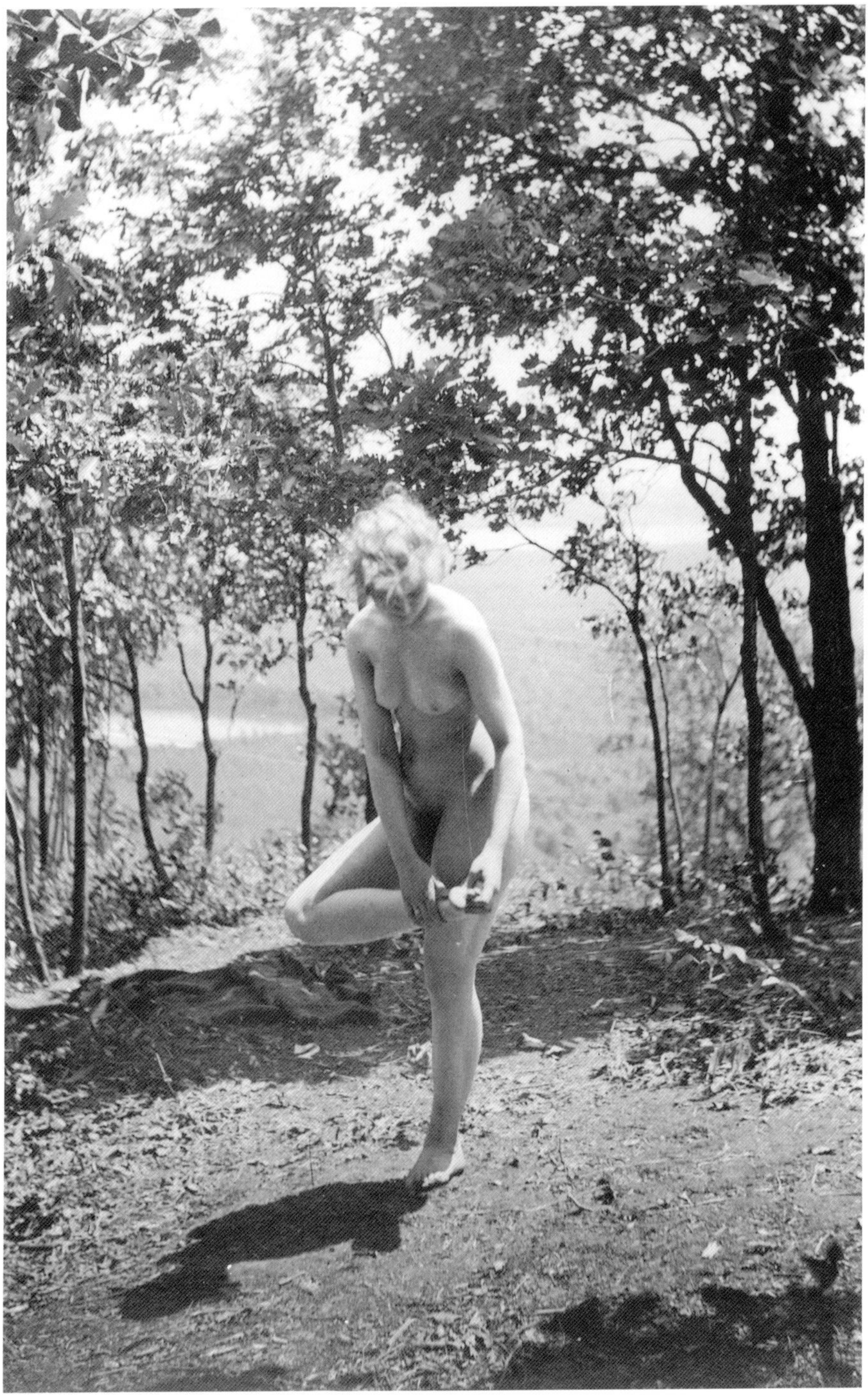

48. J. Laurie Wallace, *Nude Model Outdoors*, ca. 1890s. Joslyn Art Museum, Omaha, Nebraska. Gift of Mr. and Mrs. Joseph I. Barker in Memory of George Barker, 1966.

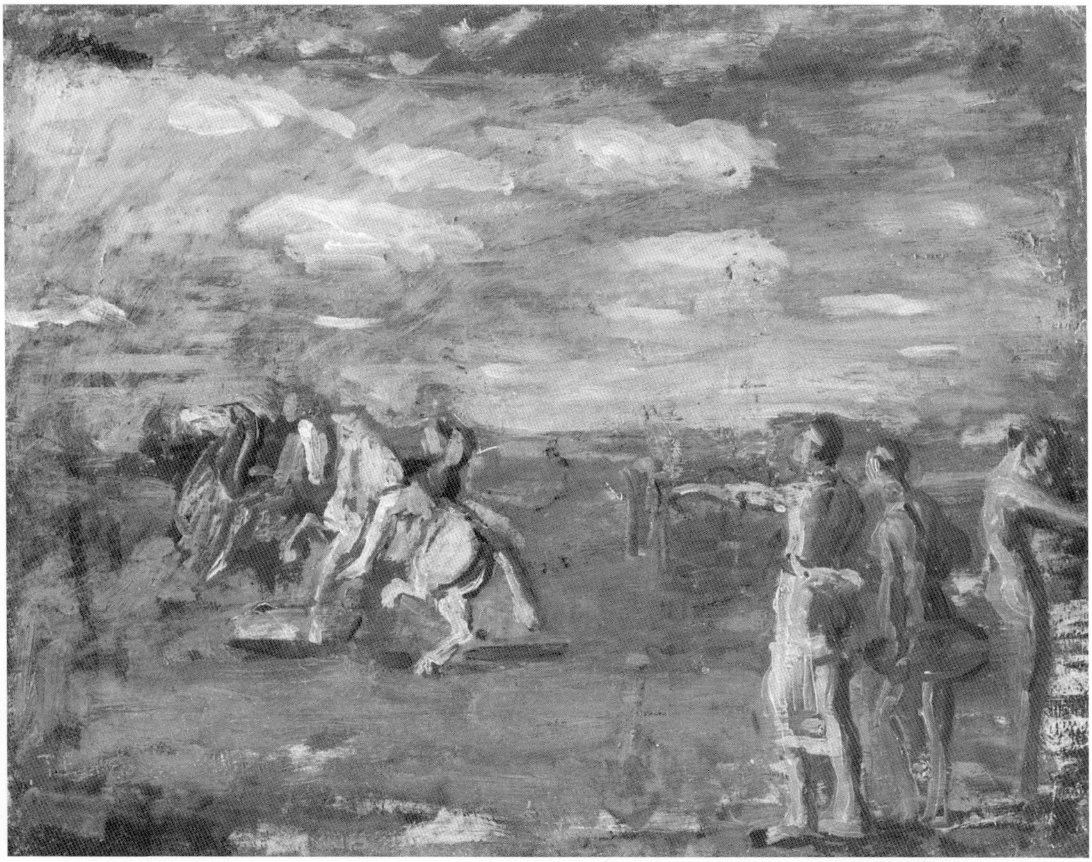

49. Thomas Eakins, *Phidias Studying for the Frieze of the Parthenon*, ca. 1890. Oil on wood, 10⅝ × 13¾ in. Collection of the Eakins Press Foundation, New York.

feels sure that Pheidias watched them passing through the streets of Athens."[67] Eakins produced two sketches (Figure 49) that visualize Lecoq's example. Each of these undated oils shows the Greek sculptor working on the Parthenon's cavalry frieze outdoors with live horses and models before him—in fact, echoing the same approach that Eakins would use a decade later for his own sculptures of horses for the Brooklyn Soldiers and Sailors Memorial. Based on his study of horses in motion, Eakins believed that Phidias must have dissected horses and used sculptural models to aid his work.[68]

Lecoq's writings abound in references to the antique. In his outdoor sessions he frequently found his models transformed into Greek gods, and many of the exercises he proposed revolved around classical themes. For example, in a passage from his *Lettres*, Lecoq indicated how a student should go about preparing to depict "a faun playing with a goat" by studying the model in various poses outdoors, testing "the movement he has imagined" for the figure, followed by life study of a goat. Then, "equipped with his recollections of them both, alone with his own ideas, his own feelings and methods of expression, he should work out his composition, which must of necessity be original, because it comes entirely out of himself."[69] This is certainly suggestive of Eakins's own method of posing Wallace, Susan Macdowell, and Ben Crowell for the Arcadian paintings.

In addition to outdoor study, Lecoq advised that moving costumed figures should be observed in grand interiors to make historical subjects more vivid. For this purpose Lecoq made use of the Palais du Justice prior to its opening to the public. Of this opportunity, Lecoq wrote, "It is difficult to imagine the noble effect that was made by the figures in fine draperies as they passed through the great doorways, leaned upon the balustrades, or stepped majestically down the monumental stair."[70] He advised his students to study models wearing "garments of different styles and periods, so as to serve in the study of old costume. The attention and interest aroused by antique draperies will be keenest when the models are in action. For then the young artists looking on will see how the absence of restraint, and naturalness of the movements, cause the folds to fall into happy lines that give rise to admirable motives at every moment."[71] Lecoq continually reminded his readers that "the artists of all great periods of art, whether of ancient Greece or Rome, or at the time of the Renaissance, had continually before their eyes, in the habits, costumes, and all the circumstances of the civilization in which they lived, scenes to inspire their genius, as the strong influence of such sights upon their works distinctly shows us."[72] Or, as Eakins had succinctly put it, "the Greeks did not study the antique," but rather "modeled from life."

Eakins's Arcadian photographs of costumed figures indoors suggest this aspect of Lecoq's program.[73] Many of these photographs depict students in classical dress, some posed with casts of antique sculpture. Eakins began his costume studies in 1881 with the colonial revival photographs of female students "in Trot's yard." The photographs from this session are informal, yet the models seem more self-conscious of their activity than in the later sessions of nude athletes. Subsequent images show male students dressed in togas and women wearing classical dress as well as eighteenth- and early nineteenth-century costumes. Some of these photographs, including one of the singer Weda Cook in classical dress (Figure 50), feature models in such hastily constructed settings as to make clear that these were conceived as studies, not fine art objects. In the photograph of Cook, for example, a wrinkled cloth hangs unceremoniously behind her. Eakins had not invested in creating an aesthetic environment—instead, he placed the emphasis on the figure.

In other photographs, the architecture and the Academy's cast collections

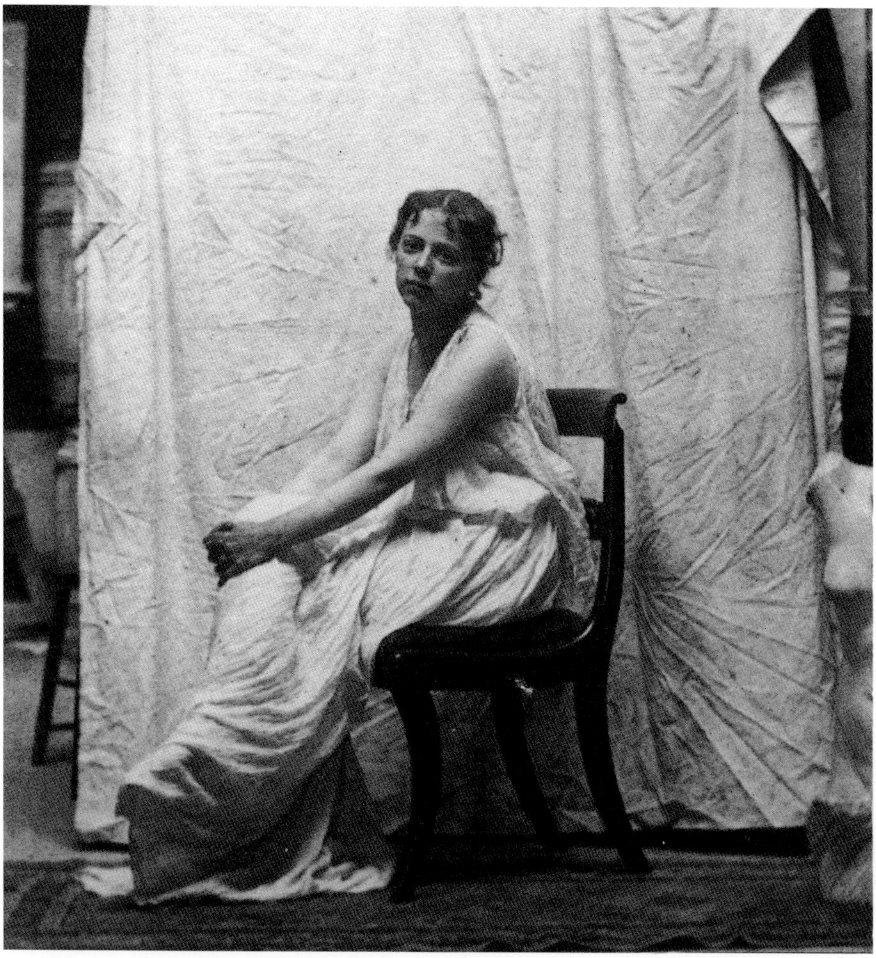

50. Thomas Eakins, *Weda Cook in Classical Costume, Sitting in Empire Chair*, ca. 1892. Platinum print, 3⅞ × 3⅝ in. Courtesy of the Pennsylvania Academy of the Fine Arts, Philadelphia. Charles Bregler's Thomas Eakins Collection. Purchased with the partial support of the Pew Memorial Trust.

seem integral to the images. In one, dramatically lit male models clad in togas pose with the casts of the Academy galleries arrayed behind them (Figure 51). In another group of photographs, costumed female models pose alone with classical busts or torsos. In these images, the direct pairing of a live model with an antique cast again suggests a comparative relationship, illustrating Eakins's belief that classical works derived from life study.[74] The photographs of women posing with antique casts resemble those Eakins took of two women with his own *Pastoral* (*Arcadia*) relief (Figure 52). In these images, Eakins presented two models in classical dress as modern, living Arcadians, situated next to his relief, a modern sculpture based on "the Greek method."

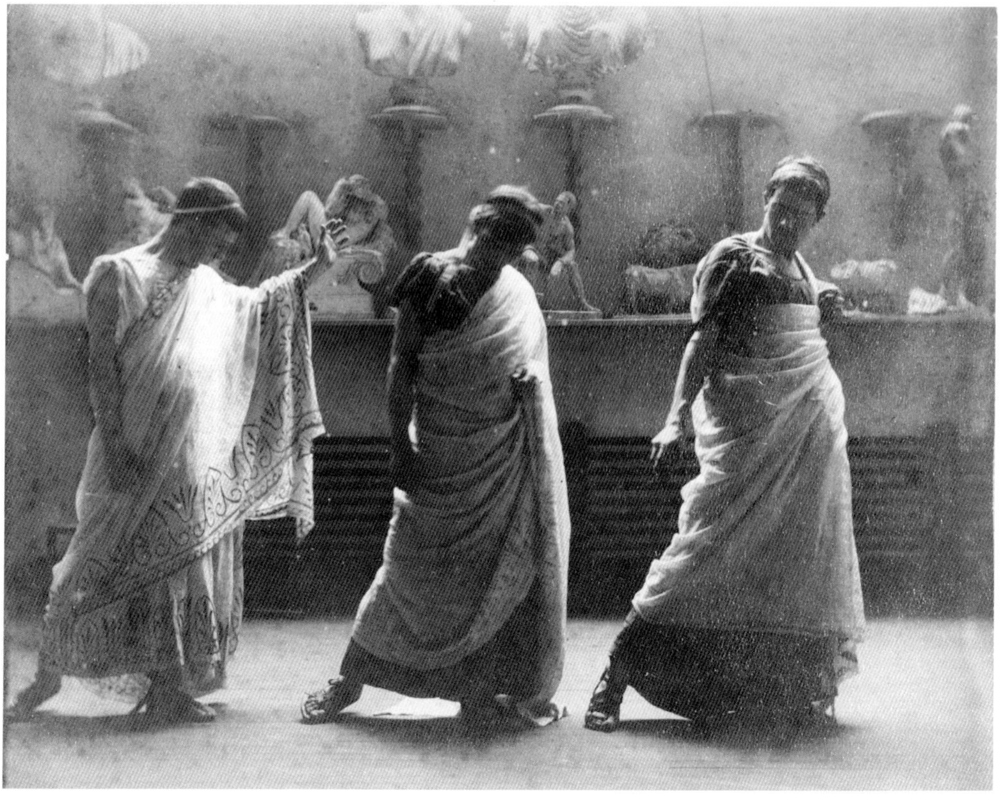

51. Circle of Thomas Eakins, *Men in Classical Costume*, ca. 1882–83. Photographic print on board, sepia, 9 × 12 cm, on board 16 × 22 cm. Courtesy of the Thomas Anshutz Papers, ca. 1870–1942, Archives of American Art, Smithsonian Institution.

Another Look at Swimming

Swimming similarly insinuates modern bodies into a classical tradition through the evocation of antique sculpture, but it also suggests other aspects of Lecoq's system. Eakins studied his swimmers outdoors and included the unusual image of the figure diving at the right, who is suspended in motion above the water. Combining so many of his interests, Eakins undoubtedly hoped that this image would mark the beginning of a long and collegial relationship with Coates. This seemed assured when Coates "confidentially" told Eakins that he hoped this painting "might someday become part of the Academy collection."[75] Therefore Eakins must have been disappointed when Coates politely declined *Swimming* shortly after its appearance at the Academy annual in 1885.

Coates diplomatically claimed that he wanted something "more representative" and acquired *Singing a Pathetic Song* in place of the picture that he had commissioned. Indeed, *Swimming* was not "representative" insofar as it

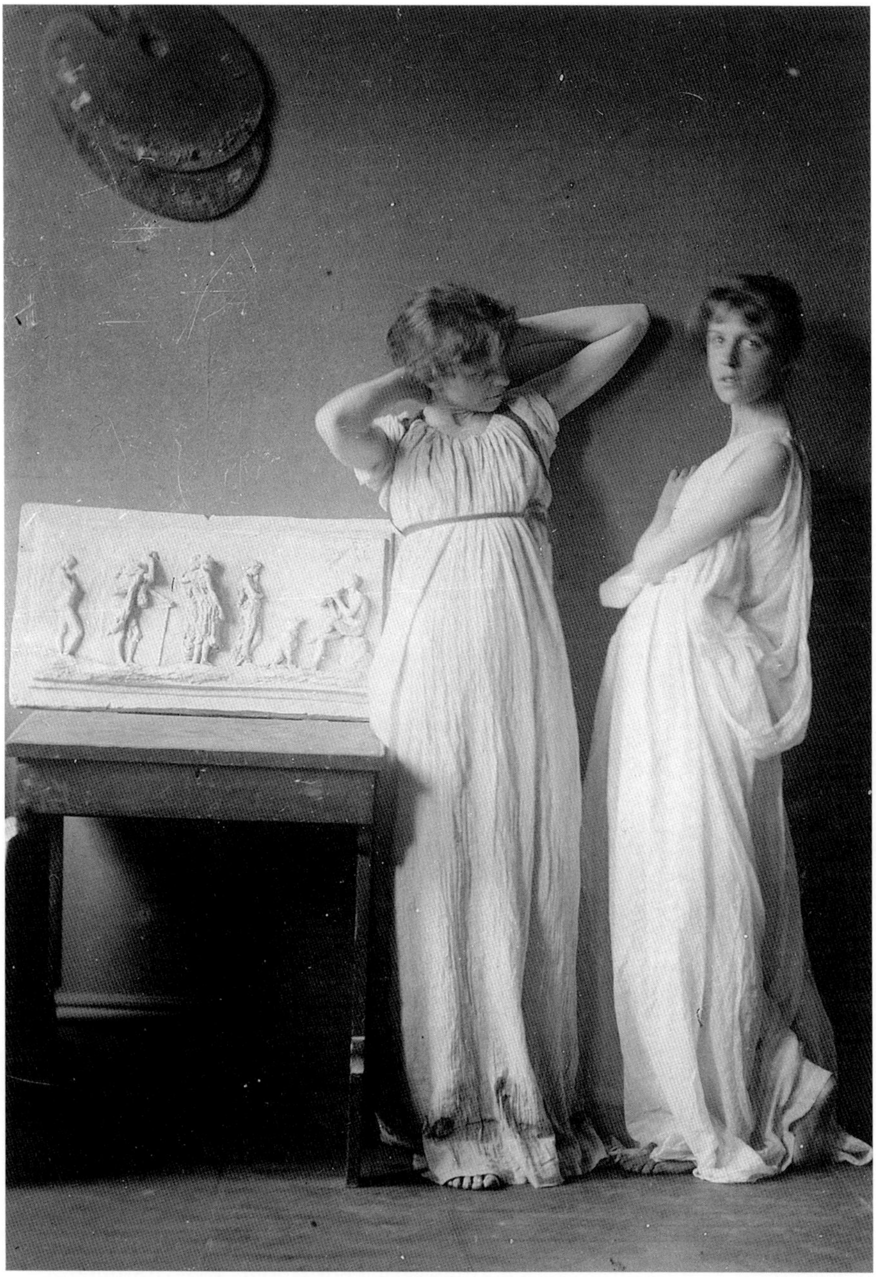

52. Thomas Eakins, *Two Pupils in Greek Dress*, 1883. Platinum print, 14½ × 10½ in. The Metropolitan Museum of Art, David Hunter McAlpin Fund, 1943 (43.87.17).

appeared unlike anything Eakins had exhibited before. One is struck by the conflicting compositional strategies at work in the image. While the figures in *Swimming* are so realistically delineated that each model has been identified—including the artist's self-portrait as the only swimmer in the water—the artifice of the painting threatens to undermine its realism. The evocation of the antique, established through the fussy triangular placement of the figures to the left of the center, seems at odds with the artist's equally self-conscious interest in the modern study of motion evidenced by the diver. Randall Griffin rightly perceives such disjunctions in the painting as Eakins's attempt to reconcile "the artistic traditions of Classicism and Naturalism—two divergent artistic modes of perceiving the world."[76] For example, the figure of the red-haired boy in the water is reasonably naturalistic, while the reclining man on the rocks seems like a static reference to classical art. These juxtapositions—real and ideal, movement and stillness, and modern and classical subjects—are central to Eakins's conception, but they also lend a jarring artificiality to the painting that is absent from *Singing a Pathetic Song.*

Although Coates said that he did not "depreciate" *Swimming* and encouraged Eakins to send it "to exhibitions in N.Y., Boston & Chicago," Eakins exhibited the painting only twice more during his lifetime following its Academy debut.[77] Consequently, *Swimming* remained virtually unknown in the artist's studio until his death in 1916. Since that time it has become one of Eakins's best-known realist masterpieces. As such, the painting has been subject to intense scrutiny, with much recent scholarship taking a psychosexual bent. Among the more controversial studies have been Whitney Davis's and Michael Hatt's speculations on Eakins's sexuality and the extent to which *Swimming* reveals the presence of male desire.[78] Toward the other end of the spectrum, the 1996 exhibition *Thomas Eakins and the Swimming Picture*, organized by the Amon Carter Museum, contextualized the work down to a minute level.[79] The show identified each of Eakins's models, examined the circumstances of the commission, and pinpointed the location of the setting. More recently, Martin Berger has suggested that the communion of Eakins and his students demonstrates "the power of same-sex communities to reinforce one's identity within and against larger cultures," while Amy Werbel posits that "the painting teaches both anatomy and physiology" through the varied poses of the figures.[80] All of this analysis has added to our understanding of this complex painting, yet Eakins's intentions in creating such an unusual work remain murky. Most puzzling is why Eakins would think that presenting a director of the Academy with a painting depicting himself and his students in the nude was a good idea. Given the importance of the patron and Coates's intention to give the work to the Academy, the selection of this subject must have been carefully considered.

Twentieth-century scholars have often regarded Edward Coates's rejection of *Swimming* with its six male nudes in favor of a genre painting with fully clad figures as evidence that nineteenth-century audiences might have found the nude subject indecorous.[81] Yet the focus on nudity and sexuality in this work appears to be a modern preoccupation not explicitly discussed in Eakins's day, in spite of intense and public debate about certain types of nudity in fine art.[82] As Werbel suggests, "Men, swimming, boxing, and even wrestling together naked were simply not an unusual occurrence in the nineteenth century."[83] While there is no evidence that Coates requested this subject from Eakins, he must have known what the artist had in mind. In May 1885, months before *Swimming*'s unveiling at the Academy that October, the journal *Art Age* reported that Eakins's painting of "The Bathers, ordered by a Director of the Academy of Fine Arts" was "already well advanced."[84] Further, as Kathleen Foster has noted, nude subjects, including bathers, had appeared on the Academy walls before.[85] Indeed, in the very exhibition in which Eakins showed *Swimming*, the artist Alexander Harrison exhibited without controversy his *Bord de Mer*, with a "party of urchins" "denuding themselves" for an ocean bath.[86] And Eakins's swimmers, carefully arrayed to avoid the depiction of their genitals, appear arguably more chaste than the eroticized academic female nudes that already hung on the Academy's walls.[87] Coates's rejection of *Swimming* could not have been solely on account of its nude figures.

Much of what has been written about *Swimming* is rooted in the knowledge of Eakins's "fall from grace" shortly after its completion. A few months after *Swimming* made its public debut at the Academy, Eakins would face scandal over the use of nude models, prompting his forced resignation from the school. However, he had every reason to feel confident about his position when the painting went on view. Indeed, at the time of the commission, Eakins was more professionally secure than he would ever be again. Unfortunately, the tendency to read Eakins's future backward onto the painting has focused attention exclusively on the one aspect of the work most relevant to his decline at the Academy: his obsession with the nude. Henry Adams has gone so far as to suggest that Eakins intended the painting to embarrass his students, his patron, and his wife by "violating accepted patterns of behavior" through his use of the nude.[88] More reasonably, *Swimming* is often regarded, along with *William Rush Carving His Allegorical Figure of the Schuylkill River*, as Eakins's manifesto on the primacy of the nude in the Academy's program. Undoubtedly, Eakins hoped that his choice of a nude subject would affirm Coates's support of his program, but *Swimming* is not just about the nude. The painting also reflects Eakins's growing interest in classical art, his study of nude figures outdoors, and his documentation of human motion—all of which formed an integral part of Lecoq's program.

Although *Swimming* has been compared to the poetry of Walt Whitman and James Whitcomb Riley, Lecoq's description of his first outing with his students provides the best textual corollary for Eakins's image:

> It was agreed that master and pupils should meet in a most beautiful spot, a sort of natural park. The deep shadows thrown by the great trees in full leaf contrasted sharply with the blaze of light with which the open glade was flooded. A pond full of reflections lay at their feet. It was a perfect place, offering endless backgrounds for the human figure, with every possible effect and range of light and shade, exactly satisfying the purpose I had in view. The models I had hired for the occasion had to walk, run, sit, and stand about in natural attitudes . . . naked like the fauns of old.[89]

In this statement we see the full expression of Lecoq's method. Students would reach this goal only after having completed numerous memory exercises increasing in complexity. Lecoq's description reveals the realist philosophy that underlies the classicism of *Swimming* and the Arcadian works. The "fauns of old" appear to Lecoq through a reenactment of the Greek method.

In another of Lecoq's outdoor sessions, his students similarly found themselves struck by the transformation of one model, "a man of splendid stature, with a great sweeping beard," who "lay at rest upon the bank of the pond, close to a group of rushes, in an attitude at once easy and beautiful. The illusion was complete—mythology made true lived before our eyes, for there before us was a river-god of old, ruling with quiet dignity over the course of the waters."[90] This recalls the reclining figure in *Swimming* (identified by Sarah Cash in the Amon Carter exhibition as the journalist Talcott Williams), who resembles, but does not replicate, the poses of antique rivers gods, such as the Parthenon's *Ilissos* or the *Nile* of the Vatican collection.[91] Although the reclining man evokes the classical tradition, he is, like the figures in the *Pastoral* (*Arcadia*) relief, clearly a modern individual. Similarly, the three male figures on the rocky outcropping suggest classical pedimental sculpture without quoting from any particular ancient example. Instead of turning directly to classical models, Eakins based his painting, in some part, on the nude photographs he had taken of his male students at Dove Lake. But, unlike the two Arcadian oils, none of the extant photographs are the exact source for any of the figures in the painting. Minute marks on the canvas indicate that Eakins likely transferred his figures from lost photographs. The tension between real and ideal throughout the composition suggests that he used the same synthetic approach that he had with *Arcadia* and *Mending the Net.*[92]

Contemporary critics of the painting complained not about the nude subject matter but about the same compositional problems that they found in *A May Morning in the Park.* The most specific charge was that the work was marred by a diving figure that failed to suggest motion. This failure was attributed to Eakins's effort "to show the results of instantaneous photography."[93] Although it does not appear as if Eakins used such studies in preparation for the painting, motion photography probably did influence his decision to include the diving figure. As they had with *May Morning in the Park,* most critics remained skeptical of Eakins's attempts to reconcile scientific concerns with the enterprise of picture making. While critics could dismiss *May Morning in the Park* as a scientific painting, *Swimming,* with its references to antiquity, undeniably referred to artistic tradition. Yet the influence of "instantaneous photography" added an incongruous reference to modernity that critics perceived as eccentric.

What was not apparent was that Eakins's addition of this moving figure into what is essentially an Arcadian subject represented a complete integration of Lecoq's ideas into his work. This painting gave Eakins the opportunity to publicly present his adaptation of Lecoq's theories before the Academy. And not only that, but Eakins's easily recognizable self-portrait as the swimmer in the water indicated his ambition to advance this program under his direction at the Academy. With *Swimming,* Eakins solicited Coates's support for more than just the use of nude models—he hoped to make additional changes to the Academy's curriculum based on the pedagogical theories of Horace Lecoq de Boisbaudran. By the time Eakins painted *Swimming,* he felt himself in a position to implement this program—a step that posed problems for Coates.

Lecoq acknowledged that finding opportunities to study the nude outdoors would be difficult. Therefore he counseled that only "a great school of art" could implement his method, and that "in the name of art it would have no difficulty in getting placed at its disposal parks and public buildings" where it could carry out the study of the nude in the manner he had outlined.[94] Eakins's use of his students in a painting for the chairman of the Academy's Committee on Instruction suggests that he was trying to get official support for just such a move. Unfortunately, Eakins's dismissal from the Academy in February 1886 intervened. Although Eakins continued lecturing at art schools on anatomy and perspective, he never again attained a position to implement Lecoq's program at "a great school of art."

Lecoq's method had proven similarly controversial in France. Shortly after his appointment, he was ousted from the Petite Ecole. Both Eakins and Lecoq continued to pursue their unconventional methods through private instruction with a loyal core of devoted students. After Eakins's departure from the Academy, a group of his students organized the Art Students League of Philadelphia, with Eakins at its head. Nude photography sessions continued both indoors and out, but the league's impact and resources were limited—the tiny group would not transform art education in America. Eakins never painted another work quite like *Swimming*, because the goals he celebrated in this image were no longer possible for him to achieve. This perhaps explains why he stopped exhibiting *Swimming*—more than any of his works it represented failure.

CHAPTER FOUR

Behold the Man: Eakins's *Crucifixion*

During the summer of 1880, Thomas Eakins began work on *Crucifixion* (Figure 53), his largest history painting and the only overtly religious work he undertook. This unusual life-size rendering of one of the central devotional subjects in Christian art has few parallels in American art history. Most American Crucifixions appear in religious contexts, and those that exist outside of these settings treat the subject either on a smaller scale or without Eakins's graphic presentation of the body of Christ. Following his colonial revival subjects and contemporary genre scenes, *Crucifixion* was entirely unexpected.

Eakins's selection of this subject has puzzled some art historians who, unable to reconcile what appears to be an anomalous religious image by a reputedly agnostic artist, have related it solely to Eakins's desire for realism, thus divesting the painting of its religious content.[1] Lloyd Goodrich, for example, considered this illustration of Christ's suffering completely devoid of "religious sentiment" and suggested that Eakins intended it simply as a realist study of the male nude body.[2] As a result, art historians have frequently associated *Crucifixion* (like *Swimming*) with Eakins's strong interest in anatomy and the nude.[3] No doubt, these interests informed the painting, but it seems unlikely that Eakins selected the most symbolically loaded image in Christian iconography simply to exercise his skill at rendering the nude figure.

In 1989, Elizabeth Milroy reestablished *Crucifixion*'s pivotal place in Eakins's career in a seminal article in which she situated the painting within the context of contemporary French art and argued that Eakins regarded the work as his reception piece—a French academic tradition demonstrating "the high level of technical expertise and sophisticated understanding of literary and artistic

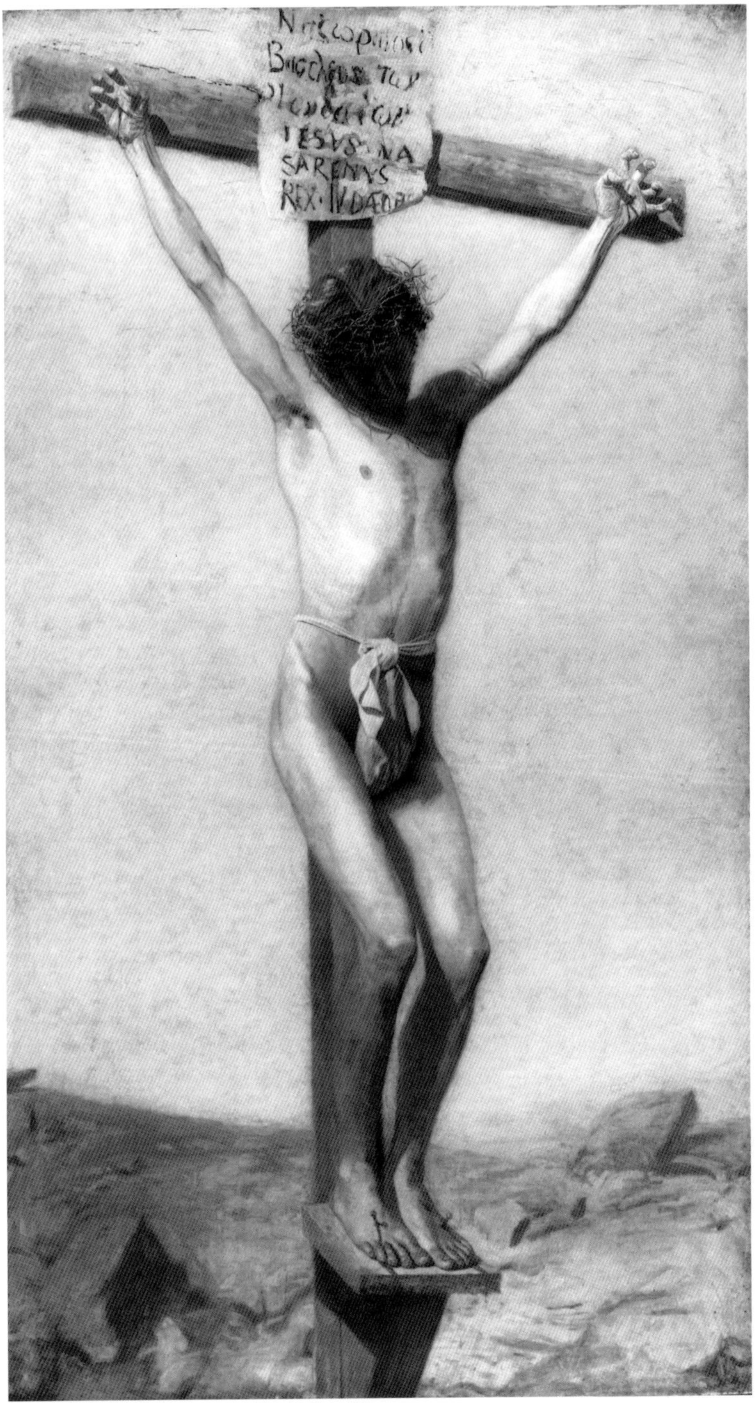

53. Thomas Eakins, *Crucifixion*, 1880. Oil on canvas, 96 × 54 in. Philadelphia Museum of Art. Gift of Mrs. Thomas Eakins and Miss Mary Adeline Williams, 1929.

sources required of mature academicians."[4] Milroy also considered the painting's religious subject matter by linking *Crucifixion*'s meaning with a precise moment in the Catholic liturgy, the *Consummatum* of the Good Friday service. Milroy further suggested that Eakins hoped to attract Catholic patronage with his painting. Yet Eakins's well-known ambivalence about organized religion, at times bordering on outright hostility, raises questions about this aspect of Milroy's interpretation.[5]

While the ambitious scale and subject of the work suggest that it was deeply important to Eakins, it is unclear why he would need a reception piece at this stage of his career, following such significant pictures as *The Gross Clinic* and *William Rush Carving His Allegorical Figure of the Schuylkill River.*[6] He may more boldly have considered the work his masterpiece, not just addressing his status in relation to the contemporary art world, but as a more enduring legacy. *Crucifixion*, like Eakins's painting of William Rush, refers to artistic tradition. Eakins hoped to insinuate himself into the art historical canon by reinterpreting this time-honored theme in a distinctly modern manner. In this way, *Crucifixion* continued Eakins's dialogue with the art historical past while remaining grounded in the present. Prepared for accolades and perhaps even some controversy, Eakins sent the painting to major exhibition venues around the country, where it generated considerable discussion. Although *Crucifixion* faced some vituperative criticism, the painting also won important admirers who defended the picture in the press. Whether loved or hated, *Crucifixion* probably received greater critical notice than any other Eakins painting. The significance of the painting is further heightened by Eakins's personal belief that it represented his "best" work.[7]

Though completed in 1880 and widely exhibited in the years following, much of *Crucifixion*'s exhibition history comes after Eakins's 1886 ouster from the Academy. If Eakins proudly exhibited the piece prior to 1886, the work may have acquired a different meaning after his disgrace. Colored with bitterness and irony in the immediate aftermath of his dismissal, *Crucifixion* perhaps briefly came to have darker associations for the artist. As the painting's meaning evolved for him, so also did it for its critics: as time went on, the painting was accepted without controversy at major venues, including the World's Columbian Exposition in 1893 and the 1915 Panama-Pacific International Exposition in San Francisco.

As much as the painting refers to artistic tradition and Eakins's standing as a professional artist, it also unavoidably addresses religion. Scholars who view the painting through the lens of Eakins's realist identity have tended to view anticlerical statements made by Eakins in his youth as evidence that he was irreligious—lending credence to Goodrich's assertion that *Crucifixion* lacks "religious sentiment."[8] When scholars have addressed the religious content of the image, they have usually read the influence of Catholicism on *Crucifixion*, based on Eakins's much later acquaintances with Catholic clergy at St. Charles Borromeo Seminary in Overbrook, Pennsylvania. Yet Eakins chose not to make any iconographic concessions on behalf of Catholic viewers. While Eakins's largely Protestant audience no doubt associated the subject with Catholicism, Catholics would likely have had problems with Eakins's painting.

Eakins's criticism of organized religion should not be viewed as a reflection of the absence of religion in his life, but instead deserves further consideration as an expression of his belief. An examination of Eakins's thoughts regarding religion reveals that he probably intended a specific reading of *Crucifixion* that was both religious and not Catholic. In fact, nineteenth-century critics debated the religious implications of the painting in precise terms. A review of Eakins's beliefs, coupled with the reception of the religious content of *Crucifixion*, suggests that Eakins's painting argues for a particular interpretation of Jesus as a strictly human figure, not a divine one. Eakins's *Crucifixion* is not irreligious; rather, it reflects liberal theological debates roughly contemporary with the painting.[9] An exploration of Eakins's content choices in *Crucifixion* not only makes clear his desire to revise the iconography of the Crucifixion for a modern audience but also elucidates the reasons for the painting's initial critical shortcomings.

Tradition

Crucifixion had its beginnings in the summer of 1880 when Eakins took his sixteen-year-old pupil, J. Laurie Wallace, on a trip across the Delaware River to southern New Jersey, near Pennsauken Creek. There, the artist found "a secluded spot" where he erected the wooden cross that he had made for the occasion.[10] Wallace then disrobed and climbed into position on the cross, wearing a crown of thorns that Eakins had also made and brought with him to the site. A sketch for *Crucifixion* (Hirshhorn Museum and Sculpture Garden, Washington, D.C) showing the effects of natural light on Wallace's face and upper torso probably resulted from this outdoor session. According to Wallace, Eakins also took photographs at the site, none of which have survived. However, a pencil grid beneath the paint surface of the final image indicates that Eakins probably made a complete compositional sketch, which he transferred to the canvas.[11] It remains possible that several other steps in the preparatory process for this large and ambitious painting have been lost.

Despite the seclusion of the Pennsauken site, hunters interrupted the two men, forcing Eakins to finish the modeling sessions at his home and studio on

Mt. Vernon Street in Philadelphia. Eakins reputedly erected the cross on the roof of his studio in order to continue studying the effects of natural light on his model, leading Goodrich to wonder, not unreasonably, what the neighbors might have thought of such a display.[12] As improbable as this scenario sounds, Eakins used the roof of his home as part of his working practice on several occasions.[13] In 1881, for example, Eakins painted two children in *Mending the Net* from a photograph of family members taken on the roof earlier that year.

The story of Wallace on the cross became legend among Eakins's students and even warranted mention in the press.[14] But it also echoed a story told about Eakins's teacher Léon Bonnat's use of a cadaver for his own painting of the Crucifixion, *Le Christ* (Figure 54). Although Bonnat completed this painting years after Eakins left Paris, it gained notoriety as part of a polemical debate regarding naturalism and religious art in France. The *Magazine of Art* featured a small reproduction of Bonnat's image in 1879, the year before Eakins painted his *Crucifixion.* American artists and critics also took note of Bonnat's work, providing Eakins with ample opportunity to consider the painting.

The American artist J. Alden Weir gave a compelling eyewitness account of Bonnat's model:

> After the lecture I went into the dissecting room and saw Mr. Bonnat and Prof. [Gérôme]. They had just received a subject, and at the opposite side of the room I saw an immense cross, but thought nothing. Bonnat said he had not much time to stay and wanted the gendarme to hurry up, so two of these soldiers and a hired man took the subject out of the room, brought the cross out and laid it on it. It was then whispered about that Bonnat had a commission to paint a crucifixion, had bought the subject and had the cross fixed, so as to be able to study the action of the muscles. Some of the students, hearing what was up, crowded in; this attracted Bonnat's attention, and he got the gendarme to close the door and lock it. We went back to the lecture room where we draw the bones, and while sitting there we heard the nails driven in. We finished; Mr. [Walter] Blackman and myself went out together after all had gone. At the door we met a guardian and bribed him to let us see the subject, which he did, and standing up against the wall was the large cross and the subject crucified on it, a horrid sight; but it shows how those French artists believe in truth.[15]

Eakins's students later conflated this story with the one of Wallace on the cross: "I was told by a friend of his that 'Tommy' took a corpse on the roof and nailed it to a wooden cross he had made, and then painted it with a thorough real-

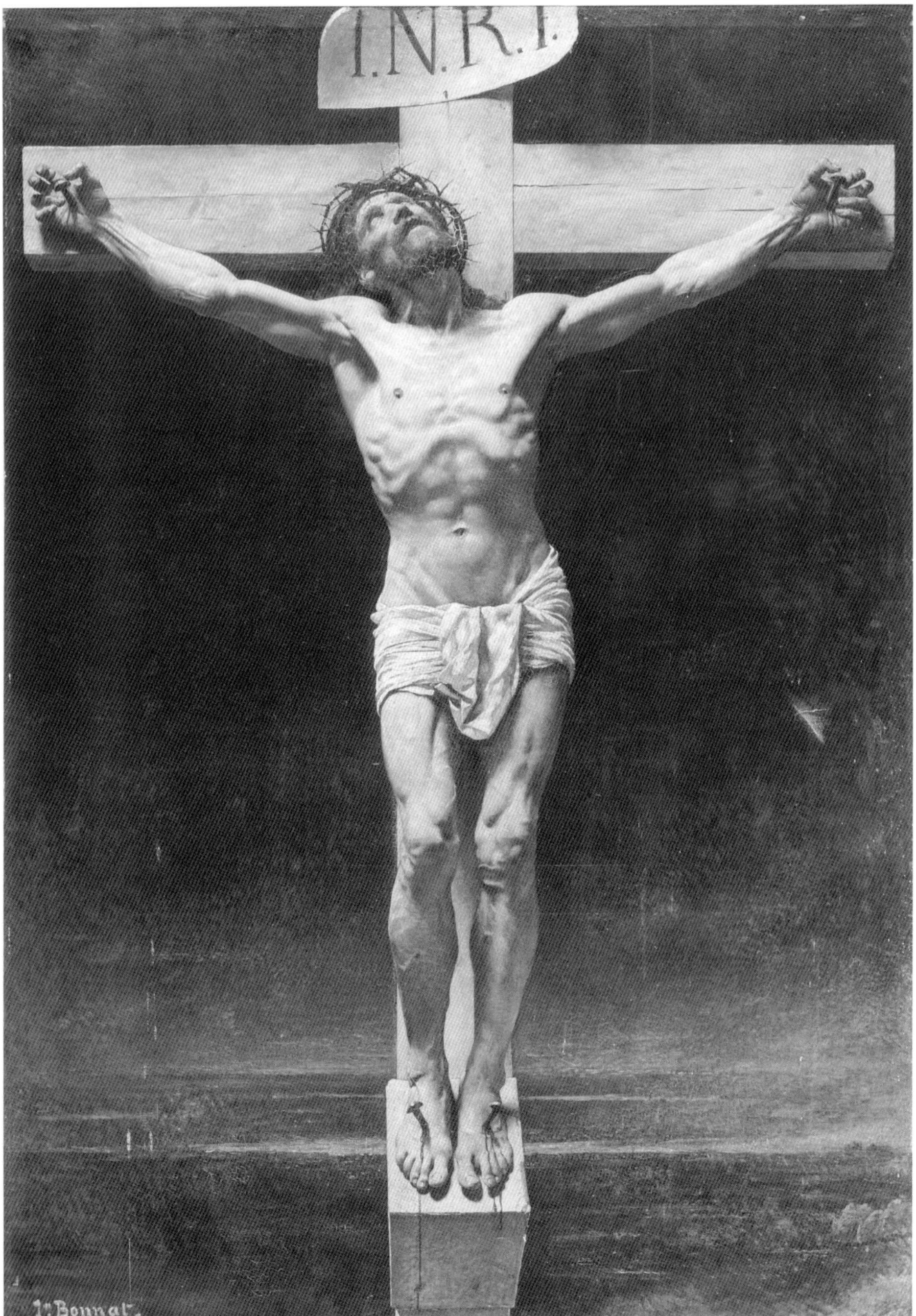

54. Léon Bonnat, *Le Christ (Christ)*, 1874. Oil on canvas, 90⅛ × 63 in . Musée du Petit Palais, Paris, France. Photo: Réunion des Musées Nationaux/Art Resource, New York.

ism."[16] The general contours of the story surfaced again when Eakins's student Samuel Murray asked a young ambulance driver to hang "from his hands from a chain" attached to a cross that he had constructed in his studio in order to model a Crucifixion for St. Patrick's Cathedral in Harrisburg, Pennsylvania.[17]

Each of the stories regarding these artists' heroic efforts to create a realist image recalls an ancient artistic tradition, of which the famed competition between the Greek painters Xeuxis and Parrhasios, recorded by Pliny the Elder, may be the earliest. In the well-known story, the two painters each sought to paint a more realistic work than the other. Xeuxis's convincing portrayal of grapes deceived the birds who came down to peck at the canvas. However, Parrhasios's illusionistic depiction of a curtain fooled Xeuxis into believing that a painting lay underneath. An apocryphal story told by Seneca provides an even more fitting parallel with regard to images of the Crucifixion. According to Seneca, Parrhasios purchased a slave for the express purpose of torturing him in order to study his agony. The unfortunate slave thus unwittingly became Parrhasios's model for a painting of Prometheus.[18] While gruesome in its details, the story provides a model of artistic integrity, reiterated again and again in the art historical tradition. As that tradition evolved, the story became particularly associated with the subject of the Crucifixion.[19]

The progression of crucifixions from Bonnat to Eakins to Murray suggests a degree of intergenerational artistic competition between these men. One detects Eakins and Murray each embracing the subject in friendly rivalry with their teachers, following another theme of artistic biography, also found in antiquity, of the student who surpasses his or her master.[20] If this Oedipal desire at all influenced Eakins, he had adequate reason for selecting the Crucifixion as the subject of his struggle. Although a strong relationship exists between Bonnat's and Eakins's paintings, particularly with respect to realism, Eakins may also have been confronting the work of his other master, Jean-Léon Gérôme.

During Eakins's student days at the Ecole, Gérôme painted a Crucifixion scene, now titled *Jérusalem (Consummatum est)* (Figure 55).[21] Influenced by his travels to the Middle East, Gérôme's treatment of the subject places the emphasis on archaeological accuracy in the depiction of a panoramic view of the Holy Land, with the city of Jerusalem in the distance. Gérôme, perhaps wisely, avoided the depiction of the body of Christ by having the three crosses and the forms of Jesus and the two thieves who were executed with him appear only as shadows in the lower right portion of the landscape. Gérôme exhibited the work at the Salon of 1868, while Eakins was still studying in his atelier in Paris. Gérôme also sent the painting to the United States, where it hung in at least three New York City venues, including an exhibition at the National Academy

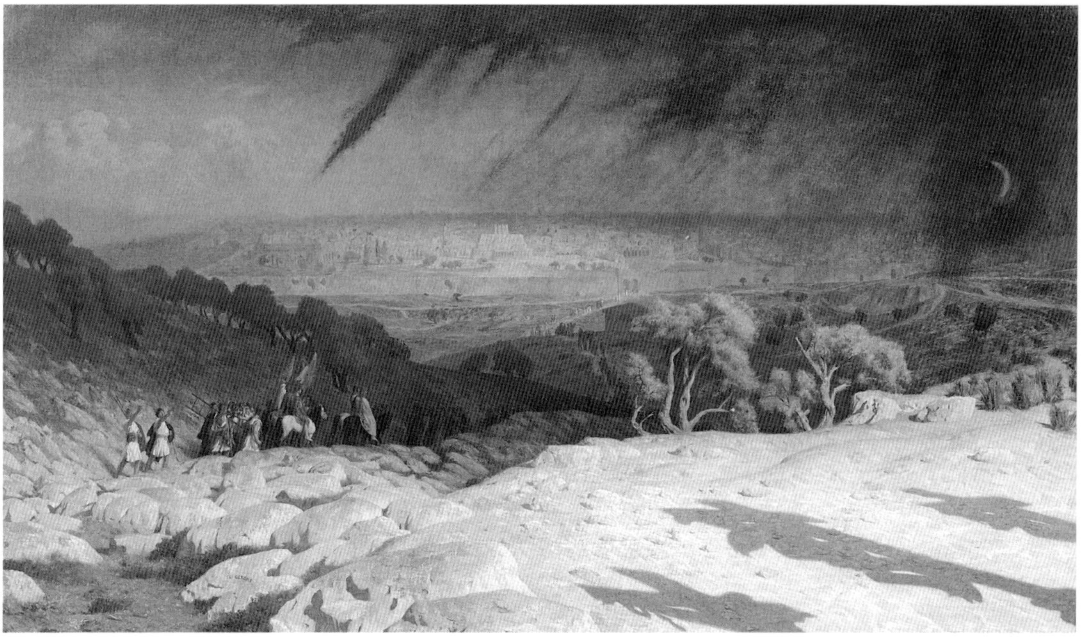

55. Jean-Léon Gérôme, *Jersusalem (Consummatum est.)*, 1867. Oil on canvas, 81.3 × 146 cm. Musée d'Orsay, Paris, France. Giraudon, The Bridgeman Art Library.

of Design (NAD). While Eakins's composition more closely reflects Bonnat's work, it is important to keep Gérôme's treatment of the subject in mind.

Eakins certainly did not emulate Gérôme's reluctance about depicting the body of Christ. In his painting of the subject, Jesus dominates a barren landscape, appearing alone, with relatively few of the narrative details that traditionally accompany the scene. Only the scroll above his head identifies him as the "King of the Jews." Although he wears the crown of thorns, he, significantly, lacks a halo. In addition, Jesus's head slumps downward in shadow, without the least suggestion of holy light. The otherwise brightly illuminated composition hides none of the attenuated body's flaws. The positioning of Jesus's body—close to the picture plane and on a diagonal—is also unusual. Rather than placing the body frontally in the center of the canvas, as Christ appears in so many Crucifixion scenes (including Bonnat's), Eakins turned the body with its right side toward the viewer. This approach to Jesus's figure accentuates his three-dimensionality, highlighting his physical presence.[22]

Several critics found Jesus's body in the Eakins painting disturbing and used terms like *ghastly* or *repulsive* in describing it. Eakins's selection of a slender sixteen-year-old model may have increased the antipathy of those inclined to find the painting unpleasant. Eakins complicated his representation of an unidealized Christ by placing him in a position that stressed his physical weakness. By turning the crucifix on a diagonal, Eakins made Jesus's thin body appear even more vulnerable. The blood streaming from his wounds and the clawlike contraction of his hands further emphasize the physical nature of his suffering. Eakins approached Christ entirely from the perspective of his human frailty and eliminated any suggestion of his omniscient strength.

Eakins would have considered each of these choices carefully. By the time he painted *Crucifixion*, Eakins was well acquainted not only with the Crucifixions done by his teachers but also with the long art historical tradition of the subject. At the Pennsylvania Academy he had access to a collection of prints and reproductions of great works of art from European collections. This included James Claghorn's well-known collection of European engravings, which in the 1870s hung in the Lecture Room and the Director's Room at the Academy.[23] Perhaps more important, as a student in Europe, Eakins visited numerous Catholic churches, including the Vatican, where he would have seen striking examples of European devotional art.[24] He also visited art museums in France, Italy, Germany, and Spain. His trips to the Museo del Prado in Madrid seem to have been particularly influential. Eakins recorded his thoughts about many of the works that he saw there, taking special note of paintings by the Spanish Baroque master, Diego Velázquez.

Although Eakins chose a different approach, his *Crucifixion* reflects the influence of Velázquez, whose *Christ on the Cross* (Figure 56) he likely saw on one of his visits to the Prado. Velázquez's earthy materialism made him particularly popular with nineteenth-century painters, including realists such as Edouard Manet. But he also merited high esteem from more conservative academic artists, such as Eakins's teacher, Bonnat, who encouraged his students to study the work of the Baroque master. Bonnat's own *Le Christ* shows the distinct influence of Velázquez's *Christ on the Cross*. The solidity of Velázquez's Christ would have appealed to Eakins, who aimed at a similarly material presence in his own work. However, Velázquez's masterful painting also presents a traditional view of the Crucifixion, set against a dark background without "even a hint of earth," which allows "the radiant Christ" to appear "suspended in time and place for all eternity."[25] As much as Velázquez influenced Eakins's treatment of the body of Christ, Eakins had no interest in replicating this sense of eternity in his own work. Instead, Eakins's Jesus seems palpably present in his historical moment.

Although the works of Bonnat and Velázquez influenced Eakins stylistically, both artists approached their paintings of the Crucifixion from an entirely different ideological perspective from that of Eakins. Unlike Eakins, for whom this was his sole religious painting, both Bonnat and Velázquez produced an

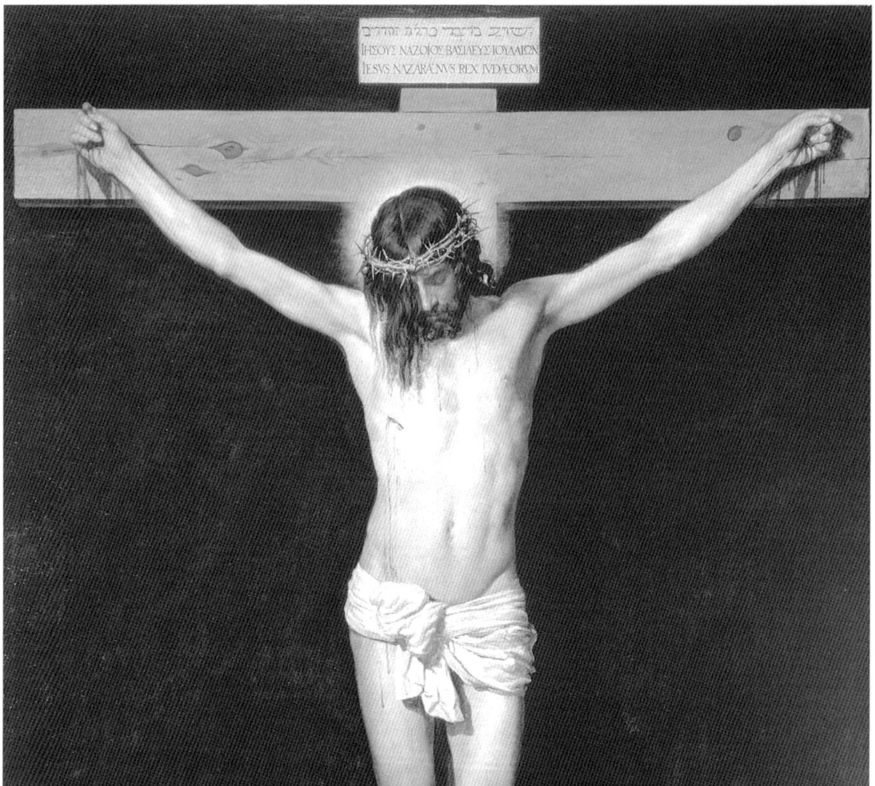

56. Diego Rodriguez de Silva y Velázquez, *Christ on the Cross*, ca. 1630. Oil on canvas, 248 × 169 cm. Prado, Madrid. The Bridgeman Art Library.

impressive body of religious art, often for church patrons. While each introduced realist elements that challenged more traditional artistic conventions, neither artist invested his work with Eakins's skepticism of religious doctrine. This was largely because Bonnat and Velázquez were both Catholic. In fact, each created his paintings for display in Catholic contexts. Velázquez's *Christ on the Cross* originally hung in the sacristy of a convent. Bonnat's painting, commissioned by the Catholic-leaning French government for the Palais du Justice, served as a reminder to convicted sinners of Christ's sacrifice and the possibility of redemption.[26] Following iconographic tradition, both artists situated their Christ figures frontally in the center of the canvas. Velázquez revealed the divine presence through the aureole of light emanating from behind Christ's head, while Bonnat similarly allowed an unnaturalistic light to fall from above onto the uplifted face of his Christ.

In another significant departure from Bonnat's and Velázquez's works, Eakins chose to set his *Crucifixion* during the daytime—a decision that many critics felt added to the brutality of his image. Typically Crucifixions appear as if they are night scenes, with the cross set against a miraculously darkened noonday sky. This tradition derives from three of the Gospel texts, which each record that the afternoon sky blackened from the sixth through the ninth hours of the Crucifixion and that Christ died in the ninth hour. By depicting Christ against a bright daylit sky, Eakins deliberately rejected the supernatural event of the darkened sky. In fact, conservation evidence suggests that Eakins originally painted a bright blue sky, which he later toned down, perhaps in an effort to temper criticism.[27]

Following in the footsteps of great European painters like Velázquez and his own teachers, Eakins selected this well-known religious theme to assert his place in the art historical tradition at a point when his career seemed to be flourishing. However, his substantial deviations from the conventional iconography of the subject shocked some elements of his American audience. Eakins signaled his work as a distinctly modern take on a traditional subject by exhibiting it first at the progressive Society of American Artists (SAA) exhibition in New York in 1882. Although many critics commented on the painting's brutally realistic treatment of the subject, Eakins's iconographic choices should not be discounted as merely part of his adherence to a realist artistic doctrine. He could have chosen any number of subjects for a major new realist composition, but instead he chose to depict Jesus, for religious as well as artistic reasons.

The Divinity of Jesus

Eakins's emphasis on Jesus's human physicality and his denial of any of the supernatural or extrahuman traits that marked Jesus as the son of God reflect

Eakins's own beliefs about the divinity of Christ. Although regarded as an agnostic with a caustic disrespect for organized religion, Eakins, like many of his rationalist contemporaries, did indeed think about religious issues. Despite his claim as a young man that he belonged to "no church," he was raised in the Protestant tradition.[28] As an adult he continued to read the Bible, and friends remarked upon his fondness for the New Testament.[29] Unfortunately, few of his letters reveal much about his thoughts on religious issues beyond his general mistrust of the clergy, an important point to which we will return shortly.

In one notable instance, however, Eakins compared Christ to the Prophet Muhammad, contrasting Muhammad's human relationship with God to that of the "three in one & one in 3" of "the contemptible Catholic religion," writing, "There's no God but God & Mahomed [*sic*] is his prophet. . . . How Christ like."[30] This statement reveals a significant distinction in Eakins's thinking: he did not deny the existence of God but rejected the Trinity. In its stead, Eakins perceived a Unitarian godhead and identified Jesus as his human prophet. Years later he clarified his position by explicitly telling his friend Dennis Cardinal Dougherty that he did not believe in the divinity of Christ.[31] While Eakins did not accept Christ's divinity, neither did he reject his important role within the Christian faith. His references to Jesus in personal correspondence are always respectful, even reverential, as in his "How Christ like." Eakins acknowledged Jesus's exemplary status, even while limiting his powers to the terrestrial sphere.

Much has been made of Eakins's rejection of religion, yet he made clear on several occasions that he objected to organized religion largely because he could not accept the role of the clergy as mediators between man and God. He lamented that "a fact as simple as the religion of Jesus Christ" had been complicated by men.[32] While he admired individual priests for their learning, he espoused strongly anticlerical opinions when it came to larger religious questions. He especially despised the fund-raising efforts of "nasty low priests" within the church itself, making him "think of Christ kicking the money changers out of the temple."[33] What little we know of Eakins's reading habits further allies him with anticlerical movements in France. He enjoyed Rabelais, "a writer priest doctor of medicine and hater of the priesthood."[34] He also read Voltaire and Victor Hugo, both of whom were associated with anticlerical thought. In addition, he periodically sent copies of the anticlerical journal *Charivari* home to his family.

Eakins envisioned a religion without ministers or priests, a concept that he briefly associated with Islam. Using Gérôme's paintings of the Near East as the basis for his understanding of Islamic belief, Eakins expressed admiration for the simplicity of Muslim prayer. Of Islam, Eakins wrote, "Their religion [is] a silent prayer to the unknown immense God. The sun is going down. The man

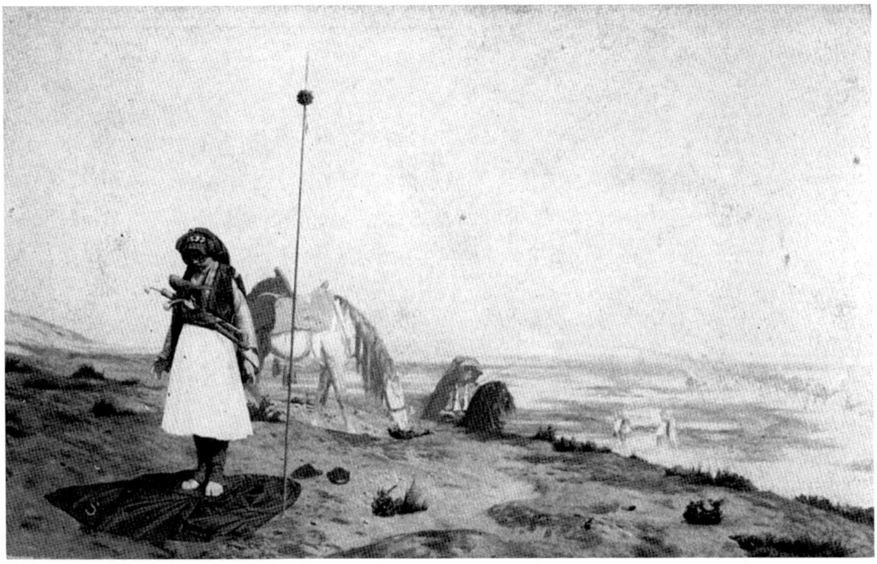

57. *Eakins's carte de visite of Jean-Léon Gérôme's "Prayer in the Desert,"* ca. 1866–70. Bryn Mawr College Library, Pennsylvania, Seymour Adelman Collection.

of the desert stops his horse, spreads out his little carpet[,] sticks his spear up in the ground[,] takes off his shoes, everything is silent there, he forgets he is of the world & prays to his Allah." Although Eakins does not explicitly state it, this passage clearly describes Gérôme's painting *Prayer in the Desert* (Figure 57). Using the image as the basis for a broader commentary on religion, Eakins continued that "healthy" religion "will always affect you like a Turk. You would get into the big quiet, the desert or the top of the house. You won't go to church to see their little parades[,] their gildings & tinsel[,] their little bells[,] to hear the money clinking for the Society of Jesus for the new chapel . . . the nasty low priests. . . . The Turk don't pray like a Christian. For he don't pay any one to pray for him. We will now sing the 917th Psalm the 1st[,] 3d[,] & 5th verses."[35] Throughout his letters, Eakins argued for a personal, unmediated religious experience, but he never denied the existence of God.

In these thoughts Eakins was not alone. Eakins's beliefs and his painting of the Crucifixion echo a range of liberal religious texts published in the second half of the nineteenth century that challenged the authority of the clergy by submitting the life of Christ to historical and scientific scrutiny. Eakins surely knew Ernest Renan's *Life of Jesus*, which circulated in France shortly before his arrival as a student and was quickly translated into several languages, including English. Taking a determinedly anticlerical position, Renan argued for "a pure worship, a religion without priests and external observances, resting entirely upon the feelings of the heart."[36] Moreover, Renan suggested that the notion of "pure worship" was one of the most innovative religious ideas to come out of Jesus's early ministry.

Influenced by German biblical scholarship of the preceding decades, Renan's controversial book also attempted to recover the historical Jesus, at the expense of miracles and supernatural interventions. Replete with geographical and archaeological details that added life to the ancient story, Renan's text was both innovative in its approach to biblical history and thoroughly readable. Renan became the most famous of a host of liberal thinkers who similarly questioned the accuracy of the Gospels and sought a more human and historically accurate picture of the events of the Bible. As Daniel Pals has written, "Especially after 1860 Lives of Christ became in fact a sort of vogue among the Victorians, to which every type of writer—devotional, radical, clerical, or eccentric—was sooner or later attracted."[37] Americans, by no means exempt from this obsession, devoured and discussed the European texts and produced their own works on the subject. Individual authors applied varying degrees of revision to the Gospel story, the most extreme of which suggested that, while well intentioned, Jesus suffered from delusions, the most egregious being his self-proclaimed status as the son of God. These scholars acknowledged his talent and charisma as a preacher but questioned his Messianic role.[38]

These texts had an immediate and multivaried influence on European artists. Gérôme's interpretation of the Crucifixion as essentially a depiction of the Holy Land as landscape reflects one of the least controversial implications of the new literature. Gérôme's painting recalls the concerns of many of the new texts with atmospheric and archaeological accuracy in its emphasis on geography and historical authenticity. Eakins did not pursue this trend in his own work, but he no doubt knew of it, writing, "Who that has read . . . the Bible or any traveller's stories but wants to see the east."[39] Eakins may also have based his generalized Eastern landscape on those seen in Gérôme's paintings. Despite the innovation of Gérôme's approach, his painting did not challenge the religious dogma that often influenced artistic treatments of the subject. On account of Gérôme's discretion, the American critic Susan Nicholls Carter upheld the painting as a model: "In Gérôme's famous picture of the *Crucifixion* our readers will recall how the artist suggests the horror by throwing upon the ground the *shadows* of the three crosses, which do not themselves appear. This is a worthy artistic rendering of a subject too solemn to be realistically treated."[40]

The rise of realism, or the broader tendency toward naturalism, had a tremendous impact on French religious art. Although in the minds of its practitioners, artistic naturalism did not necessarily require an acceptance of liberal religious thinking, critics tended to view naturalistic paintings of biblical subjects as reflecting the influence of blasphemous critical approaches to the life of Jesus. Church hierarchy sanctioned this belief when Pope Pius IX in his 1864 *Syllabus of Errors* associated naturalism and rationalism with heretical thought. Pius IX specifically condemned the modern tendency to elevate reason over faith. Along these lines, some critics felt that Bonnat's painting displayed the taint of Renan's thinking, largely because of the intense naturalism of the work.[41]

Bonnat's painting *Le Christ* caused a sensation at the Salon of 1874 where it faced criticism for its brutal realism. As one critic perceived the painting, "It is more repulsive than touching. It is not the Redeemer emaciated by fasts, nor the Son of God suffering but resigned; it is a vulgar man, who has lived a common life, and whose body undergoes tortures in which the soul does not share." For this critic, it could not follow that one who believed could represent Christ in this fashion, and he concluded that "the moral meaning of the subject has assuredly not been understood."[42] This type of criticism based its conclusions solely on Bonnat's artistic choice of representing Christ as an unidealized individual. It discounted that Bonnat had titled his painting *Le Christ*, rather than using Renan's humanizing "Jesus." More important, it ignored the presence of the unnatural light from above in Bonnat's painting, which affirmed that it was not the work of an unrepentant skeptic.

Eakins took the subject a step further by eliminating this final vestige of Christ's divinity. In this way, Eakins went beyond painting just another naturalist depiction of Jesus; he pointedly stripped the figure of its godliness. This opened the artist up to criticism, not unlike that handed to Bonnat, but with more directed charges leveled against his decision to render Jesus as a man. Artist and critic Leslie Miller clearly detected the influence of Renan and his kind in Eakins's work: "I confess that to me it only seems to say 'Come away and leave him alone in the white sunshine; it was all nonsense that we have heard about the darkness and the heavens themselves being moved. It was cruel to kill him, of course, but it is done now and cannot be helped; the clamoring mob was inhuman, we know, but it was not so very blind after all; there is one less delusion in the world at any rate.' "[43] Another critic called Eakins's Jesus "a materialistic Savior: a human and not a divine." Condemning the painting as a spiritual failure, the author continued, "There is no divinity in the picture, no mystery. It has no spiritual atmosphere to touch the soul with love and compassion."[44] A critic in Detroit concurred, writing that "[Eakins] instead of giving us a divinity has revealed a most revolting spectacle in the form of a man with emaciated figure, with wiry hair, and a face anything but God-like."[45]

This criticism of the face is unusual. Despite the polemical ambitions of the painting, Eakins remained cautious in his depiction of Jesus's visage. Just as

Gérôme avoided the physical description of Christ's body, so too did Eakins evade the depiction of Jesus's face by placing it in shadow. Some critics charged that Eakins used shadow to intentionally frustrate criticism.[46] While this may be true, Eakins's decision may also represent an acknowledgment that, despite the efforts of biblical historians, a lack of credible eyewitnesses made it impossible to ascertain Jesus's appearance. Frustratingly, the most authoritative texts, the Gospels themselves, contained no physical description of Jesus. This remained the primary stumbling block in any pictorial representation of the historical Jesus. Theologians debated the issue of Christ's personal appearance for centuries largely on doctrinal grounds, with some arguing for his intense beauty and others for his plainness.

The only historical document describing Jesus, the well-known Epistle of Publius Lentulus, allegedly the work of a Roman eyewitness, in fact dated no earlier than the eleventh century. Under scrutiny, anachronistic language and historical details in the letter indicate that the text could not date to the Roman period. Nor does the description of Jesus conform to early Christian imagery; rather it reflects the artistic conventions in place at the time of its actual creation. When viewed less critically, the document provides historical validation for an iconographic tradition that emerged in the centuries after Jesus's death. Following this tradition, Lentulus's Jesus has a beard, reddish-brown hair, and blue-grey eyes.[47] In spite of the letter's well-known unreliability, some argued that the epistle had its basis in an earlier lost text and that the inaccuracies resulted from its transmission by countless individuals through time. The potency of the image described in the letter is witnessed by the currency it still holds today.[48]

In the absence of other texts, the letter and its associated art historical tradition may have influenced Eakins's representation of Jesus. Despite his talent as a portraitist, he chose not to paint a portrait likeness of Wallace on the cross. In his depiction of Jesus's face, Eakins altered Wallace's features to conform to accepted notions of Christ's appearance, largely as they exist in the Lentulus letter. If one compares Wallaces's face as Jesus with Eakins's portrait of him from 1885 (Figure 58), there are some telling differences, most notably that Eakins changed Wallace's hair color from almost black in the portrait to reddish-brown in *Crucifixion.* Further, Eakins obscured Wallace's features in shadow, making him almost unrecognizable as an individual. This raises an important point: unlike Bonnat's Christ, which critics identified "as a vulgar man, who has lived a common life," Eakins did not want his Jesus to be specific and knowable. Yet he also did not offer the traditional alternative of an idealized Savior. Eakins presented his viewers with an earthbound Jesus and hid his undeniably human features from their gaze.

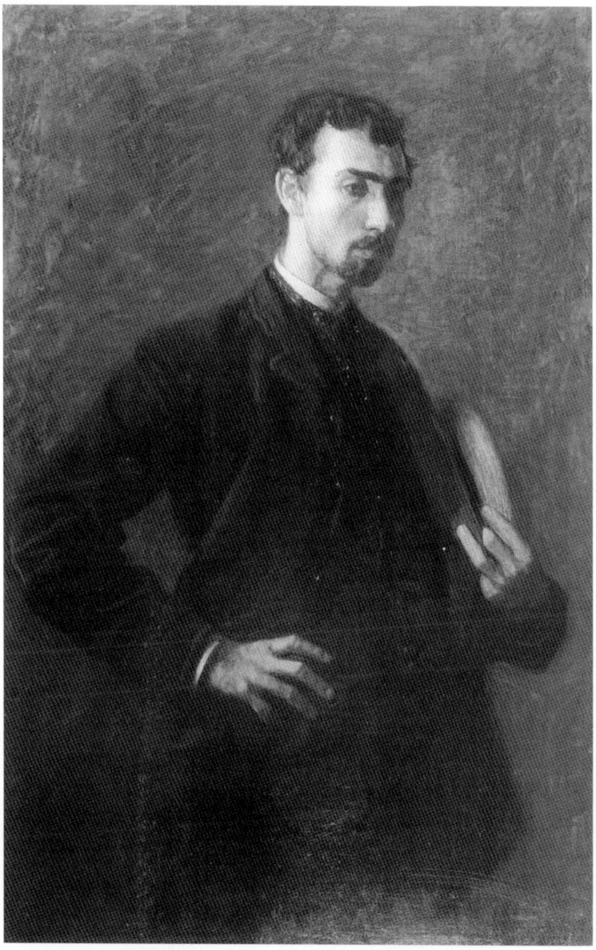

58. Thomas Eakins, *Professor John Laurie Wallace*, 1885. Oil on canvas on masonite panel, 50¼ × 32½ in. Joslyn Art Museum, Omaha, Nebraska. Gift of the James A. Douglas Foundation.

Audience

Eakins must have known of the controversy caused by Bonnat's painting *Le Christ.* An 1874 letter to his friend Earl Shinn indicates his continuing interest in Bonnat's work, and Eakins's lifelong friend William Sartain remained a student in Bonnat's atelier during this period. Eakins most certainly knew of the scandal caused by Renan's book, which figured so prominently in the press in the years prior to his painting and which his friend Shinn had read.[49] Given that he had already faced criticism for the realism of *The Gross Clinic,* he must have known that a realist representation of Christ would be even more controversial. It seems likely that he even counted on it.

Crucifixion did not create controversy solely because Eakins determined to show a man rather than a god, but also because he displayed the painting before a largely Protestant audience already uncomfortable with the image of the Crucifixion. While American Protestants did not disapprove of religious imagery—far from it—they tended to avoid certain themes, among them the Crucifixion. Jesus appeared in other Protestant images, but rarely in the Crucifixion. Protestant renderings of the theme either diminished Christ's presence or absented him altogether. For example, Elihu Vedder's sketches for a planned painting of the Crucifixion called *The Ninth Hour* depict a crowd in the foreground, with the three crosses in the distance, offering only a glimpse of Christ's body.[50] Similarly, Robert Walter Weir's *Evening of the Crucifixion* (unlocated) showed mourners leaning upon a cross without the body of Christ.[51]

Protestants understood more traditional depictions of the Crucifixion as symbolic of the Catholic tradition. The critic for the *New York Times* implied as much when he called Eakins's *Crucifixion* "an unnecessary picture" and asked, "Will the devoutest Roman Catholic be moved by it? Hardly."[52] In a survey of "The Cross in Art," a writer for the *Ladies Repository* briefly traced the history of the representation of the cross from symbol to Crucifixion. What at first seems a casual survey of the tradition quickly becomes invested with sectarian bias as the author laments the introduction of the Crucifixion in the seventh century as representative of "a decline of both artistic and religious purity." Examining the methods by which artists associated the cross with its victim, from representations of the lamb at the base of the cross to its culmination in Christ crucified with four nails, the author felt that "the grandeur of the early symbolism" had been replaced in the Crucifixion with a "most material and repulsive literalness."[53] This material imagery repelled Protestant viewers of Eakins's painting, who much preferred Gérôme or Weir's subtler renderings of the subject.

Protestants consumed material depictions of the Crucifixion featuring the body of Christ in illustrated Bibles, gift books, and prints made after European masters, but as relatively private objects made for personal contemplation, these images belonged to a different category of images than Eakins's large canvas. Protestants encountered painted Crucifixions less frequently. They admired European examples seen abroad, but strictly as the products of a foreign culture.[54] In Europe, Protestants viewed Catholic art while attempting to avoid the taint of the religion. At home, painted Crucifixions were typically confined to two environments: the panorama and the sacred spaces of Catholic interiors. The innate theatricality of the panorama prepared the Protestant spectator for the scene. In addition, the most famous of the Crucifixion panoramas to visit Philadelphia, copied from a European example, included a cast of thousands and received praise for its allegedly historically accurate rendering of Jerusalem, but the actual scene of the Crucifixion comprised a relatively minor aspect of the overall composition.[55]

The interiors of Catholic churches provided Protestants with an entirely different type of spectacle. The diaries of Eakins's sister Frances and his wife, Susan, indicate that the artist visited a number of Catholic churches while studying in Europe and later upon his return to Philadelphia.[56] He often visited these churches to attend musical performances. However, in 1876, Eakins went to Philadelphia's newly built Cathedral of Saints Peter and Paul to make sketches inside the church. While there, Eakins must have seen the altar Crucifixion painted by Italian émigré Constantino Brumidi, even if he did not sketch it. Brumidi's *Crucifixion* (destroyed) included all of the narrative details that Eakins's painting lacked. Brumidi depicted an iconic Christ, displayed frontally in a flood of holy light, following the traditional iconography. Mourners lamented Jesus below, with angels in the spandrels above, a supernatural feature prefiguring his ascent to heaven. Several Catholic churches in Philadelphia had similar painted Crucifixions over the altar.[57] With Eakins's frequent church visits, he would have had ample opportunity to view Catholic altar Crucifixions within their religious context.

Although Milroy has suggested that Eakins may have wanted to court Catholic patronage with *Crucifixion*, this seems unlikely given his reinterpretation of the subject.[58] While Eakins's image referenced a Catholic iconography, his presentation of a strictly human Jesus rejected Catholic belief, which acknowledges that both the human and the divine exist in hypostatic union in Christ. Further, Eakins divorced the subject from the church and placed it in the secular and commercial realm of the art exhibition. Late in his career, Eakins lent the painting to the Catholic Seminary of St. Charles Borromeo at Overbrook, but only after he had befriended several members of the clergy at the seminary, some of whom he also painted. Yet as Milroy recounts, the seminary seemed at a loss over what to do with the painting, never placing it on public view within their sacred spaces. In fact, the seminarians hid the painting behind a door, where a doorknob poked a hole through the canvas, causing extensive damage.[59]

If Eakins's Protestant audience viewed his subject in Catholic terms, they found his reinvention of the theme doubly troubling. Eakins's friend William J. Clark wrote, "[Eakins's *Crucifixion*] invites comparisons, such as few of his previous works invite, with the performances of very distinguished painters."[60] As Clark suggested, Americans, whether Protestant or Catholic, brought to Eakins's painting their familiarity with Old Master—primarily Catholic—treatments of the theme. Against this unconscious visual memory it was obvious to anyone viewing the painting that Eakins deliberately chose a canon-breaking approach. By selecting such a staple of the Old Master tradition, Eakins invited this comparison. His audience found the work unlike previous Crucifixions not only on artistic grounds but also because of his representation of a new Jesus.

Neither Protestants nor Catholics would have been comfortable with the painting in a sacred interior. Although Eakins put a price on the work when he exhibited it, *Crucifixion* was not a painting that was really intended for sale to a private patron either. An American might buy a distinguished European religious image, but a realist, life-size picture of Jesus on the cross by an American painter had no place on the art market.

The Art of the Crucifixion

What Eakins hoped for with *Crucifixion* was not Catholic patronage but an artistic succès de scandale. Toward this end, he carefully orchestrated *Crucifixion*'s introduction to the public. Although he signed *Crucifixion* in 1880, he delayed its exhibition until 1882. What happened to the painting in the intervening years remains unclear. However, the work was nowhere in evidence when the critic Mariana van Rensselaer visited Eakins's studio during the summer of 1881. Van Rensselaer made the trip to Philadelphia specifically to interview Eakins for an article that she planned to write about him for the *American Art Review*.[61] In a letter to her editor, Sylvester Koehler, Van Rensselaer complained, "He has evidently painted very few pictures as he could tell me of nothing of his that I had not already seen." In reference to *The Gross Clinic*, she wrote, "I do not see why it is so much worse than other things that are passed without comment & enjoyed—such as battle scenes to say nothing of crucifixions."[62] Her mention of Crucifixions in this context makes clear that she did not see Eakins's treatment of the subject. If Eakins had his new painting in the studio, he chose not to show it to the critic.

For its debut, Eakins sent the painting in 1882 to the SAA's annual exhibition. It is perhaps significant that he chose not to send the painting to the NAD's annual, which overlapped with the SAA show in its timing. The SAA was formed in 1877 by a group of young, foreign-trained artists, as a response to what was seen as the increasing conservatism of the NAD's juries. The conflict was generational, but it also revolved around questions of style, subject matter, and national identity. In contrast to the NAD annual's staple of landscape and genre subjects, the exhibitions of the SAA generally favored the French academic tradition rooted in the human figure. From its inaugural exhibition in 1878 until the rejection of his sculptures *Knitting* and *Spinning* in 1884, Eakins sent some of his most important works, including *William Rush Carving His Allegorical Figure of the Schuylkill River* and *The Gross Clinic* to the SAA exhibitions. He also frequently participated in the NAD annuals but tended to submit smaller outdoor and genre subjects to their shows. For example, in 1882, he exhibited two pictures of figures in landscapes at the NAD: *Shad Fishing at*

Gloucester on the Delaware River and *Mending the Net*. Therefore it seems likely that he specifically reserved his French-influenced *Crucifixion* for debut at the SAA show.[63]

Initially, the SAA hanging committee rejected *Crucifixion*, along with paintings by many other artists, on account of its large size. Due to the space constraints of the exhibition, the SAA organized a second show immediately following the first, which included *Crucifixion*. Eakins sent the painting to New York sometime prior to the exhibition to have it framed by C. M. Silleck.[64] Although the Philadelphia Museum of Art removed this frame (which subsequently disappeared), it is known through photographs and has recently been reproduced. Eakins often chose fairly standard gilt frames purchased from suppliers, sometimes with apparently little thought. The Silleck frame is an exception, a highly carved, almost Baroque design, it physically crowns the painting with the importance that Eakins invested in it. With this frame, Eakins linked his modern *Crucifixion* to the Baroque art historical tradition that inspired his interest in the theme.

Although the painting faced substantial criticism, the SAA showing of *Crucifixion* proved to be quite a coup for Eakins. The prominent New York venue assured him extensive press coverage, and for once every major review addressed his work and at some length. While critics disagreed about the painting's success, the reviewer for the *Art Journal* deemed it "one of those works, which it is well for an exhibition to be provided with, because it provokes discussion."[65] Many critics found the painting irreverent and unappealing. However, even those who panned the work often could not help but praise the audaciousness of the subject or the technical skill of the painter. The *Independent*, for example, found the painting "revolting beyond expression," yet conceded that it was "a bold piece of realism, in which there is some good painting."[66]

But the painting also had its admirers. Although he found fault with the religious content of the painting, Clarence Cook began his review for the *Tribune* by characterizing *Crucifixion* as "the most important study of the nude that we remember by an American artist."[67] Mariana van Rensselaer, one of the most influential critics of the Gilded Age, crafted two lengthy and insightful reviews praising the painting. For the *American Architect and Building News*, Van Rensselaer acknowledged that, while one expected anatomical skill from Eakins, she found the spiritual element in *Crucifixion* surprisingly powerful. She considered the emotional impact of the work appropriate to the subject, displaying "an intensity of pathos touched with horror." Noting the unusual iconography of the strongly illumined canvas, she praised the technical accomplishment of the daylit scene, which she felt also added "the very spirit of desolation and abandonment" to the subject. "With its aid one receives an impression that is very characteristic of the sentiment that is to be aimed at in such a work." She concluded, "I can only speak for myself, when I say that after seeing a hundred crucifixions from modern hands this one seemed to me not only a quite original but a most impressive and haunted work."[68] Van Rensselaer also praised the painting in more or less the same tone for the *New York World*, writing that Eakins "succeeded in giving the main features of the idea with distinctness and no little degree of impressive pathos. These ideas are those of sacrifice, desolation, abandonment and the thrice pathetic accomplishment of an unrighteous deed."[69]

Despite Van Rensselaer's suggestion that Eakins invested *Crucifixion* with religious feeling, most of the negative reviews argued that it appeared absent from Eakins's modern interpretation of the subject. As a result, some of the painting's harshest critics focused not on the artistic merits of the piece but rather on the appropriateness of Eakins's iconographic intervention. The critic for the *Art Journal*, for example, considered the work a "nineteenth century treatment" of an old theme and suggested that "in an age tending so strongly toward realism, there are subjects which should be left untouched."[70] Another felt that "the mere presentation of a human body suspended from a cross and dying a slow death under an Eastern sun cannot do anybody any good, nor awaken thoughts that elevate the mind."[71] The notion that a realist treatment of the subject effectively divorced the painting from any and all religious feeling had parallels with the type of criticism that Bonnat had faced with *Le Christ*. Eakins's *Crucifixion* shocked because of its religious implications, which again suggests that he did not have a Catholic audience in mind.

The critic William J. Clark wrote at length about *Crucifixion*, directly addressing its religious content. Coming from a close friend of the artist, Clark's interpretation no doubt reflects Eakins's own and is worth quoting at length:

> Whether or not Mr. Eakins' painting is to be approved . . . would appear to depend on whether the spectator has ever conceived or is willing to conceive of the crucifixion as an event which actually occurred under certain understood conditions. Certainly, if that event meant all that Christendom believes and has for centuries believed it to mean, it would seem that, if it is to be represented at all, the most realistic treatment ought to be the most impressive. It is undoubtedly the case, however, that many who believe themselves good Christians fail altogether to appreciate their religion or the events upon which it is based as realistic: and to such, a picture like this has no message to deliver.[72]

Clark believed that Eakins's painting had a "message to deliver" and that its realism did not dispense with religious feeling, but rather added to it.

Eakins's "realistic treatment" was "impressive," even to those who hated the piece. The audacity of the subject, so French in its conception and entirely unique to the realm of American art, garnered Eakins the success for which he had hoped. In the face of some strong criticism, Eakins continued to send *Crucifixion* to major exhibition venues throughout his career. In the years prior to his dismissal from the Academy, the painting traveled from New York to Chicago and then on to Philadelphia, Detroit, and New Orleans.[73] Unfortunately, as the painting toured the country, provoking comment in every city, Eakins's status as an artist again shifted. In the summer of 1886, when Eakins sent the painting to the Southern Exposition in Louisville, Kentucky, his career had been derailed by his dismissal from the Pennsylvania Academy earlier that year.

The Martyrdom of Thomas Eakins

When Eakins sent *Crucifixion* to Louisville, in the painting's first exhibition following his resignation from the Academy, it was submitted under the title *Ecce Homo*.[74] The title change is unusual, for the iconography of the *Ecce Homo* differs significantly from that of the Crucifixion. The subject of the *Ecce Homo* derives from the Gospel of John, wherein Pontius Pilate presents Christ to the people, adorned with the mock trappings of kingship. Pilate announces Christ by saying "Ecce Homo," or "Behold the Man," and the people then call out for his execution. Artists depicting the *Ecce Homo* typically chose to render the scene in two ways: either as a devotional image, usually showing at half-length the scourged body of Christ, or as a narrative subject illustrating the scene as it is described in John. In Louisville, Eakins's new title not only reinforced the corporeal presence of the subject but also pointedly alluded to the injustice of Christ's execution at the hands of an unruly mob, a situation that he may have believed, perhaps even unconsciously, paralleled his own.

On February 9, 1886, Eakins tendered his resignation from the position of director of the schools to Edward H. Coates, chairman of the Committee on Instruction at the request of the directors of the Pennsylvania Academy. In spite of the gravity of such a request, the records of the Academy are notably silent regarding this affair. The circumstances of Eakins's firing can be pieced together only from the numerous letters that the artist wrote in the wake of his dismissal. The Academy's drastic action, ostensibly precipitated by Eakins's removal of a loincloth from a male model in a classroom that included female students, actually began with a group of disgruntled students, some quite close to Eakins, who initiated a whisper campaign against him.[75]

The Academy's sudden decision left Eakins understandably stunned and anguished. Although his own actions surely contributed to his downfall, Eakins had no warning about the closed-door meeting of the directors that decided his fate. He railed against the secrecy of these proceedings, writing that "if anything suspicious appeared [to the Academy directors], they should have told me just what it was, and have asked of me the explanation. The whole conspiracy against me was so secret that I could only guess at my accusers and of what they might have accused me, nor would any one enlighten me. The subsequent action of the Directors was to my mind cowardly[,] cruel[,] and dishonorable."[76]

Over the course of the month of February, Eakins began to "see many things clearer now than I did when in my first surprise I was stabbed from I knew not where." He gradually realized that among the small group of students who inflicted the most damage were his brother-in-law Frank Stephens and Thomas Anshutz, one of Eakins's closest assistants. Eakins accused those involved in the campaign for his removal of acting in "a petty conspiracy in which there was more folly than malice, weak ambitions and foolish hopes, and the actors in it are I think already coming to a sense of their shame." Indeed, it appears that Anshutz had acted out of his own self-interest and eventually succeeded to Eakins's former position at the Academy. But Stephens had acted not out of "folly" but with "malice" and continued to slander Eakins in the coming months.[77]

Stephens and his cohort followed their success at the Academy with an effort to strip Eakins of his honorary membership at the Philadelphia Sketch Club. In March, Eakins defended himself in the Sketch Club against what he considered "an organized movement to do me mischief."[78] By this time, Eakins had steeled himself for a fight and demanded to know the charges against him. Yet into April he complained that he had "in vain endeavored to get a proper presentation of these charges, but from the character of the correspondence with the committee, from rumor, and from the irregular, secret action instigated by the same party in another club, I easily conclude the whole affair to be a dastardly attempt to injure me, and to use the club as a cat's paw to further the injury."[79]

Eakins remained deeply embroiled in the scandal in June, when he gave Charles M. Kurtz, director of the art department, a list of the paintings he hoped to send to the Louisville exposition.[80] A few weeks prior, Eakins complained in a letter to his sister Frances of "being cut deliberately on the street by those who have had every occasion to know me" and hoped that "the affadavit my father signed today & Billy's [Frances's husband, William Crowell] letter with his & your affadavit will do much good as undoing some of Frank's harm."[81] Eakins made the decision to send *Crucifixion* to Louisville in the midst of a struggle to combat his accusers and rescue his reputation.

Following his dismissal from the Academy and his expulsion from the Sketch Club, Eakins may have viewed the subject of his painting in a different light. In the midst of his own public humiliation, Eakins changed the title of *Crucifixion* to *Ecce Homo.* Apart from his overwhelming sense of the injustice of his situation, Jesus's story offered other parallels in keeping with his own religious and professional sensibilities. The humanization of Jesus led to an increasing focus on his acts. As a result, nineteenth-century writers often acknowledged Jesus's role as a teacher. Yet as a teacher he directly challenged orthodox religion, which ultimately led to calls for his execution. Eakins could have identified with this behavior and its consequences—just as Jesus's unconventional beliefs led to his death, Eakins's own unconventional teaching methods led to his downfall. In addition, Eakins felt bitterly betrayed by those whom he most trusted. Eakins's students were *his* disciples. The idea that his students would unjustly expose his reputation to a mob deeply pained him.[82]

Eakins's personal anguish may have influenced his decision to exhibit *Crucifixion* in Philadelphia in February 1887, almost a year to the day after his forced departure from the Academy. Here again the painting could have taken on poignant significance for Eakins, as he chose not only to bring the painting back to Philadelphia but also to show it at the Pennsylvania Academy in the inaugural reception of the Philadelphia Art Club. This newly founded organization had no official relationship with the Academy and no acrimonious history with the troubled artist. Eakins's great painting of Christian sacrifice hung on the Academy's walls but in an exhibition entirely separate from the institution that had shunned him. Eakins's Art Club showing was strong, drawing upon some of his best work of the past decade. He perhaps used the occasion to highlight his versatility, for he included a portrait (*Portrait of William D. Marks*), a watercolor genre subject (*Dancing Lesson/Negro Boy Dancing*), two sculptures (his *Knitting* and *Spinning* panels), and his largest history painting (*Crucifixion*).

Although Eakins's unorthodox methods led to the Academy scandal, he clearly felt persecuted. His later characterization of his own so-called honors as "misunderstanding, persecution & neglect" reflects his bitterness over what he perceived as a great injustice done to his career.[83] Although he never again showed the painting under the title *Ecce Homo*, in the context of the Academy scandal *Crucifixion*, his greatest history painting, the European-inspired masterpiece meant to crown his career, temporarily took on new meaning for the ruined artist.

Ironically, around this period, negative criticism of *Crucifixion* began to subside, to be replaced with greater acclaim. In 1889, William C. Brownell called *Crucifixion* Eakins's "masterpiece."[84] Shortly thereafter, Eakins sent the painting, along with two other works, to Paris for exhibition in the annual Salon. For reasons that remain obscure, the Salon of 1890 included only one painting by Eakins, *The Writing Master*. *Crucifixion* appears not to have been exhibited at all in France, but Eakins had high expectations for showing his work there, as he wrote to the secretary of the Treasury that he wanted to bring all of his paintings back into the country following their exhibition, "unless fortunately they be sold abroad."[85]

Undaunted, in the following years, Eakins sent *Crucifixion* primarily to international venues in the United States. In an exhibition of works by Philadelphia artists to be included in the Columbian Exposition of 1893, one critic noted the change in status of both Eakins as an artist and his painting *Crucifixion*, writing that, judging from Eakins's paintings "now being on the line," when in earlier years they had been rejected altogether, it appeared that "there had come from the good men of Philadelphia a change of heart."[86] *Crucifixion* was now considered to number among Eakins's "strongest" and "most ambitious" works.[87]

In part, one could ascribe the "change of heart" to the greater influence of French art during the decade between the painting's first appearance and the Columbian Exposition. This was certainly the case by 1902, when Sadakichi Hartmann used those aspects of the work that had so bothered critics in the 1880s—its "nineteenth century treatment" of the subject—to describe the painting's power. "[Eakins's] *Christ on the Cross*, a lean, loan figure set against a glaring sky—austere, uncouth, and diabolically realistic as it is—is a masterpiece of artistic anatomy, in the knowledge of which nobody approaches him in this country."[88]

Eakins continued to show *Crucifixion* until his death in 1916.[89] In 1900, Eakins sent the painting along with one of his most compelling male subjects, *The Thinker: Portrait of Mr. Louis N. Kenton,* (Figure 59) to the Carnegie Institute's Fifth Annual Exhibition in Pittsburgh. The compositional similarities witnessed in this pairing reinforce the humanity of Eakins's Jesus. Although the austere painting of Kenton reflects Eakins's late portrait style, the representation of a single male figure turned at an oblique angle to the viewer roughly parallels that seen in the *Crucifixion*. In both works, Eakins limited the settings, keeping the viewer focused on the figure. Kenton appears thoughtful, even intellectual, yet he came from a working-class background.[90] He married Eakins's sister-in-

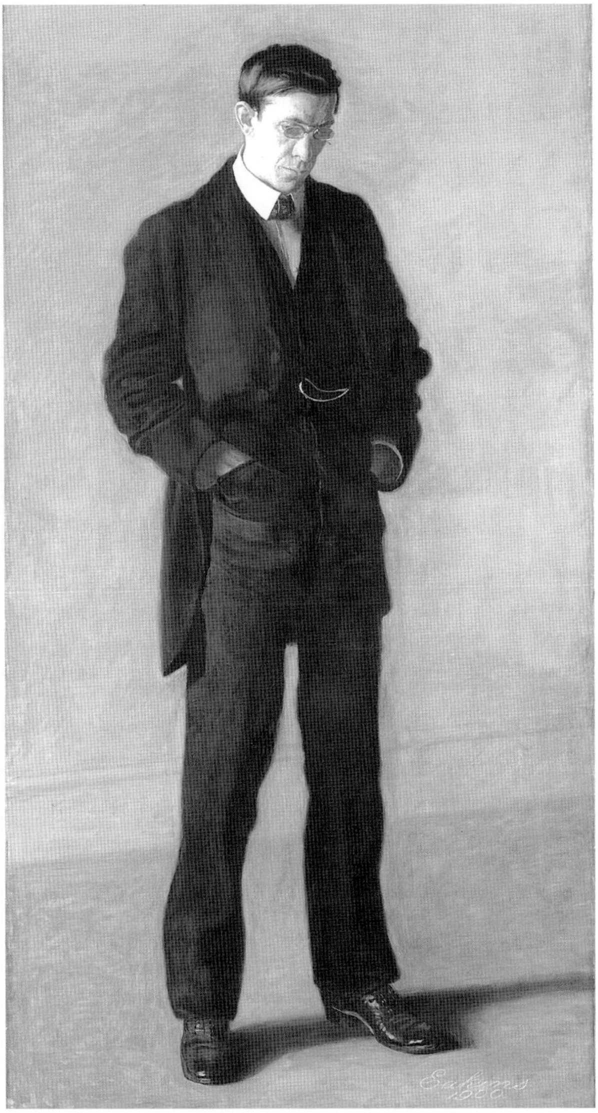

59. Thomas Eakins, *The Thinker: Portrait of Mr. Louis N. Kenton*, 1900. Oil on canvas, 82 × 42 in. The Metropolitan Museum of Art, John Stewart Kennedy Fund, 1917 (17.172).

law, Elizabeth Macdowell, and despite his contemplative appearance, his violent temper led to the dissolution of the marriage. In this deeply flawed individual Eakins did not so much suggest a comparison with Christ as offer the same intense scrutiny of character that he presented earlier in *Crucifixion.* Eakins's desire to draw forth Jesus's humanity lends *Crucifixion* the strength of his best portraits, even as it evades giving us a likeness.

Eakins made his ambitions for *Crucifixion* clear in a letter to John W. Beatty of the Carnegie Institute: "In all events I think I shall send my Crucifixion which is probably my best painting, and which I hope may be acquired by some public gallery."[91] This may have been Eakins goal all along, as he painted *Crucifixion* shortly after *In Grandmother's Time* entered the collection at Smith College in 1879. Given its powerful subject and impressive scale, it seems unlikely that the painting would have been purchased for a private collection. In April 1910, Eakins offered the painting to the Metropolitan Museum of Art. The museum declined.[92] After her husband's death, Susan Eakins faced similar difficulties in finding a home for the painting, but perhaps for entirely different reasons than those of 1882 when critics perceived the work as too realistic for a religious subject. By 1917, when it was shown in the Eakins Memorial Exhibition at the Metropolitan Museum of Art, the reviewer at the *New York Times* claimed that the painting had "nothing to say of modern feeling, but might have been painted by Courbet had the Master of Ornans been a master of anatomy."[93] Time had caught up with Eakins's picture, and viewers no longer found the religious implications of the work particularly controversial. *Crucifixion* had become an example of Eakins's realist devotion to anatomical study rather than a provocative image of a "materialistic Savior." In 1929, the Philadelphia Museum of Art finally accepted Susan's offer of *Crucifixion* as part of a larger gift of Eakins's work.[94]

CHAPTER FIVE

Collaboration and Commemoration in Public Sculpture

Although Eakins is usually thought of as a painter, he placed relief sculpture at the pinnacle of artistic achievement. From the start, sculpture held a prominent place in his explorations of historical subject matter.[1] In his painting of William Rush he celebrated a sculptor as the model for his own self-definition as an artist. In *Crucifixion* he heightened the sculptural qualities of the figure to further his interpretation of a human Jesus. In the 1880s he concluded his colonial revival series with the *Knitting* and *Spinning* reliefs and completed the three Arcadian panels that signaled his interest in classical art. Those who know of his sculpture typically think of these small reliefs, yet Eakins also produced two large-scale Beaux-Arts monuments in the 1890s and quietly continued to assist his protégé, Samuel Murray (1869–1941), with his own public sculpture projects into the twentieth century. In these monumental works Eakins hoped to emulate his artistic heroes—William Rush and Phidias—by producing enduring public sculptures. Unfortunately, complications with these commissions led to disappointment.

Eakins entered the arena of public sculpture through his friendship with New York sculptor William Rudolf O'Donovan (1844–1920). Instead of retiring into obscurity after he had been dismissed from the Pennsylvania Academy and ostracized from Philadelphia's principal art organizations, Eakins collaborated with O'Donovan on the largest Civil War monument of the period: the Brooklyn Soldiers and Sailors Memorial Arch (Figure 60), a grand triumphal arch prominently situated outside the grounds of the newly created Prospect Park.[2] Simultaneously, the pair undertook another sculptural commission for the

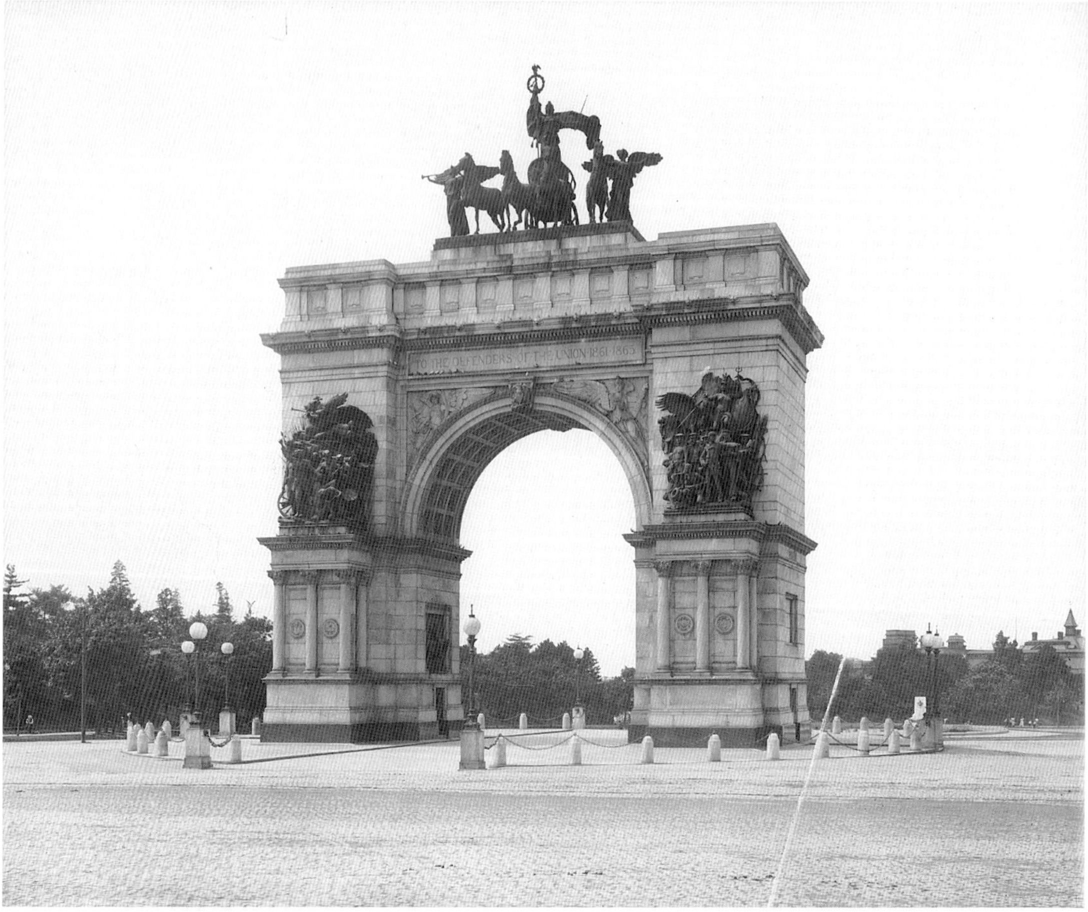

60. John H. Duncan, William R. O'Donovan, and Thomas Eakins, *Soldiers and Sailors Memorial Arch*, Brooklyn, New York. Smithsonian American Art Museum, Photograph Archives S0001596.

Trenton Battle Monument (Figure 61) in New Jersey, erected to commemorate events of the Revolutionary period.[3] In these two monuments Eakins finally had an opportunity to pursue his interest in sculpture on a large scale. Although the sculptures lack the artistic appeal of some his paintings, the shift to public sculpture was perhaps the most difficult and ambitious move of his career. These sculptural projects would dominate his artistic output for more than three years.[4]

Significantly, both of these projects brought Eakins back into the realm of American historical themes. Yet the public nature of these works forced Eakins to face the immediate consequences of their reception. The reliefs for the Brooklyn arch, though compositionally less complex than Eakins's work at Trenton, proved the more conceptually difficult of the two projects because in them the

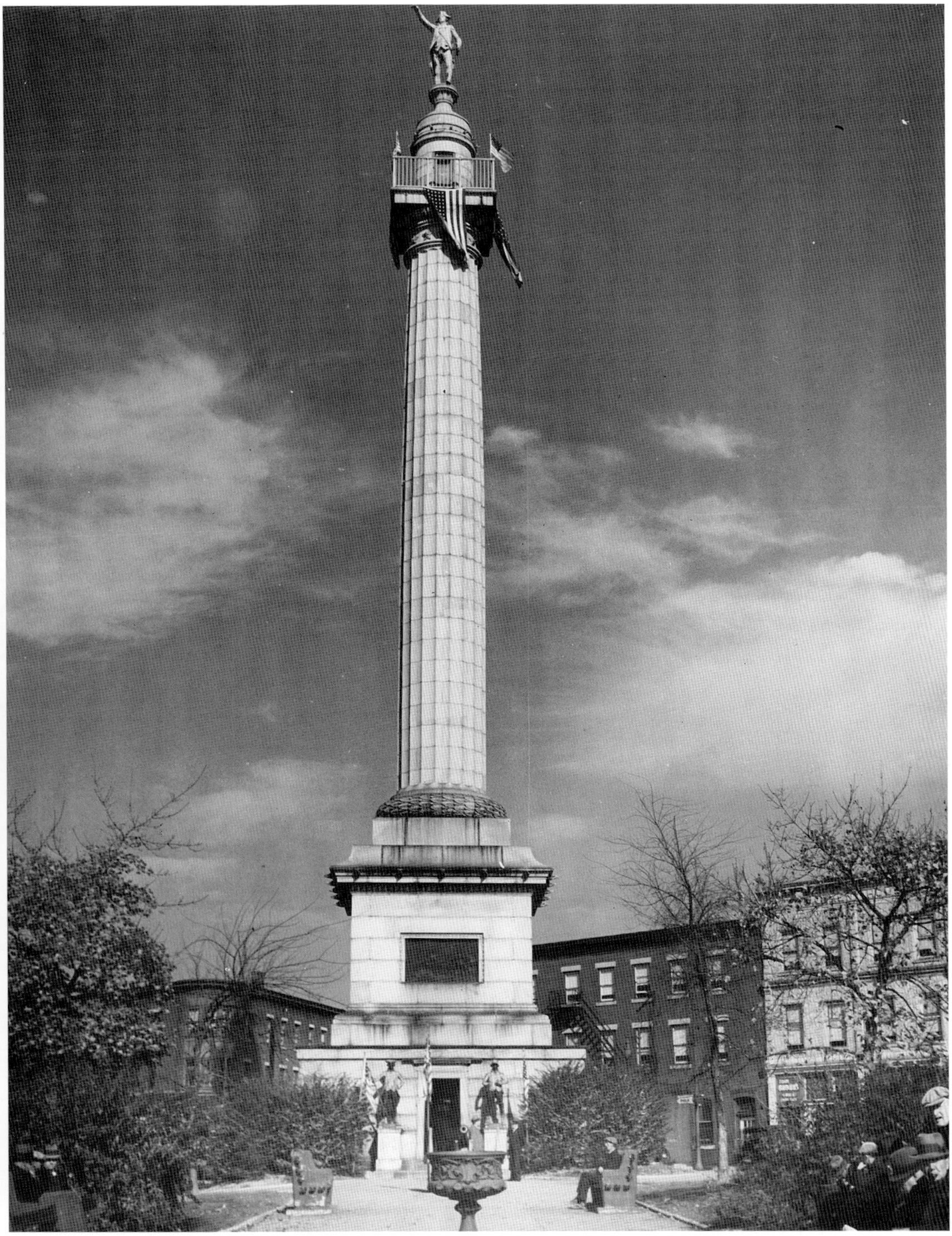

61. John H. Duncan, William R. O'Donovan, and Thomas Eakins, *Trenton Battle Monument*, Trenton, New Jersey. Smithsonian American Art Museum, Photograph Archives S0001831.

artists had to address relatively recent historical events. For the arch, the sculptors ran into problems both in creating the aura of authenticity and in satisfying the public demand for hero worship. The Trenton panels did not face such scrutiny. Despite the general satisfaction with these reliefs, Eakins received no further commissions for large-scale public monuments following their completion.

The presence of these two monuments in Eakins's oeuvre has always seemed a puzzling anomaly within his career. Why did he undertake these projects? And given his continuing involvement with sculpture through the work of his pupil Murray, why didn't he produce more on his own? As the following discussion makes clear, Eakins's failure to produce subsequent sculptural work had less to do with the lackluster public reception of the Brooklyn arch than with the artist's inability to satisfy O'Donovan's network of patrons in New York.[5]

Eakins and Sculpture

As a student in Paris, Eakins's first encounter with sculpture did not bode well for his future interest in the medium. Although he found the marble sculptures in the Louvre "much better than the miserable imitations at Philadelphia," they still made him "shiver." He left the sculpture galleries almost immediately, preferring to view the pictures.[6] Yet as Eakins began his training at the Ecole des Beaux-Arts he grew to understand the value that sculpture held for a young painter. Although he disliked studying from casts, he listed the Ecole's collection of "casts from all the good antique and many modern statues" among a description of "the advantages of the Imperial School."[7]

In March 1868 he decided to undertake the study of sculpture in order to improve his painting and entered the atelier of the sculptor Augustin-Alexandre Dumont, the author of numerous public monuments. As he explained to his father, "I am going to model in clay every once in a while. I think I will thus learn faster. When I am tired of painting I will go to the class and be fresh and I will see more models."[8] Months later, Eakins found that his hard work had indeed helped him to "construct my men more solid, springy & strong."[9] Although he did not stay long in Dumont's studio, Eakins continued to use sculpture to aid his painting while living abroad. In April 1869, for example, he bought several casts for his studio, and an August 1869 list of expenses includes the purchase of a cast of Houdon's "Cold Girl" and "modeling wax and tools."[10]

Eakins's technical interest in sculpture as a tool for studying three-dimensional form further cultivated his appreciation of the medium as an art. Following his training with Dumont, Eakins began to express admiration for Phidias and for Greek sculpture generally. Phidias had risen so high in his estimation that when he praised the French painter Thomas Couture (1815–79), Eakins referred to him as "the Phidias of painting & drawing."[11] He also took notice of the work of Jean-Baptiste Carpeaux and sent a photograph of his sculpture *The Dance* (1869), done for the Paris Opera, home to his father. Eakins declared that Carpeaux probably modeled "better than anyone in the world" and took pride in the fact that Carpeaux had also attended the Ecole.[12] This appreciation near the end of his stay in Paris contrasts sharply with his first appraisal of sculpture in France and reflects how strongly the Ecole's training influenced Eakins.

When Eakins returned to the United States, he integrated the use of sculpture into his painting practice. For several important paintings of the 1870s and 1880s Eakins turned to sculptural models to work out compositional difficulties and to solidify his figures.[13] He also advocated the use of sculpture in his teaching, urging any Pennsylvania Academy student who lost "sight of the solidity, weight, and roundness of the figure" to spend time "across the hall" in "the modeling-room."[14] Indeed, he believed that "if you do good modeling it follows that you will do good painting."[15] To aid his students he also made a set of anatomical models and would often "assist and advise the students in the making of plaster casts from life."[16] In addition to these sculpted studies and teaching tools, Eakins began to explore the possibilities of independent relief sculpture at the height of his teaching career.[17]

Eakins found the *Knitting* and *Spinning* panels, commissioned by the architect Theophilus Chandler for James P. Scott's residence, "much to my taste." Intended to adorn a fireplace in Scott's Walnut Street home, the panels provided Eakins with his first opportunity to work in relief. He invested the project with an importance that probably surprised his patron, who rejected the panels. Eakins's justification of his work to Scott expanded into a defense of his craft and of the medium. After elaborating on his training, credentials, and the extent of his labor, Eakins asserted that "relief work too has always been considered the most difficult composition and the one requiring the most learning. The mere geometrical construction of the accessories in a perspective which is not projected on a single plane but in a variable third dimension is a puzzle beyond the sculptors whom I know."[18] Still advocating for the panels a month later, Eakins compared his own work with that of Phidias. In order to make the case for the sculptures and to explain the complexities of his efforts, Eakins invited Scott to "stop at the Academy of Fine Arts" to "examine there casts of the most celebrated reliefs in the world, those of the frieze of the Parthenon."[19]

Eakins's comparison to Phidias's Parthenon frieze is unusual given the simplicity of his small, single-figure subjects and their intended use as decoration in the interior of a wealthy man's home. But the comparison suggests the elevated status that Eakins granted to sculpture in the 1880s. Eakins was not merely boasting of his own skills but acknowledging his respect for Phidias's work, writing, "No one has ever yet equaled in finish the modelling of those frieze surfaces."[20] Relief sculpture fascinated Eakins because of the intellectual challenges it posed, involving keen mathematical skills to "keep inside" of its limits.[21] "Relief," he argued, "holds a place between a painting or a drawing on a flat surface and a piece of full sculpture."[22] The difficulty arose in applying the principles of painting to a three-dimensional surface, and he warned that "if you make the least error in a relief it won't look right."[23]

Shortly after his work on the panels for Scott, Eakins began to codify his beliefs about relief sculpture and perspective, writing them down in an unpublished manuscript. Essentially based on his teaching practices, Eakins's manuscript offered his readers detailed rules for working in relief, which he punctuated with occasional aphorisms, such as "the best examples of relief sculpture are the ancient Greek." In contrast, he complained that "modern sculptors do not generally understand the beauty of relief & I have often seen an ear in a profile head as deep as the rest of the head."[24] Eakins offered his manuscript as a corrective and illustrated his text with copious examples. It seems likely that Eakins hoped to publish his manuscript, but circumstances never permitted this to happen.[25]

Within the manuscript Eakins continued to explore art historical precedents by considering the merits and disadvantages of the Italian Renaissance master Lorenzo Ghiberti's method as compared with that of Phidias. While Eakins believed that the Greeks produced "the best examples of relief sculpture," he understood that Ghiberti's panels for the Baptistry doors of Florence Cathedral addressed a more complicated problem than that of the Parthenon frieze. For the Baptistry doors, Ghiberti varied the depth of his relief in combination with the use of linear perspective to create the illusion of fully realized three-dimensional spaces. Eakins admired Ghiberti's solution of rendering "near figures which are of the greatest interest . . . in full or nearly full relief, and the distant parts" in "a very flat relief." But he cautioned that "a great disadvantage in such relief as Ghiberti's is that when viewed in the light most favorable for showing the form, the near figures throw shadows on the distant landscape and other parts."[26]

Although Eakins seems to have preferred the example of Phidias, Eakins never emulated the Greek sculptor's style in his own work. In the reliefs for the Trenton monument, one could even argue that he chose a Ghibertian solution to his complex multifigured compositions. In any case, the challenges of relief remained much on his mind, even after the disappointing rejection of *Knitting* and *Spinning*. In this period, Eakins said that he worked in relief "not on any order or hope of reward but merely to study & gain knowledge & strength; and so has my whole life gone in hard study."[27] For Eakins, sculpture had become the summa of the arts, the intellectual plain on which to exercise one's talent and critical beliefs. Within this context, William Rudolf O'Donovan's offer to work on two public sculpture projects must have seemed a tremendous proving ground to put all of Eakins's "knowledge" and "hard study" to work.

Eakins and O'Donovan

Eakins probably met William Rudolf O'Donovan in 1879. In April of that year the directors of the Pennsylvania Academy of the Fine Arts invited the Society of American Artists (SAA) to send their recent New York exhibition to Philadelphia. The SAA protested when the Academy decided to make changes to the show, notably by consigning Eakins's *Gross Clinic* to a corridor, while including a work by Thomas Moran that had been rejected for the SAA's New York show. In response, SAA president Walter Shirlaw wrote to the Academy threatening to withdraw the entire exhibition if changes were not made.[28] Six days later O'Donovan and William Merritt Chase visited Philadelphia as representatives of the SAA. In the end, the two organizations reached a compromise: *The Gross Clinic* would remain in place, but the Academy agreed to remove the Moran. Because Eakins was both at the center of the controversy and a fixture at the Academy, it seems likely that he met the gregarious O'Donovan at this time.

Although not well known today, O'Donovan achieved success as a sculptor in the last quarter of the nineteenth century due in no small part to his aggressive self-promotion. Born in Virginia, O'Donovan served in the Confederate army during the Civil War before establishing himself as a sculptor in New York. There O'Donovan proved especially skilled at cultivating influential friends who helped him gain entry into New York's arts establishment. Through his friendships with several important academicians, he became an associate of the National Academy of Design (NAD) in 1878, decades ahead of Eakins. He also took an interest in professional organizations, becoming an active member of the SAA and a founder of the Tile Club. On the merit of his work, he developed a solid reputation as a portraitist, which earned him several commissions for war memorials. Through his professional contacts, O'Donovan shrewdly managed to produce both Confederate and Union memorials in spite of his previous allegiance to the Southern cause.

O'Donovan's friendship with Maurice J. Power, the owner of the National Fine Art Foundry in New York, proved the most important professional association of his career. Aside from his ownership of the foundry, Power was a political operative with important connections within the Democratic Party.[29] An ally of Samuel J. Tilden and a holder of numerous political appointments, Power also headed the Democratic Party in New York's Sixteenth District. Power's political clout served him well as he negotiated contracts for public art commissions. He also "took an active interest in Celtic organizations," which may explain his patronage of fellow Irishman O'Donovan.[30]

Early in his career, O'Donovan approached Power about a project for a public monument of Irish leader Daniel O'Connell, fully cognizant of Power's political connections. He described Power's influence in a letter to his sister: "He has had several large contracts from the City Government for Soldiers Monuments . . . it would be a good idea to give him a chance to use his political friends still further in Art Enterprises! . . . I will try to get Powers to use his influence in this direction."[31] Thereafter, the two men formed a close working relationship, with O'Donovan moving his studio into Power's foundry.

Throughout the 1870s and 1880s, O'Donovan sculpted monuments cast by Power's firm. A third Irishman, the New York architect John Hemenway Duncan, joined Power and O'Donovan to work on the Tower of Victory Memorial in Newburgh, New York, in 1886.[32] The three men worked together again in 1888 on a monument to the Irish Brigade at Gettysburg. Eakins would subsequently collaborate with all three on the Brooklyn Soldiers and Sailors Memorial and on the Trenton Battle Monument.[33] As O'Donovan was the primary sculptor for both commissions, it was probably he who introduced Eakins to Duncan and Power. Eakins's Democratic leanings in this period, coupled with his Irish ancestry, probably aided his cause with Power and Duncan more than their belief in his artistic talent.

Photographs of Eakins and O'Donovan, taken in the former's Chestnut Street studio sometime in the 1890s, show the easy camaraderie between the two men (Figure 62). In these images, a smiling Eakins listens to a gesturing O'Donovan, with glasses of whiskey on the table between them. O'Donovan's bust of Winslow Homer, a gift from the sculptor to Eakins, also appears on the table. In the background sits a bust of their mutual friend, Walt Whitman: both O'Donovan and Eakins served as honorary pallbearers at Whitman's funeral in 1891. Although the candid warmth and intimacy of the image suggests a private moment, it later appeared as a publicity photograph in an article about the Brooklyn arch.[34]

In spite of their friendship, O'Donovan and Eakins were unlikely creative partners. O'Donovan demonstrated keen political skill throughout his career, while Eakins's independence and artistic ideals often put him at odds with his patrons as well as the cultural establishment. Eakins typically labored over his art, particularly his few commissions, in a meticulous effort to produce high-quality work. O'Donovan took a more expedient view of commissions.

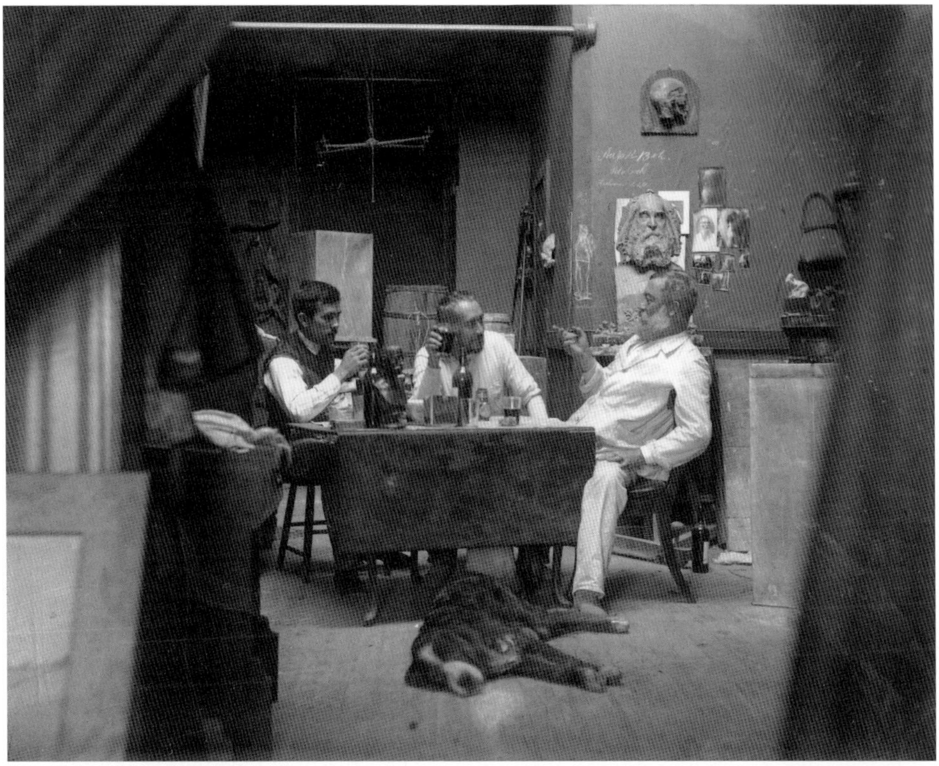

62. Susan Macdowell Eakins, *Samuel Murray, Thomas Eakins, and William R. O'Donovan in Chestnut Street Studio*, 1891–92. Dry-plate glass negative, 4 × 5 in. Courtesy of the Pennsylvania Academy of the Fine Arts, Philadelphia. Charles Bregler's Thomas Eakins Collection. Purchased with the partial support of the Pew Memorial Trust.

Although his portraits attest to his talent as an artist, he could also churn out banal, derivative pieces if necessary. Quality aside, O'Donovan met deadlines and generally satisfied his patrons' expectations in ways totally foreign to Eakins.

The two also differed in their training. While Eakins acknowledged his debt to his teachers at the Ecole des Beaux-Arts, O'Donovan exploited an age-old theme in artistic biography in the false claim that he was self-taught. In fact, he possessed an artistic pedigree more common to American sculptors of the previous generation: after an apprenticeship with a stonecutter in his youth, he then trained in New York with the sculptor James Wilson MacDonald. Newspaper accounts mention O'Donovan's intentions to travel to Europe on several occasions, but it seems that he never actually went. Given O'Donovan's skill at self-promotion, it remains possible that he never had any intention of traveling abroad but used these newspaper reports as a means of credentialing himself as a cosmopolitan artist.[35] Eakins and he may have gotten along well personally, but in many ways they followed opposite professional paths.

Despite such differences, the two men espoused similar concerns regarding authenticity in historical representations. While Eakins had often introduced anachronistic details in his own historical subjects, his identification with realism and empirical observation lent an aura of authenticity to his work, particularly in contrast to the countless idealized allegories produced by other Beaux-Arts-trained sculptors. Similarly, O'Donovan cultivated a reputation for accurate likenesses in his public sculpture and became especially well known for his depictions of historical figures, including George Washington. O'Donovan established this reputation, in part, by challenging critics and competitors over issues of historical accuracy. In one instance, O'Donovan used the pages of the *New York Post* to launch a heated and public debate with Benson Lossing, a historian of the American Revolution, regarding the authenticity of the Washington life mask in the possession of his mentor MacDonald. O'Donovan not only questioned Lossing's expertise but publicly reinforced his self-proclaimed status as an expert on matters related to the Revolutionary era and on Washington in particular.[36]

Despite undertaking several major public commissions throughout the Gilded Age, O'Donovan never attempted the allegorical female figures popularized by Augustus St. Gaudens and his contemporaries. In fact, he sought to distance his work from that of his successful Beaux-Arts-trained peers. In a series of letters to the *New York Tribune*, O'Donovan attacked the critic Clarence Cook over his assertion that O'Donovan had received preferential treatment at St. Gaudens's expense at the NAD's 1877 Annual.[37] The ensuing debate eventually degenerated into an attack by O'Donovan on the "art for art's sake" ideals preferred by Cook over his own realistic methods. O'Donovan clarified his position in an 1878 article in the *Art Journal* when he criticized Frédéric Bartholdi's *Liberty Enlightening the World* (*The Statue of Liberty*) for being an "exotic" allegory and "not an outcome of our civilization." As he explained, "[Americans] do not think in allegories as the ancients did."[38] Through such public statements, O'Donovan suggested that life study and historical authenticity were hallmarks of a distinctly American art.

By the time O'Donovan invited Eakins to work on the two monuments, the painter had slowly recovered from his dismissal from the Academy and the general rejection by the Philadelphia arts community. He achieved this, in part, by directing his energies beyond Philadelphia and by reestablishing his ties to New York, where he continued to hold a faculty position at the Women's Art School of the Cooper Union from 1887 until 1897 and regularly lectured on artistic anatomy at the NAD from 1888 to 1895. By 1891 he had resumed an aggressive exhibition schedule, showing more of his work than he had in the years immediately following the Academy scandal. By adding public sculpture to his list of professional accomplishments, Eakins sought to prove himself to his peers.

The Brooklyn Arch

In 1887 the state of New York authorized the creation of a memorial in Brooklyn dedicated to the soldiers and sailors who fought for the Union during the Civil War. The Brooklyn Common Council accepted a proposal for a ninety-foot-high shaft adorned with allegorical figures by the German American sculptor Henry Baerer. However, Alfred Chapin, Brooklyn's Democratic mayor, objected to the design, claiming that he found it too conventional.[39] At his insistence the council held a second competition during the summer of 1888, this time calling for a "memorial arch." Most of the thirty-odd submissions were either Gothic or Romanesque in style.[40] An exception was John Hemenway Duncan's winning design, which proposed a Roman-inspired arch, ornamented with relief and freestanding sculptures, similar to the *Arc de Triomphe* in Paris. The popular Parisian design also served as the basis for architect Stanford White's nearly contemporary Washington Square Arch in Greenwich Village.[41]

General William Tecumseh Sherman laid the cornerstone of the arch in an elaborate ceremony on October 30, 1889. With the construction of the monument underway, attention shifted to the sculptural program. Duncan saw to it that the commission went to his friend William Rudolf O'Donovan, who in 1891 was asked to create two life-size bronze equestrian reliefs: one of Abraham Lincoln (Figure 63), the other of General Ulysses S. Grant (Figure 64). For the Brooklyn project, O'Donovan said that he aspired to "show in these two statues real men on real horses." He asked his "old friend" Thomas Eakins to collaborate with him because he wanted a fellow artist "who possessed such expert knowledge of the horse's anatomy as would render impossible any error in the modeling." In that regard, Eakins's years of anatomical study made him extremely well qualified.[42]

An 1895 article by Cleveland Moffett for *McClure's Magazine* documents the collaboration between Eakins and O'Donovan in great detail. Appearing just months before the unveiling of the bronzes on the arch, the article features several illustrations of the two artists working, including the image of Eakins and O'Donovan socializing in the Chestnut Street studio. The well-connected Power probably orchestrated the piece as a promotional tool. This use of the press was entirely new to Eakins. The article explains the sculptors' working

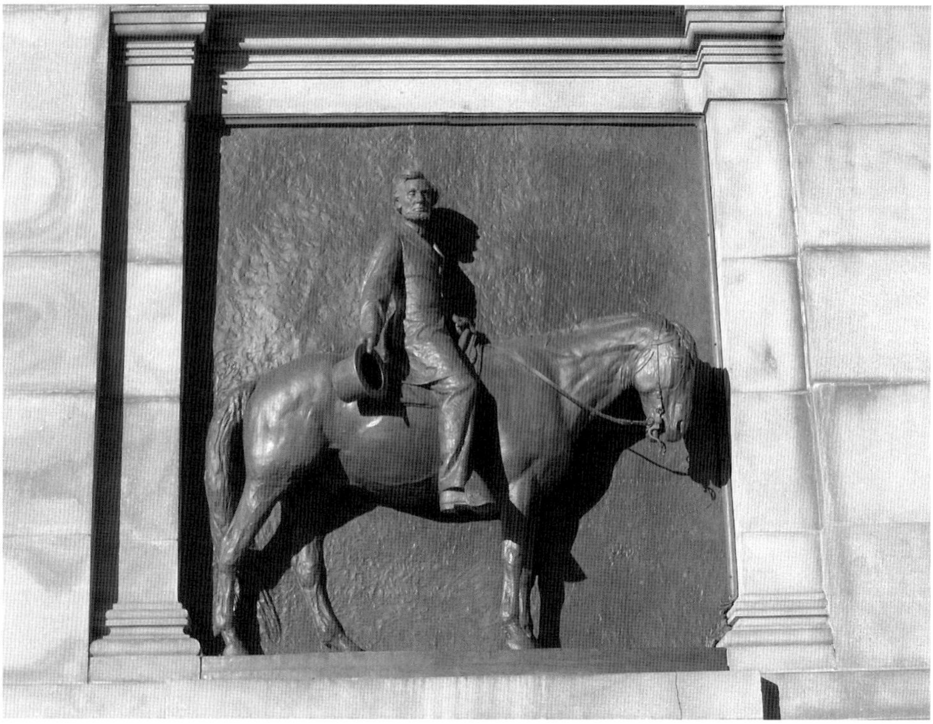

63. Thomas Eakins and William R. O'Donovan, *Abraham Lincoln on Horseback, Soldiers and Sailors Memorial Arch*, Brooklyn, New York. Courtesy of Margaret Stenz.

methods in exacting detail, making it the most explicit description of Eakins's practices as a sculptor published during his lifetime.

Moffett's article outlines a clear division of labor for the project: Eakins created the horses while O'Donovan sculpted the likenesses of the men. Yet it also maintains that the two artists collaborated on all matters, particularly those relating to the historical authenticity of the work. Eakins and O'Donovan reportedly decided against the standard method of "presenting a composite horse, patched together from fragments of many horses, taking the best points of each and avoiding the defects."[43] Instead, they embarked on a search for two horses possessing all of the qualities that they desired. In effect, the artists sought a living ideal for each of the horses, not as a matter of anatomical interest, but in order to render them as historical figures appropriate to the dignity and temperaments of their riders.

As the late president "never cared for a showy charger," Eakins modeled Lincoln's horse on his own "cowboy horse," Billy, whom he had brought back to Philadelphia following an 1887 trip to the Dakota Territory.[44] Grant, who had been particular about his horses, posed more of a problem. His statue called for

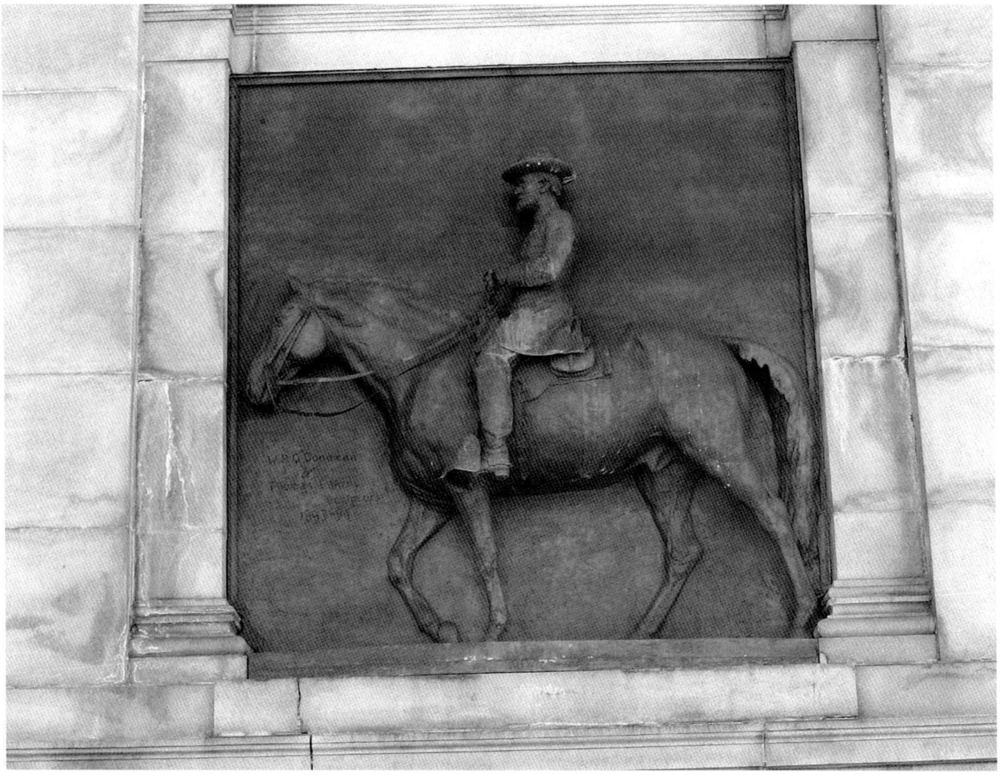

64. Thomas Eakins and William R. O'Donovan, *Ulysses S. Grant on Horseback, Soldiers and Sailors Memorial Arch*, Brooklyn, New York. Courtesy of Margaret Stenz.

"a charger of ideal proportions, a creature of great strength and race, a splendid animal fit to carry a great commander into battle."[45] The search for an appropriate horse took the artists to West Point, where Eakins made instantaneous studies of cavalrymen on horseback, but they were unable to find an acceptable horse for the general. The artists continued the search for another two months, visiting circuses and horse shows as well as examining horses at Newport and Long Branch. In the end they selected "'Clinker,' a saddle horse owned by Alexander J. Cassatt, of Philadelphia."[46]

Working at his sister Frances's farm in Avondale, Pennsylvania, Eakins began the painfully slow process of sculpting the horses. Although Eakins's "expert knowledge of the horse's anatomy" surely informed his work, he did not generalize the figures by relying upon it. Instead, he worked extensively with his equine models to capture the unique details of their appearances, creating portrait likenesses of each.

Given Eakins's preoccupation with Greek sculpture, especially throughout his work on the Arcadian series, it is not surprising that he became wholly absorbed in the creation of these life-size horses. Much as he had with *Crucifixion*, Eakins contended with an age-old art historical tradition in his equine figures for the Brooklyn arch. That the bronzes specifically reflect Eakins's admiration for Phidias's cavalry frieze for the Parthenon is suggested by two oil sketches that he made of Phidias at work on the frieze.[47] In these paintings Eakins depicted the Greek sculptor working outdoors from live horses, a method he found reflected in the writings of Horace Lecoq de Boisbaudran but which he believed had its origins in ancient Greek art. According to his student Adam Emory Albright, the Parthenon frieze stood for Eakins as "one shining example of absolute correctness" in the rendering of the horse, "which gave rise to a speculation by Eakins that Phidias might have dissected horses and made little jointed and movable models from his findings."[48] Eakins posed for photographs (two of which appear in Moffett's article) showing him working on the Brooklyn horses outdoors, standing in nearly the same pose that Phidias assumes in the oil sketches. In these photographs (Figure 65) Eakins literally stands in the place of his artistic hero, a theme he would repeat in his reprisal of the William Rush subject in 1908.

Deeply invested in noble artistic ideals, Eakins lavished attention on the bronzes. He began by making wax models in the field, a technique that he adapted from his painting method. He had used wax models to aid with several of his more complex compositions, notably in *William Rush Carving His Allegorical Figure of the Schuylkill River* and *A May Morning in the Park*. At this early stage, Eakins "studied every step and movement" as Billy and Clinker were ridden around the farm, "making in wax now and then some quick correction with his thumb"—a step that followed his notion of Phidias's use of "moveable models" for the Parthenon frieze.[49] A roughly modeled one-sixteenth scale wax version of Clinker in the Hirshhorn Museum and Sculpture Garden shows the horse in essentially the same pose he would assume in the monument. As was often the case with his paintings, it appears that Eakins settled on the final composition in this sketching phase. Also following his painting practice, Eakins squared the study at three-fourth-inch intervals so that it could be enlarged to a quarter-size clay model, which he "finished, also in the field, and cast into permanent plaster form."[50]

The conditions of the commission stipulated that Eakins and O'Donovan submit the quarter-size models to the Brooklyn committee for their acceptance before proceeding with the final life-size figures.[51] Eakins added greater detail to the figure at this stage. The surviving quarter-size plaster relief of Clinker reflects the final work as completely as possible. In this version, Clinker's face and muscular structure are fully realized, and a saddle has been added to his back. Eakins also fitted his clay horse with a nude male rider, which he subse-

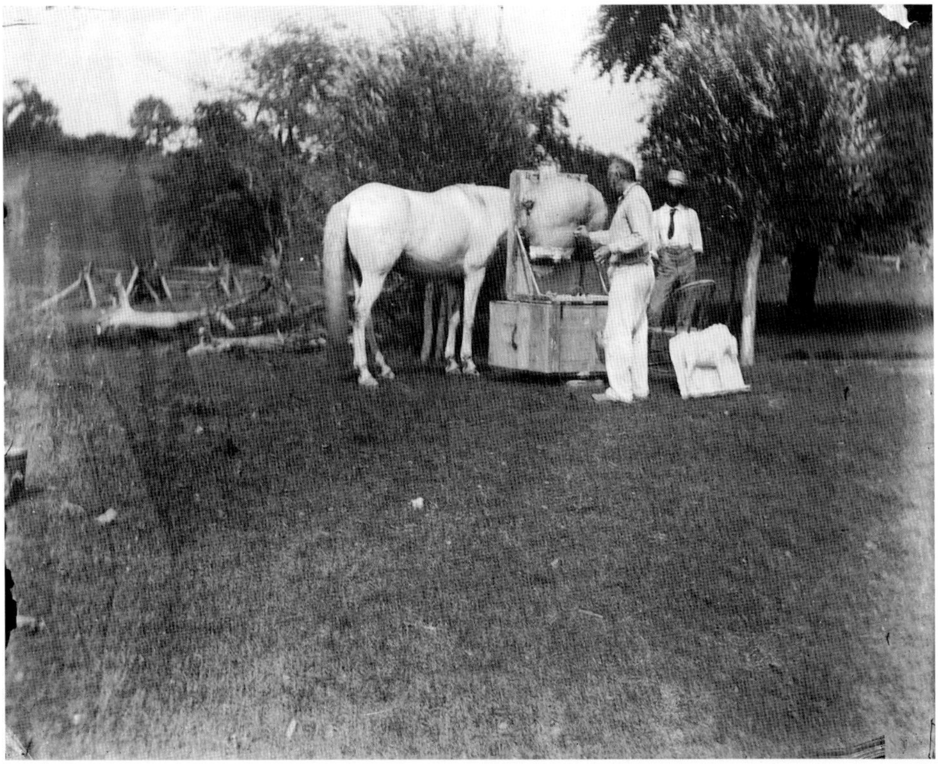

65. Circle of Thomas Eakins, *Thomas Eakins at Right, Modeling the Horse Billy at Avondale, Pennsylvania*, 1891–92. Albumen print, 3³⁄₁₆ × 4³⁄₁₆ in. Courtesy of the Pennsylvania Academy of the Fine Arts, Philadelphia. Charles Bregler's Thomas Eakins Collection. Purchased with the partial support of the Pew Memorial Trust.

quently removed. Ghostly traces of the figure remain in the plaster on the saddle and in the background just above it. Once all of the details had been resolved, Eakins then squared the quarter-size model for transfer to the life-size version.

Eakins's method was painstaking. He made the cast for the full-size sculpture in ten separate pieces, "constructed of wood . . . and covered with wire netting . . . [and] over this core the sculptor spread his clay an inch deep."[52] Following this, the modeling of the horses began for the third and final time, with Eakins again referring directly to the living horses in the field for accuracy. Photographs accompanying Moffett's article show both O'Donovan and Eakins at work in Avondale, suggesting that O'Donovan knew the extent of Eakins's meticulous working methods. Working a section at a time, Eakins "would copy in clay every curve and muscle and vein of that part of the horse."[53] He then cast each clay model in plaster and carefully fitted the pieces together to create the entire horse.[54]

Moffett's article implies that the production of the bronzes proceeded smoothly and collegially. It did not. Although the often troubled Eakins worked well in collaboration with O'Donovan, he found himself unable to adapt his artistic method to the exigencies of a public commission. The political consequences of his failure to meet deadlines led to an inevitable conflict with Duncan, and Power, who became tremendously frustrated with Eakins when he single-mindedly began work on the life-size versions of the horses prior to the acceptance of the quarter-size model by the Brooklyn committee. By this time, the two men had also engaged Eakins to prepare three relief panels for the Trenton Battle Monument. Although the Brooklyn commission came first, the timetable for the Trenton monument made it a priority. According to Moffett, Eakins finished the life-size model of Clinker in April 1892 and sent it to O'Donovan in New York to fit with his rider. As Eakins continued working on the other horse into September 1893, Power sent Eakins an angry letter rebuking him for his unwillingness to switch his attention from the Brooklyn horses to the Trenton reliefs. Eakins's rift with Duncan and Power had the unfortunate consequence of permanently foreclosing any future collaboration with O'Donovan.

The Trenton Battle Monument

The records regarding the commission for the Trenton Battle Monument present a vivid picture of the political maneuverings of Maurice Power and John Hemenway Duncan. In March 1891 the Trenton Battle Monument Association solicited Duncan's advice in evaluating three proposals for a monument commemorating Washington's celebrated victory at Trenton. The association received two of the proposals favorably, each of which called for Roman-inspired columns. In criticizing the two plans, Duncan dismissed "one as impractical for sculpture and the other suited only as a mortuary shaft."[55] Having eliminating his competition, Duncan was invited by the association to "prepare a plan himself, embodying the best parts of the 2 plans."[56] While Duncan offered his "advice" to the design committee, Power praised Duncan's work to General William S. Stryker, president of the Monument Association.[57] Shortly thereafter, the association hired Duncan as the architect for the monument.

Emulating the designs of his competitors, Duncan also modeled his proposal upon Roman victory columns. In its final form, the monument called for several reliefs as well as freestanding figures, including a statue of George Washington crowning the top of the column. Once Duncan had secured the commission, he quickly demanded control over the sculpture, writing to the Monument Association, "I would not be willing to have my name associated with any structure that I could not have a voice in selecting the artist."[58] For the next several months Duncan consulted with sculptors and foundries, including Power and O'Donovan. As he had done with the architect's proposals, Duncan found ways of eliminating all of Power and O'Donovan's competition. The sculptor Frank Edwin Elwell, for example, was "too expensive." He described Bureau Brothers' Gettysburg Monument as "inferior work," accepted only because of the dedication deadline. He also felt that neither Karl Bitter nor Philip Martiny was "the equal of Mr. O'Donovan at portraits." Duncan concluded that the association could not "obtain as satisfactory a piece of work as at Monmouth for anything like the same price." The Monmouth monument to which he referred, of course, came from Maurice Power's foundry.[59]

In February 1892, Duncan submitted "Messrs. O'Donovan and Eakins's" cost estimates for the Trenton Monument. After some additional negotiations, Duncan told Stryker on March 23, 1892, that he had "sent notices to all sculptors that Mr. O'Donovan has been awarded the commission."[60] The acceptance of O'Donovan also clearly meant the acceptance of Power, for in the interim Power wrote to Stryker requesting that his firm act as the exclusive foundry for the monument. Stryker could not agree to this, as he hoped to receive additional funding for the project from other states whose troops had participated in the battle. Stryker insisted that he could only offer Power and O'Donovan those sculptures funded by the association and the state of New Jersey. He could not force another state to accept the artists that the association had selected if it did not approve of them. Power, however, would find a way around this. Duncan proceeded with a contract "with Maurice J. Power for Messrs. O'Donovan and Eakins in accordance with my recommendation."[61]

Eakins's name appears second to O'Donovan's in virtually all of the correspondence regarding the commission. The minutebook of the association explains Eakins's involvement in the project, stating that "a large number of prominent sculptors sent in estimates of their work. Unfortunately . . . many of these men were crowded with orders for sculpture to be exhibited at the World's Columbian Exposition, Chicago and we feared that they would do crude and hasty work." But Duncan brought "to his aid Mr. Thomas Eakins who has for several years been head instructor in the Pennsylvania Academy of Fine Arts and who is the lecturer on Anatomy in the Academy of Design in New York City, and according to reputation and the Cyclopedia of American Biography . . . stands very high as an artist and as a designer."[62]

The minutebook also outlines Eakins's specific role: "He is now engaged in preparing some new and if possible some historically accurate sketches of the Crossing of the Delaware, the Opening of the Fight and the Surrender of the Hessians. It is expected that Mr. Eakins in collaboration with Mr. O'Donovan will execute these three relieves [*sic*]."[63] While the reliefs were to be done "in collaboration" with O'Donovan, the rest of the sculptural program would be carried out by O'Donovan himself. In other words, it was O'Donovan's commission, with Eakins serving in a supporting, collaborative role.

Yet, as with the Brooklyn arch, the responsibilities soon became clearly divided, this time to Eakins's great advantage. He was given total control over the three reliefs, with O'Donovan preparing all of the freestanding sculpture. Each of Eakins's nearly eight-foot-long panels would depict an important historical subject, involving multiple figures in elaborate settings. As much as he labored over the Brooklyn horses, he faced greater compositional challenges in the Trenton panels. Never before had Eakins attempted such complex compositions. Phidias's processional frieze was an unsuitable model for the episodic subjects of the Trenton panels. Eakins had to integrate his figures into their settings in a more Ghibertian way. Yet he did not want to duplicate the unnatural shadows cast by Ghiberti's figures onto the background landscape. Eakins finally had a major project on which to test his own theories of relief.

In spite of the tremendous challenge posed by the Trenton panels, Eakins did not begin the reliefs until several months after receiving the commission. Although he presented his sketches to General Stryker in Trenton in February 1893, he still intended to undertake extensive research for the project. That April, Eakins wrote to Stryker requesting someone to guide his pupil Samuel Murray to "the exact place that Washington crossed the Delaware" so that Murray could photograph the spot for him. His approach to historical research combined the method with which he had tackled his painting of William Rush with the need for direct visual re-creation that had informed his Arcadian series. Eakins wondered if he could "ask the natives" in Trenton for assistance, "trusting to local tradition."[64] He interviewed his friend General Burd Grubb and other military men about the specifics of the battle and the accuracy of his conception. But he also had his student Charles Bregler borrow "continental suits from a lodge of Mechanics to which he belonged" so that he could study his models in authentic dress.[65]

While Eakins immersed himself in artistic concerns, Power, O'Donovan, and Duncan became engaged in political machinations behind the scenes to secure full control of the commission. These tactics were completely new to Eakins, who often either sold his work below market value or retained possession of pieces because he was not able to secure his asking price. Eakins's position probably seemed equally alien to Power, whose true talent rested in such political horse trading.

In February 1893, Power personally lobbied the New York Legislature for an additional appropriation for the Trenton Monument. Power accompanied

Stryker's representatives to Albany to be "nearby in case my advice may be in [*sic*] use—and I will get them letters to the best Republicans and anti-machine Democrats altho' they should probably only confer *officially* with the Machinists at Albany."[66] Three days later, Power "hoped that the application" would not be "delayed too long" and expressed disappointment that Stryker had not taken matters into his own hands by coming to Albany himself. But Power assured him that he would do all he could: "I will see all but the Machine Crowd before next Sunday and get their support for the matter if I can get it."[67] The next day Power enlisted the support of Senator McClellan and the governor and noted that O'Donovan hoped to use his "pleasant acquaintance with Liet. Gov. Sheehan" to their advantage.[68] By May, with all of his political cards in play, Power gleefully reported his success to Stryker. The appropriations bill passed the Albany legislature and received the governor's signature.

Meanwhile, Eakins continued to struggle with the commission. The sketches that he presented to Stryker that February had been rejected, and "an exchange of views on the subject" between Eakins, Duncan, and Power necessitated arbitration with "those whose judgement you [Stryker] invite on these subjects." As Power saw it, Eakins had opted for an unacceptable "pictorial effect while Mr. Duncan has been urging on Mr. Eakins and I think very properly a sculpturesque effect by massing the figures in relief." Power suggested that a committee meet to come to some agreement on Eakins's compositions first, followed by a discussion of the issue of the "pictorial effect" of the reliefs. Power's complaint was directed at the subtlety of the low relief that Eakins employed to combat the problem of Ghiberti's shadows. Eakins, unaccustomed to interference with his work, was reportedly "very much disappointed." But this only marked the beginning of his conflicts with Power and Duncan. His friend and collaborative partner, O'Donovan, remained silent during all of the ensuing controversies.[69]

Having won relatively few public or private commissions, Eakins rarely worked with deadlines imposed upon him. And although he encouraged his students to please their patrons, he had limited success with this himself. Indeed, his first sculpture commission, for *Knitting* and *Spinning*, had not gone well. It took Eakins years of protracted negotiations with the patron to receive payment for his rejected work.[70] Some of Eakins's sitters expressed similar dissatisfaction with their portraits and either rejected them outright—as Edward Coates had with the genre painting *Swimming*—or hid them from view. Eakins produced his best work without regard for reception or patronage. It is therefore not surprising that his own meticulous and contrarian methods led to conflict with the machinery of Power's system.

Things reached a critical impasse in August 1893 when Eakins made clear to

Stryker that he would not be able to meet his October deadline. Eakins seems to have utterly failed to understand the urgency of the situation and cavalierly told the general that he was too busy "working at horses now in the country and shall continue to do so until the cold weather." He suggested that they use his sketches and have them enlarged for casting in staff. He also indicated that they should employ Samuel Murray (for a fee of $275) to complete a plaster of *Opening of the Fight* because, he argued, "with all the care I am bestowing upon it even if I devoted all my time to it" it could not be done in time.[71] Eakins's letter prompted a firestorm.

Stryker, Power, and Duncan were outraged by Eakins's irresponsible and unprofessional behavior. Power lambasted Eakins, "I don't think it is fair to the Trenton Committee, or fair to me, that the Trenton work should have been abandoned in the manner in which it has been. . . . It is painful to have so wide disagreements with you on matters that seem so simple. It is a mortification I did not expect to experience."[72] He further told Eakins that if he could not complete the plasters for the commission himself then he should assume responsibility for Murray's fees. Power assured Stryker that he had written "a most urgent letter" to Eakins stating "that the mortification will be great to the committee and the blame will be his if the monument is not completed" on time. Power continued, "I confess I don't expect much satisfaction from the prospect of his changing his purpose. He is incomprehensible to me." He also made clear that he had no part in Eakins's decision to prioritize the Brooklyn horses: "As to the work he is doing on the model of the horse at Avondale, he has been definitely advised on the part of Mr. Duncan and myself that it may be time wasted, unless Duncan and the committee for whom the work is designed, will accept the small model of which this is the large copy, together with another small model which has not been given, and which he and Donovan [*sic*] are to do in collaboration."[73]

Eakins was mystified. In consequence of his failure to adhere to his deadlines, he lost the commission for the monument's third panel, which Power reassigned to the sculptor, Charles Niehaus, who agreed to hire his own assistant to quickly meet the committee's demands. Eakins's behavior cost him the possibility of ever working with Power and Duncan again, which meant an end to future collaboration with O'Donovan. His only opportunity to continue in the realm of public sculpture was through the assistance he offered to Samuel Murray throughout his career, but credit for these works always went to Murray. Murray proved himself capable and willing to use his own political and social connections to secure commissions, but he also ably managed his commitments and met his deadlines, ensuring his future employment.

Eakins's self-destructive behavior seems baffling, but the two life-size horses for the Brooklyn arch provided him with an opportunity to challenge Phidias, whom he considered his most accomplished sculptural predecessor. From his work on the William Rush painting onward, Eakins sought to place himself within the grand art historical tradition, even as he failed to achieve the successes of his contemporaries. As time went on, Eakins increasingly measured his success, not against his peers, but against ideals established by the Greeks, the Old Masters, and his own revered teachers. In Brooklyn he had an American subject worthy of the Greek tradition, two heroes, both dead, of the greatest conflict the nation had yet faced.

Eakins's intensive labor on the horses reflects not just a keen interest in equine anatomy but also his belief that he was continuing his work, begun with the Arcadian series, "after the Greek methods of relief." In many ways the memorial can be seen as an extension of the Arcadian series. His painstaking effort to study the individual nuances of each of the horses' bodies and his observation of the horses in motion followed the same methods that he used for the Arcadian works. The Brooklyn arch and its prominence in New York also put Eakins in a continuum with sculptors like Phidias and William Rush, whose public monuments endured. Yet Eakins's personal engagement with the art historical tradition set him at odds with Power. Power's political influence had turned his foundry into a veritable factory for public commissions, many of which were not destined for art historical greatness. Neither man understood the other's position. As it turned out, Eakins may have aspired to commune with the artists of the past, but he failed to appease his contemporaries.

The Brooklyn bronzes were finally installed without fanfare in December 1895.[74] Shortly thereafter, the press began to complain about the reliefs. Much of the comment centered on the figures, but a surprising amount of criticism focused on the horses. The critic for the *Brooklyn Eagle* felt that the two were inappropriate for their riders and should have been exchanged. Censuring the selection of the steeds, the writer felt that Grant's horse was "tubby in the loins and wobbly in the knees" and Lincoln's too "spunky" and "skittish."[75] More than one critic felt that the placement of Lincoln on horseback made him "ridiculous." Indeed, among the profusion of Lincoln sculptures produced after the Civil War, Eakins and O'Donovan's may well be the only equestrian example. One complaint against the Lincoln was that his placement on horseback seemed in itself a misguided effort at idealization, "as offensive to the eye as the Roman toggery on the bodies of British admirals in the mortuary sculpture of Westminster."[76]

Aside from the problems with the sculptures themselves, their position on the arch was not flattering—they were situated too high and without enough distance between them to view the works properly. The critic for the *Art Amateur* touched on this when he complained that the figure of Lincoln offered "for public inspection the interior of a shockingly bad hat." The same critic continued to expound upon the faults of the sculptures, writing that "if this bit of 'realism' was intended to distract attention from the faults of the horse and the figure, it fails of its object. The figure is poorly modeled, and the horse's legs are notably weak. The Grant figure has one good point: it sits the horse well. But the latter is one of the ugliest beasts we have seen in bronze, and trails his right foreleg like a tired donkey."[77]

An unfortunate consequence of the placement of the figures combined with the artists' decision to use a very high relief was that both Grant's and Lincoln's bodies were truncated on the side attached to the panel. The appearance from below gives the disconcerting sense that the arms of the figures have been amputated, an unpleasant association to invoke for a war memorial, especially as the war had left so many soldiers maimed and disfigured. As the *Eagle* critic observed, "The lack of Lincoln's left arm and of Grant's right certainly calls for protest; for the men look as if those limbs have been amputated. The whole impress of the work is that of awkwardness and insipidity."[78]

Aside from such specific complaints, most of the criticism revolved around a perceived lack of heroism in the two figures, understandable given the subjects and the veristic approach of the two artists. The *Eagle* critic, for example, groused that although Lincoln and Grant were both "plain and modest" men, they had been treated by the sculptors as if they "were riding to business on a trolley car."[79] Part of the problem was that Eakins and O'Donovan had to confront recent history, fresh in public memory. As authors of a commemorative work in honor of "the Defenders of the Union," the sculptors faced criticism from individuals who had experienced the war and had opinions about how Grant and Lincoln should be represented. These were not abstract heroes like Washington; these were men known to the public, a public that still included veterans of the war.

Eakins and O'Donovan therefore faced two conflicting types of criticism: some found the work antiheroic while others criticized the accuracy of the reliefs. In some reviews the sculptors found themselves subjected to both types of criticisms simultaneously: "Neither in the case of the President nor the general have the sculptors secured either an obvious likeness nor an amending bravery."[80] The credibility of the likenesses of the two men was challenged, with one critic complaining that Grant's head was too large and awkward. All of which must have perplexed Eakins, who had taken such pains to consider his subjects as "real men on real horses." It seemed that no matter what criteria were used, the sculptures had failed in their aim, causing some to urge their removal from the arch. A writer for the *Eagle* offered this withering assessment: "As the city has become the absolute owner of these bronzes it is free to correct the mistake—or worse—of a former administration that inflicted us with bad pavements at high prices and betrayed the town into the control of conscienceless scamps. We can now destroy these things, or put them into an obscure part of some public reservation . . . or give them to an asylum for the blind."[81]

Sophia Antoinette Walker, writing for the *Independent,* was among the few critics to praise the sculptures in any way. She found the bronzes deeply flawed but blamed Duncan for proposing "figurative subjects rather than decorative tablets" and for ordering the sculptures "from a bronze-casting company known chiefly for its soldiers' monuments of mercantile rather than artistic quality." Although she criticized the sculptors for choosing such a high relief and for their "unheroic conception of our two war heroes," she urged the commission not to commit a "final error in melting down the tablets." Walker further defended Eakins's work: "Probably horse anatomy has never been better rendered in bronze than by Mr. Eakins in these two tablets, and if for this reason alone it would be wise to provide a place for them, possibly in the new Art Institute of the city."[82] Despite the general dissatisfaction with the two reliefs, they were ultimately accepted under protest by the park commissioners. An attempt to withhold the final payment to Power failed when attorneys representing the borough could find no legal grounds to do so.[83]

Many of the problems with the commission arose from differing aesthetic ideals on the part of the sculptors, their patrons, and the public. In 1894, Frederick MacMonnies was contracted to produce three additional figural groupings for the project, *Quadriga: The Triumphal Progress of Columbia* (Figure 66), to surmount the arch and *Navy: American Sailors at Sea Urged On by the Genius of Patriotism* and *Army: Genius of Patriotism Urging American Soldiers On to Victory* for the piers on the arch's south side. A Beaux-Arts-trained sculptor, MacMonnies was a native Brooklynite who spent the bulk of his career living abroad in France. When MacMonnies's much-anticipated sculptures finally arrived, the press hailed them as masterpieces.

Allegorical and idealizing, all three of MacMonnies's sculptural compositions are distinctly heroic. MacMonnies's quadriga grouping, for example, includes three idealized female figures. Foremost among them is the figure of Columbia driving the Roman quadriga. She is flanked by two winged Victories in flowing gowns who herald her triumph with trumpets. It was not merely MacMonnies's female allegories that differed from Eakins's realist vision—even the horses of the quadriga reveal the contrast. The four stylized horses pulling

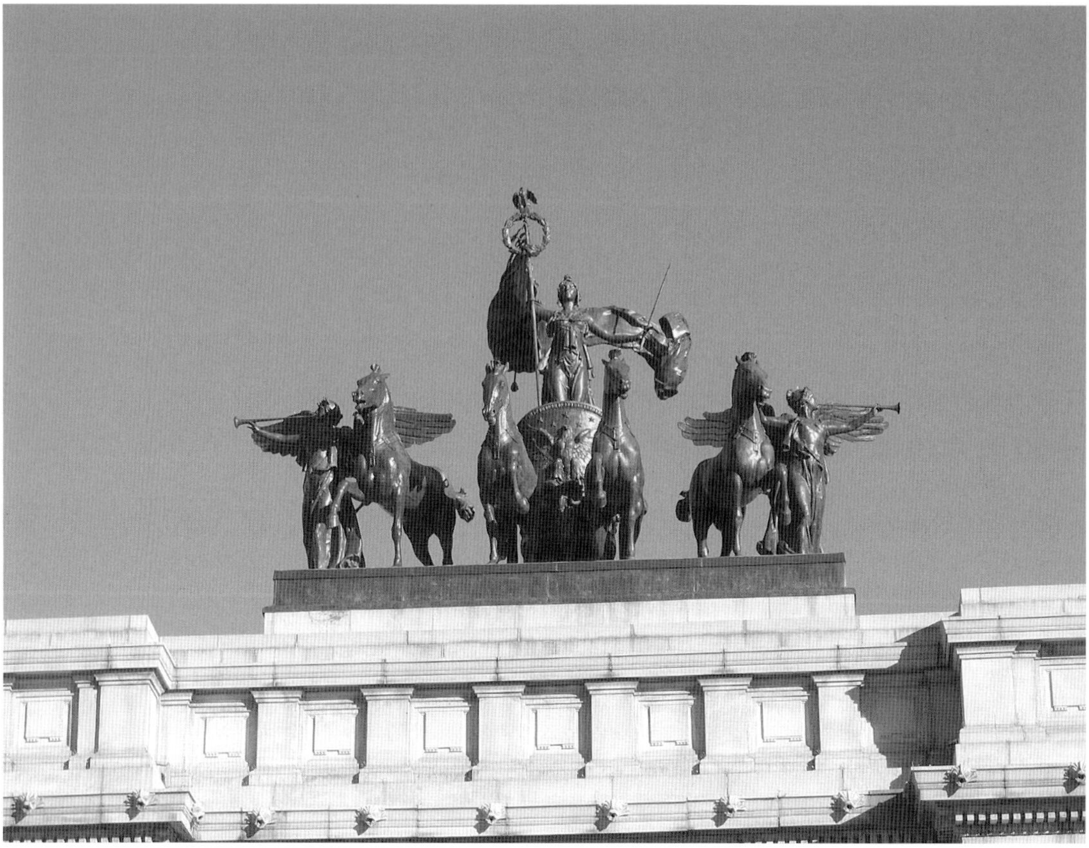

66. Frederick Macmonnies, *Quadriga, Soldiers and Sailors Memorial Arch*, Brooklyn, New York. Courtesy of Margaret Stenz.

the quadriga are based not on living ideals but on the Hellenistic or Roman horses now in Venice at Saint Mark's. MacMonnies's interest in motion was purely aesthetic. Although life study was also critical to MacMonnies's method, his eclectic work was inspired by Baroque and Hellenistic precedents.

Although O'Donovan believed that Americans "do not think in allegories," for MacMonnies it proved a better solution for commemorating recent history. To those who found Eakins's and O'Donovan's reliefs without artistic merit, MacMonnies's work seemed "as fine sculpture as any in the modern world."[84] MacMonnies soon became known as *the* sculptor of the monument and Eakins's and O'Donovan's works receded from memory, easily overlooked on the interior piers of the arch.

The artist Will Low unwittingly articulated the problem with Eakins's and O'Donovan's sculptures when he praised MacMonnies and his good fortune in coming "upon the scene when our Civil War has left great deeds to perpetuate, when the people of these states have relaxed their toil to look about them and seek to beautify their surroundings."[85] For MacMonnies and his contemporaries, strict realism was not considered inherently artistic; beauty needed to be created by the artist and enhanced through idealization. Art, rather than years of anatomical study, shaped MacMonnies's figures. Eakins did not eschew beauty in favor of a gritty reality, but rather he felt that the scrupulous representation of unidealized individuals was beautiful. In the case of the Brooklyn arch, Eakins and O'Donovan simply failed to meet expectations.

The sculpture for the Trenton Battle Monument did not stir controversy; indeed, critics rarely singled out the works for praise or criticism. One mitigating factor may have been that the monument commemorated less recent history. Because the witnesses to the events commemorated were long dead, Eakins and O'Donovan merely had to claim to be historically accurate.

The Trenton monument is not a particularly noteworthy memorial of the Beaux-Arts period. The relationship between the architectural elements and the sculptures seems awkward. O'Donovan's Washington, which crowns the monument, is indistinguishable from several other Washingtons made by him. Two other figures by O'Donovan, situated outside the entrance to the monument, appear unnervingly wooden. Duncan's criticism of Eakins's "pictorial effects" proved valid. In order to avoid the intrusive shadows of Ghiberti's Baptistry doors, Eakins used an extremely low relief, much subtler than any of the sculptural work he had done before. While passages of these enormous panels show an amazing mastery of form, without the rigidity of some of Eakins's earlier efforts, the decision to employ such delicacy for works that would be placed above eye level makes it difficult to read the panels from below.

Eakins crafted these subtle works with the skill of a draftsman, not a sculptor. He had relatively limited practical experience with the materials of sculpture and accordingly based much of his theory of relief on his work as a painter. While Phidias created his Parthenon frieze with a clear understanding of how his work would be viewed in its architectural setting, Eakins's panels were best seen when they were exhibited in Philadelphia and in New York in 1894–95. Closer to paintings than any of his other reliefs, Eakins's panels demand to be hung on the line. In *Opening of the Fight* (Figure 67), Eakins varied the relief, which is never terribly high, to such a degree that the houses in the distance barely project from the panel. Over this entire scene is a delicate haze of smoke from the recently fired cannon. This effect, barely discernable in a clean cast of the panel, is all but lost in the patina of the original. Eakins's principles of relief sculpture did not take this aspect of his materials into account. Nor did he seem to consider the siting of the panels. For example, in *The Continental Army Crossing the Delaware* (Figure 68), the figure of George Washington is placed in

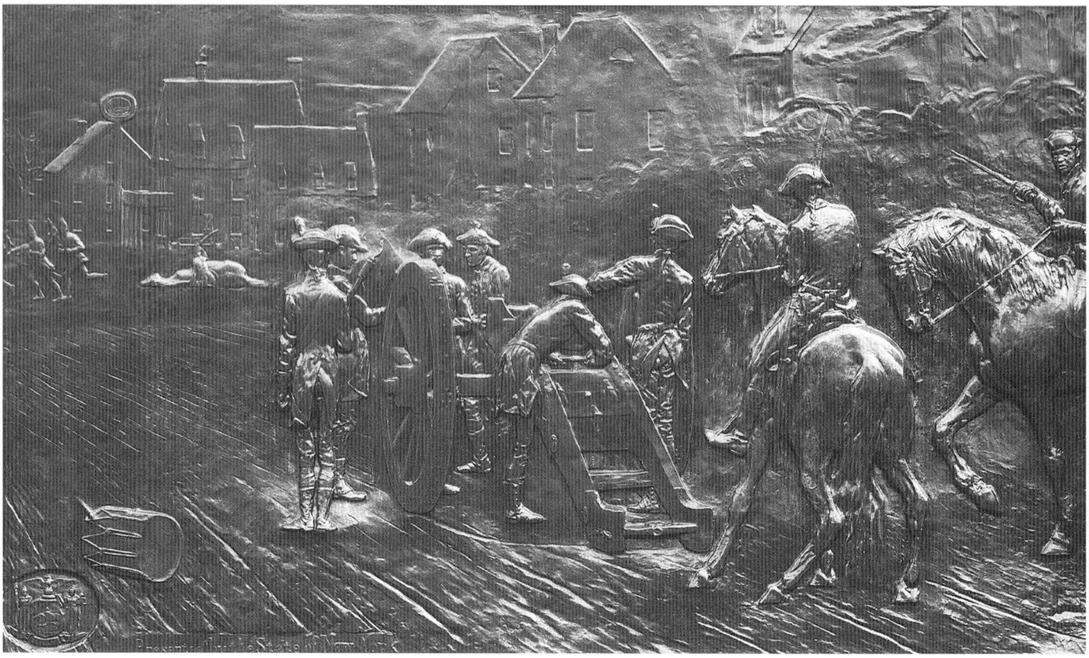

67. Thomas Eakins, *The Opening of the Fight*, 1893 (cast 1969). Bronze, 54¾ × 93⅞ × 3¼ in. Hirshhorn Museum and Sculpture Garden, Smithsonian Institution. Gift of the Joseph H. Hirshhorn Foundation, 1972. Photo: Lee Stalsworth.

the center, but not in the foreground. Washington instead occupies a boat in the middle distance that gets lost from the vantage point of the viewer looking at the monument.

In this panel, Eakins contended with the well-known but inaccurate and bombastic image of *Washington Crossing the Delaware* by Emmanuel Leutze. His efforts at historical accuracy corrected some of the obvious flaws of the Leutze work. While Leutze's Washington navigated through a river populated by mini-icebergs in inauthentic boats that would not support their cargo, Eakins placed his men in accurate Durham boats carrying a feasible payload across a realistically icy river. But Eakins also sacrificed the dramatic heroism of Leutze's painting through his placement of Washington in the distance.

Overlooking such faults, the panel elicited extended praise during its Philadelphia exhibit from the *Press*, a paper often supportive of Eakins: "Mr. Thomas Eakins has a powerful relief of 'Washington Crossing the Delaware,' which breaks loose from all the canons and justifies the act by the result. Here is atmosphere suggested in bronze as it has not been since the earlier Italians, the figure handled with a complete freedom and a sense of movement unrivaled. Such work is to be judged not by rule, but by result."[86] Despite this praise,

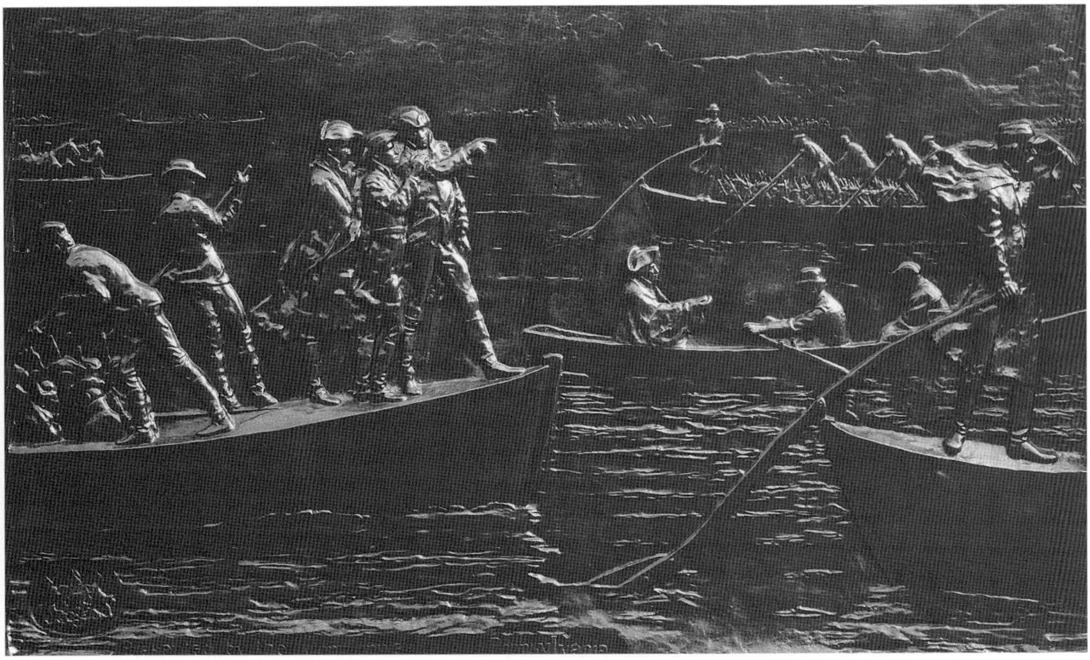

68. Thomas Eakins, *The Continental Army Crossing the Delaware*, 1893 (cast 1969). Bronze, 55 × 94⅛ × 3⅞ in. Hirshhorn Museum and Sculpture Garden, Smithsonian Institution. Gift of the Joseph H. Hirshhorn Foundation, 1972. Photo: Lee Stalsworth.

Eakins attempted only one other relief sculpture, a small portrait of Mrs. Mary Hallock Greenwalt, which he did not exhibit.

Collaborations with Samuel Murray

While Eakins proved unsuited to managing public commissions, he did not seem willing to give up sculpture altogether. Eakins continued to assist his pupil Samuel Murray on sculptural projects into the twentieth century. Unlike his work with O'Donovan, Eakins seems to have genuinely collaborated with Murray. However, Murray secured all of the commissions and, for the most part, received the credit for each project. Eakins's activities as a sculptor are difficult to piece together after the Trenton panels because there are few public mentions of his involvement. It is likely that he assisted Murray in some capacity with all of his larger commissions, as he and Murray shared a studio.[87]

Murray had assisted Eakins with both the Brooklyn and Trenton monuments. He and Eakins began sharing the Chestnut Street studio in 1892, in the middle of the Brooklyn arch commission. Murray probably assisted Eakins throughout the project and even appears in two of the photographs accompanying Moffett's article on the Brooklyn bronzes.[88] Eakins also relied on Murray throughout the Trenton commission, but it remains unclear how much work Murray contributed to the panels.

In October 1895, Eakins wrote to his sister Frances that "Murray and I are promised an order for some nude sculpture."[89] This commission appears not to have materialized, but suggests that someone had considered offering both men a project. A year later, Murray received a commission for ten terra-cotta Old Testament prophets to adorn the Witherspoon Building, owned by the Presbyterian Board of Publication and Sabbath School Work, at Walnut and Juniper streets in Philadelphia. Although Murray had worked as a sculptor for a few years, this was his first major public commission. Perhaps the scope and scale of the project (the figures were ten and a half feet tall) led Murray to ask Eakins for assistance.[90] Murray may also have suggested that Eakins collaborate on the prophets in order to help his mentor recover from ongoing criticism directed at the Brooklyn arch bronzes. Murray alluded to his concern many years later in a letter to Lloyd Goodrich about the Brooklyn and Trenton projects: "I must see you to tell you of some of these sinister ways Mr. E. was used. I cannot write anymore. I get mad all through thinking about them."[91]

Because of the large size of the works, the two men rented an additional studio on Wissahickon Avenue, which they referred to as the "Tioga studio." In February 1897, Eakins wrote to Harrison Morris of the Pennsylvania Academy that he would "be very busy all day tomorrow at the Tioga studio," indicating his active participation on the Witherspoon figures.[92] In July 1897, Eakins traveled to Seal Harbor, Maine, to work on a portrait of Professor Henry A. Rowland. The trip was to be particularly fruitful for the development of the Witherspoon figures. Murray joined Eakins sometime that month, when the two scheduled a rendezvous in Boston to "see the Sargent things."[93] The letter undoubtedly refers to John Singer Sargent's murals in the north gallery of the Boston Public Library.

Sargent's complex mural cycle, known as *Triumph of Religion,* marked a shift for the well-known society portraitist into the sphere of public art. Sargent's epic undertaking would occupy him for decades and remain unfinished at his death in 1925. The installation of the first panels of the cycle in the north gallery in 1895 received extensive press coverage. Eakins and Sargent shared a mutual admiration of one another's work, which is borne out by Eakins's decision to take the time to view the Boston murals. According to Murray, the two artists would also spend time together in Philadelphia in 1903 during Sargent's visit to the city and had considered painting each other's portraits.[94] In Boston, Eakins and Murray were probably eager to see one of Sargent's most popular mural compositions in the north gallery, the *Frieze of the Prophets.*

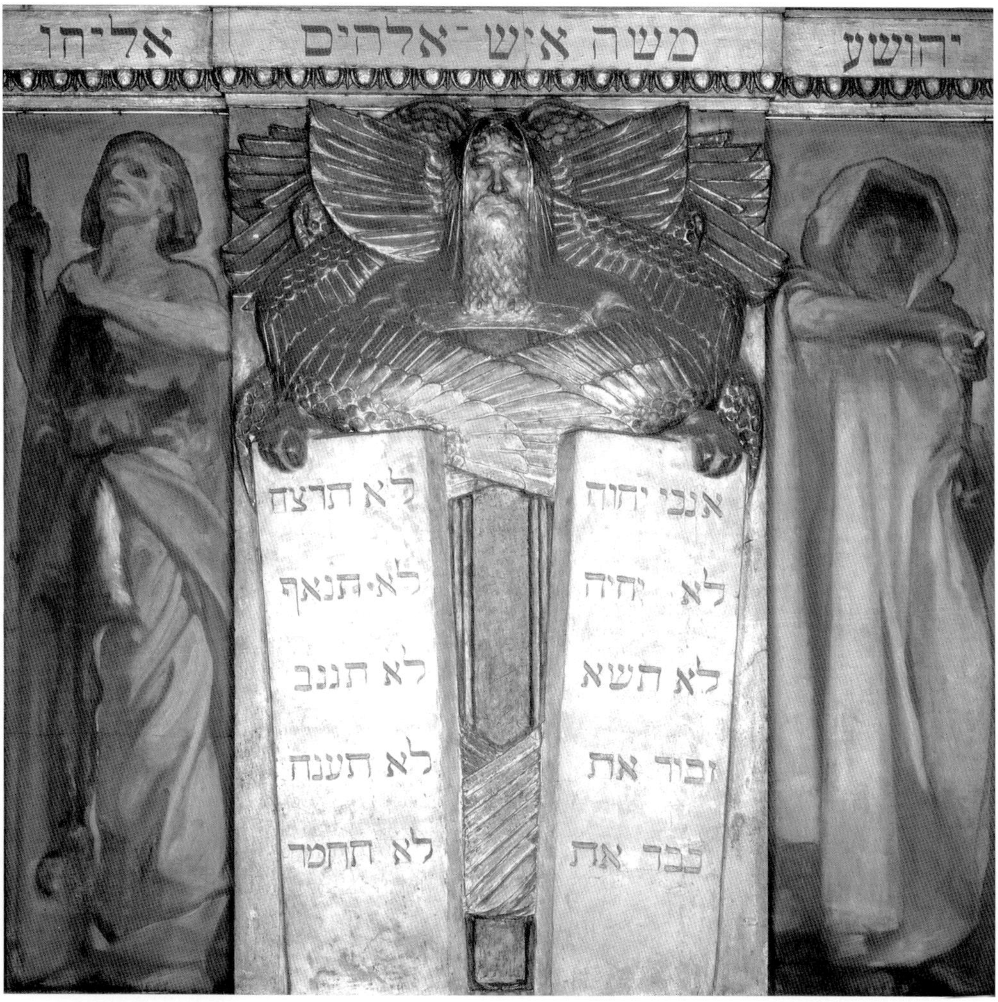

69. John Singer Sargent, *Frieze of the Prophets*, Boston Public Library, Sargent Hall, north wall, center panel, installed 1895. Oil on canvas with relief elements of gilded and painted papier-mâché and plaster. Trustees of the Boston Public Library.

As Sally Promey has shown, Sargent's conception of the *Prophets* derived from "French painting theory" and from Ernest Renan's *History of the People of Israel* in which Moses is defined by his antiquity. Eakins had been similarly influenced by his French training and the writings of Renan when he painted *Crucifixion* in 1880. Sargent visualized Renan's notion of Moses (Figure 69) by treating him in a stylistically different manner from the other, more naturalistically rendered prophets. Sargent set his Moses apart by depicting him in partial relief, surrounded by a winged divine presence, holding the tablets upon which is written God's law. This "oddly petrified" *Moses* suggested a model for Eakins and Murray, who crafted a similarly hieratic figure for their Witherspoon *Moses* (Figure 70).[95]

Sargent's work also offered Eakins and Murray a model for their naturalistic rendering of the other prophet figures, several of whom may have been based on family or close friends of the two artists.[96] Although Mariah Chamberlin-Hellman proposed Walt Whitman, who had died in 1892, as the model for Eakins and Murray's *Moses*, the work is far less portraitlike than the other prophets on the building, who do appear to possess the physiognomies of specific individuals. Murray acknowledged that Eakins's father-in-law, William G. Macdowell, served as the model for the figure *Jeremiah*. Macdowell was chosen not only for his appearance but because Murray perceived him as a "modern Jeremiah."[97] *Jeremiah,* in a contemplative posture suggestive of conscious thought and feeling, is more naturalistic than the impassive *Moses*. The other Witherspoon figures are similarly individuated and distinctive. *Deborah*, for example, is highly animated, striding forward, with one arm upraised. By contrast, the *Moses* appears as a static icon.

As work on the project continued, Eakins wrote to his friend Henry Rowland in October 1897 to explain his slow progress on Rowland's portrait: "I have been very busy with the big statues for the Witherspoon Building and have not done much to the picture."[98] However, in spite of the collaborative nature of the project, when *Jeremiah* appeared in the Pennsylvania Academy's annual exhibition in 1898, Murray was credited as the sole artist of the piece. While Eakins publicly ceded the credit for the prophets to Murray, he did not keep his participation secret and even posed for a photograph with Murray and the sculpture of *Jeremiah* (Figure 71). Moreover, several biographical dictionary entries published during Eakins's lifetime specifically mention his work on the prophets.[99]

The critic Riter Fitzgerald praised the prophets as being "full of character, executed with splendid breath and power . . . in every respect first class Works of Art, worthy to be placed in a more prominent position."[100] Perhaps on account of his success with the Witherspoon Building, Murray soon began to receive additional commissions. Murray also began to demonstrate a talent for soliciting support for commissions from influential people and following through by fulfilling his commitments in ways that Eakins could not. His efforts fell far short of Power and O'Donovan's aggressive manipulations, but he may have learned how to negotiate the system of patronage from O'Donovan's Irish clique. Admiral George Wallace Melville, for example, offered Murray extensive support and encouragement, particularly regarding the commission for the monument to Commodore John Barry in Independence Park in Philadelphia.[101]

Eakins's involvement with Murray's projects becomes murky at this point.

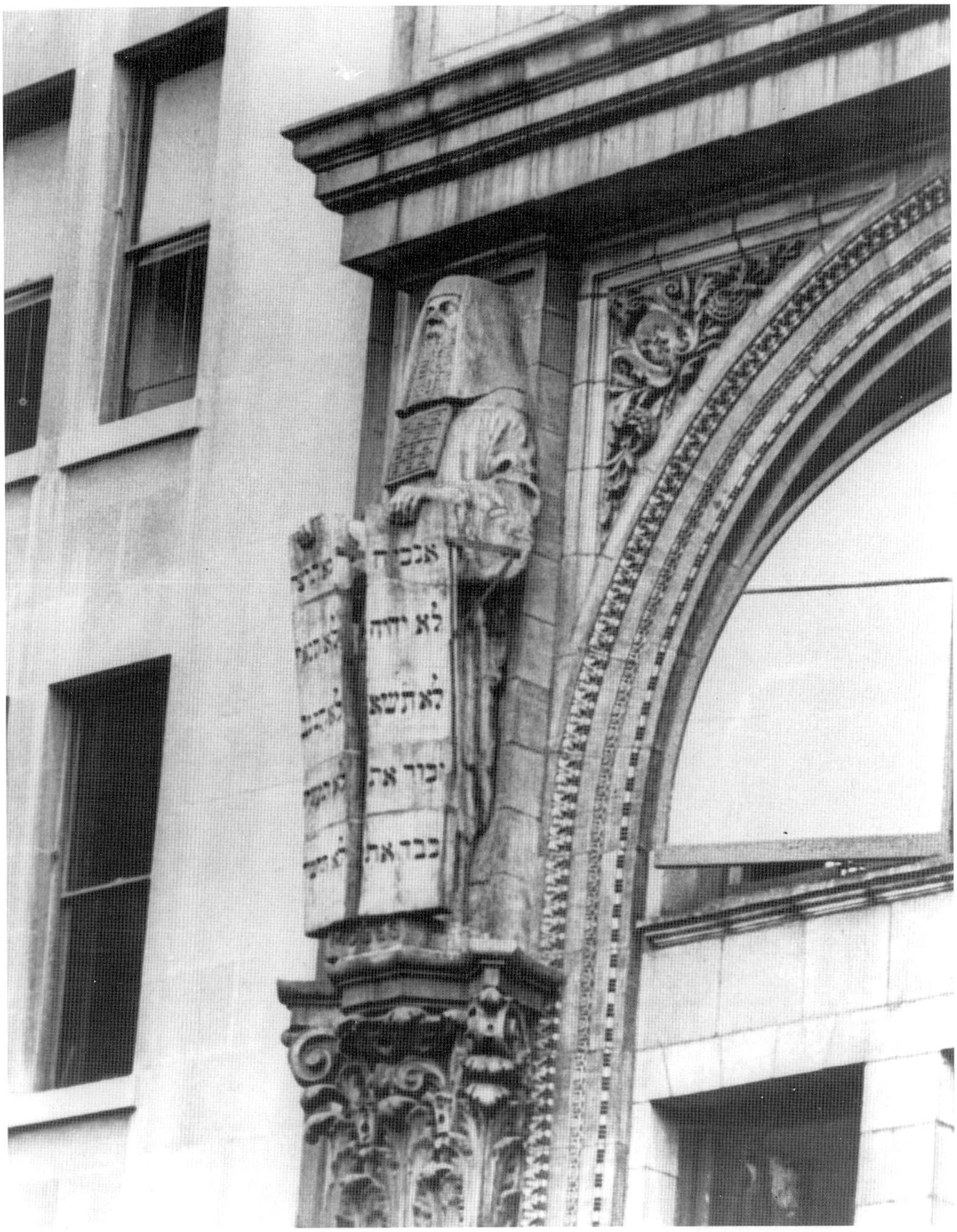

70. Unidentified photographer (Samuel Murray and Thomas Eakins, sculptors), *Moses Statue on the Witherspoon Building.* Witherspoon Building Records, 1895–1973. Presbyterian Historical Society, Presbyterian Church (U.S.A.) (Philadelphia, Pennsylvania).

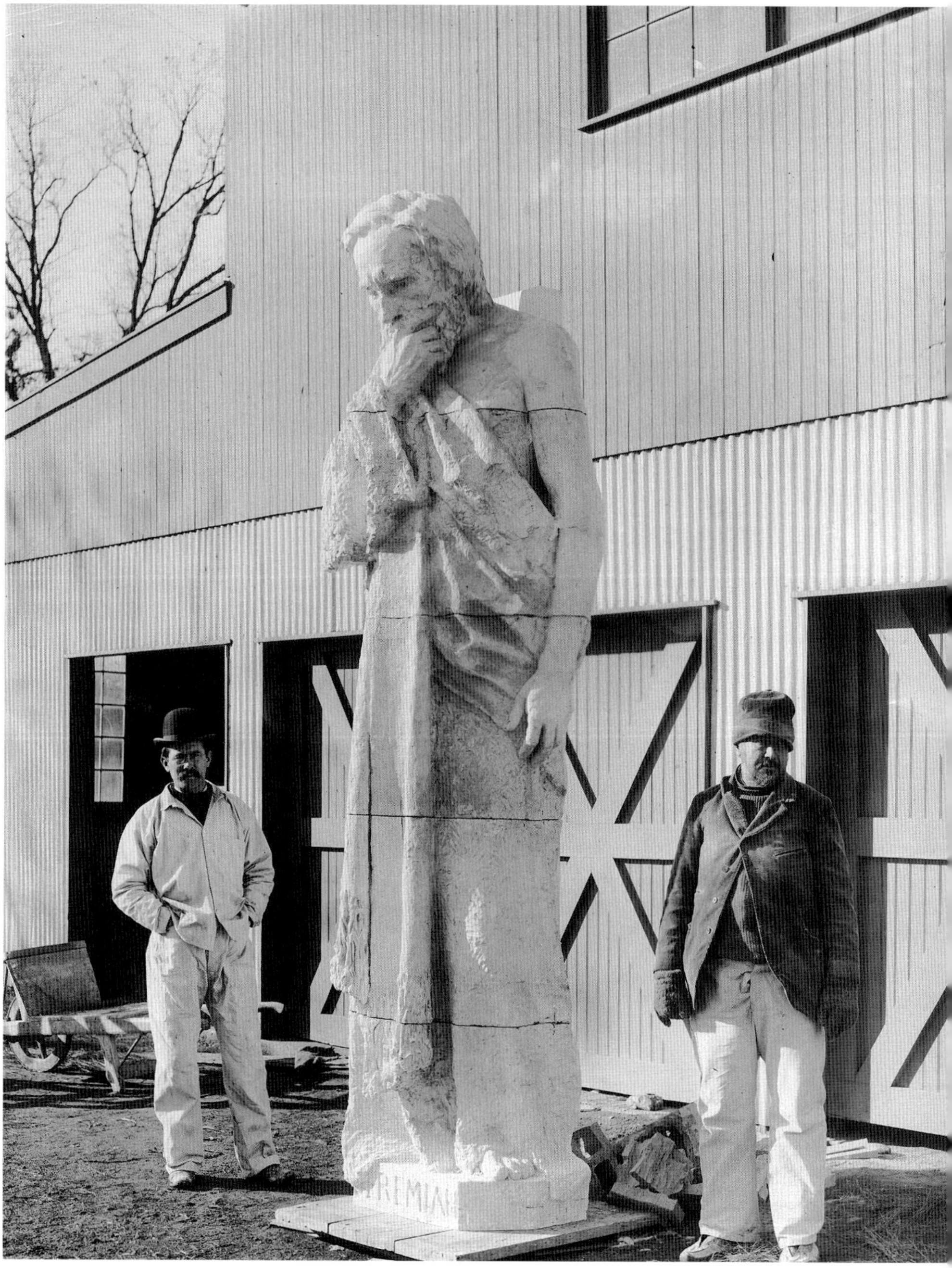

71. Circle of Thomas Eakins, *Samuel Murray and Thomas Eakins Posing with the Jeremiah Statue for the Witherspoon Building*, ca. 1897–98. Bryn Mawr College Library, Pennsylvania, Seymour Adelman Collection.

In 1907, Eakins mentioned his participation in the Barry commission in a letter to a friend: "Artistically the statue is I believe the best in the country and I am proud to have assisted Murray in its execution."[102] This is the last acknowledgment of his collaboration with his pupil. Around the time of the Barry commission, Eakins completed his last independent relief sculpture, the portrait of Mrs. Mary Hallock Greenwalt (unlocated).[103] These may well have been Eakins's last sculpted works, for there are no other references to sculpture projects in his letters after this point. Yet as he concluded his work in the medium, his thoughts returned to William Rush, and a year after the Barry commission, he undertook a reexamination of the Philadelphia sculptor.

The Greenwalt portrait was the only piece of sculpture Eakins completed that did not have a historical subject. Sculpture had always provided Eakins with a reference point in terms of the art historical tradition. He identified with William Rush, Phidias, and Ghiberti, and ultimately these were the men he hoped to equal. His meticulous work habits and his high-minded ideas about the nature of sculpture as an art made him particularly ill suited to work with someone like Maurice Power. Yet these projects seemed to hold the greatest potential value to Eakins because, like the Parthenon reliefs and William Rush's public work, civic sculpture had the potential to endure. With all that Eakins invested in the medium, it is not surprising that Murray, his closest student, became a sculptor and not a painter.

CONCLUSION

Rush Revisited: Eakins as Old Master

In 1905 Eakins completed his last independent sculpture, a relief (now lost) of his friend Mary Hallock Greenwalt, whom he had painted two years earlier. Yet the true conclusion of his career as a sculptor seems to have come when Samuel Murray's *Monument to Commodore John Barry* was unveiled in Independence Square in 1907. Although Murray received the commission and the credit for the work, Eakins expressed pride in the assistance that he had been able to offer his closest student in the completion of this public monument.[1] After decades of interest in sculpture, Eakins's work on three-dimensional projects ceased. Yet he still found himself preoccupied with the idea of sculpture, so much so that he uncharacteristically returned to an old subject, *William Rush Carving His Allegorical Figure of the Schuylkill River.*

Around 1908, Eakins not only revived the 1877 subject but treated it in a manner that he had never used for any of his finished projects.[2] Although Eakins's working methods varied throughout his lifetime, he often made rough compositional oil studies for his paintings.[3] Almost from the start of his career, the defining characteristic of these sketches was their close adherence to the final painting. The difficult task of assembling the composition appears to have taken place in his head prior to painting. For his return to *William Rush*, Eakins made many compositional sketches, each showing a different variant of the scene. In these sketches, Eakins experimented with his subject, modifying not only the configuration of the composition but also the number of characters in the painting. In addition, he worked up several of the sketches to a much higher degree of finish than was typical of his earlier compositional sketches. Never before had he visualized a subject on canvas in so many ways.

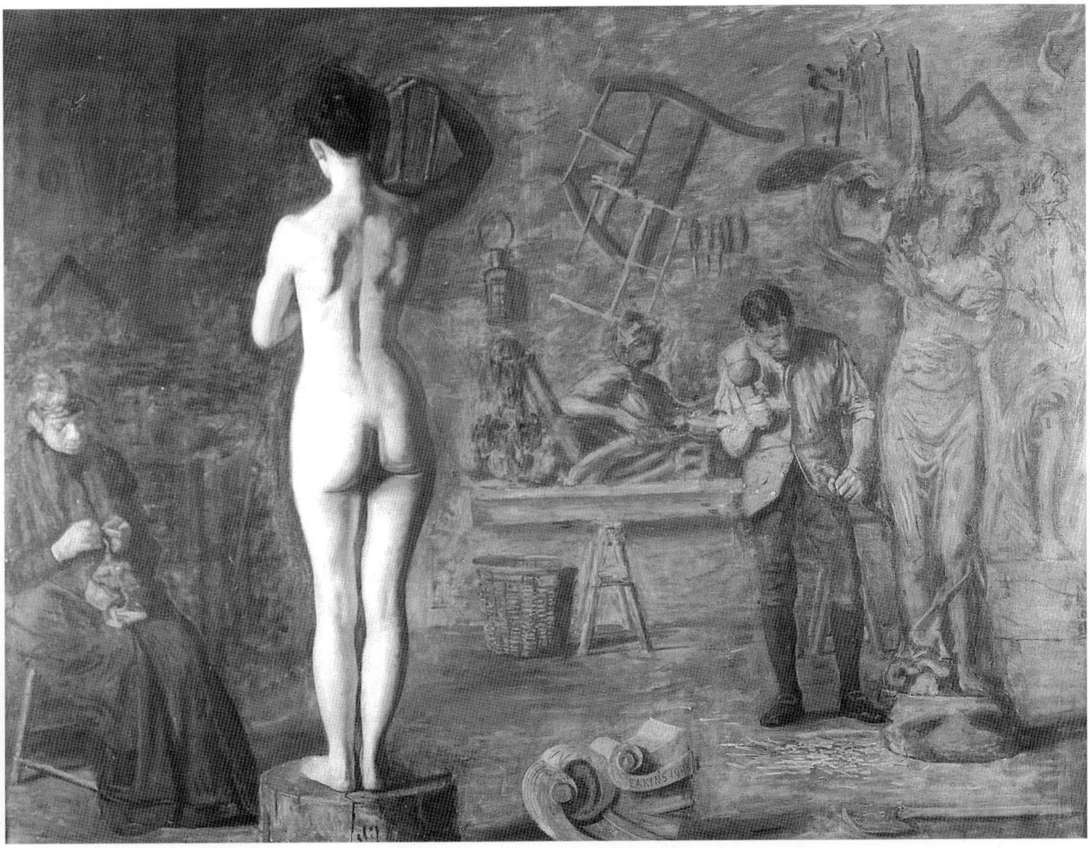

72. Thomas Eakins, *William Rush Carving His Allegorical Figure of the Schuylkill River*, 1908. Oil on canvas, 35$^{15}/_{16}$ × 47$^{13}/_{16}$ in. Brooklyn Museum 39.461. Dick S. Ramsay Fund.

Despite their abundance, almost none of the 1908 Rush sketches were used to craft the one finished version of the subject (Figure 72). This image, now in the Brooklyn Museum, though substantially larger than the 1877 painting, represents the least inventive of his reworkings of the composition. In the Brooklyn painting, Eakins retained most of the elements of the original, but he shuffled them into a less logical arrangement. Eakins shifted the positions of the sculptor and the chaperone to opposite sides of the canvas. The model stands without the contrapposto of the 1877 image and seemingly faces the chaperone instead of the artist. The interior of Rush's workshop reads more coherently, but it also seems more mundane. The figurative sculptures are arranged closer to one another in the crowded right corner of the room. The sculpture of *George Washington* looks off to the right, squeezed between the *Nymph* and the right edge of the composition, and *Allegory of the Waterworks* is situated on a work-

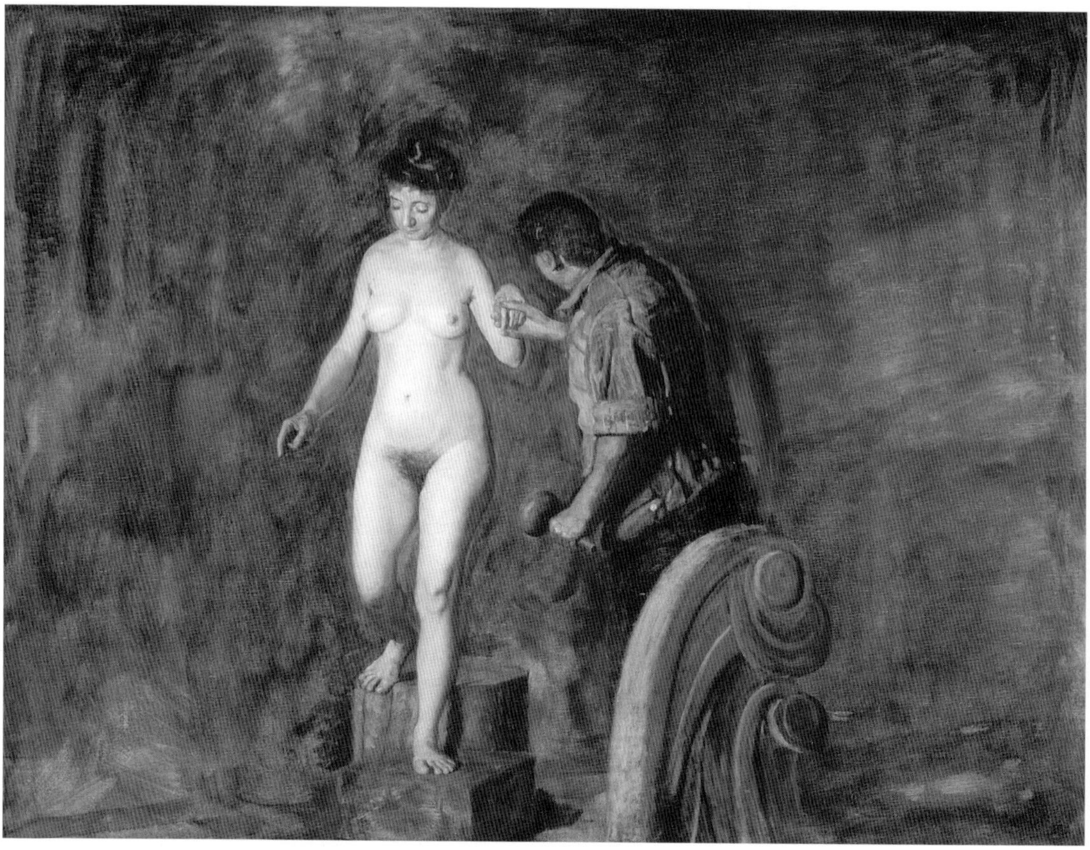

73. Thomas Eakins, *William Rush and His Model*, 1908. Oil on canvas, 35¼ × 47¼ in. Honolulu Academy of Arts. Gift of the Friends of the Academy, 1947.

table, surrounded by equally prominent woodworking tools. Rush himself appears workman-like rather than gentlemanly. Of the substantive changes, the most significant is the transformation of the chaperone from an elderly white matron to an African American woman. Eakins also eliminated the beautiful still life of discarded clothing so prominent in the original. While the painting does not thoroughly reconceive the subject, the sketches show a surprisingly imaginative reconsideration of the theme.

In addition to the handful of studies that relate to aspects of the Brooklyn picture, Eakins also made many sketches for a painting that he never fully realized. This project completely reimagined the exchange between model and sculptor into a kind of collaborative partnership. The unfinished painting, *William Rush and His Model*, now in Honolulu (Figure 73), is almost identical in size to the Brooklyn painting. This too constitutes a change for Eakins, as he appears to have had at least two large-scale versions of the Rush subject in mind in this period. The Honolulu painting shows the sculptor, who previously faced the viewer in earlier iterations, with his back to us as he hands the model down from her stand. The model, this time, is situated frontally. Only in this compositional arrangement of the theme, in all of Eakins's painted work, does he present a nude figure fully exposed to his audience. In the Honolulu picture she seems entirely unaware that she is observed and, looking downward, concentrates on her footing. The sculptor and model stand alone in a nearly barren composition, with only the model's pedestal and an enormous ship's scroll to define the studio.

The most complete compositional sketch for the Honolulu painting (Figure 74) suggests that Eakins conceived of the image with an additional figure present: a woman standing to the left who offers the model a gown as the sculptor hands her down. Eakins studied the model and this other female figure in at least one additional sketch—in both instances in which this second woman appears, she also seems to be nude. The scene has the feel of allegory, with two lovely goddesses standing in the artist's studio. Yet when Eakins worked the image into the larger version, there was no sign of this figure—no interloper between artist and model. And as many scholars have noted, Rush now very much resembles the older Eakins.[4] What are we to make of all this?

In one sense, Eakins may have been reflecting upon the changes in his profession since he painted the first version in 1877, but he also surely must have been thinking of himself—his career, the meaning of his art, and his place within the art historical tradition. In the case of his profession, the later Rush images completely change the relationship between artist and model to reflect the realities of 1908. In the Brooklyn painting, Eakins achieves this by altering the race of the chaperone.[5] In early twentieth-century America, let alone the early Republic of Rush's day, the African American woman would not have been the social equal of the model or the artist. The chaperone's ability to protect the chastity of the nude society belle in her charge diminished considerably when Eakins changed her skin color. The chaperone disappears altogether in the unfinished Honolulu picture, as she had in the studios of artists in the 1900s.[6]

When Eakins painted the first Rush oil in 1877, it followed his suggestion that the Academy should hire better models, drawn outside the ranks of prostitutes. In order to get these demure young ladies to pose, he recommended that they be allowed to bring their mothers with them. By the turn of the century, this idea seemed quaint. When Eakins exhibited the 1877 Rush at the Exhibition of Contemporary Art held at the Brooklyn Museum in 1915, the critic for the *New York Times* wrote, "In the foreground stands his model, the true theme of the composition, and near her sits her duenna, a naïve commentary on the

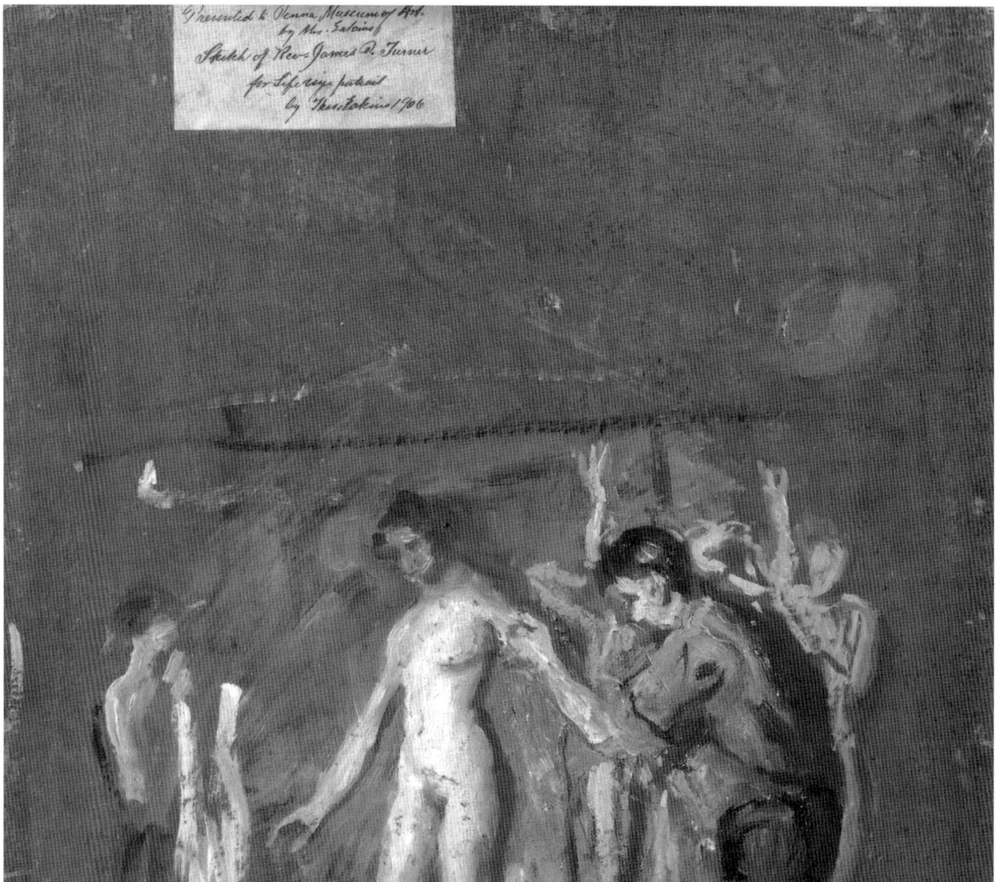

74. Thomas Eakins, *Sketch for "William Rush and His Model,"* ca. 1908. Oil on cardboard, 14½ × 10½ in. Philadelphia Museum of Art. Gift of Mrs. Thomas Eakins and Miss Mary Adeline Williams, 1930.

period."[7] The idea of having a chaperone seemed preposterous in an era when models were becoming celebrities. Indeed, in 1907, the *Times* ran an article titled "The Women Who Served as Models for the Coins," in which two models, Mary Cunningham and Nannie Williams, recounted their experiences posing for artists. Williams, who served as the model for Louisa Vanuxem in Eakins's 1877 painting, publicly described not only her sittings for the head on the Morgan dollar but also her connection with Eakins.[8]

In addition to reflecting the changing status of artists' models, Eakins's 1908 Rush series also seems a poignantly personal project. Although Eakins thoroughly contemplated the subject, made elaborate sketches, crafted one large-scale painting, and began another, he never exhibited any of the works in this group. The degree to which he experimented with the subject on canvas also suggests that Eakins had a private interest in these works. As with the chaperone, the artist also undergoes changes throughout the sketches and the more finished paintings. In one version, Rush appears as a balding man, dressed in attire that is not as gentlemanly as the 1877 original but also not as workman-like as in the Honolulu painting.[9] In the Brooklyn picture he becomes younger and more of a workman. In the sketches for the Honolulu composition, Rush is a slender figure. Finally, in the Honolulu image, what we see of Rush's form looks older and heavier than in the sketches and, indeed, resembles Eakins in his later years. In 1877, Eakins had highlighted the aspects of Rush's career that most pertained to his own goals as an artist; in 1908, Eakins became Rush. If Eakins considered Rush in the context of the art historical tradition in the 1877 painting, in 1908 Eakins depicted himself in the place of an American Old Master.

By the time he painted the Honolulu oil, the winds had shifted more favorably in Eakins's direction. Starting in the 1890s, his work received more positive attention from critics. Commissions also materialized in this period.[10] In 1896 he had a large one-man show at Earles Galleries in Philadelphia. Five years later he shared another focused show with Samuel Murray. Then, in 1902, he was elected both an associate and an academician of the NAD. He received several awards: gold medals at the Pan-American Exposition in Buffalo (1901), the Louisiana Purchase Exposition in St. Louis (1904), and the American Art Society of Philadelphia (1907). The Pennsylvania Academy of the Fine Arts also awarded Eakins the Temple Gold Medal in 1904. The twentieth century brought Eakins honors, commissions, and praise.[11]

Also in this period he began serving regularly on exhibition juries. He became a frequent juror for the Carnegie Institute's annual exhibitions starting in 1899. In addition, he sat on juries in Worcester, Philadelphia, and New York.[12] Through these experiences, Eakins interacted with his artistic peers on a regular basis—he also clearly had a keen sense of the sort of work being submitted to these exhibitions. In Pittsburgh, for example, Eakins must have seen the Carnegie's portrait of the violinist Pablo de Sarasate by James A. McNeill Whistler, as he included a small replica of it in the background of his 1904 painting *Music.*[13] Eakins's reinvigorated connection to the art world is also witnessed by the sheer numbers of portraits of artists, dealers, and curators that he painted after 1900. Eakins had often painted his students, especially as they frequently posed as models, but the artist portraits that he began around the turn of the century, with his 1899 painting of William Merritt Chase, suggest as potent an interest in art professionals as his better documented fascination with doctors or the Catholic clergy.[14]

When Eakins painted himself as an American Old Master in the form of Rush in 1908, his work was increasingly being compared to that of European Old Masters. That Eakins also began appearing in historical surveys of American art around the turn of the century may have contributed to this trend. In 1901, Eakins made it into Sadakichi Hartmann's *A History of American Art.*[15] Hartmann celebrated the "brutal" realism of Eakins's work, praise that would resonate so profoundly with later Depression-era scholars. Echoing Hartmann, many critics noted the strength of Eakins's "prosaic" pictures, using words such as *truthful* and *honest* to characterize the style. One such evaluation of *The Cello Player* claimed, "It is unmitigated truth and not the poetry of elegance or refinement."[16] In such assessments, Eakins's "outsider" status and lack of popular appeal in earlier years was touted as a virtue, a badge of integrity and artistic principle.

Others suggested that Eakins's work was more a modern equivalent of the masters of the Baroque period. When Charles H. Caffin published his *The Story of American Painting* in 1907, Eakins numbered among the artists mentioned in this study, which surveyed painting in the United Stated from the colonial era to the early twentieth century. While Caffin included Eakins in the section devoted to realism, the most in-depth discussion of the artist's work centered on *The Gross Clinic* and its close ties to Rembrandt's *Anatomy Lesson of Dr. Tulp.*[17]

In one sense, the desire Eakins expressed during his student days in Paris to produce only "worthy painting" found its reward in these later accolades. When Eakins received the Academy's Temple Medal for his *Portrait of Archbishop Elder of Cincinnati*, the press hailed the picture as "a substantial piece of painting," though one critic felt that the "beautiful and poetic" portrait *The Oboe Player*, which Eakins exhibited at the same time, was equally worthy of the prize. In either case, the critic felt that Eakins deserved the prize not merely for the work itself but because Eakins had the strength to "adhere to those high canons which those who know the history of art are aware last."[18] In the *Portrait of Archbishop*

Elder, a Velasquez-influenced representation of the Catholic archbishop, critics recognized the hand of a master. This type of tribute would continue until the artist's death in 1916.[19] One of the most glowing appreciations of Eakins's work came just a year before his death, when he exhibited the unfinished portrait of Mrs. Talcott Williams, known as *The Black Fan.* The *Inquirer* compared the painting with Titian's *Man with a Glove* and declared that Eakins's "place in the history of American painting is of utmost importance."[20]

As Eakins received these tributes and prizes he clearly began to worry about the future of his work. Early in 1910, he wrote to Bryson Burroughs, curator at the Metropolitan Museum of Art, "I have always felt inadequately represented in the Metropolitan Museum. Hearing that the Museum was now buying some American pictures I have hopes that something of mine might be included."[21] Eakins pursued Burroughs over the next several months, meeting him in New York in April of that year and suggesting that the Metropolitan consider buying *Crucifixion.*[22] A few months later he sent Burroughs "a Spanish picture," one of the very first paintings he ever completed, made when he was in Spain in 1869–70.[23] Neither painting was acquired by the museum.

A year later, ill with influenza, Eakins worried that his *Portrait of Henry T. Rowland* "should be in a public gallery or museum out of the danger."[24] As Eakins embraced his status as an American Old Master, he hoped that his work would find its way into public collections, where it could continue to be seen. Eakins appears never to have fully recovered from this bout with the flu, and, in fact, his health would only continue to decline in the remaining years of his life. But just before he died, in 1916, he had the pleasure of seeing the Metropolitan Museum purchase one of his works, *Pushing for Rail,* a realist hunting scene. Though he was pleased to see more of his work enter this collection, Eakins expressed his disappointment that the museum had not "chosen a larger and more important picture."[25]

When the Metropolitan Museum of Art held a memorial exhibition for Eakins in November 1917, it was by no means comprehensive, and yet this show did not portray just the realist Eakins. Although Eakins had been heroized in the press for at least a decade, it was not strictly as a realist. His status as an American Old Master rested on *William Rush* and *Crucifixion* as well as *The Agnew Clinic.* In the memorial exhibition, *Crucifixion* hung next to *The Pair-oared Shell* and *Portrait of Elizabeth Coffin.* Spinning subjects occupied the same wall with his much-admired portrait of his father, *The Writing Master.* The 1877 version of *William Rush Carving His Allegorical Figure of the Schuylkill River* was there as well. Susan Eakins also lent *Swimming,* which had not been publicly shown since 1887. Nearly all of Eakins's historical subjects were represented in one form or another, except for sculpture. Though this was a notable omission, it was not neglected in his obituaries, which remarked upon his "equestrian statues for the Brooklyn Memorial Arch and reliefs on the monument at Trenton, N.J."[26] Eakins was represented in the show as a sculptor in one way—through the inclusion of a bronze sculpture of himself by Samuel Murray. While Eakins remained best known for his paintings, Murray's sculptural work represented the legacy of his teaching.

Although Eakins might not be pleased to find that few art historians would agree with his assessment that *Crucifixion* represents his "best work," he would no doubt be happy to see that his name has not been forgotten. From the start of his career, Eakins seems to have had a strong desire to make his mark in art history, even if he could not make a fortune with his art. The distinction he made between talent and success was all too clear when he wrote to a young student in 1906, "The life of an artist is precarious. I have known very great artists to live their whole lives in poverty and distress because the people had not the taste and good sense to buy their works. Again I have seen the fashionable folk give commissions of thousands to men whose work is worthless."[27] Although there may be a certain amount of bitterness in his letter, there is also the implicit belief that sales did not reflect true worth.

Eakins's youthful admiration of "big painting" remained with him throughout his career. He came to link such work with a singular method: life study. His notion that this was the basis of all good work, from Phidias to William Rush and, perpetuated by the French tradition of Gérôme and Bonnat, is at the heart of many of his historical subjects. In each decade of his career, Eakins undertook at least one of these historical themes, all of which relate to his regard for his profession. A complex amalgam of tradition and modernity, Eakins used these images to assert his deepest held beliefs about art. In his desire to become part of the art historical tradition himself, he numbered these works among his best and hoped that they would continue to speak for him after his death. To Eakins, these were "big paintings."

Notes

INTRODUCTION

1. Cecilia Beaux, December 1917, Cecilia Beaux Papers, Archives of American Art.

2. Cecilia Beaux, *Background with Figures: Autobiography of Cecilia Beaux* (Boston: Houghton Mifflin, 1930), 98, quoted in Sylvia Yount, ed., *Cecilia Beaux: American Figure Painter* (Berkeley and Los Angeles: University of California Press, 2005), 15.

3. For a discussion of the consequences of Eakins's dependency on his father for support, see Martin A. Berger, *Man Made: Thomas Eakins and the Construction of Gilded Age Manhood* (Berkeley and Los Angeles: University of California Press, 2000), 11–12.

4. Beaux, *Background with Figures*, 98.

5. Carol Vogel, "Eakins Masterwork Is to Be Sold to Museums," *New York Times*, November 11, 2006, B7. The comparisons to Rembrandt in relation to *The Gross Clinic* predate the artist's death but tended to come toward the end of his career.

6. Thomas Eakins (hereafter TE) to John W. Beatty, September 25, 1900, Carnegie Institute Museum of Art records, Archives of American Art.

7. There are several studies of history painting in America, including William H. Gerdts and Mark Thistlewaite, *Grand Illusions: History Painting in America* (Fort Worth, Tex.: Amon Carter Museum, 1988); William Ayres, ed., *Picturing History: American Painting, 1770–1930* (New York: Rizzoli, 1994); and Patricia M. Burnham and Lucretia Hoover Giese, *Redefining American History Painting* (Cambridge: Cambridge University Press, 1995).

8. Kathleen Foster and Amy Werbel have written the most extensive studies of Eakins's technique. A good overview of his practices is Kathleen Foster, ed., *A Drawing Manual by Thomas Eakins* (Philadelphia: Philadelphia Museum of Art, 2005). This work reproduces a drawing manual written by Eakins detailing his methods.

9. Randall C. Griffin, *Homer, Eakins, and Anshutz* (University Park: Pennsylvania State University Press, 2004), 78.

10. See Amy Werbel, "The Critical Reception of Thomas Eakins's Work: I, Lifetime," in *Thomas Eakins*, ed. John Wilmerding (Washington, D.C.: Smithsonian Institution Press, 1993), 192. For example, on February 7, 1874, *The Daily Graphic* called two of Eakins's rowing pictures "muscular studies" and declared that they were not "of a very high class of art."

11. Elizabeth Milroy, "'Consummatum est . . .': A Reassessment of Thomas Eakins's *Crucifixion* of 1880," *Art Bulletin* 71 (June 1989): 269–84.

1. The earliest sketches for the painting date to 1875. The work was not exhibited until January 1878. The most exhaustive study of Eakins's William Rush subject remains Elizabeth Johns, *Thomas Eakins: The Heroism of Modern Life* (Princeton, N.J.: Princeton University Press, 1983), 82–114. Other extended discussions of the theme include Lloyd Goodrich, *Thomas Eakins* (Cambridge, Mass.: Harvard University Press, 1982), 1:145–57; Michael Fried, *Realism, Writing, Disfiguration: On Thomas Eakins and Stephen Crane* (Chicago: University of Chicago Press, 1987), 2–89; Kathleen A. Foster, *Thomas Eakins Rediscovered* (New Haven, Conn.: Yale University Press, 1997), 144–50; Gordon Hendricks, "Eakins's *William Rush Carving His Allegorical Statue of the Schuylkill*," *Art Quarterly* 31 (Winter 1968): 382–404; Norma Lifton, "Representing History: From Public Event to Private Meaning," *Art Journal* 44 (Winter 1984): 345–51; Phyllis D. Rosenzweig, *The Thomas Eakins Collection of the Hirshhorn Museum and Sculpture Garden* (Washington, D.C.: Smithsonian Institution Press, 1977), 63–75; Darrel Sewell, *Thomas Eakins: Artist of Philadelphia* (Philadelphia: Philadelphia Museum of Art, 1982), 46–57; Darrel Sewell, ed., *Thomas Eakins* (Philadelphia: Philadelphia Museum of Art, 2001); Theodor Siegl, *The Thomas Eakins Collection* (Philadelphia: Philadelphia Museum of Art, 1978), 67–72; John Wilmerding, ed., *Thomas Eakins* (Washington, D.C.: Smithsonian Institution Press, 1993), 90–93; and Henry Adams, *Thomas Eakins Revealed: The Secret Life of an American Artist* (New York: Oxford University Press, 2005), 244–55.

2. Johns, 99.

3. Johns, 99. For the Old Master precedent, see Gerald M. Ackerman, "Thomas Eakins and His Parisian Masters Gérôme and Bonnat," *Gazette des Beaux-Arts* 73 (April 1969): 235–56; Johns, 91–95; H. Barbara Weinberg, *The American Pupils of Jean-Léon Gérôme* (Fort Worth, Tex.: Amon Carter Museum, 1984), 35–47. Of course, Eakins was well aware of this tradition; he purchased at least two European cartes de visite of such subjects while he was a student in Paris. Both are now in the Seymour Adelman Collection in the Mariam Coffin Canaday Library at Bryn Mawr College. They are Charles-François Jalabert's *Raphael's Studio*, showing the Renaissance master working from a live (and fully clad) model for a painting of the Madonna and Child, and Jean-Léon Gérôme's *Rembrandt Etching a Plate in His Atelier* (both published by Goupil).

4. The two essential sources on William Rush are Henri Marceau, *William Rush, 1756–1833: The First American Sculptor* (Philadelphia: Philadelphia Museum of Art, 1937); and Linda Bantel, ed., *William Rush, American Sculptor* (Philadelphia: Pennsylvania Academy of the Fine Arts, 1982).

5. Kathleen Foster also notes that Rush's heavy attire does not correspond to other seasonal cues in the painting that suggest that the time of the scene is midsummer. Foster, 146–47.

6. It is possible that Eakins did not know the chronology of the sculptures. Dates for these works appeared in some local histories, but the earliest source that I have found that includes dates for all three works was published in 1884. See J. Thomas Scharf and Thompson Westcott, *History of Philadelphia, 1609–1884* (Philadelphia: L. H. Everts & Co., 1884), 2:1066. I have found no evidence to suggest that artists in America during this period made use of nude models (male or female). It is possible that artists' wives or prostitutes served as models, but I have not found accounts of this practice in contemporary sources. I would like to thank Wendy Bellion, Cheryl Leibold, Ellen Miles, Guy Jordan, William Gerdts, and David Ward for sharing their thoughts on this matter.

7. Earl Shinn, "Fine Arts: The Lessons of a Late Exhibition," *Nation*, April 11, 1878, 251.

8. Foster, 144. In 1886, the directors of the Pennsylvania Academy forced Eakins to resign his position as director of the schools over the use of life models. In March 1895, Eakins was

similarly ousted from a teaching position at the Drexel Institute for using a nude model. Augustus St. Gaudens also faced obstacles in his use of nude models while teaching at the Art Students League in New York. See "Mr. St. Gaudens Has Not Resigned," *New York Times*, May 15, 1890, 8. This is only one of several instances in St. Gaudens's career where the propriety of his work was called into question over the nude.

9. Sewell, *Thomas Eakins: Artist of Philadelphia*, 48.

10. William C. Brownell, "The Art Schools of Philadelphia," *Scribner's Monthly* (September 1879): 742.

11. "The Fine Arts: The Philadelphia Society Exhibition at the Academy, Third Notice," *Philadelphia Press*, December 2, 1881, 5.

12. Thomas Eakins (hereafter TE) to Frances (Fanny) Eakins (hereafter FE), October 30, 1866, Charles Bregler's Thomas Eakins Collection, Pennsylvania Academy of the Fine Arts (hereafter PAFA). Sarah Burns discusses Eakins's immaturity in "Ordering the Artist's Body: Thomas Eakins's Acts of Self-Portrayal," *American Art* 19 (Spring 2005): 84.

13. TE to Benjamin Eakins (hereafter BE), January 16, 1867, Bregler Collection, PAFA. Philadelphia's Great Central Fair of June 1864 was held in Logan Square, not far from the Eakinses' home. It included works by Europeans as well as Americans, but these were generally minor pictures by minor artists.

14. In addition to his work with Gérôme, Eakins studied briefly with the sculptor Augustin-Alexandre Dumont in March 1868. Gustave Boulanger also occasionally took charge of Gérôme's classes, while the latter traveled in the Middle East with his friend Léon Bonnat in search of Orientalist subject matter. Later, Eakins spent a month in Bonnat's studio.

15. TE to BE, March 6, 1868, Bregler Collection, PAFA.

16. TE to BE, March 17, 1868, Bregler Collection, PAFA.

17. TE to BE, October 29, 1868, Bregler Collection, PAFA.

18. TE to BE, May 7, 1869, Bregler Collection, PAFA.

19. TE to BE, December 2, 1869, Bregler Collection, PAFA.

20. Thomas Eakins's Spanish notebook, Bregler Collection, PAFA.

21. The Lee sketches are not dated, but most scholars place all three of these historical projects around the time of the 1876 Centennial Exhibition. Eakins began his painting of Rush shortly after he abandoned *Hiawatha*. On the Columbus painting, see Foster, 384–85; Margaret McHenry, *Thomas Eakins, Who Painted* (Oreland, Pa.: Privately printed, 1946), 33; and Lloyd Goodrich, *Thomas Eakins: His Life and Work* (New York: Whitney Museum of Art, 1933), 169. For the Lee painting, see Rosenzweig, 55; and Carol Troyen, "The Surrender of General Lee to General Grant: Thomas Eakins and History Painting," *Apollo* 157 (May 2003): 30–31. William Innes Homer has discussed the Lee and Columbus projects as images of "defeated men" and relates them to Eakins's own professional disappointments. See William Innes Homer, *Thomas Eakins: His Life and Art* (New York: Abbeville Press, 1992), 100.

22. "Eakins Chats on Art of America: Veteran Painter Vigorous and Enthusiastic as in Days Past," *Philadelphia Press*, February 22, 1914, 8.

23. In that year, he was still working on colonial revival subjects, he had painted but not yet exhibited *Crucifixion*, and was developing his Arcadian works.

24. "The Fine Arts: Artists and Art Doings," *Daily Evening Telegraph*, October 17, 1881, 4.

25. See Marc Simpson, "Eakins's Vision of the Past and the Building of a Reputation," in *Thomas Eakins*, ed. Darrel Sewell (Philadelphia: Philadelphia Museum of Art, 2000), 211–23.

26. TE to Earl Shinn, January 30, 1875, Richard T. Cadbury Papers, Friends Historical Library, Swarthmore College. Eakins mentioned his progress on the painting to Shinn, securely dating it to late 1874.

27. The oil has been characterized both as a study for the watercolor and as an unfinished work. When the oil appeared at Knoedler in 1944 it measured 20 × 30 inches. It was subsequently cut down, probably by Charles Bregler. See Rosenzweig, 53–54.

28. Henry Wadsworth Longfellow, *The Poems of Henry Wadsworth Longfellow* (New York: Modern Library, n.d.), 154.

29. Rosenzweig, 54.

30. TE to Earl Shinn, January 30, 1875, Richard T. Cadbury Papers, Friends Historical Library, Swarthmore College.

31. Eakins compared himself with New Yorkers in at least two instances. Writing of one of his rowing subjects, he noted that "the long sweeps are all better expressed than I see any New Yorkers doing." TE to Earl Shinn, March 26, 1875, Richard T. Cadbury Papers, Friends Historical Library, Swarthmore College. When the work was inexplicably returned to him unexhibited, he maintained that it was "a much better figure picture than any one in N.Y. can paint." TE to Earl Shinn [April ? 1875], Richard T. Cadbury Papers, Friends Historical Library, Swarthmore College.

32. TE to Earl Shinn, January 30, 1875, Richard T. Cadbury Papers, Friends Historical Library, Swarthmore College.

33. TE to Earl Shinn, March 26, 1875, Richard T. Cadbury Papers, Friends Historical Library, Swarthmore College.

34. There are two sketches for this project, but Carol Troyen suggests that Eakins's student Charles Bregler may have cut a single composition in half to make the two images. Troyen, 30–31.

35. Mark Thistlewaite, "A Fall from Grace: The Critical Reception of History Painting, 1875–1925," in *Picturing History: American Painting, 1770–1930*, ed. William Ayres (New York: Rizzoli, 1993), 178–82. Carol Troyen and Douglass Paschall have suggested that Eakins may have embarked on this subject with the Union League of Philadelphia in mind. Troyen, 30–31. For Homer, see Margaret C. Conrads, *Winslow Homer and the Critics: Forging a National Art in the 1870s* (Princeton, N.J.: Princeton University Press, 2001), 9–11. For a discussion of historical paintings of the Civil War, see Bruce Chambers, "Painting the Civil War as History," in *Picturing History*, ed. Ayres, 117–34.

36. Ann Uhry Abrams has studied the theme in the antebellum period. Ann Uhry Abrams, "Visions of Columbus: The 'Discovery' Legend in Antebellum American Paintings and Prints," *American Art Journal* 25 (1993): 75–101. Many of the images at the Centennial were in the Italian section.

37. This sketch may also have been cut from a larger canvas. It now measures only approximately 6 × 7 inches.

38. Also in the sketchbook is a list of navigation texts that Kathleen Foster suggests may relate to the Columbus project. On the verso of this sheet are notes regarding early nineteenth-century costumes probably taken for the Rush project. See Foster, 384–93.

39. Foster, 384–85.

40. Kathleen Foster has suggested that Eakins sketched Houdon's sculpture of George Washington in the Capitol as a study for some of the details in his painting of Rush. She describes Eakins's sketches of Federal-era portraits as costume studies for Rush. Foster, 384–93.

41. Foster, 388–89. As Foster notes, the list also does not include John Sartain. She suggests the possibility that the list may relate to the writings and lectures of Eakins's friend Earl Shinn. Shinn spoke at the Pennsylvania Academy on "The History of Aesthetics" in October 1876. For Marchant, see Andrew L. Thomas, "Edward Dalton Marchant's *Abraham Lincoln*," in *Philadelphia's Cultural Landscape: The Sartain Family Legacy*, ed. Katharine Martinez and Page Talbot (Philadelphia: Temple University Press, 2000), 62–71.

42. TE to BE, December 2, 1869, Bregler Collection, PAFA.

43. For a discussion of these transformations see Sarah Burns, *Inventing the Modern Artist: Art and Culture in Gilded Age America* (New Haven, Conn.: Yale University Press, 1998), 1–16; and David B. Dearinger, "An Introduction to the History of American Art Criticism to 1925," in *Rave Reviews: American Art and Its Critics, 1826–1925*, ed. David B. Dearinger (New York: National Academy of Design, 2000), 16–29.

44. See Elizabeth Johns, "Histories of American Art: The Changing Quest," *Art Journal* 44 (Winter 1984): 338–44; and Dearinger, 16–29.

45. E[arl] S[hinn], "The First American Academy, First Paper," *Lippincott's Magazine* 9 (February 1872): 143–53; and E[arl] S[hinn], "The First American Academy, Second Paper," *Lippincott's Magazine* 9 (March 1872): 309–21.

46. Annual Meeting of the Stockholders and Members of the Brooklyn Art Association, April 22, 1872, Minutes of the Brooklyn Art Association, Brooklyn Museum Library. See also Kate Nearpass, "The First Chronological Exhibition of American Art," *Archives of American Art Journal* 23 (1983): 21–30.

47. The lenders to the show included Yale University, Harvard University, the Pennsylvania Academy of the Fine Arts, John Taylor Johnston, Samuel P. Avery, John Falconer, Henry Ward Beecher, and the collections of Philadelphians James Claghorn and Joseph Harrison.

48. Shinn, "Second Paper," 320.

49. A few years later, Eakins's familiarity with PAFA's history was explicitly outlined in a letter to Charles M. Kurtz in which he extracted information from "the old minutes of the Academy." TE to Charles M. Kurtz, February 20, 1881, Charles M. Kurtz Papers, Archives of American Art.

50. Foster, 146.

51. According to Doris Devine Fanelli, Etting acquired ninety-nine portraits (both originals and copies of eighteenth- and early nineteenth-century works) between 1870 and 1878. Doris Devine Fanelli and Karie Diethorn, *History of the Portrait Collection, Independence Historical Park* (Philadelphia: American Philosophical Society, 2001), 44.

52. Foster, 146.

53. For a discussion of American art at the Centennial, see Kimberly A. Orcutt, "Canonicity and Modernity: Building an American Art History at the Centennial" (unpublished paper, 2004).

54. For a discussion of the quality of the work on view at the Centennial, see Ethan Robey, "John Sartain and the Contest of Taste at the Centennial," in *Philadelphia's Cultural Landscape: The Sartain Family Legacy*, ed. Katharine Martinez and Page Talbot (Philadelphia: Temple University Press, 2000), 87–99.

55. For a discussion of professionalization in America, see Burton J. Bledstein, *The Culture of Professionalism: The Middle-Class and the Development of Higher Education in America* (New York: W. W. Norton & Co., 1976). Amy Werbel describes the process of professionalization that took place within the Academy under Eakins. She perceptively argues that Eakins "implemented many of the aspects of medical college pedagogy into artistic education as director at the Pennsylvania Academy." Amy Werbel, *Thomas Eakins: Art, Medicine, and Sexuality in Nineteenth-Century Philadelphia* (New Haven, Conn.: Yale University Press, 2007), 66–68.

56. Sarah Burns, *Inventing the Modern Artist*, 23.

57. Werbel, 67.

58. The *Nymph* and the city's waterworks were always major public attractions in Philadelphia, whether in their original location in Centre Square or after they relocated to the banks of the Schuylkill River in 1829. The Washington sculpture became a fixture of Independence Hall after the city acquired it in 1831.

59. The Academy once owned more portraits by Rush, but they have subsequently disappeared. See Johns, *Thomas Eakins: The Heroism of Modern Life*, 88n11.

60. Typescript labeled "William Rush, copy of original writing by Thomas Eakins," Bregler Collection, PAFA (hereafter William Rush typescript).

61. Johns, *Thomas Eakins: The Heroism of Modern Life*, 95–99.

62. *Illustrated Catalogue: Exhibition of Paintings, Nov. 1st to Dec 26th, 1881* (Philadelphia: Pennsylvania Academy of the Fine Arts, 1881). A shorter version appeared in the catalogue for the Society of American Artists exhibition in 1879.

63. Johns, *Thomas Eakins: The Heroism of Modern Life*, 95. Eakins's wife, Susan, also suggested this in interviews with Lloyd Goodrich.

64. Johns, *Thomas Eakins: The Heroism of Modern Life*, 97–98.

65. John F. Watson, *Annals of Philadelphia* (Philadelphia: E. L. Carey and A. Hart, 1830), 350–52. The Pennsylvania Academy owned a copy of the Watson book prior to 1864 according to records in the PAFA Archives.

66. Elizabeth Johns discusses the relationship between Watson and Dunlap's texts in Johns, *Thomas Eakins: The Heroism of Modern Life*, 97–98.

67. William Dunlap, *A History of the Rise and Progress of the Arts of Design in the United States*, vol. 1 (1834; repr., New York: Dover Publications, 1969), 315–16. His many portraits, including the one of Washington, were also modeled from life.

68. Johns summarizes Rush's decline, noting his diminished status as "a mere figurehead carver" by 1875. Johns, *Thomas Eakins: The Heroism of Modern Life*, 95–99.

69. Johns, *Thomas Eakins: The Heroism of Modern Life*, 109–11.

70. Elizabeth Johns and Michael Fried have each discussed the link between artisanal labor and high art in Eakins's career, and in the William Rush painting in particular. Like Rush, Eakins began his career as an artisan. In his case, he first followed his father's profession of writing master before turning to the fine arts. See Johns, *Thomas Eakins: The Heroism of Modern Life*, 100–101; and Fried, 19–21. For a more recent interpretation of the influence of artisanal labor on Eakins, see Emily Dana Shapiro, "Machine Crafted: The Image of the Artisan in American Genre Painting, 1877–1908 (Thomas Eakins, George de Forest Brush, Charles Ulrich, Jefferson David Chalfant)" (Ph.D. diss., Stanford University, 2003), 123–60.

71. William Rush typescript. When Eakins exhibited the painting at the Academy he did mention PAFA's collection of Rush portrait busts.

72. G. W. Samson, *Elements of Art Criticism . . . Designed as a Text Book for School and Colleges, and as a Hand-book for Amateurs and Artists* (Philadelphia: J. B. Lippincott & Co., 1867), 362.

73. S. G. W. Benjamin, "Early Attempts at Sculpture in America," *Daily Evening Transcript* (Boston), March 18, 1879, 4.

74. Johns, *Thomas Eakins: The Heroism of Modern Life*, 98.

75. Charles Akers, "Sculpture in the United States," *Atlantic Monthly*, November 1868, 558–59.

76. William C. Brownell, 740–42.

77. TE letter, July 7, 1892, in *Edmund Stewardson* (Philadelphia: Privately printed, 1893), 45–46. For a discussion of the controversy over *The Bather*, see Susan James-Gadzinski and Mary Mullen Cunningham, *American Sculpture in the Museum of American Art of the Pennsylvania Academy of the Fine Arts* (Seattle: University of Washington Press, 1997), 143–46.

78. TE to James P. Scott, June 18, 1883, Lloyd and Edith Havens Goodrich Papers, Philadelphia Museum of Art.

79. Bantel, 23. William Rush may have used woodcutters to rough in the form.

80. Foster, 147–48.

81. William Rush typescript.

82. TE to BE and Caddy Eakins, May 9, 1868, Collection of Mr. and Mrs. Daniel W. Dietrich II, Phoenixville, N.Y. William Innes Homer transcription, Thomas Eakins Archive, Philadelphia Museum of Art.

83. Shinn, "First American Art Academy, First Paper," 145. Several sources recount how the first life model at the Columbianum was a young baker who fled under the scrutiny of the artists. For the Peale story, see also Maria Chamberlin-Hellman, "Thomas Eakins as a Teacher" (Ph.D. diss., Columbia University, 1981), 9; Felix Régamey, *L'Enseignment du Dessin Aux États-Unis* (Paris: Librairie Ch. Delgrave, 1881), 65.

84. Fanny Trollope, *Domestic Manners of the American People*, Pamela Neville-Sington (New York: Penguin Books, 1997), 253–54.

85. It is also possible that these were made during private modeling sessions in the artists' studios. See Foster, 28–29. See also Doreen Bolger, "The Education of the American Artist," in *In This Academy* (Philadelphia: Pennsylvania Academy of the Fine Arts, 1976), 29.

86. Chamberlin-Hellman, 45.

87. William Rush typescript.

88. Vanuxem's gown was based upon a sketch that Eakins made from a 1807 fashion plate. See Foster, 146. Sarah Burns has noted that, by the 1890s, American artists tried to project a sense of professionalism through dress. Eakins's William Rush is similarly attired in gentleman's clothing. See Burns, 19–45.

89. The first mention I have found of Louisa Vanuxem serving as Rush's model is Charles S. Keyser, *Fairmount Park* (Philadelphia: Claxton, Emsen, and Haffelfinger, 1871), 14. Eakins's friend Earl Shinn also mentioned Vanuxem in this connection in his 1872 article, "First American Academy, First Paper," 151. Neither indicates that Louisa Vanuxem posed nude.

90. Johns, *Thomas Eakins: The Heroism of Modern Life,* 109–14.

91. Scharf and Westcott, 1:543. This account was repeated in E. Leslie Gilliams, "A Philadelphia Sculptor," *Lippincott's Monthly Magazine* (August 1893): 251. By 1937 the story had evolved to such an extent that Henri Marceau could write, "The recital of the criticism which arose when the figure was placed in Centre Square is too well known to bear repetition here." Marceau, 28.

92. This tradition prevailed until the 1980s.

93. *Poulson's American Daily Advertiser*, August 18, 1809, quoted in Charles Coleman Sellars, "William Rush at Fairmount," in *Sculpture of a City: Philadelphia's Treasures in Bronze and Stone*, ed. Fairmount Park Art Association (New York: Walker Publishing, 1974), 10. Trollope, 203. In 1810, Sister Catherine Fritsch wrote about the sculpture, which she referred to as "Rush's exquisite art creation of a nymph" during a visit to Philadelphia with another Moravian sister. See A. R. Beck, ed., "Notes of a Visit to Philadelphia, Made by a Moravian Sister in 1810," *Pennsylvania Magazine of History and Biography* 36 (July 1912): 358. A positive description of the sculpture appeared in the short story "Gertrude; or, The Fatal Prophecy," by Joseph R. Chandler in *Godey's Lady's Book*, May 1843, 231. Set in 1812 when the nymph still stood in Centre Square, Chandler wrote of "Rush's finely carved female figure" and the popularity of Centre Square as a place of "much resort," where "thousands flocked" and children played. As a genre scene, Krimmel's painting suggests a range of responses to the work.

94. "Academy of Fine Arts: Annual Meeting of Stockholders," *Times* (Philadelphia), February 4, 1879, n.p.

95. There are several Eakins life drawings of women in the collections of the Pennsylvania Academy and the Philadelphia Museum of Art. In images where masks are not worn, the

women turn their faces from the viewer so that they are unrecognizable. These have been dated to both the years before Eakins's travel to France and after. Kathy Foster has offered persuasive evidence for an 1860s date for the drawing of the masked model. See Foster, 26.

96. For a discussion of the association of the professional artists' model with prostitution in France, see Susan Waller, *The Invention of the Model: Artists and Models in Paris, 1830–1870* (London, Ashgate, 2006), 49–72.

97. Shinn, "First American Art Academy, First Paper," 145.

98. "Academy of Fine Arts: Annual Meeting of Stockholders," n.p.

99. TE to the Committee on Instruction, January 8, 1877, PAFA Archives.

100. Charlotte Adams, "Artists' Models in New York," *Century Illustrated Magazine*, February 1883, 569.

101. "The Nude Models: Who They Are, and How They Act in the Studios," *National Police Gazette*, August 9, 1884, 6; "The Trilby's of Boston," *National Police Gazette*, February 9, 1895, 6.

102. Susan Waller, "Realist Quandaries: Posing Professional and Proprietary Models in the 1860s," *Art Bulletin* 89 (June 2007): 239–65, Eakins may have been more familiar with the Realist milieu than usually assumed if, as Alan Braddock has argued, he made use of the black female model seen in two paintings by Frédéric Bazille, while he was studying in France. See Alan C. Braddock, *Thomas Eakins and the Cultures of Modernity* (Berkeley: University of California Press, 2009), 74–79.

103. For an overview of Nannie Williams's modeling, see Goodrich, *Thomas Eakins*, 1:148–50. The April 1878 issue of the *American Journal of Numismatics* gave details about Williams's modeling for the coin without mentioning her by name, though the press found her out the following year. See also "The Women Who Served as Models for the Coins," *New York Times*, December 15, 1907, X2. I have not found any evidence to suggest that her nude modeling for Eakins ever became public knowledge during her lifetime. Her role as the model for Vanuxem was discovered by Goodrich during the 1930s.

104. Life study remained controversial but became a common practice in most American art schools. Concerns were raised about the damage that exposure to the nude inflicted upon young morals. Eakins felt the effects of this concern when a mother complained that the Academy curriculum was corrupting her daughter in 1882. "R. S." to James L. Claghorn, April 11, 1882, PAFA Archives.

105. TE to Edward Hornor Coates, September 12, 1886, Bregler Collection, PAFA.

106. The literature on Praxiteles' Aphrodite is extensive. Some helpful sources are Christine Mitchell Havelock, *The Aphrodite of Knidos and Her Successors* (Ann Arbor: University of Michigan Press, 1995); Aileen Ajootian, "Praxiteles," in *Yale Classical Studies*, vol. 30, *Personal Styles in Greek Sculpture*, ed. Olga Palagia and J. J. Pollitt (Cambridge: Cambridge University Press, 1996), 91–129. J. J. Pollitt, *The Art of Ancient Greece: Sources and Documents* (Cambridge: Cambridge University Press, 1990).

107. Lucian, quoted in Havelock, 11.

108. Havelock, 49–54, traces how the Knidias's degraded reputation developed in the nineteenth century.

109. Richard Westmacott Jr., quoted in Havelock, 50–51.

110. Clara Erskine Clement, "Stories of Art and Artists, Second Paper," *Lippincott's Magazine* (March 1881): 399.

111. "The Nude in Art," *Evening Telegraph* (Philadelphia), November 12, 1878, n.p., clipping in the Bregler Collection, PAFA. For a discussion of the controversy, see Alison Smith, "The 'British Matron' and the Body Beautiful: The Nude Debate of 1885," in *After the Pre-Raphaelites: Art and Aestheticism in Victorian England*, ed. Elizabeth Prettejohn (New Bruns-

wick, N.J.: Rutgers University Press, 1999), 217–39. For the English context, see Alison Smith, *The Victorian Nude: Sexuality, Morality, and Art* (Manchester: Manchester University Press, 1996).

112. "Nude in Art," n.p.

113. Alma-Tadema exhibited the painting in London as *A Sculptor's Model (Venus Esquilina)*. The *Venus Esquilina* (Musei Capitolini, Rome) was excavated in Rome in 1874 and was widely attributed at the time to the Greek sculptor Skopas. It is more likely a later Roman work.

114. In one of the most unusual discussions of the model, Henry Adams suggests that her body is actually "a composite of male body parts." Adams, 255.

115. The professional disappointment of his forced resignation from PAFA was followed by estrangement from his youngest sister, Caroline, over his controversial methods. In the 1890s, his eldest sister, Frances, similarly broke with her brother over the suicide of her daughter, Ella. Frances seems to have blamed Eakins for Ella's instability because he had pressured her to model for him. For a discussion of the incident, see Kathleen A. Foster and Cheryl Leibold, *Writing about Eakins: Manuscripts in Charles Bregler's Thomas Eakins Collection* (Philadelphia: University of Pennsylvania Press, 1989), 105–22.

CHAPTER TWO

1. The term *colonial revival* is used here in its broad sense to define the movement in the fine and decorative arts. This usage embraces not only colonial images but also those depicting subjects up to around 1830. Among the Eakins works that I include in this category are *In Grandmother's Time* (1876, oil, Smith College Museum of Art), *Seventy Years Ago* (1877, watercolor, The Art Museum, Princeton University), *Fifty Years Ago* (1877, watercolor, Metropolitan Museum of Art), *The Spinner (A Sketch)* (1878, oil, Worcester Art Museum, Mass.), *Courtship* (ca. 1878, oil, Fine Art Museums of San Francisco), *Retrospection* (1880, watercolor, Philadelphia Museum of Art; oil, Yale University Art Gallery), *Homespun* (1881, watercolor, Metropolitan Museum of Art), *Spinning* (1881, watercolor, private collection), and the sculptures *Knitting* and *Spinning* (1882–83, Pennsylvania Academy of the Fine Arts). There are also several sketches, numerous photographs, and at least one lost work. For a thorough discussion of these works, see Marc Simpson, "Eakins's Vision of the Past and the Building of a Reputation," in *Thomas Eakins*, ed. Darrel Sewell (Philadelphia: Philadelphia Museum of Art, 2000), 211–23.

2. The award was granted for his watercolor entries to this exhibition, which also included *Study of Negroes (Negro Boy Dancing)* and a rowing subject, *Turning the Stake*.

3. Helen L. Earle, *Biographical Sketches of American Artists* (Lansing: Michigan State Library, 1912), 62. Similar language was used in other biographical dictionaries of the period; see, for example, John William Leonard and Albert Nelson Marquis, *Who's Who in America, 1903–1905* (Chicago: A. N. Marquis, 1903), 3:431. Modern scholars have not always been as appreciative of the series. Sylvan Schendler, for example, called them "works of emasculation." Sylvan Schendler, *Eakins* (Boston: Little, Brown, 1967), 64. More recently Henry Adams has viewed these historical pictures as marking a period of diminished "emotional intensity." Henry Adams, *Eakins Revealed: The Secret Life of an American Artist* (New York: Oxford University Press, 2005), 257.

4. Lloyd Goodrich, *Thomas Eakins* (Cambridge, Mass.: Harvard University Press, 1982), 1:158.

5. See Kathleen Spies, "Figuring the Neurasthenic: Thomas Eakins, Nervous Illness, and Gender in Victorian American," *Nineteenth Century Studies* 12 (1998): 85–109; Norma Lifton, "Thomas Eakins and S. Weir Mitchell: Images and Cures in the Late Nineteenth Century,"

in *Psychoanalytic Perspectives on Art*, ed. Mary Mathews Gedo (Hillsdale, N.J.: Analytic Press, 1987), 247–74; David Lubin, "Modern Psychological Selfhood in the Art of Thomas Eakins," in *Inventing the Psychological*, ed. Joel Pfister and Nancy Schnog (New Haven, Conn.: Yale University Press, 1997), 133–66. Lifton, 247–49, 263–69, discusses *Retrospection*, one of the colonial revival images. For a discussion of the disease in relation to art in the Gilded Age, see Sarah Burns, *Inventing the Modern Artist: Art and Culture in Gilded Age America* (New Haven, Conn.: Yale University Press, 1996), 122–56; and Katherine Williams, Zachary Ross, Kathleen Spies, Amanda Glesmann, and Claire Perry, *Women on the Verge: The Culture of Neurasthenia in Nineteenth-Century American Art* (Stanford, Calif.: Iris and B. Gerald Cantor Center for Visual Arts at Stanford University, 2004).

6. Alan Axelrod, ed., *The Colonial Revival in America* (New York: Norton, for the Henry Francis du Pont Winterthur Museum, 1985); Karal Ann Marling, *George Washington Slept Here: Colonial Revivals and American Culture, 1876–1986* (Cambridge, Mass.: Harvard University Press, 1988).

7. In another venture into the international art world, Eakins submitted two hunting pictures to the Paris Salon of 1875.

8. "A Re-United Country," *Centennial and Journal of the Exposition* 2 (August 1874): 1.

9. Rodris Roth, "The New England, or 'Olde Tyme,' Kitchen Exhibit at Nineteenth-Century Fairs," in *The Colonial Revival in America*, ed. Axelrod, 159–83. See also Christopher Monkhouse, "The Spinning Wheel as Artifact, Symbol, and Source of Design," in *Victorian Furniture: Essays from a Victorian Society Autumn Symposium*, ed. Kenneth L. Ames (Philadelphia: Victorian Society in America, 1983), 155–71.

10. Donald G. Mitchell, "In and about the Fair," *Scribner's Monthly* (September 1876): 747.

11. William Dean Howells, "A Sennight of the Centennial," *Atlantic Monthly* (July 1876): 100–101.

12. Goodrich, 1:158.

13. "The Art Museum Exhibition: Water-colors Crayons and Charcoals," *Daily Evening Transcript* (Boston), May 10, 1879, 8.

14. Simpson, 215. See also John Davis and Jaroslaw Leshko, *The Smith College Museum of Art: European and American Painting and Sculpture, 1760–1960* (New York: Hudson Hills Press, 2000), 148; and Amy Kurtz, "*In Grandmother's Time*, the Colonial Revival and Smith" (unpublished paper, Smith College Museum of Art object files, 1996).

15. Marling, 60–61. See also Celia Betsky, "Inside the Past: The Interior and the Colonial Revival," in *The Colonial Revival in America*, ed. Axelrod, 241–77.

16. See also William Merritt Chase's *Ready for the Ride* (1877, Union League Club, New York) and J. Alden Weir's *Still Life in the Studio* (ca. 1878, Yale University Art Gallery).

17. These were shown at the Pennsylvania Academy of the Fine Arts in 1877.

18. For a discussion of geraniums, see Ellen G. Miles, "Rubens Peale with a Geranium," in *American Paintings of the Nineteenth Century*, pt. 2, ed. Robert Wilson Torchia, Deborah Chotner, and Ellen G. Miles (Washington, D.C.: National Gallery of Art, 1998), 51–52.

19. Simpson, 212.

20. Several artists gave their works titles that indicated they were costume pieces of present-day women. An example is Francis Davis Millet's *Lady in Costume of 1740*, exhibited at the Centennial. It depicts a woman "in the dress worn by her great-great grandmother . . . on the occasion of her wedding in 1740." See Marling, 60.

21. See Charles H. Woodman, "Love a Hundred Years Ago," *Appleton's Journal* 15 (March 25, 1876): 390–94; Margaret Hunt, "Literary Success a Hundred Years Ago," *Appleton's Journal* 9 (November 1880): 432–37; Mary Chase Granger, "One Hundred Years Ago,"

Ladies' Repository, August 29, 1875, 151–55. Simpson indicates that Eakins's title was inspired by the article "An American Lady's Occupations Seventy Years Ago," which appeared in *Lippincott's Magazine* in April 1875. See Simpson, 404n15. However, the language was so common both in the press and even among artists in the period that it is difficult to establish a singular source. Eakins's friend William Sartain exhibited a work at the National Academy of Design in 1879 also titled *Seventy Years Ago.*

22. Frances Crowell interview, Lloyd and Edith Havens Goodrich Papers, Philadelphia Museum of Art (hereafter Goodrich Papers). By 1838, Benjamin Eakins was working as a teacher and living with his cousin William Fife, a writing master at 67 Locust Street. See Advertisement, *Pennsylvania Inquirer and Daily Courier* (Philadelphia), September 13, 1838. By 1843, the two men had moved to 10 Sergeant Street. In October of that year, Benjamin left Fife and moved into the home of his mother-in-law, "Margaret Cowperthwait, gentlewoman," at 4 Carrolton Square. The surname was originally spelled "Akins." It changed to "Eakins" sometime around 1828 when Alexander Eakins petitioned for U.S. citizenship.

23. Adrienne D. Hood, "The Gender Division of Labor in the Production of Textiles in Eighteenth-Century Rural Pennsylvania (Rethinking the New England Model)," *Journal of Social History* 27 (Spring 1994): 537–62; and Adrienne D. Hood, "The Material World of Cloth: Production and Use in Eighteenth-Century Rural Pennsylvania," *William and Mary Quarterly* 53 (January 1996): 43–66.

24. Alexander Eakins's will, "Inventory of the Estate September 13, 1839," Chester County, Pa.

25. BE to Henry Huttner, July 29, 1874, Charles Bregler's Thomas Eakins Collection, Pennsylvania Academy of the Fine Arts (hereafter PAFA).

26. Goodrich, 1:158.

27. The two other works are the watercolor *Spinning* and the oil *The Courtship.*

28. For a different interpretation of these images, see Martin A. Berger, *Man Made: Thomas Eakins and the Construction of Gilded Age Manhood* (Berkeley and Los Angeles: University of California Press, 2000), 54–58.

29. Laurel Thatcher Ulrich, *The Age of Homespun* (New York: Alfred A. Knopf, 2001), 93.

30. See Sylvia Yount, "A 'New Century' for Women: Philadelphia's Centennial Exhibition and Domestic Reform," in *Philadelphia's Cultural Landscape: The Sartain Family Legacy*, ed. Katharine Martinez and Page Talbott (Philadelphia: Temple University Press, 2000), 149–60.

31. Rebecca Fussell to her daughter, April 2, 1871, quoted in Goodrich, 1:76. Caroline Eakins may have suffered with her condition for several years. In January 1867, Eakins wrote to his sister Frances, "Why haven't I got [Mommy's] photograph. I cant [*sic*] help worrying when I hear of something strange." TE to FE, January 8, 1867, Bregler Collection, PAFA. This cryptic exchange suggests that Eakins worried about his mother even during his student days in Paris. Henry Adams suggests that Eakins was "his mother's primary caregiver." However, there is no evidence proving that this was the case. Adams, 170. See also Sarah Burns, "Ordering the Artist's Body: Thomas Eakins's Acts of Self-Portrayal," *American Art* 19 (Spring 2005): 84–85.

32. A friend of the family, Sallie Shaw, whom Goodrich interviewed in the 1930s, claimed that Eakins was not smitten with Kathrin Crowell. Goodrich, 1:79–80. Gordon Hendricks possessed a partial copy of a lengthy text by William Crowell, which documents the severance of ties between Crowell and his sister Elizabeth over moral differences. William Crowell account, ca. 1892, Gordon Hendricks Papers, Archives of American Art (hereafter Hendricks Papers).

33. William Crowell account, Hendricks Papers.

34. Eakins's contact with the doctors began very early in his career. Wood studied penmanship with Eakins's father, and during the Civil War Mitchell collaborated with Dr. William W. Keen, who would become the instructor for anatomy at the Pennsylvania Academy. Mitchell owned Eakins's painting *Negro Whistling Plover* by 1877.

35. G. M. Beard, "Neurasthenia, or Nervous Exhaustion," *Boston Medical and Surgical Journal* 3 (April 29, 1869): 217. See also Francis G. Gosling, *Before Freud: Neurasthenia and the American Medical Community, 1870–1910* (Urbana: University of Illinois Press, 1987).

36. Eakins probably underwent Wood's cure in 1887 when the doctor arranged for him to spend several months at the B-T Ranch in the Dakota Territory following the artist's forced resignation from the Pennsylvania Academy.

37. Sally Mills, "The Spinner (A Sketch)," in *Thomas Eakins*, ed. John Wilmerding (Washington, D.C.: Smithsonian Institution Press, 1993), 95.

38. *Courtship* file, Goodrich Papers. In her retrospective diary, Susan Eakins remembered the purchase as happening in 1889. However, Eakins exhibited the sketch for *Courtship* in 1878 at the Social Art Club in Philadelphia, suggesting that he was working on the painting in that year. Wood's son's account of his father's snatching the unfinished canvas from the artist remains the accepted version of the story. Bregler Collection, PAFA.

39. The signature is no longer visible with the naked eye. The fugitive red pigment on the bench once read "Eakins." Thanks to Jane Glover in the American Art Department of the San Francisco Fine Art Museums for confirming this.

40. Kathleen A. Foster, *Thomas Eakins Rediscovered* (New Haven, Conn.: Yale University Press, 1997), 394; and Roger Stein, "Gilded Age Pilgrims," in *Picturing Old New England: Image and Memory*, ed. William H. Truettner and Roger B. Stein (New Haven, Conn.: Yale University Press, 1999), 47.

41. Horatio C. Wood, *Brain-Work and Overwork* (Philadelphia: Presley Blakiston, 1880), 85. Eakins's friend Dr. William W. Keen was the editor of this series.

42. Silas Weir Mitchell, *Wear and Tear or Hints for the Overworked* (J. B. Lippincott, 1887; repr., New York: Arno Press, 1973), 8.

43. At least two sales of Mitchell's collections were held at Wm. D. Morley's art galleries in Philadelphia. The first sale of the "Library of Dr. S. Weir Mitchell" was held on May 19, 1941, and included "books, autographs, prints, and historical relics." The second sale of "Selected, Choice and Labeled Early American Furniture, Silver, Lowestoft, Paintings, Etc. from the Biddle, Newbold, Roberts, Earnshaw and Mitchell Families" was held on May 28, 1942. This second sale included a reproduction "Philadelphia Chippendale-Style Carved Mahogany Side Chair" copied after a chair retained by the Mitchell family. Mitchell specialized in collecting revolutionary-era material, including, for example, documents autographed by Signers, Washingtoniana, and a diary kept by Benedict Arnold. For a discussion of Wood's chair, see Lifton, 345–50.

44. Goodrich transcription, TE to James P. Scott, June 18, 1883, Goodrich Papers.

45. Silas Weir Mitchell, 8–9.

46. M.E.W.S., "Arachne and Penelope," *Appleton's Journal* 4 (January-February 1878): 62–63.

47. Silas Weir Mitchell, 30.

48. Burns, "Ordering the Artist's Body," 82, suggests that Eakins may have feared mental illness because of his mother's disease.

49. Academy president James L. Claghorn received one letter dated April 11, 1882, and signed "R.S.," identified as a parent of one of the female students, which complained of Eakins's methods. In 1884, Diana Franklin, an Academy student, launched a protest over the use of male models in the schools. PAFA, Archives.

50. Margaret McHenry, *Thomas Eakins, Who Painted* (Oreland, Pa.: Privately printed, 1946), 29.

51. TE to Edward H. Coates, September 11, 1886, Bregler Collection, PAFA.

52. TE to Edward H. Coates, September 11, 1886, Bregler Collection, PAFA. Eakins's attitudes toward his female students may also be acknowledged in the Art Student's League (ASL) of Philadelphia that was organized by PAFA students after Eakins's dismissal from the Academy. The ASL was a predominantly male enclave, with very few female students in attendance. Of the names listed in a record book of attendees kept by Edward Boulton, only three women who were not related to Eakins are listed. Eakins Archive, Philadelphia Museum of Art.

53. Silas Weir Mitchell, 36.

54. Silas Weir Mitchell, 44.

55. Silas Weir Mitchell, 33, 36.

56. Silas Weir Mitchell, 47.

57. The Ecole did not admit women until 1897. Tamar Garb has discussed the fears that French male artists voiced about women attending the school and the notion that women were too weak to handle contact with life models. According to Garb, critics of women artists even suggested that admission to the Ecole would "reduce the nation's birthrate . . . because [women's] reproductive capacities would inevitably deteriorate as a result of excessive mental stimulation." Tamar Garb, "The Forbidden Gaze," *Art in America* 79 (May 1991): 147–51, 186.

58. Amy Werbel, *Thomas Eakins: Art, Medicine, and Sexuality in Nineteenth-Century Philadelphia* (New Haven, Conn.: Yale University Press, 2007), 68–72.

59. For a history of the college's collection, see Linda Muehling, ed., *Masterworks of American Painting and Sculpture from Smith College Museum of Art* (New York: Hudson Hills Press, 1999), 8–13; and Charles Cheltenham, "The Smith College Museum of Art," *Magazine Antiques* (November 1969): 768–75.

60. Silas Weir Mitchell, 44.

61. Office of the President, Annual Report, Smith College, 1875–76. For additional information about Smith College and Seelye, see Harriet Seelye Rhees, *Laurenus Clark Seelye* (Boston: Houghton Mifflin, 1929); and L. Clark Seelye, *The Early History of Smith College, 1871–1910* (Boston: Houghton Mifflin, 1923).

62. Elizabeth Johns, *Thomas Eakins: The Heroism of Modern Life* (Princeton, N.J.: Princeton University Press, 1983), 28–30; Berger, 8–46. Although Eakins had ceased painting rowing subjects by the time he began the colonial revival images, he frequently exhibited these subjects together.

63. H. Barbara Weinberg, "Thomas Eakins and the Metropolitan Museum of Art," *Metropolitan Museum of Art Bulletin* 52 (Winter 1994–95): 25; Foster, 96; Marc Simpson, "The 1880s," in *Thomas Eakins*, ed. Sewell, 109.

64. Goodrich, 1:158.

65. Will Homespun, *Aurora*, August 16, 1809, 2.

66. M.E.W.S., "Arachne and Penelope," 63. Another classical connection can be found in Diego Velázquez's painting, *Las Hilanderas* (Museo del Prado, Madrid), which features women at the spinning wheel and alludes to Arachne's competition with the goddess Athena. Eakins admired this painting during his visit to the Prado as a student.

67. Marc Simpson, "Thomas Eakins and His Arcadian Works," *Smithsonian Studies in American Art* 1 (Fall 1987): 83.

68. Lloyd Goodrich transcription, TE to James P. Scott, June 18, 1883, Goodrich Papers.

69. TE to James. P. Scott, July 11, 1883, Bregler Collection, PAFA. Eakins continued the comparison with Phidias's work, writing, "To make an analogy then, my panels should be

finished 12/2 just 6 times as much as the Phidias work." He also recommended that Scott look at "some little Greek reliefs at the Academy" as well.

70. David Sellin, "Eakins and the Macdowells and the Academy," in *Thomas Eakins, Susan Macdowell Eakins, Elizabeth Kenton* (Roanoke, Va.: North Cross School, 1977), 27–28. Similarly, Susan's watercolor *Chaperone* (1879) focuses on the chaperone figure from Eakins's painting of William Rush.

71. Undated clipping, Bregler Collection, PAFA.

72. This award was given by the Academy for accurate drawing. In 1879, Susan won the Mary Smith Award for her painting *The Rehearsal*, given for the best painting by a woman native of Philadelphia.

73. Susan Eakins's retrospective diary, Bregler Collection, PAFA. It is interesting that these photographs were taken two weeks before Susan completed the sketch for *The Old Clock on the Stairs*, which she records on July 1, 1881.

74. A similar photograph of Eakins's sister Caroline (Caddie) served as the basis for Elizabeth Macdowell's painting *Day Dreams*. In both the painting and the photograph, a prominently placed spinning wheel was one of the primary props.

75. Ellwood C. Parry III, "The Thomas Eakins Portrait of Sue and Harry; or, When Did the Artist Change His Mind?" *Arts Magazine* 53 (May 1979): 146–53. Parry identifies a number of possible influences on the painting.

76. Parry was the first to discuss these changes. Parry also notes the setting of the work. Subsequent consideration of the conservation data can be found in Natalie Spassky with Linda Bantel, Doreen Bolger Burke, Meg Perlman, and Amy L. Walsh, ed. Kathleen Luhrs, assisted by Jacolyn A. Mott, *American Paintings in the Metropolitan Museum of Art*, vol. 2 (New York: Metropolitan Museum of Art, 1985), 613–19.

77. Scholars have also characterized the painting in this way. The most extreme reaction is perhaps Henry Adams's statement that the portrait is "a study in ugliness and weakness." Adams, 326.

78. Spassky et al., 616.

79. Henry Adams has suggested that the presence of the Japanese book demonstrates that Eakins intended the work as "a parody of a voguish mode of painting at the time—the representation of women in Japanese costume." Adams, 327. However, Eakins never ventured into parody in his professional work. Susan collected Japanese books, some of which are in the Bregler Collection, PAFA. Other Japanese items owned by the Macdowell sisters are in the collection of the Taubman Museum of Art in Roanoke, Virginia.

80. Using the dimensions of the *Arcadia* plaster as a guide, the image of *Figure Study: Woman Sewing* in Eakins's painting is slightly larger than it is today. However, files at the Pennsylvania Academy suggest that Susan's sketch was trimmed by Bregler before mounting on its current support. My thanks to Barbara Katus for bringing this to my attention.

81. I would like to thank Aileen Riberio, Linda Eaton, and Paula Richter for identifying the gown. For a discussion of red stockings, see Margaret F. MacDonald, "Maud Franklin and the 'Charming Little Swaggerers,'" in *Whistler, Women, and Fashion*, by Margaret F. MacDonald, Susan Grace Galassi, and Aileen Ribeiro, with Patricia de Montfort (New York: Frick Collection in association with Yale University Press, 2003), 147–53.

82. Roger B. Stein, "Artifact as Ideology: The Aesthetic Movement in Its American Cultural Context," in *In Pursuit of Beauty*, Doreen Bolger Burke, Jonathan Freedman, Alice Cooney Frelinghuysen, David A. Hanks, Marilyn Johnson, James D. Kornwolf, Catherine Lynn, Roger B. Stein, Jennifer Toher, and Catherine Hoover Voorsanger, with the assistance of Carrie Rebora (New York: Metropolitan Museum of Art, 1986), 41; and Simpson, "The 1880s," 116.

83. Karal Ann Marling, "Portrait of the Artist as a Young Woman: Miss Dora Wheeler," *Bulletin of the Cleveland Museum of Art* (February 1978): 53. Marling also identified the setting as Wheeler's studio.

84. Amelia Peck and Carol Irish, *Candace Wheeler: The Art and Enterprise of American Design, 1875–1900* (New Haven, Conn.: Yale University Press, 2001), 174.

85. Susan Eakins to Bryson Burroughs, quoted in Spassky et al., 616.

86. Laura R. Prieto, *At Home in the Studio: The Professionalization of Women Artists in America* (Cambridge, Mass.: Harvard University Press, 2001), 116.

87. Kirsten Swinth, *Painting Professionals: Women Artists and the Development of Modern American Art, 1870–1930* (Chapel Hill: University of North Carolina Press, 2001), 94–95.

88. See Spies, 84–109.

89. Silas Weir Mitchell, 32.

90. Sarah Burns has discussed the ways in which women artists were belittled and, at times, viewed as unfeminine; see Burns, *Inventing the Modern Artist*, 181–86.

91. Silas Weir Mitchell, 33.

92. Carroll Smith-Rosenberg, *Disorderly Conduct: Visions of Gender in Victorian America* (New York: Oxford University Press, 1985), 258. Rosenberg cites the work of another physician writing in this period, William Goodell, whose *Lessons in Gynecology* of 1879 was part of a series edited by Eakins's friend, Daniel G. Brinton. As Goodell wrote, "Our great-grandmothers got their schooling during the winter months and let their brains lie fallow the rest of the year. They knew less about Euclid and the classics than they did bout housekeeping and housework. But they made good wives and mothers, and bore and nursed sturdy sons and buxom daughters and plenty of them at that." William Goodell, *Lessons in Gynecology* (Philadelphia: D. G. Brinton, 1879), 353.

93. TE to William Crowell, September 21, 1868, Betsy Wyeth Collection, Brandywine River Museum, Chadds Ford, Pa.

CHAPTER THREE

1. TE to Edward H. Coates, late February 1886, Charles Bregler's Thomas Eakins Collection, Pennsylvania Academy of the Fine Arts (hereafter PAFA).

2. The most complete discussion of the series appears in Marc Simpson, "Thomas Eakins and His Arcadian Works," *Smithsonian Studies in American Art* 1 (Fall 1987): 71–95.

3. Leslie W. Miller, "Art: The Awards of Prizes at the Academy," *American*, November 7, 1885, 45.

4. According to Eakins's account book, he hired an unnamed model to pose for a work he called "Panel Piper" from June 1884 to late December 1884. This is likely one of the smaller Arcadian reliefs now known as *A Youth Playing the Pipes.* Collection of Mr. and Mrs. Daniel W. Dietrich II, copy, Eakins Archive, Philadelphia Museum of Art. In addition to the references to antiquity, Martin Berger sees the presence of the past in the old ruins upon which the men stand. He views these eighteenth- or early nineteenth-century foundations as a symbolic platform of tradition upon which the students intend to launch the modern artistic practice advocated by Eakins. Martin A. Berger, *Man Made: Thomas Eakins and the Construction of Gilded Age Manhood* (Berkeley and Los Angeles: University of California Press, 2000), 96.

5. Lecoq's influence on Eakins has been noted in Kathy Foster, "Paris and Philadelphia: Thomas Eakins and the Beaux-Arts" (M.A. thesis, Yale University, 1972), 16–18; Elizabeth LaMotte Cates Milroy, "Thomas Eakins' Artistic Training, 1860–1870" (Ph.D. diss., University of Pennsylvania, 1986), 168; and Anne McCauley "'The Most Beautiful of Nature's Works': Thomas Eakins's Photographic Nudes in their French and American Contexts," in

Eakins and the Photograph, ed. Susan Danly and Cheryl Leibold (Washington, D.C.: Smithsonian Institution Press, 1994), 49–50.

6. Randall C. Griffin, *Homer, Eakins, and Anshutz: The Search for American Identity in the Gilded Age* (University Park: Pennsylvania State Press, 2004), 76. Griffin relates the style of the landscape more directly to Barbizon painting but also suggests a comparison to works painted by Americans George W. Sheldon and William Morris Hunt.

7. Lloyd Goodrich referred to the Arcadian works as forming "a curious interlude in Eakins' art," and Gordon Hendricks considered them "among the artist's least successful projects." Lloyd Goodrich, *Thomas Eakins* (Cambridge, Mass.: Harvard University Press, 1982), 1:230; Gordon Hendricks, *The Life and Work of Thomas Eakins* (New York: Grossman, 1974), 188.

8. Kathleen A. Foster, "The Making and Meaning of *Swimming*" in *Thomas Eakins and the Swimming Picture*, ed. Doreen Bolger and Sarah Cash (Fort Worth, Tex.: Amon Carter Museum, 1996), 16; John G. Lamb Jr., "Eakins and the Arcadian Themes," in *Eakins at Avondale and Thomas Eakins: A Personal Collection*, ed. William Innes Homer (Chadds Ford, Pa.: Brandywine River Museum, 1980), 19–20.

9. Goodrich, 1:236–37.

10. Eakins's "troubles" almost always involved transgressions of gender boundaries—the removing of the loincloth of a male model in a class that included women is the most well known. Nudity itself was not the issue that destroyed Eakins's career at the Academy; rather, opportunities for the mixing of both genders in a sexualized environment led to his dismissal. During his tenure as the chairman of the Committee on Instruction, Fairman Rogers acknowledged the acceptability of the nude in a single-sex environment: "The male figure is more familiar to the male students . . . through opportunities afforded in swimming and the like." This suggests to me that the content of *Swimming*, with its all-male subjects, would have been less controversial in the 1880s than it is today. See Fairman Rogers, "The Schools of the Pennsylvania Academy of the Fine Arts," *Penn Monthly* (June 1881): 456.

11. The few reviews that mention the Arcadia relief do not include aesthetic evaluations of the work. One reviewer called it "clever," but that is the extent of the nineteenth-century reception available. See "Fine Arts: A Display of Studies and Sketches," *New York Herald*, October 20, 1883, 5.

12. Samuel Murray and Frank Linton were among those who owned a plaster. The relief also appears in the home of Lucy and Anna Lewis in Susan Macdowell Eakins's painting *At Home (The Lewis Sisters)* (1932, private collection).

13. Goodrich, 1:230.

14. Elizabeth Johns, *Thomas Eakins: The Heroism of Modern Life* (Princeton, N.J.: Princeton University Press, 1983), 129–30.

15. Henry Adams, *Eakins Revealed: The Secret Life of an American Artist* (New York: Oxford University Press, 2005), 303.

16. Simpson's conclusion that the "Arcadian theme is essentially elegiac" is based partly on the head on hand gestures of two of the figures, which he links with classical mourning iconography. Although this pose is melancholic, Simpson compares it with that of the first century *Pudicity* (Vatican Museum), which displays a different gesture than that seen in the Eakins panel. *Pudicity* is shown tugging at her veil, a pose that is found on Attic grave stelae that typically has marital associations.

17. At the sale of the William Merritt Chase estate, the *Arcadia* oil was titled *Idyl*. Whether Eakins used this title is not known.

18. Art historians have generally not probed too deeply into questions of attribution regarding the photographs. The consensus has been that, although Eakins did not take all of

the photographs himself, he oversaw and shaped the content of these projects. I will be following this tradition, but feel that more research is needed. The assumption that a male gaze influenced all of these images has had a strong impact on recent interpretations, yet there were many talented women photographers in the Eakins circle, including his wife, Susan.

19. Kathleen A. Foster, *Thomas Eakins Rediscovered* (New Haven, Conn.: Yale University Press, 1997), 117. More specifically, Foster and others have reasonably postulated that Eakins's preference for certain negatives is revealed by the greater numbers of prints of those images and the use of the more expensive platinum process in printing them. Foster has also suggested that the multiple prints may reflect Eakins's experimentation with development processes.

20. Simpson, 76. Less convincingly, Henry Adams has suggested that Greek subjects merely provided Eakins with "a pretext for beginning to undress his students." Adams, 299. Life study alone would have provided a pretext if any were needed to study the nude.

21. A useful discussion of Lecoq in a French context can be found in Petra ten-Doesschate Chu, "Lecoq de Boisbaudran and Memory Drawing: A Teaching Course Between Idealism and Naturalism," in *The European Realist Tradition*, ed. Gabriel P. Weisberg (Bloomington: Indiana University Press, 1982), 242–89.

22. Horace Lecoq de Boisbaudran, *The Training of the Memory in Art, and the Education of the Artist*, trans. L. D. Luard (London: Macmillan, 1911), 85. For the sake of clarity, I have used Luard's English translation of Lecoq's three texts. Luard simultaneously reprinted the texts in French in 1911. Possibly due to his work on the two publications simultaneously, Luard's English translation adheres closely to the French.

23. Luard, 95. Georges Bellenger and Léon Lhermitte were part of this demonstration.

24. Eakins purchased a copy of Thomas Couture's *Méthode et entretiens d'atelier* in 1868. TE to BE, March 17, 1868, Bregler Collection, PAFA.

25. William Sartain manuscript in Gordon Hendricks Papers, Archives of American Art. A loose sheet from 1869 written by William Sartain lists the "professors of the 'Petit [*sic*] Ecole'where I go." His list includes twelve professors who regularly taught at the school in the late 1860s and into the 1880s. Eakins and Sartain intermittently shared a studio at this time.

26. TE to BE, November 30, 1867, Bregler Collection, PAFA.

27. TE to BE, January 17, 1868, Lloyd and Edith Havens Goodrich Thomas Eakins Research Collection, Philadelphia Museum of Art.

28. TE to BE, March 6, 1868, Bregler Collection, PAFA.

29. Luard, 18.

30. Kathleen A. Foster and Cheryl Leibold, *Writing about Eakins* (Philadelphia: University of Pennsylvania Press, 1989), 298–99.

31. Gordon Hendricks Collection, Archives of American Art, undated manuscript. The dictum "Strain your brain more than your eyes" appears in Charles Bregler's notes on Eakins's teaching. Susan's use of it here in regard to memory suggests a more specific context for its application to Eakins's pedagogical method.

32. TE to Edmund Clarence Messer, July 3, 1906, Archives of the Corcoran Gallery of Art, Washington, D.C.

33. Régamey published an appreciation of his teacher, titled *Horace Lecoq de Boisbaudran et ses élèves: Notes and souvenirs* (Paris: Champion, 1903).

34. Régamey visited the Sketch Club on June 15, 1876. Sketch Club Records, Archives of American Art.

35. Felix Régamey, *L'enseignement du dessin aux Etats-Unis* (Paris: Delagrave, 1881). In

his book, Régamey used statistics for the Academy's 1878–79 season but named Eakins as "le directeur actuel" of the school, a position he could only have claim to after September 1879. In his account, Régamey also mentions the first exhibition of the Society of Artists in November 1879, further pinpointing the date of his visit to the Academy.

36. Mark Tucker and Nica Gutman, "Photographs and the Making of Paintings," in *Thomas Eakins*, ed. Darrel Sewell (Philadelphia: Philadelphia Museum of Art, 2001), 225–38.

37. W. Douglass Paschall, "The Camera Artist," in *Thomas Eakins*, ed. Sewell, 247.

38. Eakins's method is detailed in Tucker and Gutman, 225–38.

39. Luard, 21.

40. Luard, 16–17.

41. Pennsylvania Academy of the Fine Arts, *Circular of the Committee on Instruction, 1882–83* (Philadelphia: PAFA, 1882), 3.

42. Luard, 136.

43. Goodrich, 1:141, from a letter dated June 13, 1877, to Geo. D. McCreary.

44. William C. Brownell, "The Art Schools of Philadelphia," *Scribner's Monthly* (September 1879): 745.

45. Amy Werbel, *Thomas Eakins: Art, Medicine, and Sexuality in Nineteenth-Century Philadelphia* (New Haven, Conn.: Yale University Press, 2007), 51.

46. Luard, 34.

47. Muybridge's work was published in several journals worldwide and also became available in the photographic portfolio *The Horse in Motion* (1878). According to the annual report of the Academy for 1878, Rogers donated a set of Muybridge photographs to the school. Pennsylvania Academy Minutes, February 3, 1879, Archives of American Art.

48. Michael Leja, *Looking Askance: Skepticism and American Art from Eakins to Duchamp* (Berkeley and Los Angeles: University of California Press, 2004), 66–71.

49. "The Academy," *North American* (Philadelphia), November 19, 1880.

50. Eadweard Muybridge gave two lectures on animal locomotion at the Pennsylvania Academy in February 1883. In the years following, Eakins's interest in motion photography grew. He observed Muybridge's continued experiments at the University of Pennsylvania and even devised a camera and method for producing motion photographs of his own.

51. Adam Emory Albright, "Memories of Thomas Eakins," *Harper's Bazaar* (August 1947): 139.

52. Sketch Club Records, Archives of American Art.

53. Pennsylvania Academy Records, Archives of American Art.

54. Ellwood C. Parry III, "Thomas Eakins's 'Naked Series' Reconsidered: Another Look at the Standing Nude Photographs Made for the Use of Eakins's Students," *American Art Journal* 20 (1988): 53–77.

55. See Danly and Leibold, 192, cat. nos. 363–65.

56. Luard, 29.

57. Luard, 159.

58. Luard, 35 (emphasis mine).

59. Luard, 30.

60. The disjointed nature of the human and landscape elements is not unlike that found in Eakins's more realist paintings, such as his rowing subjects. Here the effect may be complicated by the unfinished state of the works, as Eakins often added a toning layer to his finished works that would likely have unified these compositions.

61. Kathleen Foster has noted that a platinum print of this image in the Bregler Collection has been enlarged to the same scale as the figure in the painting, which may suggest that Eakins used this photograph directly for his transfer to the canvas. See Foster, *Thomas Eakins, Rediscovered*, 183.

62. Simpson, 78.

63. Simpson, 74–75.

64. Phyllis D. Rosenzweig, *The Thomas Eakins Collection of the Hirshhorn Museum and Sculpture Garden* (Washington, D.C.: Smithsonian Institution Press, 1977), 104–5.

65. Brownell, 742.

66. Both Eakins and Lecoq were opposed to awarding prizes to art students. Lecoq believed that prizes stifled innovation by teaching students to conform to a style that pleased conservative juries.

67. Luard, 85.

68. Albright, 184.

69. Luard, 152–53.

70. Luard, 32.

71. Luard, 159.

72. Luard, 39.

73. The Academy owned a large collection of costumes.

74. Eakins took the theme a step further and painted a sketch of one of these compositions, known as *Sketch of Woman with Torso* (private collection).

75. Edward H. Coates to TE, November 21, 1885, Bregler Collection, PAFA.

76. Griffin, 75.

77. Edward H. Coates to TE, November 21, 1885, Bregler Collection, PAFA. After its PAFA debut, *Swimming* was shown at the Southern Exposition in Louisville, Kentucky (1886), and the Inter-State Industrial Exposition in Chicago (1887).

78. Whitney Davis, "Erotic Revision in Thomas Eakins's Narratives of Male Nudity," *Art History* 17 (September 1994): 301–41; and Michael Hatt, "The Male Body in Another Frame: Thomas Eakins' *The Swimming Hole* as a Homoerotic Image," *Journal of Philosophy and the Visual Arts: The Body* 4 (1993): 9–21. See also Randall C. Griffin, "Thomas Eakins' Construction of the Male Body, or 'Men Get to Know Each Other across the Space of Time,'" *Oxford Art Journal* 18 (1995): 70–80. Of course, as Werbel, 43, observes, "Homosexuality was almost completely nonexistent in public discourse" during the nineteenth century. For an extended discussion of homosexuality in this cultural context, see also Werbel, 126–49.

79. Doreen Bolger and Sarah Cash, eds., *Thomas Eakins and the Swimming Picture* (Fort Worth, Tex.: Amon Carter Museum, 1996).

80. Berger, 106; Werbel, 51.

81. For a discussion of the work in this context, see Foster, "Making and Meaning of Swimming," 26; and Rosenzweig, 114.

82. Henry Adams feels that Eakins had a somewhat sinister obsession with nudity. See Adams, 279–326. See chapter 1 for a discussion of Alma-Tadema's *A Sculptor's Model.* Much of the concern over nudity seemed to focus on the female figure and the potential of such images to "cause mischief" for young men.

83. Werbel, 43.

84. "Philadelphia Art Notes: Studio Notes," *Art Age* 2 (May 1885): 159. Some of Eakins's students clearly knew the subject of the painting as well. Thomas Anshutz (who did not pose for the painting) wrote to J. Laurie Wallace on August 25, 1884, "Eakins is painting a picture for Mr. Coates of a party of boys in swimming." Goodrich typescript of Anshutz letter from the Joslyn Museum Collection, Goodrich Papers, Philadelphia Museum of Art.

85. Foster, "Making and Meaning of Swimming," 26.

86. "Pennsylvania Academy Exhibition," *Art Amateur* 14 (December 1885): 5. Harrison's painting was destroyed by fire in 1886. Critics also praised John Singer Sargent for his *Neapolitan Children Bathing* (1878), featuring four nude boys on a beach, which he exhibited at the

National Academy of Design in 1879. Over a decade earlier a composition remarkably similar to *Swimming* had even appeared in the pages of the London *Art Journal*, complete with diving figure.

87. I do not contend that Eakins's images are devoid of eroticism, but rather that his works are far less explicit than other imagery of the period. Eakins had access to two landmark examples of the erotic female nude at the Academy: Cabanel's *Birth of Venus* and Vanderlyn's *Ariadne Asleep on the Island of Naxos.* Both were owned by Philadelphia collectors and eventually entered the Academy's collection. Cabanel's work was exhibited at the PAFA annual in 1877 along with Vanderlyn's *Ariadne*, which also appeared in the annual of the following year. In each, the figure is on erotically charged display. In Eakins's own exploration of the female nude, *William Rush Carving His Allegorical Figure of the Schuylkill River*, first shown at the Boston Art Club in January 1878, in contrast, the model turns her back to the viewer. Some scholars have suggested that Eakins's similar discretion in *Swimming* was intended to protect his models. Yet only two men in the painting are clearly seen—Eakins and the reclining man identified in the Amon Carter show as Talcott Williams. None of the figures identified as Eakins's students show their faces, making the need to obscure their anatomy unnecessary.

88. Adams, 325.

89. Luard, 29. For a discussion of Riley and Whitman's poetry, see Foster, "Making and Meaning of Swimming," 28–29. See also Berger, 89–90.

90. Luard, 31.

91. Since Eakins situated the figure next to a body of water, it is probable that he had classical river gods in mind. These were also the source images for William Rush's *Allegory of the Schuylkill River in Its Improved State.*

92. Tucker and Gutman, 235–36.

93. "At the Private View: First Impressions of the Autumn Exhibition at the Academy of the Fine Arts," *Times* (Philadelphia), October 29, 1885, 2. For the diving figure, Eakins created a sculptural wax model that he suspended on a string to give the impression of being in middive. Leja discusses the disjunctions in representation here as well, noting that "the splash is rendered schematically rather than illusionistically." Leja, 259n33.

94. Luard, 66.

CHAPTER FOUR

1. An important discussion of the work appears in Lois Dinnerstein, "Thomas Eakins' *Crucifixion* as Perceived by Mariana Griswold Van Rensselaer," *Arts Magazine* (May 1979): 140–45. However, the first extended discussion of the painting came only in 1989, with Elizabeth Milroy, "'Consummatum est . . .': A Reassessment of Thomas Eakins's *Crucifixion* of 1880," *Art Bulletin* 71 (June 1989): 269–84. The pre-1989 literature often mentioned the painting but typically as an anomaly. As Milroy has noted, the Philadelphia Museum of Art (which owns *Crucifixion*) did not even include the painting in its 1982 exhibition of Eakins's work. Since Milroy's article, the painting's significance has been acknowledged, yet it remains a difficult work to integrate into Eakins's oeuvre.

2. Lloyd Goodrich, *Thomas Eakins* (Cambridge, Mass.: Harvard University Press, 1982), 1:196. Henry Adams reiterates Goodrich's notion: "It eliminates the sort of spiritual or religious content usually associated with the subject." Henry Adams, *Eakins Revealed: The Secret Life of an American Artist* (New York: Oxford University Press, 2005), 296. Similarly, the catalogue entry for the sketch for *Crucifixion* in *The Hand and the Spirit* reads, "It is quite certain that it was done without reference to any religious body or beliefs." See Jane Dillenberger and Joshua Taylor, *The Hand and the Spirit: Religious Art in America, 1700–1900*

(Berkeley, Calif.: University Art Museum, 1972), 156. Martin Berger has also discussed how Eakins's emphasis on the body effectively "drained the image of religious significance." Martin Berger, *Man Made: Thomas Eakins and the Construction of Gilded Age Manhood* (Berkeley and Los Angeles: University of California Press, 2000), 87–89.

3. Amy Werbel suggests that *Crucifixion* reveals "rather than an interest in spirituality or history" Eakins's "fascination with human anatomy." Amy Werbel, *Thomas Eakins: Art, Medicine, and Sexuality in Nineteenth-Century Philadelphia* (New Haven, Conn.: Yale University Press, 2007), 37–38. The link with anatomy was affirmed in the 2001 Eakins retrospective at the Philadelphia Museum of Art. Although Marc Simpson's catalogue essays nicely handle the religious content of the painting, in the exhibition itself, viewers found the painting displayed next to bronze anatomical casts that Eakins used for teaching. It was also one of the few major paintings in the exhibition that was hung without any wall text. See Marc Simpson, "The 1880s," and "Eakins's Vision of the Past and the Building of a Reputation," in *Thomas Eakins*, ed. Darrel Sewell (Philadelphia: Philadelphia Museum of Art, 2001), 108–9, 221–22.

4. Milroy, 283.

5. In her article on the painting, Elizabeth Milroy used the absence of the wound in Christ's side to pinpoint the exact moment depicted as the "Consummatum": the moment just after Christ cries out "It is finished" and dies, but before the wound is inflicted in his side by a Roman soldier. Milroy associates this episode with the liturgical moment of the "Consummatum," a pregnant pause in the Good Friday service, in the Catholic tradition. While I agree with her identification of the scene itself, I find the relation to the Catholic liturgy less likely. I see the image as being more universal and question the notion that Eakins would have wanted to paint devotional subjects for the church. Kristin Schwain has also related the painting to Catholicism in "Figuring Belief: American Art and Modern Religious Experience" (Ph.D. diss., Stanford University, 2001). Schwain provides a compelling discussion of Eakins's later clerical portraits, but I feel that the much earlier *Crucifixion* is less easily defined by his interest in Catholicism, which blossomed later in his career.

6. Although the work came before the public in 1882 at an auspicious moment for Eakins, just months after he had been promoted to director of the academy's schools, he would not have known that when he completed the work in 1880.

7. For a list of exhibitions and reviews, see Elizabeth Milroy, ed., *Guide to the Thomas Eakins Research Collection with a Lifetime Exhibition Record and Bibliography* (Philadelphia: Philadelphia Museum of Art, 1996). Only four reviews are noted in the lifetime exhibition record for the 1882 Society of American Artists (SAA) show in which *Crucifixion* appeared publicly for the first time. However, the compliers of the volume acknowledged that "the list even now must be incomplete." I have found six additional reviews for the SAA show alone. What is striking about these reviews is that the length of the coverage surpasses most other reviews of Eakins's work. I have found additional reviews for other exhibitions featuring the painting and uncovered a previously unknown venue for the painting at the Boston Mechanics Fair of 1887. TE to John W. Beatty, September 25, 1900, Carnegie Institute, Museum of Art Records, Archives of American Art. Eakins wrote to Beatty, "I think I shall send my Crucifixion which is probably my best painting."

8. Theodor Siegl reiterated Goodrich's argument in *The Thomas Eakins Collection* (Philadelphia: Philadelphia Museum of Art), 88–90. Kathleen A. Foster also examined the realist influence in the painting in *Thomas Eakins Rediscovered* (New Haven, Conn.: Yale University Press, 1997), 45. Foster frames her discussion with a thoughtful comparison to Bonnat's painting, *Le Christ*.

9. Marc Simpson discusses the painting with respect to the writings of Ernest Renan in his essay "The 1880s," 108–9.

10. Goodrich, 1:190.

11. Siegl, 89.

12. Goodrich, 1:191.

13. Foster, 169. Foster also mentions Eakins's use of the rooftop to study models of rowers that he made for the rowing series. Even earlier, Eakins studied his models on the roof of a building in Spain for his painting *Street Scene in Seville.*

14. The story was told in the press when the painting made its debut at the SAA exhibition. The critic for the *Art Amateur* wrote, "We are told that Mr. Eakins painted his picture out of doors, his model having been suspended on a cross erected on the roof of the artist's house in Philadelphia." *Art Amateur* 7 (June 1882): 2. The same version of the story was mentioned in the *New York Daily Tribune*, May 17, 1882, 5. Clarence Cook wrote for both journals, and it is probable that the two reviews reiterating this story are by him.

15. Julian Alden Weir to his father, postmarked February 21, 1874, in Dorothy Weir Young, *The Life and Letters of J. Alden Weir* (New Haven, Conn.: Yale University Press, 1960; repr., New York: Kennedy Graphics and DeCapo, 1971), 30–31. Walter Blackman, who was mentioned by Weir as witnessing this grisly scene with him, was a close friend of the Philadelphia painter Thomas Hovenden.

16. J. M. Nugent to Arthur B. Wilder, June 11, 1935, Arthur B. Wilder Papers, Archives of American Art.

17. "Zealous Soldier Reproduces Tragedy of Golgotha," *Public Ledger*, April 13, 1919, clipping in the Philip R. McDevitt Papers, J. W. Shanahan Memorial Archives, Diocese of Harrisburg.

18. The *Public Ledger* article about Murray's commission compares the sculptor's methods to a version of the story of Parrhasios: "What followed is, in many respects, reminiscent of the story of Parrhasius, one of the greatest painters of ancient Greece, most readers undoubtedly are familiar with the poem which tells of how Parrhasius, portraying on canvas the agony of an aged slave who had been nailed to a cross, implores him for forgiveness for making this use of his agony. But although his own heart is pierced with grief and horror, Parrhasius does not for an instant lose sight of his purpose." I have not been able to locate the poem mentioned in this text. Nathaniel Parker Willis wrote a poem titled "Parrhasius," but it essentially recounts the story as found in Seneca and does not involve a crucifixion.

19. Ernst Kris and Otto Kurz, *Legend, Myth, and Magic in the Image of the Artist: A Historical Experiment* (New Haven, Conn.: Yale University Press, 1979), 114. Kris and Kurz discuss how the story became attached to two Crucifixions by Michelangelo, as well as works on the same theme by other artists. Alisa Luxenberg, "Leon Bonnat (1833–1922)" (Ph.D. diss., New York University, 1990), says that the cadaver story derives from the tales surrounding Michelangelo's work. While the long-standing artistic legend no doubt informed the story, Weir's account would suggest that Bonnat did use a cadaver. Luxenberg stresses that the cadaver story only emerged in later biographies of Bonnat and did not surface at the time of the painting's exhibition in 1874. Similar stories surrounded Caravaggio's *Death of the Virgin*, which told of his use of a drowned corpse as the model for the Virgin Mary.

20. Pliny credits the painter Apollodoros with the epigram "Xeuxis stole the art from his very teachers, and carried it off with him." Quoted in J. J. Pollitt, *The Art of Ancient Greece* (Cambridge: Cambridge University Press, 1990), 149. Interestingly, the *Public Ledger* article about Murray's sculpture in no way acknowledges Eakins's treatment of the subject, yet several of the articles about Eakins's painting mention Bonnat. This, to some extent, reflects the temperaments of the two men. Murray's work was so closely linked with Eakins's for much of his career, especially in terms of subject matter, that he understandably desired more credit for his sculpture. Eakins, to the end, acknowledged his debt to his teachers and seems to have enjoyed the comparison to them.

21. The painting was exhibited at the Salon under the title *Jerusalem*. It was included in exhibitions at the National Academy of Design (1876) and the Union League (1875) as *Crucifixion*. Gérôme made a smaller replica of the work that probably served as the model for an engraving by Hermann Eichens. See Gerald M. Ackerman, *Jean-Léon Gérôme: Monographie Révisée Catalogue Raisonné mis à jour* (Tours: ACR Édition, 2000), 262.

22. As Milroy has noted, artists such as Delacroix and Rubens also turned the cross, but with a greater sense of dramatic potential that was heightened by other compositional choices such as the darkened sky or the inclusion of emotional onlookers. Eakins loathed Rubens's work, making him an unlikely model for his composition. Milroy, "'Consummatum est . . .': A Reassessment of Thomas Eakins's *Crucifixion* of 1880," 271.

23. The contents of Claghorn's collection are documented in several sources; for example, the catalogue for the Forty-ninth Annual Exhibition at the Pennsylvania Academy (1878) included a full list of the Claghorn prints on display. Among the prints were several religious subjects, including scenes of the Passion, with at least seven Crucifixions among them. The Baltimore Museum of Art now owns most of the Claghorn collection. See Catherine Stover, "James L. Claghorn: Philadelphia Collector," *Archives of American Art Journal* 27 (1987): 4–8.

24. Eakins's sister Frances kept a diary during a trip to Europe that she took with her father to see Eakins. The three spent much of August 1868 traveling through Italy and Germany, seeing, for example, "numerous churches and picture galleries" in Venice. Eakins-Crowell Selected Papers, 1795–1938, Archives of American Art.

25. Jonathan Brown and Carmen Garrido, *Velázquez: The Technique of Genius* (New Haven, Conn.: Yale University Press, 1998), 70.

26. Bonnat, a devout Catholic, had close ties to the church establishment. His aunt was the mother superior of a convent, and he even considered entering the priesthood himself.

27. Siegl, 89.

28. TE to Caroline Cowperthwait Eakins, October 1, 1866, Charles Bregler's Thomas Eakins Collection, Pennsylvania Academy of the Fine Arts (hereafter PAFA). Eakins's religious background is fairly complex. His paternal grandfather (Alexander Akins) was Presbyterian, as his paternal grandmother (Frances Fife) was likely to have been. His maternal grandmother (Margaret Jones) was Episcopalian. His maternal grandfather (Mark Cowperthwait) was a Quaker, who was written out of meeting for eleven years for marrying "out of unity" and later reinstated. Eakins's parents were married at the Methodist Protestant Church at Wood and 11th streets.

29. Eakins's Bible reading habits are recounted in Margaret McHenry, *Thomas Eakins, Who Painted* (Oreland, Pa.: Privately printed, 1946), 129.

30. TE to Caroline Cowperthwait Eakins and FE, April 1, 1869, Eakins Papers, Archives of American Art.

31. Dennis Cardinal Dougherty to Sir Shane Leslie, April 10, 1948, Lloyd and Edith Havens Goodrich Collection, Thomas Eakins Research Collection, Philadelphia Museum of Art.

32. TE to FE, June 19, 1867, Eakins Papers, Archives of American Art.

33. TE to FE, January 8, 1867, Bregler Collection, PAFA.

34. TE to BE, March 17, 1868, Bregler Collection, PAFA.

35. TE to Caroline Cowperthwait Eakins and FE, April 1, 1869, Eakins Papers, Archives of American Art. Eakins bought a carte de visite of *Prayer in the Desert* (published by Goupil & Cie) while he was a student in Europe. Seymour Adelman Collection, Miriam Coffin Canaday Library, Bryn Mawr College. Similarly, Eakins's mention of prayer on "the top of a house" was also derived from a Gérôme painting, *Prayer on the Housetops*.

36. Ernest Renan, *The Life of Jesus* (Garden City, N.Y.: Dolphin Books, n.d.), 93. This is a reprint of an 1863 English translation of Renan's text.

37. Daniel L. Pals, *The Victorian "Lives" of Jesus* (San Antonio, Tex.: Trinity University Press, 1982), 3.

38. The American minister and scholar Augustus Blauvelt surveyed this critical literature in a series of articles for *Scribner's Monthly*. One article in the series is of particular interest for Eakins's conception of Jesus: "Christ's Supernaturalism, Scientifically Considered," *Scribner's Monthly*, February 1875, 410–25.

39. TE to Caroline Cowperthwait Eakins and FE, April 1, 1869, Eakins Papers, Archives of American Art.

40. Susan Nicholls Carter, "Art at the Exhibition," *Appleton's Journal* 15 (June 3, 1876): 726. Carter used the painting as a foil for Rothermel's *Battle of Gettysburg*, which was roundly criticized when it was exhibited at the Centennial. For a similarly positive review, see "Art: The 'Golgotha' of Gérôme," *Eclectic Magazine of Foreign Literature* 15 (March 1872): 381.

41. The most thorough discussion of the religious implications of naturalism in French art is found in Michael Paul Driskel *Representing Belief: Religion, Art, and Society in Nineteenth-Century France* (University Park: Pennsylvania State University Press, 1992). In his book, Driskel briefly discusses Bonnat's painting and places it within the context of "the counterdiscourse to the Aesthetics of Ultramontanism." He cites a lack of documentation regarding Bonnat's beliefs as an impediment to understanding that artist's intentions. However, in her dissertation on Bonnat, Alisa Luxenberg quotes extensively from Bonnat's correspondence, which indicates that he was a practicing Catholic.

42. Clara Erskine Clement and Laurence Hutton, *Artists of the Nineteenth Century and Their Works* (Boston: Houghton Mifflin, 1879), 75–76. The authors reprinted this review by Réne Ménard from the May 1875 issue of the *Portfolio*.

43. Leslie Miller, "Art in Philadelphia," *American Architect and Building News* 12 (November 25, 1882): 252.

44. Undated clipping (1883) discussing "the devotional chamber" of the Art Loan Exhibition, the Detroit Art Loan Scrapbook in the Detroit Art Loan Association Records, Archives of American Art.

45. Undated clipping (1883), the Detroit Art Loan Scrapbook in the Detroit Art Loan Association Records, Archives of American Art.

46. The unnamed Detroit critic of the previous note wrote that Eakins "had undertaken to so thoroughly conceal his features in shadow that any attempt to criticize would be baffled." The Detroit Art Loan Scrapbook in the Detroit Art Loan Association Records, Archives of American Art.

47. John McClintock and James Strong, *Cyclopedia of Biblical, Theological, and Ecclesiastical Literature*, vol. 5 (New York: Harper, 1891), 348–50.

48. Inexpensive prints circulated in America showing Jesus with the Lentulus letter printed below. See David Morgan and Sally M. Promey, *Exhibiting the Visual Culture of American Religions* (Valparaiso, Ind.: Brauer Art Museum, Valparaiso University, 2000), 62–63. Newspapers also reprinted the letter, and Americans continued to debate the legitimacy of the document in the early twentieth century. For a discussion of depictions of Christ by American artists, see John Dillenberger, *The Visual Arts and Christianity in America* (New York: Crossroad, 1989), 141–55.

49. TE to Earl Shinn, April 2, 1874, Richard T. Cadbury Papers, Friends Historical Library, Swarthmore College. See also Earl Shinn's Commonplace Book, Historical Society of Pennsylvania, Archives of American Art.

50. Jane Dillenberger discusses the absence of Christ's body in "Between Faith and Doubt: Subjects for Meditation," in *Perceptions and Evocations: The Art of Elihu Vedder*, Joshua C. Taylor, Jane Dillenberger, and Richard Murray (Washington, D.C.: Smithsonian Institution Press, 1979), 154–56.

51. Kent Ahrens, "The Religious Paintings of Robert Walter Weir," *Antiques* (April 1973): 744–49. For the Protestant use of the cross, see Ryan K. Smith, "The Cross: Church Symbol and Contest in Nineteenth-Century America," *Church History* 70 (December 2001): 705–34. Smith traces the Protestant acceptance of the cross as a symbol long associated with the Catholic Church. Although Protestants gradually embraced the symbol of the cross, the Crucifixion maintained its association with popery.

52. "Society of American Artists," *New York Times*, May 4, 1882, 5.

53. "Art Notes: The Cross in Art—I," *Ladies Repository* 11 (April 1873): 307–8.

54. Henry James's *Italian Hours* or the earlier *French and Italian Notebooks* by Nathaniel Hawthorne are among the most famous works by Protestant writers who record their encounters with Catholic art. Although the two authors were often moved by the religious works that they saw in Italian churches, each maintained a detachment from the culture that created them, assiduously avoiding masses in favor of more secularized moments in which to view the art. Jenny Franchot has examined the complexities of the Protestant attraction to Catholicism in *Roads to Rome: The Antebellum Protestant Encounter with Catholicism* (Berkeley and Los Angeles: University of California Press, 1994).

55. Karl Frosch, Wilhelm Heine, and August Lohr exhibited a panorama of the Crucifixion in Philadelphia in 1890, overlapping with the exhibition history of Eakins's *Crucifixion*. Frosch, Heine, and Lohr based their composition on that of a panorama of the same subject by Bruno Piglhein, which had earlier completed a successful European tour. See Stephan Oettermann, *The Panorama: History of a Mass Medium* (New York: Zone Books, 1997), 274–85. Michael Leja suggests that Eakins's *Crucifixion* "carried an implicit critique of the sensationalism and gimmickry of popular spectacular versions of the subject." Leja, *Looking Askance: Skepticism and American Art from Eakins to Duchamp* (Berkeley and Los Angeles: University of California Press, 2004), 81. John Davis also discusses panoramas of the Holy Land in *The Landscape of Belief: Encountering the Holy Land in American Art and Culture* (Princeton, N.J.: Princeton University Press, 1996), 53–72. A variant on this type of spectacle were three-dimensional wax figures; one such group depicting the Crucifixion was rescued from a fire in Philadelphia's Temple Theater in 1887 and was reported in "Entertainments," *Public Ledger*, February 18, 1887, 4.

56. Frances's diary is in the Eakins-Crowell Papers, Archives of American Art. Susan Eakins's diaries are in the Bregler Collection, PAFA.

57. Holy Trinity, the Church of St. Charles Borromeo, St. Mary's, and the Church of St. Vincent de Paul (Germantown) were among those with altar Crucifixions. See Historic American Buildings Survey, http://lcweb2.loc.gov/ammem/collections/habshaer/.

58. Milroy, "'Consummatum est . . .': A Reassessment of Thomas Eakins's *Crucifixion* of 1880," 280–83.

59. Milroy, "'Consummatum est . . .': A Reassessment of Thomas Eakins's *Crucifixion* of 1880," 283. The loan is confirmed by a 1911 inventory that Eakins made of his possessions. Bregler Collection, PAFA. The damage to the painting was noted in Eakins's Paintings Register in the Philadelphia Museum of Art.

60. "The Fine Arts," *Evening Bulletin* (Philadelphia), November 1, 1882, 5.

61. The magazine went bankrupt before Van Rensselaer published her article.

62. Mariana van Rensselaer to Sylvester R. Koehler, June 12, 1881, Sylvester R. Koehler Papers, Archives of American Art.

63. In 1878, Eakins sent three works to the SAA's inaugural exhibition: *William Rush Carving His Allegorical Statue of the Schuylkill River*, *Spinning*, and a photograph of his painting *The Gross Clinic*. The following year he was more circumspect, sending only *The Gross Clinic*. This set the tone for the next four years, wherein he sent only one painting each year

to the SAA show. These included *Elizabeth at the Piano* (1880), *The Pathetic Song* (1881), *Crucifixion* (1882), and *The Writing Master* (1883). In 1884 his streak with the SAA was interrupted by the rejection of his two panels, *Knitting* and *Spinning*. Eakins did not exhibit at the NAD in 1880 and 1883. See also Marc Simpson, "Eakins's Vision of the Past and the Building of a Reputation," in *Thomas Eakins*, ed. Sewell, 214–16.

64. TE to Frederick Diehlman, March 18, 1882, Diehlman Papers, National Academy of Design.

65. "Art Notes," *Art Journal* 8 (June 1882): 190.

66. "Fine Arts: Exhibition Notes," *Independent*, May 11, 1882, 9.

67. [Clarence Cook], "Society of American Artists: Fifth Annual Exhibition—New Pictures [First Notice]," *New York Daily Tribune*, May 17, 1882, 5.

68. Mariana van Rensselaer, "Society of American Artists, New York—II," *American Architect and Building News* 11 (May 20, 1882): 231.

69. [Mariana van Rensselaer], "The Society of American Artists—Conclusion," *New York World*, May 15, 1882, 5.

70. "Art Notes," *Art Journal* 8 (June 1882): 190.

71. "The American Artists' Supplementary Exhibition," *Art Amateur* 7 (June 1882): 2.

72. "The Fine Arts," *Evening Bulletin* (Philadelphia), November 1, 1882, 5.

73. Eakins offered the painting at the high price of $1,200 throughout all of these pre-1886 exhibitions. With other works, he often lowered his price as time went by, even with his relatively popular colonial revival paintings.

74. Susan M. Eakins for Thomas Eakins to George Corliss, Secretary of the Pennsylvania Academy, July 14, 1886, PAFA Archives. In the letter, Susan wrote, "Please let the bearer have the picture by Thomas Eakins—entitled—'Ecce Homo' for James S. Earle and Sons collectors for Charles M. Kurtz Director of Art Depart. Louisville Ky." Susan was handling some of Eakins's correspondence in this period, during which he was directing his attention to his defense against the various charges against him. Kurtz visited artist studios in Philadelphia on June 22 or 23, 1886. Charles M. Kurtz Papers, Archives of American Art. In a letter to J. Laurie Wallace, written by Eakins on June 24, 1886, Joslyn Art Museum, Omaha, Nebraska, he wrote, "I am ashamed to see the date of your letter to me. I was very busy when I received it & so Susie commenced to answer it for me." In this same letter he mentioned having just seen "Mr Kurtz—who takes pictures to Louisville. I had marked down your portrait to go there but since his list came I got a circular from Chicago asking me for pictures. I asked Kurtz therefore to change off your portrait for another of my works & I send yours then to Chicago." This letter makes clear that Eakins had direct contact with Kurtz, suggesting that he probably sanctioned the use of "*Ecce Homo*" in Susan's letter, for the painting was exhibited under that title in Louisville.

75. The most thorough discussion of the episode appears in Kathleen A. Foster and Cheryl Leibold, *Writing about Eakins: Manuscripts in Charles Bregler's Thomas Eakins Collection* (Philadelphia: University of Pennsylvania Press, 1989). It is unclear if the class was composed entirely of women or if it was a mixed class.

76. TE to Edward H. Coates, February 1886, PAFA Archives.

77. TE to Edward H. Coates, February 1886, PAFA Archives.

78. TE to John V. Sears, March 13, 1886, Philadelphia Sketch Club, Archives of American Art.

79. TE to the President and Members of the Philadelphia Sketch Club, April 17, 1886, Philadelphia Sketch Club, Archives of American Art.

80. TE to J. Laurie Wallace, June 24, 1886, Joslyn Art Museum. The list itself no longer exists.

81. TE to FE, June 4, 1886, Bregler Collection, PAFA.

82. In Gérôme's atelier, Eakins witnessed a hazing ritual enacted on one student "disliked by all the school." He was "tied to an easel upside down or *crucified* as it is called" (emphasis mine). TE to BE, November 1867, Bregler Collection, PAFA. The same treatment happened to Eakins's student Henry Ossawa Tanner while he was studying at the Pennsylvania Academy. See Dewey F. Mosby, *Henry Ossawa Tanner* (New York: Rizzoli, 1991), 60. There are other important links between Jesus and the artistic profession, which have perhaps less relevance for Eakins. Foremost among these is the relationship between the two, if one accepts Christ's divinity, as creators. There is also the example of Dürer's *Self-Portrait* in which he appears, for entirely different reasons, as Christ. See "The Artist as Christ," in Joseph Leo Koerner's *The Moment of Self-Portraiture in German Renaissance Art* (Chicago: University of Chicago Press, 1993), 63–79.

83. TE to Harrison Morris, April 23, 1894, PAFA Archives. Sarah Burns has suggested that Eakins portrayed himself as a victim in his 1902 self-portrait for the National Academy of Design. See Sarah Burns, "Ordering the Artist's Body: Thomas Eakins's Acts of Self-Portrayal," *American Art* 19 (Spring 2005): 101.

84. William C. Brownell, "French Traits—The Art Instinct," *Scribner's Monthly* (February 1889): 249.

85. TE to Secretary of the Treasury, March 11, 1889, Bregler Collection, PAFA. It remains possible that Gérôme placed the paintings with a private gallery when the Salon rejected them, but as yet little research has been undertaken in France regarding Eakins's later exhibitions there.

86. Martin Church, "The Fine Arts: Philadelphia Exhibit of Works for the World's Fair," *Daily Evening Transcript* (Boston), January 17, 1893, 6. At the Columbian Exposition itself, the painting hung in a prominent location on an exterior wall of the second floor of the Fine Arts Building, visible from the first floor galleries.

87. *Public Ledger* (Philadelphia), January 16, 1893, 6; and *Philadelphia Press*, January 15, 1893, 8.

88. Sadakichi Hartmann, *A History of American Art*, 2 vols. (Boston: L. C. Page, 1902), 1:204. Biographical dictionary entries for Eakins in the 1890s and 1910s also started mentioning the painting as one of Eakins's major works.

89. After 1886, Eakins showed the painting in 1887 at the Philadelphia Art Club and the Boston Mechanics Fair. In 1893 the *Crucifixion* again hung at the Academy in its showing of "Works to Be Exhibited at the World's Columbian Exposition," before traveling on to the Chicago fair. In 1900, Eakins sent it to the Carnegie Exhibition. In 1904 it was shown in St. Louis in the Louisiana Purchase Exposition. Between 1908 and 1914, Eakins lent the painting to the Seminary of St. Charles Borromeo at Overbrook, Pennsylvania. Finally, Eakins shipped the painting to San Francisco for the Panama-Pacific International Exposition in 1915. *Crucifixion* remained in San Francisco in 1916 for a Post-Exposition Exhibit. The 1887 Boston show recently came to light thanks to Col. Merl Moore, which suggests the possibility that there are more exhibitions to be uncovered.

90. Kathleen A. Foster, "Portraits of Teachers and Thinkers," in *Thomas Eakins*, ed. Sewell, 313.

91. TE to John W. Beatty, September 25, 1900, Carnegie Institute Museum of Art records, Archives of American Art.

92. H. Barbara Weinberg, "Thomas Eakins and the Metropolitan Museum of Art," *Museum Bulletin* 52 (Winter 1994–95): 37.

93. "Art at Home and Abroad," *New York Times*, November 4, 1917, SM7.

94. Those interested in seeing the painting at the Philadelphia Museum today are

directed not to the Eakins galleries but rather to the European galleries on the other side of the building, where the painting seems more at home with its French counterparts than among other American works of the period.

CHAPTER FIVE

1. For an overview of Eakins's work as a sculptor, see Moussa M. Domit, *The Sculpture of Thomas Eakins* (Washington, D.C.: Corcoran Gallery of Art, 1969).

2. Michael Kammen, *Mystic Chords of Memory* (New York: Alfred A. Knopf, 1991), 116. For Eakins's work on the arch, see Michael W. Panhorst, "The Equestrian Sculptures for the Brooklyn Memorial Arch," in *Eakins at Avondale and Thomas Eakins: A Personal Collection*, ed. William Innes Homer (Chadds Ford, Pa.: Brandywine River Museum, 1980), 24–26.

3. The most extensive discussion of the Trenton Battle Monument can be found in Zoltan Buki and Suzanne Corlette, eds., *The Trenton Battle Monument Eakins Bronzes* (Trenton: New Jersey State Museum, 1973).

4. Lloyd Goodrich's 1933 catalogue raisonné lists only five dated paintings by Eakins between 1892 and 1894. Lloyd Goodrich, *Thomas Eakins: His Life and Work* (New York: Whitney Museum of Art, 1933), 184–85.

5. The history of the commission has recently come to light through a group of newly discovered letters that sat mislabeled for nearly a century in the New Jersey State Archives. I wish to thank Beth Colosimo at the Archives for allowing me to view the letters in the middle of her effort to catalogue this important collection.

6. TE to FE, October 30, 1866, Charles Bregler's Thomas Eakins Collection, Pennsylvania Academy of the Fine Arts (hereafter PAFA).

7. TE to BE, December 23, 1866, Bregler Collection, PAFA. In a March 7, 1867, letter to his father, Eakins noted that during antique week only about a dozen of "the most studious and peaceful" students attended. Bregler Collection, PAFA.

8. TE to BE, March 6, 1868, Bregler Collection, PAFA.

9. TE to BE, September 8, 1867, Lloyd Goodrich transcription, Eakins Archive, Philadelphia Museum of Art.

10. TE to Caroline Cowparthwait Eakins (hereafter CE), April 14, 1869, Eakins Papers, Archives of American Art; TE to CE, August 30, 1869, Bregler Collection, PAFA.

11. TE to CE and FE, April 1, 1869, Eakins Papers, Archives of American Art.

12. TE to BE, September 28, 1869, Lloyd Goodrich transcription, Eakins Archive, Philadelphia Museum of Art.

13. Eakins made rough three-dimensional models out of a cigar box and some fabric for his first major painting, *The Champion Single Sculls*. He modeled more academic studies for *William Rush Carving His Allegorical Figure of the Schuylkill River* and *A May Morning in the Park (Fairman Rogers's Four-in-Hand)*, as well as for *Swimming*.

14. William C. Brownell, "The Art Schools of Philadelphia," *Scribner's Monthly* (September 1879): 742.

15. Charles Bregler, "Thomas Eakins as a Teacher," *Arts* 17 (March 1931): 385.

16. Charles Bregler, "Thomas Eakins as a Teacher," *Arts* 18 (October 1931): 35.

17. Kathleen Foster has noted the connection between teaching and sculpture in Eakins's career. She has also been among the few to acknowledge the importance of sculpture to Eakins apart from his teaching. See Kathleen A. Foster, *Thomas Eakins Rediscovered* (New Haven, Conn.: Yale University Press, 1997), 98–105.

18. TE to James P. Scott, June 18, 1883, Lloyd Goodrich transcription, Eakins Archive, Philadelphia Museum of Art.

19. TE to James P. Scott, July 11, 1883, Bregler Collection, PAFA.

20. TE to James P. Scott, July 11, 1883, Bregler Collection, PAFA.

21. Bregler, "Thomas Eakins as a Teacher," March 1931, 385.

22. Thomas Eakins Relief Manuscript, Philadelphia Museum of Art.

23. Bregler, "Thomas Eakins as a Teacher," March 1931, 385.

24. TE Relief Manuscript, Philadelphia Museum of Art.

25. Philadelphia artist Leslie Miller published his own perspective book around this time, which may have curtailed Eakins's plans, or perhaps the scandal at the Academy led to its being shelved. The illustrations came to light with the recovery of PAFA's Charles Bregler Collection. The Philadelphia Museum of Art owns Eakins's texts. The two parts of the manual have recently been reunited in Kathleen A. Foster, ed., *A Drawing Manual* (New Haven, Conn.: Yale University Press, 2005).

26. TE Relief Manuscript, Philadelphia Museum of Art.

27. TE to Edward H. Coates, n.d. (late February 1886?), Bregler Collection, PAFA.

28. Lloyd Goodrich, *Thomas Eakins* (Cambridge, Mass.: Harvard University Press, 1982), 1:137–38.

29. For information about the politics behind New York sculpture commissions in the Gilded Age, see Michele H. Bogart, *Public Sculpture and the Civic Ideal in New York City, 1890–1930* (Chicago: University of Chicago Press, 1989).

30. Maurice Power obituary, *New York Times*, September 12, 1902, 9. O'Donovan often signed his work with a shamrock.

31. O'Donovan to Janet O'Donovan Abraham, undated letter, quoted in Virginia Baird Kelly, "William Rudolf O'Donovan and the Business, Politics and Art of Sculpture" (M.A. thesis, Syracuse University, 1992), 9.

32. The commission was actually awarded to Power, according to David M. Kahn, "The Grant Monument," *Journal of the Society of Architectural Historians* 41 (October 1982): 224.

33. At some point, Eakins gave Duncan his painting *Cowboys in the Badlands*, but there is no evidence that the two were friends either before or after the work on the monuments.

34. Several versions of these photographs exist. During this period the two men also made portraits of one another. Unfortunately, both portraits are now missing.

35. On July 31, 1879, the *Evening Post* noted that O'Donovan had "relinquished his studio in the Tenth street building preparatory to his departure for a prolonged stay in Europe." Six months later, the *Evening Post* reported that O'Donovan "will go to England in the spring and remain there an indefinite time." *Evening Post,* January 30, 1880, 3.

36. O'Donovan's dispute with Lossing began in March 1877 and continued through June of that year. Articles on the matter appeared in the *Evening Post* on March 31, 1877; April 10, 1877; April 13, 1877; and June 1, 1877.

37. *New York Tribune,* May 19, 1877, 6. The debate continued through the month of June. See Kelly, 40–42.

38. William Rudolf O'Donovan, "A Sculptor's Method of Work," *Art Journal* 4 (1878): 63.

39. It seems likely that Power influenced the awarding of the commission. He clearly knew Chapin, who was an attendee at a political dinner held in Power's honor in February 1888.

40. It is unclear exactly how many proposals were submitted. Newspaper accounts record different numbers in their coverage of the competition, ranging from as many as forty-six submissions to as few as thirty-four.

41. David M. Kahn provides the most thorough description of John Hemenway Duncan's career as an architect, including an account of the Brooklyn arch commission.

42. Cleveland Moffett, "Grant and Lincoln in Bronze," *McClure's Magazine* (October 1895): 420.

43. Moffett, 421.

44. Moffett, 421.

45. Moffett, 422.

46. Moffett, 423. Alexander J. Cassatt was president of the Pennsylvania Railroad and brother of the artist Mary Cassatt. Perhaps as compensation for his help, Eakins offered to paint Cassatt's portrait a few years after the Brooklyn project. Cassatt's letterbook index lists a November 27, 1901, letter received from Eakins. Although the letters no longer exist, the letterbook index records the subject of each of the letters that Cassatt received. Selections from Alexander Johnston Cassatt's letterbook index, Archives of American Art. The American Philosophical Society owns the original letterbook. There is no evidence that Eakins ever painted Cassatt.

47. The date of these works is uncertain—they may have been made around the time of the Arcadian series in the early 1880s, but they could also date to the 1890s when Eakins was working on the Brooklyn bronzes.

48. Adam Emory Albright, as told to Evelyn Marie Stuart, "Memories of Thomas Eakins," *Harper's Bazaar,* August 1947, 184.

49. Moffett, 423.

50. Moffett, 423.

51. Moffett, 423.

52. Moffett, 424.

53. Moffett, 424.

54. Neither of the life-size casts of the horses is extant, but photographs of the plasters, made before they were shipped off to New York, show the seams where the individual casts were fitted together. See Foster, *Thomas Eakins Rediscovered*, 105.

55. Trenton Battle Monument Association Minutebook, April 6, 1891, New Jersey State Archives (NJSA).

56. Trenton Battle Monument Association Minutebook, April 6, 1891, NJSA.

57. Power did not appear to have any affiliation with the association at this point.

58. John H. Duncan to Commission of the Trenton Battle Monument, March 19, 1891, NJSA.

59. John H. Duncan to General Stryker, February 1, 1892, NJSA. Although the Monmouth Battle Monument was the work of several individuals, Power was fabricator, and his National Fine Art Foundry was the founder for the project. Also, in May 1891, Duncan told Stryker that he would soon be sending him the cost of Mr. Power's work at Monmouth.

60. John H. Duncan to General Stryker, March 23, 1892, NJSA

61. John H. Duncan to General Stryker, December 5, 1892, NJSA.

62. Trenton Battle Monument Association Minutebook, December 26, 1892, NJSA.

63. Trenton Battle Monument Association Minutebook, December 26, 1892, NJSA.

64. TE to General Stryker, April 5, 1893, NJSA.

65. Margaret McHenry, *Thomas Eakins, Who Painted* (Oreland, Pa.: Privately printed, 1945), 127–28.

66. Maurice Power to General Stryker, February 20, 1893, NJSA.

67. Maurice Power to General Stryker, February 23, 1893, NJSA.

68. Maurice Power to General Stryker, February 24, 1893, NJSA.

69. Maurice Power to General Stryker, February 14, 1893, NJSA.

70. Finally, in 1885, after arbitration, Eakins received a little more than half of the amount owed him for the commission. The rejected panels were later acquired by Edward Hornor Coates and given to the Pennsylvania Academy. See Theodor Siegl, *The Thomas Eakins Collection* (Philadelphia: Philadelphia Museum of Art, 1978), 99–101.

71. TE to General Stryker, August 29, 1893, NJSA.

72. Maurice Power to TE, September 4, 1893, NJSA.

73. Maurice Power to General Stryker, September 5, 1893, NJSA.

74. "Arch Bas Reliefs in Place," *Brooklyn Eagle*, December 19, 1895, 4. The article also notes that the works faced severe criticism.

75. "Dissatisfying Sculpture," *Brooklyn Eagle*, December 22, 1895, 6.

76. "Dissatisfying Sculpture," 6.

77. "Public Sculpture in Brooklyn," *Art Amateur* 34 (February 1896): 60.

78. "Dissatisfying Sculpture," 6.

79. "Dissatisfying Sculpture," 6.

80. "Dissatisfying Sculpture," 6.

81. "Gallery and Studio: Architecture in the Annual Exhibitions of New York," *Brooklyn Eagle*, July 19, 1896, 10.

82. Sophia Antoinette Walker, "Fine Arts: Art Notes," *Independent*, January 23, 1896, 7.

83. *Thirty-sixth Annual Report of the Department of Parks of the City of Brooklyn for the year 1896* (Brooklyn: Eagle Press, 1897), 36; "M. J. Power Is Sanguine," *New York Times*, February 21, 1896, 5. A year later there was still public debate about the fate of the sculptures, and the Brooklyn chapter of the American Institute of Architects issued a report condemning the works as "disreputable examples of the art of sculpture and design" and urging that "the proper authorities should be requested to have them removed." "Local Architects Protest against the Bronzes in Arch at the Entrance to Prospect Park," *Brooklyn Eagle*, January 19, 1897, 16.

84. "Dissatisfying Sculpture," 6.

85. H. H. Greer, "Frederick MacMonnies, Sculptor," *Brush and Pencil* 10 (April 1902): 3.

86. *Press* (Philadelphia), December 15, 1894, 4. Eakins's friend Talcott Williams was an editor at the *Press* and was often responsible for the kind reviews the artist received. Williams was also a friend of O'Donovan's.

87. Murray's work has been little studied. See Michael W. Panhorst, *Samuel Murray* (Washington, D.C.: Smithsonian Institution Press, 1982). See also by Panhorst, "Samuel A. Murray, Sculptor" (M.A. thesis, University of Delaware, 1982).

88. He appears opposite O'Donovan in the photographs of Eakins and O'Donovan together at Chestnut Street (the photo is sometimes called *The Consultation*). Murray also appears in the photograph captioned "A Nude Pose." Here his face has been retouched, probably to avoid identification, but an undoctored version of the image has surfaced in the Bregler Collection, making his identification possible. See Susan Danly and Cheryl Leibold, eds., *Eakins and the Photograph* (Washington, D.C.: Smithsonian Press, 1994), 199.

89. TE to Frances (Fanny) Eakins Crowell, October 22, 1895, Bregler Collection, PAFA.

90. Mariah Chamberlin-Hellman, "Samuel Murray, Thomas Eakins, and the Witherspoon Prophets," *Arts Magazine*, May 1979, 134–39. Photographs and correspondence regarding the project are in the collection of the Presbyterian Historical Society in Philadelphia.

91. Samuel Murray to Lloyd Goodrich, May 23, 1931, Lloyd and Edith Havens Goodrich Research Archive, Philadelphia Museum of Art.

92. TE to Harrison Morris, February 16, 1897, PAFA Archives.

93. TE to Susan Macdowell Eakins, "Saturday morning" (July) 1897, Bregler Collection, PAFA.

94. Goodrich, *Thomas Eakins*, 2:222.

95. Sally M. Promey, *Painting Religion in Public: John Signer Sargent's "Triumph of Religion" at the Boston Public Library* (Princeton, N.J.: Princeton University Press, 1999), 53–58.

96. Chamberlin-Hellman identified several sitters for the prophets, but these are specu-

lative. Murray only acknowledged the identity of William Macdowell as the model for *Jeremiah.* Since the sculptures are, for the most part, no longer extant, any identifications have been based on the archival photographs of each prophet in the Presbyterian Historical Society in Philadelphia. Unfortunately, it is very difficult to see clearly the features of several of the sculptures. Chamberlin-Hellman suggested Eakins's student Franklin Schenck as the model for *Samuel.* Support for her argument may be suggested by a notation in Eakins's Paintings Register at the Philadelphia Museum of Art, which calls Eakins's portrait of Franklin Schenck, known as *The Bohemian,* a "Bible character."

97. McHenry, *Thomas Eakins, Who Painted,* 128.

98. TE to Henry Rowland, October 4, 1897, Addison Gallery of American Art, Andover, Mass.

99. *Men and Women of America* (New York: L. R. Hamersly and Company, 1910), 541 and Albert Nelson Marquis, ed., *Who's Who in America,* vol. 7, *1912–13,* (Chicago: A. N. Marquis and Company, 1912), 616. Each entry records that Eakins assisted Samuel Murray in modeling "the colossal figures of the prophets" that decorate the Witherspoon Building. Several biographical dictionary entries from the turn of the century, including the former, discuss only Eakins's work as a sculptor. Many of these books received such information directly from the individuals listed.

100. Riter Fitzgerald, "Superb Statues," undated clipping in Murray Scrapbook IV, quoted in Panhorst, *Samuel Murray,* 11.

101. Letters in the Hirshhorn Museum and Sculpture Garden's Samuel Murray Collection indicate that Melville offered Murray extensive advice about the commission. Similarly, Dr. Edward Nolan seems to have advised Murray on the commission for a statue of Father Corby for Gettysburg. Nolan corresponded with several people on Murray's behalf. Letters to Nolan in the Murray Collection suggest the greatest possibility for corruption in the awards process. In one such letter, John Sullivan assures Nolan that "the contract should be awarded on the basis of ability," but then suggests that Nolan join the Alumni Sodality held at St. Joseph's College "partly to help bring about proper action in this matter." Another letter to Nolan, dated March 15, 1909, from Edward Dooner, states that he "will do all in his power to prevent the award of the Father Corby Monument to anyone but Murray."

102. TE to Mrs. Elizabeth Burton Johnston, June 21, 1907, typescript, Eakins Archive, Philadelphia Museum of Art.

103. According to Susan Eakins's diary, Eakins started the Greenwalt relief on the same day that Murray was awarded the Barry commission. Bregler Collection, PAFA.

CONCLUSION

1. He wrote to his friend Elizabeth Burton Johnston, giving an extended description of the sculpture, its unveiling, and the celebratory banquet that followed. Of the work he declared, "Artistically the statue is I believe the best in the country and I am proud to have assisted Murray in its execution." Thomas Eakins to Mrs. Johnston, June 21, 1907, typescript, Eakins Archive, Philadelphia Museum of Art.

2. The date of the series has been based on letters that suggest that Eakins hoped to exhibit the Brooklyn picture at the Carnegie Annual in 1908. TE to John W. Beatty, March 30, 1908, Daniel Dietrich Collection, copy, Eakins Archive, Philadelphia Museum of Art. TE to John W. Beatty, March 23, 1908, Carnegie Institute, Museum of Art Records. TE to August Zeller, April 10, 1908, Carnegie Institute Records. Eakins sent an extended textual description of the painting to the Carnegie, similar to his earlier texts about Rush. Unfortunately, the painting could not be exhibited because the frame was damaged in transit and required repair.

3. Eakins's use of sketches is described in Kathleen A. Foster, *Thomas Eakins Rediscovered* (New Haven, Conn.: Yale University Press, 1997), 72–80.

4. Darrel Sewell, *Thomas Eakins, Artist of Philadelphia* (Philadelphia: Philadelphia Museum of Art, 1982), 51.

5. Martin Berger has discussed the similar replacement of Eakins's own figure in *Artist and His Father Hunting Reed Birds in the Cohansey Marshes* with the figure of an African American man in the painting *Rail Shooting*. Martin A. Berger, *Man Made: Thomas Eakins and the Construction of Gilded Age Manhood* (Berkeley and Los Angeles: University of California Press, 2000), 27–40.

6. Franklin Kelly, "The Chaperone," in *American Paintings of the Nineteenth Century, Part 1*, Franklin Kelly with Nicolai Cikovsky Jr., Deborah Chotner, and John Davis (Washington, D.C.: National Gallery of Art, 1996), 185–89.

7. "Exhibition of Contemporary Art: Art at Home and Abroad," *New York Times*, April 11, 1915, Magazine Section, 22.

8. "The Women Who Served as Models for the Coins," *New York Times*, December 15, 1907, n.p.

9. Though the sketch is very loose in the area around the artist, he recalls the figure of Eakins's father, Benjamin.

10. For example, his 1903 commission to paint Robert C. Odgen or Jefferson Medical College's commission for a portrait of Professor William Smith Forbes. For an evaluation of Eakins's twentieth-century reputation, see Jennifer Hardin, "The Critical Reception of Thomas Eakins's Work II: Posthumous," in *Thomas Eakins*, ed. John Wilmerding (Washington, D.C.: Smithsonian Institution Press, 1993), 195–98; and Carol Troyen, "Eakins in the Twentieth Century," in *Thomas Eakins*, ed. Darrel Sewell (Philadelphia: Philadelphia Museum of Art, 2001), 367–76.

11. For a thorough accounting of Eakins's accomplishments after 1900, see Troyen, 367–76.

12. Eakins's involvement on the Worcester jury was recently discovered. "Art Matters of Note: At Home and Abroad," *New York Times*, March 31, 1907, X5. The New York jury was for the 1904 Louisiana Purchase Exposition in St. Louis.

13. The Carnegie acquired the painting in 1896. Whistler died in 1903, and the Copley Society in Boston held a memorial exhibition in his honor.

14. He painted roughly twenty-five portraits of art professionals between 1900 and 1910. As with all of his art, some works are more successful than others. His portraits of Chase, Elizabeth Coffin, Henry Ossawa Tanner, and Frank Linton are among the most appealing that are currently located. Others, such as his portraits of the Japanese artist Genjiro Yeto or the American William Lippincott, have yet to be traced.

15. Sadakichi Hartmann, *A History of American Art*, 2 vols. (Boston: L. C. Page, 1901). Martin Berger has discussed how Hartmann considered Eakins's strong, "manly" work an "antidote to effeminacy." Berger, 8–10.

16. Sidney Allan, "Masterpieces of American Portraiture," *Bulletin of Photography* 17 (August 4, 1915): 141.

17. Charles H. Caffin, *The Story of American Painting* (New York: Frederick A. Stokes, 1907), 230–31.

18. "Art and Artists," *Press* (Philadelphia), February 14, 1904, 6.

19. When Albert Barnes purchased Eakins's *Dr. D. Hayes Agnew*, the artist Robert Henri wrote to Barnes, "I think your purchase of his work is more significant than the purchase of a hundred old masters." Quoted in Sally Mills, "Dr. D. Hayes Agnew," in *Thomas Eakins*, ed. John Wilmerding (Washington, D.C.: Smithsonian Institution Press, 1993), 143.

20. "Academy Opens Its 110th Exhibition," *Philadelphia Inquirer*, February 7, 1915, 2.

21. TE to Bryson Burroughs, January 12, 1910, Metropolitan Museum of Art Archives.

22. For details of Eakins's exchanges with Burroughs and the Metropolitan, see H. Barbara Weinberg, "Thomas Eakins and the Metropolitan Museum of Art," *Metropolitan Museum of Art Bulletin* 51 (Winter 1994–95): 5–43.

23. TE to Bryson Burroughs, June 16, 1910. Metropolitan Museum of Art Archives.

24. TE to William Henry Holmes, April 19, 1911, Charles Bregler's Thomas Eakins Collection, Pennsylvania Academy of the Fine Arts.

25. TE to Bryson Burroughs, April 23, 1916, Metropolitan Museum of Art Archives.

26. "Obituary: Thomas Eakins," *American Art News* 14 (July 15, 1916).

27. TE to George Barker, February 24, 1906, Joslyn Art Museum.

Index

Page numbers in italics refer to illustrations.

Acknowledgments

Numerous individuals and institutions contributed to the completion of this book. In particular, I am deeply grateful to Sally M. Promey for investing so much thought and time in her careful readings of my work. I have benefited greatly from her invaluable advice and intellectual generosity. Thanks are also due to Franklin Kelly, who taught me to appreciate objects and to look carefully. William Pressley, Renee Ater, and Marjorie Venit also helped shape my ideas as the project developed.

I began to think seriously about Thomas Eakins's career while working on the Philadelphia Museum of Art's 2001 Eakins retrospective exhibition. This experience guided my research in its early stages. I am especially thankful to have worked with Darrell Sewell and Kathleen Foster, who shared their deep knowledge of this much studied artist. Douglass Paschall tirelessly and unstintingly answered my many Eakins questions, no matter how tedious. Audrey Lewis kindly tracked down documents and answered questions when I was far from Philadelphia. Mark Tucker and Nica Gutman generously shared their research on matters of conservation and technique. I also benefited from working with the scholars who contributed to the catalogue: Elizabeth Milroy, Amy Werbel, Kathleen Brown, Carol Troyen, Marc Simpson, H. Barbara Weinberg, and William Innes Homer. The staff of the museum's library and archives provided significant support for my research. In addition, I would like to thank Dee Minnite for her friendship and her kindness in hosting me during my research trips to Philadelphia.

The Smithsonian American Art Museum (SAAM) and the Hirshhorn Museum and Sculpture Garden provided critical financial and research support as I began writing. The staffs of both institutions offered me invaluable assistance during my year in residence. At SAAM, the late Richard Murray was especially encouraging and ever generous with his time. William Truettner, Pat Lynagh, Christine Hennessey, Andrew Thomas, and Cynthia Mills deserve special recognition for their help and advice. I also thank Emily Shapiro and Martin Berger, who graciously shared their own work on Eakins with me. Phyllis

Rosenzweig offered her insight and gave me access to the rich Eakins holdings at the Hirshhorn. I would also like to thank the staff at the Archives of American Art, particularly Judy Throm, for helping me locate research materials and allowing me to view unmicrofilmed collections.

Additional funding support was provided by the Henry Luce Foundation, the University of Maryland, the Terra Foundation, the Amon Carter Museum, and Georgia State University. My Terra-sponsored summer in Giverny, France, was indescribably blissful. I am particularly grateful to have met Veerle Thielemans, whose keen intelligence informed the experience. Veerle helped me understand Eakins's Arcadian works by introducing me to the writings of Horace Lecoq de Boisbaudran. Miranda Fontaine's good humor and administrative skill added immeasurably to the success of the program. I also enjoyed the camaraderie of the Terra fellows. I especially benefited from discussions of American art with Graham Boettcher and Elizabeth Lee. At the Amon Carter Museum, a Davidson Family Fellowship allowed me the opportunity to continue my research on *Swimming.* Allen Townsend and Rebecca Lawton not only aided my research but also introduced me to Fort Worth and made sure that I was never lonely that hot August. Paula Stewart patiently assisted me with the research files for the museum's 1996 "Swimming Picture" exhibition.

I would also like to thank a number of colleagues and friends who have provided intellectual, emotional, and material support over the course of the past several years. Kimberly Orcutt, Kristen Schwain, Leo Costello, Amy Kurtz Lansing, and Betsy Boone all shared unpublished work with me. The participants in the Erasmus Institute summer seminar conducted by Elizabeth Johns in 2003 helped to shape my thoughts about *Crucifixion.* In addition, Johns helpfully read an early draft of my first chapter. Her comments allowed me to significantly improve the text in subsequent revisions. I am indebted to her scholarship, and I have crudely modeled my own study upon her elegant 1983 book, *Thomas Eakins: The Heroism of Modern Life.* Sylvia Yount is owed special thanks for her encouragement and support. As a colleague, mentor, and friend, Sylvia has influenced me more than she can ever know. It is in no small part due to her that this book was ever completed. Chloe Wigston Smith, Aileen Ribeiro, Linda Eaton, and Paula Richter offered their expertise on historical costumes. Thomas Denenberg, in addition to being a good friend, was of tremendous help on all things colonial revival. Elizabeth Peters-Concha, Elissa Auther, Nancy Yeide, Heather Medlock, Lori Cavagnaro, Susan Nalezyty, Abbie Grotke, and Susan Rosenbaum offered food, friendship, and the occasional place to stay.

I am also grateful to the curators, librarians, archivists, and support staff who aided my research: Barbara Grubb at the Canaday Library, Bryn Mawr

College; Cheryl Leibold and Barbara Katus at the Pennsylvania Academy of the Fine Arts; Beth Colosimo at the New Jersey State Archives; Ellen Sklar at the Presbyterian Historical Society; Susannah Koerber and Mary LaGue at the Art Museum of Western Virginia; Brandon Fortune, Ellen Miles, and David Ward at the National Portrait Gallery; and Julian Cox at the High Museum of Art.

I would also like to thank Jo Joslyn, Yumeko Kawano, Erica Ginsburg, and the staff of the University of Pennsylvania Press for their help and patience. Thanks as well are due to the two anonymous readers who offered their insightful and constructive comments for the improvement of the manuscript.

I reserve my deepest gratitude for my family, who have lived with this project for so long. My husband, Stephen Mihm, deserves significant credit for the completion of this book. His cooking, criticism, advice, cheerleading, child care, and love sustained me throughout the project. Recognition is due to our two sons, especially Silas, who was the most tolerant of two-year-olds during the editing of this text. His new brother, Asher, arrived just as I finished my revisions. Our cats, Lily, Ernie, and Gus, offered comfort as my constant writing companions. I also thank my parents, James and Kathleen, and my sister, Quayla, for their love and support. Last, I thank my grandmother, Mary Florence Birch, for being the wonderful inspiration that she was.